Exploring Strategic Management

Gerry Johnson
Cranfield School of Management

Kevan Scholes
Sheffield Business School

Robert W. Sexty
Memorial University of Newfoundland

Prentice-Hall Canada Inc., Scarborough, Ontario

Canadian Cataloguing in Publication Data

Johnson, Gerry
  Exploring strategic management

North American ed.
First ed. (1984) published under title: Exploring corporate strategy.
Includes bibliographical references and index.
ISBN 0–13–297490–8

1. Corporate planning. I. Scholes, Kevan. II. Sexty, Robert W. (Robert William), 1942– . III. Title. IV. Title: Exploring corporate strategy.

HD30.28.J63 1988   658.4'012   C88–094151–0

Prentice-Hall, Inc., Englewood Cliffs, New Jersey
Prentice-Hall International, Inc., London
Prentice-Hall of Australia, Pty., Ltd., Sydney
Prentice-Hall of India Pvt., Ltd., New Delhi
Prentice-Hall of Japan, Inc., Tokyo
Prentice-Hall of Southeast Asia (Pte.) Ltd., Singapore
Editora Prentice-Hall do Brasil Ltda., Rio de Janeiro
Prentice-Hall Hispanoamericana, S.A., Mexico

ISBN 0–13–297490–8

Production Editors: Heather Scott McClune/Peter Buck
Production Coordinators: Matt Lumsdon/Sharon Houston
Typesetting: Colborne, Cox & Burns
Designer: Deborah-Anne Bailey

1 2 3 4 5 JD 93 92 91 90 89

Printed and bound in Canada by John Deyell Co.

Exploring Strategic Management

CONTENTS

ILLUSTRATIONS

PREFACE

This book reflects important and interesting developments in the subject of strategic management, and is written with the purpose of developing a greater capability for strategic thinking among managers and potential managers.

This book aims to provide readers with an understanding of:

- What strategic management is.
- Why strategic decisions are important.
- What approaches to use when formulating strategy.
- How implementing strategy is accomplished.

It is not a book of corporate planning techniques but rather builds on the practice of good strategic management, as researchers and practitioners in the area understand it. It is a book primarily intended for students of strategy on undergraduate, diploma, and masters courses in universities and colleges; students on courses with titles such as Corporate Strategy, Business Policy, Strategic Management, Organizational Policy, Corporate Policy, and so on. However, we know that many such students are already managers anyway and are undertaking part-time study: so this book is written with the manager and the potential manager in mind.

Traditionally, the study of strategic management in organizations has been taught using intensive case study programs. There remain teachers who argue that there can be no substitute for such an intensive case program. At the other extreme there is a growing school of thought which argues that the only reason cases were used was that there was an insufficient research base to the problems of strategy resulting in a lack of theoretical underpinning. These adherents argue that since the 1960s the strides made in research and the development of theory make such intensive case programs redundant. It seems to us that this is a fruitless division of opinion probably rooted in the academic traditions of those involved, rather than a considered view of the needs of students. The position taken here is that case work, or appropriate experiential learning, is of great benefit in the study of strategy for it allows students both to apply concepts and theories and — just as important — to build their own. However, it is also the case that the growing body of research and theory can be of great help in stimulating a deeper understanding of strategic problems and strategic management, and in the classroom discussion of cases.

Our approach builds in substantial parts of such research and theory and encourages readers to refer to more: but we also assume that readers will have the opportunity to deal with strategic problems through such means as case study work or projects or, if they are practicing managers, through their involvement in their own organizations. Our view in this respect is exactly the same as the writers of a medical or engineering text and we encourage readers to take the same view: good theory helps good practice, but an understanding of the theory without an understanding of the practice is very dangerous — particularly if you are dealing with a patient, a bridge or, as with this book, organizations.

Strategic management is a responsibility of all managers, and what is more, a responsibility that is becoming more and more important. It is not sufficient for a manager to think of management in some operational or functional context, simply to know his or her piece of the jigsaw puzzle well and trust that others know theirs equally as well. Modern organizations exist in a complex environment with an increasing demand for fast and effective strategic responses. The very least a manager requires is to understand how his or her piece of the puzzle fits into the rest in the context of the strategic problems and direction of the organization. If he or she does not, then the effectiveness of strategic management, and particularly the implementation of strategy, can be severely impaired.

In preparing this edition we have tried to bear in mind the needs of the manager in understanding strategic problems in many different organizations. To do this, certain themes have been developed in the book.

The book explicitly develops the theme that strategy and the management of strategy can be thought of in at least two rather different ways. First, it can be seen as a matter of essentially *economic analysis and planning*. Second, it can be seen as a matter of *organizational decision making* within a *social, political, and cultural process*. Both these aspects of strategic management are relevant to the study of strategy and the text incorporates both. For example, one of the themes running through the book is the importance of a clear analysis of the strategic situation facing the organization and a rational assessment of the future options available to it. In considering such issues, the book includes, for example, discussion of the value of environmental audits, structural and strategic group analysis of competitive environments, the relevance of experience curve concepts, value chain analysis, life cycle models of strategic analysis and choice, and the findings of those researchers who have tried to understand the relationship between strategic positioning of organizations and financial performance. In short, one of the themes is that the employment of rational models of analysis and choice in organizations is important to strategic management.

There is also a growing expectation that managers will be able to make decisions about change and implement change with a great deal more assurance and skill than hitherto. Yet, the evidence is that managers are not good at handling change, particularly change of the sort of magnitude involved with strategic change. Strategic management cannot be developed by providing "a bag of management techniques"; it is also to do with developing in managers a sensitivity to an increasingly turbulent environment, together with an understanding of the culture of the organization in which they work and the means whereby they can manage change within that culture. Here lies one of the fundamental problems of strategic management. The environment organizations face is increasingly turbulent, so the need for management sensitivity to change is growing. Yet the values, expectations, and assumptions of members of an organization working within a particular culture can be a very constraining and conservative influence on the understanding of strategic problems and the development of solutions.

Thus, another theme of the book is the recognition that it is important for managers to understand the processes of decision making in organizations within a social and political context. The book draws on the growing amount of research and literature on decision-making processes within a political and cultural context, considers explicitly how such influences can be analyzed, and also what mechanisms exist for managing strategic change within such systems. There is, therefore, an expectation that readers will seek to reconcile "scientific management" about the complex issues of strategy with an understanding of the human and social side of management. While this is a demanding task, it is the challenge of the effective management of strategy and a fundamental task of managers in today's organizations.

The book also recognizes that strategic management is as relevant to the government sector and not-for-profit organizations as it is to the private sector of industry and commerce. We have included sections which discuss this specifically and some references, examples, and illustrations of the application of strategic management concepts to the government sector. Unfortunately, space does not allow us to examine strategic management in such organizations in any depth.

The book, while using up-to-date theory and research, is not primarily an academic treatise, but a book for managers and those who intend to be managers: so a few words about the style of the book are in order. The reader will find that throughout the book there are "Illustrations" which enlarge on or give case material related to, a point in the text. These illustrations are all taken from actual incidents reported in the press and in journals, from case studies, or from the authors' personal experiences and, wherever possible, the organization or individuals involved are named. An attempt has been made to select well known organizations, or ones which provide products known to readers. It was felt that familiarity would make the illustrations more meaningful and interesting to the readers. This is why General Motors is used as the lead illustration in Chapter 1. In addition, we have tried to select illustrations which would be meaningful to both Americans and Canadians.

As far as terminology is concerned, we have tried to avoid some of the pitfalls of jargon management writers often fall into: if we have failed to do so on occasions it is not for the want of trying. The word "organization" has been used most frequently but there are times when "company," "enterprise," or "firm" are used: these tend to be where commercial operations are being discussed but it does not mean that the discussion only relates to the private sector. We have also chosen not to make dogmatic distinctions between descriptions of the subject of study such as "corporate strategy," "business policy," "strategic management," and so on.

The structure of the book is explained in some detail in Chapter 1. However, it might be useful to explain the basic structure of the book here. The book is in four parts. Part I comprises an introduction to strategy, first in terms of its characteristics and the elements of strategic management, (Chapter 1) and then in terms of how strategic decision actually come about in organizations (Chapter 2), in particular, the relationship between organizational strategy and culture. Part II of the book is concerned with Strategic Analysis with Chapter 3 focusing on the analysis of the environment within which organizations operate and Chapter 4 on the assessment of an organization's resources. Chapter 5 examines the ways in which the expectations and objectives of stakeholders in organizations can be understood within the context of political and cultural systems. As previously indicated, this part of the book also contains more explicit coverage of some recent research and concepts in strategic management, in particular the influential work of Michael Porter, and structural, strategic, group, and value chain analyses are discussed. Part III of the book is concerned with Strategic Choice and consists of three chapters. Chapter 6 is a review of strategic options organizations face; Chapter 7 introduces some principles of evaluation and provides general guidelines on the subject; and Chapter 8 discusses some techniques of evaluation of specific options. Finally, Part IV of the book is about Strategy Implementation. Chapter 9 discusses planning and the allocation of resources, including the use of value chain ideas in resource planning. Chapter 10 examines organizational structure as an aspect of strategy implementation and Chapter 11 discusses the influence of people and systems with emphasis given to cultural mechanisms for strategic change.

The writing of a book requires the assistance of many others and this project is no exception. I wish to especially thank Gerry Johnson and Kevan Scholes for their cooperation in the preparation of the book. They provided the thesis for the book and I have been impressed with their command of the strategy literature. The input of three reviewers is acknowledged, as they made many helpful comments: Gary Davis (University of New Brunswick, Saint John), John Mundie (University of Manitoba), and Colin Boyd (University of Saskatchewan). Also, I would like to thank the organizations which have given permission to use materials in the book's illustrations.

An author relies on many persons at the publishing house. I thank Lu Mitchell, the business editor at the time the project was initiated, and Yolanda de Rooy, the editor during later stages, for their enthusiastic support of the book. Also, there are several in the editorial and production departments whose contributions I wish to recognize: Peter

Buck, David Jolliffe, Heather Scott McClune, Monica Schwalbe, and Marta Tomins. Finally, I appreciated Maggie McDougall's assistance from Prentice-Hall International (UK) Ltd.

There is a growing recognition of the importance of strategic management in educational programs at undergraduate, graduate, and professional levels, as well as a major surge of interest in practicing it in all organizations, whether corporate, government, or non-profit. It is hoped that *Exploring Strategic Management* will be a useful and stimulating book for anyone interested in the topic.

Robert W. Sexty

Part I   *Part I*   *Part I*   *Part I*   *Part I*

Part I   *Part I*   *Part I*   *Part I*   *Part I*

Part I   *Part I*   *Part I*   **Part I**   *Part I*

Part I   *Part I*   *Part I*   *Part I*   *Part I*

Part I   *Part I*   *Part I*   *Part I*   *Part I*

Part I   *Part I*   *Part I*   *Part I*   *Part I*

Part I   *Part I*   *Part I*   *Part I*   *Part I*

Part I   *Part I*   *Part I*   *Part I*   *Part I*

Part I

INTRODUCTION

Chapter 1
STRATEGIC MANAGEMENT: INTRODUCTION

By the end of the 1970s, the North American automobile industry recognized that drastic action would have to be taken if it hoped to survive. Customers were demanding different and better quality cars, and the industry had never before been under such threats from foreign competition. Something was needed to revitalize the industry. Illustration 1.1 outlines the strategy formulated by General Motors Corporation (GM) in response to this environment, and identifies the choices and challenges confronted by the company.

General Motors was selected because the circumstances the company faced provide an insightful example of strategic management. GM is not used as an example of good or bad strategic planning. The illustration simply demonstrates that strategic planning is necessary and not easy. Not all companies face as demanding a set of circumstances as the strategists at GM did, but very few, whether large or small, can afford to ignore problems similar to those faced by GM when planning strategically.

The changes at GM have been dramatic and, it appears, will continue to be so. These changes dealt with the future direction of the business; they were long term in nature, and were bound to have far ranging implications on employment, the financing of business, and types of products produced. They were major strategic decisions which had to be made. All organizations are faced with the need to formulate strategies; they are not all faced with the problems of the magnitude confronting GM, but even the critical nature of Mr. Smith's problems are not so unusual when it comes to formulation of strategy. This book deals with why reviews of strategic direction take place in organizations, why they are important, how such decisions are made, and some of the tools and techniques managers can use to make such decisions. This chapter will draw on the General Motors illustration for the purposes of discussion, and as the book progresses, other such illustrations will be used to help develop discussion.

This first chapter deals with the questions of what is meant by strategic management, why it is so important, and what distinguishes it from other organizational decisions.

ILLUSTRATION 1.1   *Strategic Management at General Motors*

In 1979, General Motors Corporation (GM) formulated and began to implement a strategy in response to changes in the firm's environment which seriously threatened performance. This illustration outlines this strategy and identifies the choices and challenges faced by GM.

During the 1970s, several changes occurred in the market for automobiles. The types of cars North Americans wanted to drive changed. A large influence on this change was the increasing cost of fuel caused by the OPEC cartel's ability to restrict supplies and increase prices. The change in customer preference to smaller cars required a rethinking of sales techniques and marketing assumptions, and of course, there were implications for manufacturing. In addition, the government was imposing new safety, pollution-control, and fuel economy laws on the industry which provided challenges for manufacturing, and increased costs. During the 1970s, the North American automobile producers faced intense competition from Japanese cars, requiring further revamping of manufacturing and management methods to achieve greater efficiency.

GM introduced a strategic plan to produce the newly designed smaller cars demanded by the market at lower costs. This strategy was described in a "Customer Information From General Motors" advertisement as:

- To build new plants and modernize or close old ones.
- To give employees the opportunity to participate in managing the business, and to teach them to use technology as a tool.
- To use systems engineering and worldwide computer systems to help design cars, operate equipment, and move ahead of the industry in product quality and value.
- To reap the cost savings and earn the profits of this new production system — and pass its benefits along to every customer.

The result was to be a manufacturing process which could more adequately respond to volume and market share fluctuations, or in other words, which would allow GM to respond more quickly and effectively to changes in the environment. The plan was based on GM's superior financial strength over its main North American competitors, Ford and Chrysler. It was estimated that about $40 billion would be spent to implement the plan.

In 1981, Roger Smith became Chairman and was considered to be the first GM CEO with a strategic vision instead of being merely reactive to environmental changes and internal problems. However, he was confronted with many strategic choices and constraints in attempting to implement the strategy.

It was not easy to ascertain the types of cars customers wanted and the kinds of quality features they were seeking. Customers wanted smaller cars, but not too small, which still had some luxury features. It was a challenge to identify the new products the company should develop.

If smaller cars were demanded, the next problem was how to produce them, especially in the short term. Partnerships with foreign producers were possible, with cars manufactured overseas but sold as GM products in North America. Joint ventures with Japanese firms to produce cars and components in North America were also feasible. GM was faced with modernizing existing plants and building new ones to produce the cars demanded.

High technology would be much more evident in car manufacture. GM had to decide how to acquire the technology, whether to develop it on their own or to purchase it. Next came the question of how quickly and in what manner to install the technology. The impact on employees would have to be ascertained as would the capital costs and the savings in operating costs in the future.

The company's organizational structure would need to be revised. Design and manufacturing functions were highly centralized, but the marketing divisions were decentralized by car brand (Chevrolet, Pontiac, Buick, Oldsmobile, and Cadillac). The company was integrated backward and supplied most of its own components. The appropriateness of this arrangement might have to be questioned. In order to introduce high technology, new work practices, and new car models, it might be necessary to establish separate companies, such as the wholly owned Saturn Corp., established in 1985, which exists outside the GM corporate structure.

Diversification would have to be considered if the company wanted to increase its non-automotive revenues. The diversification possibilities could be designed to advance car-making activities, or be completely unrelated. The synergistic benefits would have to be determined as would the management skills available to run the different businesses.

Quite a change in corporate culture would be occurring in the company with more emphasis on innovation, product quality, customer satisfaction, and diversification; with the company being more receptive to taking risks and looking at new fields. But, GM might be too big to change and resistance might prevent improvements.

While all these strategic choices confronted the company, there was no assurance that the environment would not continue to change. Competition might increase from Ford and Chrysler, and from other foreign companies. The government might impose new regulations on automobiles or how they were manufactured.

Many strategic changes would be necessary in order for GM to accomplish its strategy. Strategic management at GM would be challenging!

Source: "Bumps Ahead for a Car Guy," *Fortune*, (September 28, 1987), pp. 105–9; "It's Time for a Tune-up at GM," *Business Week*, (September 7, 1987), pp. 22–3; "General Motors: What Went Wrong," *Business Week*, (March 16, 1987), pp. 102–10; "Can GM Manage It All?" *Fortune*, (July 8, 1985), pp. 22–8; "GM Moves Into a New Era," *Business Week*, (July 16, 1984), pp. 48–54.

One other point should be made before proceeding. The term strategic management is used here for two main reasons. First, the book is concerned with strategy and strategic decisions in all types of organizations — small and large business enterprises as well as government services and not-for-profit organizations — and the term embraces them all. Second, as the term is used in this book (discussed more fully in Subsection 1.1.2 below), strategic management denotes a general level of strategy in an organization and in this sense embraces other levels of strategy. Readers will undoubtedly come across, outside this book, terms such as: business policy, management policy, corporate policy, and corporate strategy, all of which deal with the same general area of study.

1.1 THE NATURE OF STRATEGY

Why are the changes at General Motors described as strategic changes? What sort of decisions are strategic decisions, and what distinguishes these from other sorts of decisions made in the company at the same time? Many of the characteristics of strategic decisions can be illustrated by using the GM example.

1.1.1 THE CHARACTERISTICS OF STRATEGIC DECISIONS

The characteristics usually associated with the word strategy and strategic decisions are these:

1. Strategic decisions are likely to be concerned with the *scope of an organization's activities*: does (and should) the organization concentrate on one area of activity, or does it have many? For example, should GM remain in the business of producing cars as in the past, or should it attempt to diversify into other activities, such as electronics? To what extent should it remain vertically integrated backwards? Should it continue to acquire other companies? The issue of scope of activity is fundamental to strategic decisions because it concerns the way in which those responsible for managing the organization conceive its boundaries. It has to do with what they want the organization to be like and to be about.

2. Strategy has to do with the *matching of the activities of an organization to the environment* in which it operates. Until the 1960s and 1970s, General Motors, Ford, Chrysler, and American Motors dominated the North American automobile market. However, in the 1960s and, in particular, the 1970s, the changes in the automobile industry were dramatic. Most significant, perhaps, was the growth in market power and technological competence of Japanese producers who, building on a large home market, adopted a strategy of worldwide dominance for their cars. The effect was marked. US car producers faced a major loss in market share: for example, in just one decade, GM's share of almost 50 percent of the market was reduced to under 40 percent by 1987.

Foreign competition was not the only environmental change to affect General Motors, or indeed, the automobile industry in general. The oil price increases of 1973 changed customer expectations of car performance and running costs; technological advances provided opportunities for car design which accelerated through the 1970s and 1980s and provided car manufacturers with opportunities to differentiate their products; changing demographic patterns and household earnings provided opportunities to increase car ownership in the family; pollution control regulations in different countries meant that imported cars had to meet quite rigorous performance standards; and fluctuations in exchange rates provided both constraints and opportunities in an international market.

In short, the automobile industry in general, and General Motors within it, was faced with the problems of an increasingly competitive market in a changing business environment; the need was to match the organization's activity to this environment in such a way as to take advantage of opportunities which might appear and to overcome the many threats which might arise. Since the environment is continually changing for all organizations, strategic decisions necessarily involve change: in the case of GM the environmental changes were of a major nature and the changes required were of a fundamental kind. This is not always the case; the extent and speed of environmental change will vary and the pace at which strategy must change will, of necessity, also vary. However, GM provides a good example of a company, faced with major environmental changes, that found it immensely difficult to make the sort of fundamental strategic changes necessary; a management problem which is not at all uncommon.

3. Strategy also has to do with the *matching of the organization's activities to its resource capability*. Strategy is not just about countering environmental threats and taking advantage of environmental opportunities. It is also about matching organizational resources to these threats and opportunities. There would be little point in trying to take advantage of some new opportunity if the resources needed were not available and could not be made available, or if the strategy was rooted in an inadequate resource base. For example, many of the problems faced in the 1970s and 1980s by General Motors stemmed from a failure to invest in modern plant and modern technology in the 1950s and 1960s. The result was a corporation faced with efficient low cost foreign competition when it had an insufficient base for increasing productivity. Throughout the latter 1970s and early 1980s, therefore, GM had to make major investments in plants at a time of falling markets, and at the same time, had to obtain more productivity from a smaller work force. Fortunately for GM, it had sufficient financial resources to make the more than $40 billion in investment required. However, the money may not necessarily have been spent wisely. Resource capability did not increase as workers were inadequately trained to integrate with the new technology. GM had difficulty producing cars to the quality standards expected by customers. Corporate planners were faced not only with trying to understand how a changing environment would affect their business, but also with having to project the availability and requirements of resources such as finance, plant, design, technological capability, and work force skills, for the future.

4. Strategic decisions often have *major resource implications* for an organization. These may be decisions about the disposal or acquisition of whole areas of resource. GM had to rationalize its operations by downsizing and even closing some plants. The company had

also moved into whole new areas of technology and production including robotized manufacturing operations which were necessary to compete in volume car manufacturing. And over the years, the work force had been cut significantly. In other words, the strategic decisions of the last decade had resulted in major changes in the resource base of the business.

5. Strategic decisions are likely to *affect operational decisions*; to "set off waves of lesser decisions."[1] In the General Motors case, the decision to introduce high technology, such as robots and computers, to the manufacturing operations ran into many problems. Some of the equipment did not perform as well as expected or took longer to set up and make operational than planned. Difficulties were experienced in installing electronic technology, leading to delays in introducing new cars. As a result, all sorts of day-to-day problems were encountered by plant managers and foremen. It is important to understand that strategic decisions have wide ramifications across an organization.

6. The strategy of an organization will be affected not only by environmental forces and resource availability, but also by the *values and expectations* of those who have *power* in the organization. In some respects, strategy can be thought of as a reflection of the attitudes and beliefs of those who have most influence in an organization. Whether a company is expansionist or more concerned with consolidation, and where the boundaries are drawn for a company's activities, may say much about the values and attitudes of those who most strongly influence strategy. A word sometimes used to describe attitudes and expectations about scope and posture of an organization is *mission*. Mission may comprise views about the organization's standing in relation to the competition or in terms of technological advance, product quality, or perhaps its role in society. It may also be about the ownership of a firm, particularly in the case of small companies where the desire to perpetuate family ownership may be a very important influence on strategy. Such views are not about specific aims so much as conceptions of where the organization is thought to be throughout time. In this sense, mission is a visionary view of the overall strategic posture of the organization and it is likely to be a persistent and resistent influence on strategic decisions. In the case of GM, the expectations of management and in particular, Roger Smith's more visionary approach to planning, would be very influential on the mission of the corporation.

7. Strategic decisions are likely to affect the *long term direction* of an organization. In the past, planning at GM had been short term. As a result of the changing environment, Smith and others realized that the planning horizon had to be lengthened. Instead of a reactive type of planning response, GM is now attempting to plot strategy for ten years and beyond. To critics who suggest that strategic changes have not resulted in improved performance, Smith has clearly stated that it takes years for such changes to have effect. Strategic decisions, therefore, tend to have long time horizons and/or long term implications.

8. Strategic decisions are often *complex in nature*. It can be argued that what distinguishes strategic management from other aspects of management in an organization is precisely this complexity. The complexity arises for at least three reasons. First, strategic decisions

usually involve a *high degree of uncertainty*; they may involve making decisions on the basis of views about the future which are impossible for managers to be sure about. Second, strategic decisions are likely to demand an *integrated* approach to managing the organization. Unlike functional problems, there is no one area of expertise, or one perspective, which can define or resolve the problems. Managers therefore have to cross functional and operational boundaries to deal with strategic problems and come to agreements with other managers who, inevitably, have different interests and perhaps different priorities. This problem of integration exists in all management tasks but is particularly problematic for strategic decisions. Third, as has been noted above, strategic decisions are likely to involve *major change* in organizations. Not only is it problematic to decide upon and plan those changes, it is even more problematic to implement them. Strategic management is therefore distinguished by a *higher order of complexity* than operational tasks.[2] The complexity of strategic decision making should be clear after reading about the challenges confronting General Motors!

These are the sorts of characteristics associated with the idea of strategy in an organizational context. They are summarized in Figure 1.1.[3]

Figure 1.1 *The characteristics of strategic decisions.*

Strategic decisions are concerned with:
- The scope of an organization's activities
- The matching of an organization's activities to its environment
- The matching of the activities of an organization to its resource capability
- The allocation and re-allocation of major resources in an organization
- The values, expectations and goals of those influencing strategy
- The direction an organization will move in the long term
- Implications for change throughout the organization — they are therefore likely to be complex in nature

1.1.2 LEVELS OF STRATEGY

Strategic management involves formulating and implementing strategies at a number of levels in an organization. In companies like General Motors, there are at least three different levels of strategy. The first level is the *corporate* level: here the strategy is concerned with the sorts of businesses the company should be in and is therefore concerned with decisions of scope. Corporate strategy would be concerned with which businesses to acquire or divest, or how resources should be allocated by corporate headquarters. Corporate strategy is therefore likely to involve questions about the financial structure and organizational structure of the firm as a whole.

The second level can be thought of more in terms of *competitive or business strategy*. Here strategy is about how to compete in a particular market. While corporate strategy involves decisions about the organization as a whole, competitive strategy is more likely to be related to a unit within the whole. In the case of General Motors, the corporate strategy must be translated into strategies for each division, such as Chevrolet, Pontiac, and so on. As each division markets cars appealing to different market segments, strategies have to be designed to match the circumstances in each of these segments. The business strategy for Saturn Corp., for example, differs substantially from that of the parent company (GM), as different production and marketing approaches were to be implemented. Yet, each of these competitive or business strategies must complement the company's corporate strategy.

The third level of strategy is at the operating end of the organization. Here there are *operational strategies* concerned with how the different functions of the enterprise — marketing, finance, manufacturing and so on — contribute to the other levels of strategy. Such contributions will certainly be important in terms of how an organization seeks to be competitive. Competitive strategy may depend to a large extent on, for example, decisions about market entry, price, product offer, financing, personnel, and investment in plant. In themselves these are decisions of strategic importance which are made, or at least strongly influenced, at operational levels.

The ideas discussed in this book are of relevence to all three levels of strategy but are most specifically concerned with areas of corporate and competitive strategy — what businesses (or areas of operation) should an organization be in and how should it compete in each of these?

1.2 STRATEGIC MANAGEMENT

What, then, is strategic management? The easy answer is to say that it is the management of the process of strategic decision making. However, this response fails to make a number of points important both to the management of an organization and to the area of study with which this book is concerned.

The nature of strategic management is different from other aspects of management. In most areas, the individual manager is required to deal with problems of operational control,[4] such as the efficient production of goods, the management of a sales force, the monitoring of financial performance, or the design of some new system which will improve the efficiency of the operation. These are all very important tasks, but they are essentially concerned with effectively managing a limited part of the organization within the context and guidance of a more overarching strategy. Operational control is what managers are involved in most of the time. It is vital to the effective implementation of strategy but it is not the same as strategic management.

Strategic management is concerned with deciding on strategy and planning how that strategy is to be put into effect. It can be thought of as having three main elements and it is these which provide the framework for this book. There is *strategic analysis* in which the strategist seeks to understand the strategic position of the organization. There is a *strategic choice* stage which has to do with the formulation of possible courses of action, their evaluation, and the choice between them. Finally, there is *strategy implementation* which is concerned with planning how the choice of strategy can be put into effect. This three-part approach, summarized in Figure 1.2, is not dissimilar from how corporation strategies are described by managers and in newspaper articles. Illustration 1.2 outlines the elements of strategic management in another firm and provides examples of the types of matters considered under each element.

Figure 1.2   *A basic model of the strategic management process.*

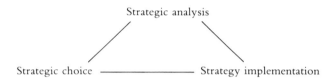

Before discussing these stages in detail, it is important to make clear how they relate to each other and why Figure 1.2 is shown in the form it is. The figure could have been shown in a linear form — strategic analysis preceding strategic choice, which in turn precedes strategy implementation. Indeed, this might seem quite logical, and many texts on the subject do just this.[5] However, in practice, the stages do not take this linear form. It is very likely that, far from being separate, the stages are very much involved with each other: it is quite possible that one way of evaluating a strategy would be to begin to implement it, so strategic choice and strategy implementation might be carried out together. It is also very likely that strategic analysis will be an ongoing activity and so will overlap with the implementation of strategy. A linear representation of the process gives the impression that one stage is totally distinct from or precedes or follows another when, in fact, they are part of the same process. The process is examined more fully in Chapter 2 in the light of research on the subject to give readers a greater "feel" for the realities of strategic management. It is for structural convenience only that the process has been divided into sections in this book.

1.2.1 STRATEGIC ANALYSIS

Strategic analysis is concerned with understanding the strategic position of the organization. What changes are going on in the environment and how will they affect the organization and its activities? What is the resource strength of the organization in the context of these changes? What is it that those people and groups associated with the organization — managers, shareholders or owners, unions and so on — aspire to and how do these aims affect the present position and the organization in the future?

ILLUSTRATION 1.2   *John Forsyth Company Inc. and the Elements of Strategic Management*

John Forsyth, one of Canada's largest apparel makers, provides an example of the three elements of strategic management.

John Forsyth has followed a very successful strategy of manufacturing and marketing a broad range of apparel in the medium price range. This appeal to the mass market allows the company to produce in volume, while making sure there is a balance between price and quality in the products produced. It produces its own brands but also markets under trademarks such as Pierre Cardin, Oscar de la Renta, and Coca-Cola Co. There is a balance between domestic and foreign supplies of materials to provide protection against the vagaries of supply. The company is planning to introduce additional lines of women's clothing and is considering retail operations.

  Some of the aspects of strategic management considered by management in terms of the three elements were:

Strategic Analysis: understanding the strategic position of the firm.
- The clothing business is very volatile, and correct identification of fads, styles, colors and fashions is critical.
- The Canadian clothing industry is fragmented: there are many domestic competitors in addition to foreign competition.
- The business is cyclical in nature, seasonal and shaped by fashion trends.
- Some large buyers can pressure manufacturers.
- Supplies of raw materials, textiles, are not always readily available in Canada and imports are often expensive.
- The firm appears to have competent managers and a strong sales force.
- The firm has a good track record and is well established in its markets.
- Financing seems adequate after recently going public.
- The firm values "quality" in its products and believes in treating managers well.

Strategic Choice: identifying, evaluating, and selecting from among possible courses of action.
- The market is segmented on several dimensions:
    - price: high, medium, low
    - type of clothing: women's, men's, children's, unisex
    - market: specialized (few customers) vs. general (volume)
- Sources of supply are available from domestic textile producers or offshore.
- The manufacture of own brands vs. other trademarks or private brands.
- The possibility of vertical integration, especially into retail operations.

- The possibility of partnership arrangements with major retailers vs. remaining independent.

Strategy Implementation: planning how the "choice" of a strategy will be put into effect.

- Attempt to level seasonal demand by encouraging retailers to order earlier allowing more efficient production scheduling.
- Control labor costs through automation.
- Modernize domestic plants and become involved in offshore manufacturing.
- Decentralize operations into profit centers.
- Decentralize production into 12 separate, largely autonomous divisions to encourage flexibility in operations.
- Recognize the need to take advantage of economies of scale by making sure each unit is of sufficient size.
- Make decentralized units responsible for the marketing of products produced.
- Change the approach to motivating managers, include the bonus system.
- Develop a close working relationship with main customers.

Source: The John Forsyth Company Inc. *Annual Report 1986*, and Barbara Aarsteinsen, "John Forsyth finds a good fit in its expanding clothing line," *The Globe and Mail*, February 16, 1987, B4.

General Motors' managers, such as Roger Smith, undertook such a strategic analysis in the late 1970s and concluded that the corporation was becoming uncompetitive in many market segments, burdened with out-of-date plants, suffering from low productivity, and operating at high cost levels. The analysis no doubt found that in order to overcome the threat of a declining market share, the corporation would have to respond to customer needs in terms of types of cars desired and the quality being demanded. As GM was large, and had been profitable, the main resource strength was financial. A major weakness was in the products being offered, but short term solutions in the form of partnerships and joint ventures to produce the smaller cars being demanded by the market were viable.

However, General Motors also illustrates that, in order to appreciate fully the strategic position of the firm, it is necessary to understand how other *stakeholders* — the government, unions, dealers and shareholders — view the situation the business faces, and where it is going. Further, it is important to understand the less explicit, but nonetheless powerful, influence of organizational culture; by culture is meant the kinds of beliefs and assumptions current in the organization and its ways of doing things, very often inherited over many years of operating. Understanding the values, expectations, objectives, and the less precise, but nonetheless key, influence of culture is therefore also a vital part of strategic analysis.

Thus, the aim of strategic analysis is to form a view of the key influences on the present and future well-being of the organization and therefore on the choice of strategy. These influences will be from many sources but they are summarized in Figure 1.3 and discussed briefly below.

1. The *environment*. The organization exists in the context of a complex commercial, economic, political, technological, ethical, and social world. This environment changes and is more complex for some firms than for others. Since strategy is concerned with the position a business takes in relation to its environment, an understanding of the environment's effects on a business is of central importance to strategic analysis. The historical and environmental effects on the business must be considered, as well as the present effects and the expected changes in environmental variables. This is a major task because the range of environmental variables is so great. Many of these variables will give rise to *opportunities* of some sort and many will exert *threats* upon the firm. The two main problems to be faced are, first, to distil out of this complexity an analytic view of the main or overall environmental impacts for the purpose of strategic choice; and second, the fact that the range of variables is so great that it may not be possible or realistic to identify and analyze each variable. Chapter 3 of this book addresses these types of problems.

2. The *resources* of the organization. Just as there are outside influences on the firm and its choice of strategies, so are there internal influences. A straightforward way of thinking about the internal strategic position of a firm is to consider its strengths and weaknesses (what it is good or not so good at doing or where it is at a competitive advantage or disadvantage, for example). These strengths and weaknesses may be identified by considering the resource areas of a business such as its physical plant, its management, its financial structure, and its products. Again, the aim is to form a view of the internal influences — and constraints — on strategic choice. Chapter 4 examines resource analysis in detail.

3. The *expectations* and objectives of different stakeholder groups are clearly important because they will directly affect which strategies advanced by management will be seen as acceptable. However, the beliefs and assumptions which make up the *culture* of an organization, though less explicit, will also have an important influence. The environmental and resource influences on an organization will be interpreted through these beliefs and assumptions; so two groups of managers, perhaps working in different divisions of an organization, may come to entirely different conclusions about strategy, although they are faced with similar environmental and resource implications. Which influence prevails is likely to depend on which group has the greatest power, and understanding this can be of great importance in recognizing why an organization has followed or is likely to follow the strategy it does. Chapter 2 discusses the important influence of culture on the formulation of strategy and this is followed in Chapter 5 by a discussion of how the culture, expectations, and power structures in an organization can be analyzed and the ways in which such beliefs and expectations are likely to affect organizational objectives.

Together, consideration of the environment, the resources, the expectations, and the objectives within the cultural and political framework of the organization provides the basis of the strategic analysis of an organization. However, to understand the strategic position an organization is in, it is also necessary to examine the extent to which the direction and implications of the current strategy and objectives being followed by the organization are in line with, and can cope with, the implications yielded by the strategic analysis. Is the current strategy capable of dealing with the changes taking place in the organization's environment or not? If so, in what respects and, if not, why not? It is unlikely that there will be a complete match between current strategy and the picture which emerges from the strategic analysis. The extent to which there is a mismatch here is the extent of the strategic problem facing the strategist. It may be that the adjustment required is marginal or it may be that there is a need for a fundamental realignment of strategy. For example, the extent to which General Motors had come to be out of line in its competitive environment in the 1970s posed Roger Smith with the problems of fundamental strategic repositioning.

Figure 1.3   *Aspects of strategic analysis.*

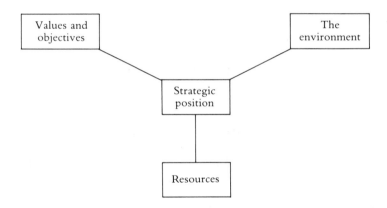

1.2.2 STRATEGIC CHOICE

Strategic analysis provides a basis for *strategic choice*. This aspect of strategic management can be conceived of as having three parts:

1. *Generation of strategic options*. There may be many possible courses of action. General Motors, for example, had to decide the *basis of competing* in a worldwide industry: could it compete on a cost-leadership basis? Would it need to differentiate itself from competitors, or perhaps select particular market segments or products to focus on? Within these broad

choices, the most sensible *strategic directions* must be determined. Should the company: modernize plants or build new ones; have cars built overseas by other producers and marketed in North America by GM divisions; enter into joint ventures overseas and in the US; attempt to maintain market share in an increasingly competitive market; or focus on product development of cars for particular market segments? Each of these possibilities is important and needs careful consideration: indeed, in developing strategies, a potential danger is that managers will not consider any but the most obvious courses of action — and the most obvious is not necessarily the best. Therefore, an important step in strategic choice is to generate strategic options.

2. *Evaluation of strategic options*. The strategic options can be examined in the context of the strategic analysis to assess their relative merits.

An organization may seek strategies which build upon strengths, overcome weaknesses and take advantage of the opportunities, while minimizing or circumventing the threats it faces — in this book this is called the search for "strategic fit" or *suitability* of a strategy. Many commentators on the General Motors situation have argued that given the company's size and the changing environmental circumstances, the strategy embarked upon in 1980 was not suitable. It is argued that an even more dramatic strategy will be necessary, such as dividing the company into smaller units, because the difficulty of introducing changes in such a large organization is too great. Although the company may have the financial capability, the chosen strategy involved major structural and cultural changes at GM which are not easy to achieve in the short term.

In other words, it is questionable whether or not the strategy is workable. A valid consideration when deciding on strategy is whether or not it could pass a test of *feasibility*. Although questions have been raised about GM's strategy, it may be to soon to pass judgment. One assumes that in the late 1970s, GM's strategists believed that the strategy was feasible.

A third criterion used in evaluation is *acceptability* of the strategy. In GM's case, employees, and especially the unions, would find it unacceptable that a large portion of GM's cars be manufactured overseas. The government would also consider foreign production questionable. Shareholders, especially institutional investors, have challenged GM's performance in recent years. Roger Smith has made efforts to assure shareholders that GM is on the correct course. The strategy selected must not only be acceptable to management, but also to the other stakeholders in the organization.

3. *Selection of strategy*. This is the task of selecting those options management is going to pursue. There could be just one strategy chosen or, as in the case of GM, the strategy may be multifaceted. There is unlikely to be a clear-cut right or wrong strategy because any strategy must inevitably have some dangers or disadvantages so, in the end, it is likely to be a matter of management judgment. It is important to understand that a selection of strategy cannot always be viewed or understood as a purely objective, rational act. Selection is strongly influenced by the values of the managers and other groups with interest in the organization and, in the end, may very much reflect the power structure in the organization.

Strategic choice is dealt with in Part III of this book. In Chapter 6 there is a discussion of the various strategic options organizations most typically consider. Chapter 7 discusses the criteria of evaluation in more detail and discusses several approaches to assessing the suitability of different types of strategies. Chapter 8 goes on to consider some techniques for evaluating specific options and the ways in which strategy selection may occur.

1.2.3 STRATEGY IMPLEMENTATION

Strategy implementation is concerned with translation of the strategy into action. A strategy for General Motors might take shape in terms of how many plants should be operated, the extent of automation in modernized or new plants, and how many workers should be employed. This problem of translating strategy into action is certainly part of strategic management, and is at least as problematic as strategic analysis or choice. Implementation can be thought of as having several parts.

Implementation is likely to involve *resource planning* in which the logistics of implemention are examined: what are the key tasks to be carried out, what changes need to be made in the resource mix of the operation, by when, and who is to be responsible for them? It is also likely that there will be changes in *organizational structure* needed to carry through the strategy. For example, while the design and manufacturing functions at GM were highly centralized, the marketing function was decentralized. Changes in structure have since occurred with design and manufacturing being decentralized into two groups of divisions, becoming more closely associated with those divisions responsible for selling the cars.

There is also likely to be a need to adapt the *systems* used to manage the organization. What will different departments be held responsible for? What kinds of information systems are needed to monitor the progress of the strategy? Is there a need for retraining of the workforce? What about the cultural systems of the organization? If strategy is to change it will be necessary to find ways of getting the people in the organization to change the way they preceive their "organizational world." How might this be done?

Part IV of the book deals with the strategy implementation. Problems of planning resource allocation are discussed in Chapter 9, issues of organizational structure are dealt with in Chapter 10, and the problems of managing the people and systems for strategic change are discussed in Chapter 11.

1.2.4 A SUMMARY OF THE STRATEGIC MANAGEMENT PROCESS

As stated earlier, there is a danger in thinking of the process of strategic management as a specific, orderly sequence of steps; the danger is that readers may not find the same stages described here as exist in reality and therefore argue that strategic management in their organization does not take place. It is important to stress that the model used in this book, and summarized in this chapter, is a useful device for the structuring of the book and a means by which managers and students of strategy can think through complex strategic problems. It is not, however, an attempt to describe how the processes of strategic management take place in the political and cultural arenas of organizations. Chapter 2 deals with how strategic decisions are made in practice and shows that a study of the process of strategic management yields somewhat different descriptive models.

With some trepidation, then, a summary model of the influences on, and elements of, strategic management is given in Figure 1.4. It is not intended as a prescription of what strategic management should be but as a framework readers can use to think through strategic problems.

Figure 1.4   *A summary model of the elements of strategic management.*

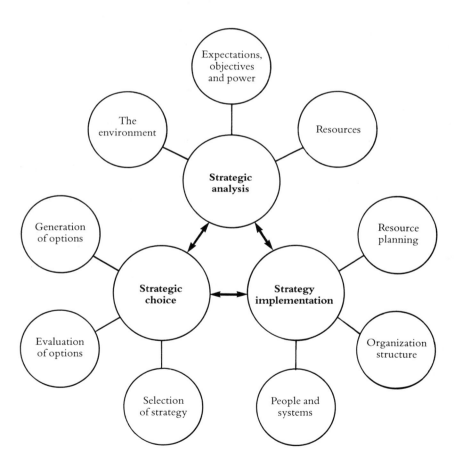

It was stated earlier that the process cannot be regarded as linear and it should now be clear why this is so. In practice, so many elements of the model are expressions of the same thing. For example, a consideration of cultures and expectations is not simply part of strategic analysis. It is also directly relevant to an assessment of the acceptability of a given strategy. Similarly, in considering the planning of resources for the purposes of strategic implementation, a study of feasibility is in fact being undertaken and so too is a reassessment of existing resources, which also might be described as strategic analysis. The point to emphasize is that the elements of strategic management are relevant one to another.

1.3 THE CHALLENGE OF STRATEGIC MANAGEMENT

It should be clear by now that the breadth of concern of strategic management is much greater than that of any one area of functional management. The concern is with organization-wide issues in the context of a whole range of environmental influences. This gives rise to some problems for those who seek to develop their skills in this area.

1.3.1 DEVELOPING A STRATEGIC PERSPECTIVE

One obvious problem is that managers have to be able to cope with overall considerations of their organization and its environment. This is not easy to do, as managers who move from functional responsibilities to general management responsibilities often find. The accountant finds that he still tends to see problems in financial terms, the marketing manager in marketing terms and so on. Each aspect in itself is most worthy, of course, but none is adequate alone. The manager has to learn to take an overview, to conceive of the whole rather than the parts.

A manager must develop the facility to take a holistic view of the situation and consider major, overall problems rather than to dwell on difficulties which, real as they may be, do not help develop a strategic perspective. Implicit in the arguments put forward in this book is the view that a manager needs to be competent both as an operator in a functional sense and as a strategist. It is not enough for a manager to simply maintain what the organization has always done, he or she must be capable of contributing to a debate about where the organization is going, and become involved in the practical tasks of making strategies work.

1.3.2 COPING WITH CHANGE

To cope with the vast variety and range of environmental inputs in the strategic decision process, managers have to operate within a simplified model of that environment. Essentially managers reduce the infinite to a personally manageable model of reality. More precisely, there is evidence that to some extent this "model of reality" is inherited by the manager in the sense that there exist *recipes*, or perceived wisdom about the key factors for business success in a particular business environment.[6] The idea of recipes is discussed more fully in Chapter 2; suffice it to say at this stage that their influence can be a significant constraint on change.[7]

For example, it has been difficult for some at General Motors — managers, supervisors, workers, and dealers — to accept the changes necessary to implement the strategy. The focus on customer consultation about design is difficult for some technical personnel to accept. The introduction of high technology involves change and is threatening to many and therefore requires extensive training of supervisors and workers. In an effort to improve customer service, GM is now evaluating dealers by surveying customers directly, which has upset many dealers. Resistance to change plagues all organizations and GM is no exception.

It is important for those who wish to understand, or develop skills in, strategic management to consider the problems of achieving changes in strategy. To achieve such changes effectively, what is being asked of managers may well be a change in the way they and their colleagues perceive their organizational world. How such changes came about, indeed whether they can be brought about at all, underlies the study of strategic management and is considered in more detail in Chapters 2, 5, and 11 of the book.

1.3.3 STRATEGY IN SMALL BUSINESSES

Most literature on strategy, including this book, focuses on large business organizations and ignores small businesses. This is unfortunate because a small business also needs organized and systematic management, and according to Peter Drucker "it needs strategy".[8]

Small businesses are always in danger of failing since they are more vulnerable to demand changes. They usually rely on a few products and/or customers for most of their revenues and demand shifts can cause major problems. They lack the diversification possible in larger businesses and have few slack resource capabilities to get them through tough times. In order to survive, small businesses must stay in tune with their environments and markets and be aware of their resource requirements. The development of a strategy is one way of accomplishing this.

A small business strategy often tries to locate a *niche* in the market where the small business would have special competence, or be able to meet a particular market need. A small business needs something to give it distinction, or a competitive advantage. This might be flexibility in production or service, or specialization in some technology or the servicing of a special market segment (refer to Illustration 1.3 for examples). Larger businesses are often unable to take advantage of these niches while small businesses often have greater operational flexibility with lower overheads which give them a cost and price advantage. But, studies have found that most owner/managers, or entrepreneurs, do not think in strategic terms. This is one aspect of the main reason given for the high failure rate of small businesses, that is, poor management.

ILLUSTRATION 1.3   *Small Businesses and New Manufacturing Technologies*

New manufacturing technologies can be introduced successfully in small businesses as well as large ones. The introduction of such technologies can have a substantial impact on the firm's strategy by leading to new products and markets.

It might be thought that only large firms benefit from new manufacturing technologies leaving small firms disadvantaged in the future. But, studies indicate that this is not the case.

New manufacturing technologies include such things as: computer-aided design; computer-aided manufacturing; flexible manufacturing systems; robotized factories; and automated storage/retrieval systems. Small firms are using this technology in novel and creative ways to gain advantages by capitalizing on flexibility, improving quality, reducing lead time, and lowering costs.

Two examples illustrate how small firms are using new manufacturing technologies to more effectively compete in the market:

Illinois Tool Works — This firm produces computer data entry devices, such as keyboards, and has used "in-line" manufacturing (group technology) to its advantage. Group technology is a non-computerized process of plant reorganization into "cells" to do in-line processing of part-families. The benefits of such a manufacturing technology include: reduced lead time (product design through production) and cycle time (production time); lower work-in-process inventories; and increased capacity. The improved manufacturing process has allowed Illinois Tool to divide their original market into small segments by providing more options, models, sizes, and colors. This ability to customize products has resulted in more satisfied customers because the firm can respond to individual requirements. The outcome is that the firm's strategy is now more "market-driven" rather than "manufacturing-driven."

Peerless Saw Company — In 1981, this firm was faced with strong foreign competition, increasing costs, and an old, out-of-date plant. Foreign competition was taking away the market for steel blades and sales were declining. The firm's president had software developed to allow the cutting of the sawblades to be performed by a laser. This technology enabled the firm to better meet the needs of customers making it able to supply more specialized blades in a shorter time. In fact, the technology changed the firm's market focus from high-volume, low-margin, standard products to a specialized one catering to a high-margin, custom-products market. The firm's strategy shifted substantially after the introduction of the new technology.

Source: Jack Meredith, "The Strategic Advantages of New Manufacturing Technologies for Small Firms," *Strategic Management Journal*, Vol. 8, No. 3 (June-July 1987), pp. 249–58.

Developing a strategy for a small business will be quite different from preparing one for a large organization. Planning is formalized in a large corporation and often involves Boards of Directors, professional planning staffs, committees, and consultants in addition to top management. In a small business, it is much more personalized in the owner/ manager. The strategy must be designed to seize opportunities in the market since it is not possible for a small business to create opportunities as a large corporation sometimes can. Small businesses often experience a scarcity of resources of every type, and this tends to focus strategy on resource attainment. As a result, the strategy must be more flexible, and more short term. Even if conceived only in the mind of the entrepreneur, a planning process, including a strategy, is needed in order to provide management discipline in a small business. Also, as the small business grows, the resource commitments become greater and operations more complex, necessitating more formalized planning practices.

1.3.4 STRATEGY IN THE GOVERNMENT SECTOR AND NOT-FOR-PROFIT ORGANIZATIONS[9]

The development of concepts and techniques of corporate strategy has in the past mainly occurred in the area of commercial enterprises; is this development applicable to public sector and not-for-profit organizations? The answer is most certainly yes. There are of course differences in such organizations, and, arguably what matters most is that managers can identify what those differences are and therefore what the focus of attention should be in considering strategic developments in the organization. For example, consider the difference between a commercial operation and a government agency. "A business company has a sales market in which it sells its products or services for money, a labor market from which it gets people to whom it pays money, a purchase market from which it gets its supplies for money, the money market from which it gets money and interest, loans or equity and to which it pays interests and dividends. The *raison d'être* of a business company lies in its sales market. It also gets there direct feedback for success or failure."[10]

However, although a government agency is in some respects similiar — it too has a labor market, a money market of sorts; it too has suppliers and users or customers — the fundamental difference is that at its heart lies a "political market which approves budgets, and provides subsidies." It is the explicit nature of this political dimension managers or officers have to cope with which particularly distinguishes government bodies, be they national or local, from commercial enterprises. This may in turn change the time horizons of decisions, since these may be heavily influenced by political considerations and may mean that analysis of strategies will require the norms of political dogma to be explicitly considered. However, although the magnitude of the political dimension is greater, the model of strategic management posed here nonetheless holds. What is different is that the emphasis placed on certain aspects of strategic analysis and choice, notably those to do with political dimensions, is the more important.

Other government sector operations may be commercial enterprises anyway. For example, in the United States, local transit systems and an electricity producer such as the Bonneville Power Administration are commercial enterprises as is Amtrak, the government operated rail passenger service, and Conrail, the railway system sold by the government in 1987. In Canada, governments own hundreds of business enterprises. Here the differences are likely to be associated with the nature of ownership and control. A state-controlled commercial enterprise may well have differences in planning horizons, different bases of finance, and require that top management more centrally control their organization for reporting purposes, for example to government ministers. Nonetheless, it is likely that the same competitive pressures will be exerted on these businesses as on private organizations.

Similarly, there will be differences in not-for-profit organizations such as educational institutions, hospitals, labor unions, political parties, churches, voluntary associations, arts and culture groups, and organized charities.[11] Illustration 1.4 provides an example of a strategy developed at one such organization, a university. Here the differences may be both to do with the different expectations of influencing bodies and also the special nature of revenue generation in terms of resources. The likelihood is that funding bodies may be diverse and, quite likely, not direct beneficiaries of the services offered. Moreover, they may well provide funds in advance of the services being offered in the form of grants for example. The implications here are several. The influence from the funding bodies is likely to be high in terms of the formulation of the strategies of the organizations; indeed the organizations may well develop strategies as much to do with, and influenced by, the funding bodies as by their clients. Moreover, since they are heavily dependent on funds which emanate not from clients, but from sponsors, a danger may be that the organization will become more concerned with resource efficiency than service effectiveness. It is also likely that there will be multiple sources of funding and this, linked to the different objectives and expectations of the funding bodies, might lead to a high incidence of political lobbying, difficulties in clear strategic planning, and a requirement to hold decision making and responsibility at the center where it is answerable to external influences rather than to delegate it within the organization. These characteristics and difficulties of strategic management in not-for-profit organizations are summarized in Figure 1.5. However, it must be pointed out that it is still necessary for such organizations to make surpluses if they are to carry out their work and, whether the focus is on the clients who use the services, or the sponsors who provide the revenue, strategies for achieving such surpluses are nonetheless necessary.

Overall, there is a need to recognize that different parts of the model of strategic management presented in this chapter and developed throughout the book, will be relevant to varying degrees according to the differences between organizations. There is no one right way of approaching the problems of strategic management and the consideration of government sector and not-for-profit organizations makes this point well.

ILLUSTRATION 1.4 *Strategic Management in Universities*

Many universities, one type of not-for-profit organization, are attempting to cope more effectively with a changing environment and resource shortages by developing appropriate strategies.

Many universities in the United States and Canada are involved in strategic management. The example in this illustration is the University of Alberta in Edmonton, Canada, but the approach used by this university is very similar to that used by others. The University of Alberta has about 24,000 students and an operating budget of over $230 million. The importance of a strategy is highlighted by this quotation from a planning document:

> Planning is essential for every organization; universities are no exception. As an institution, the University of Alberta must take charge of its future and shape it according to a deliberate and conscious strategy — a strategy derived from our best judgment of what it is that we, individually and collectively, want to be and to do.

The strategic plan analyzed the University's environment and identified several challenges: high enrollment; shifting demands for programs; new research opportunities; changing societal expectations of the role of a university; and limited availability of funds. Objectives were established: excellence in scholarship and research; excellence in teaching and learning; and excellence in service to society.

Given the environment and objectives, the University selected those things it felt should have priority, that is, the programs which would result in the accomplishment of the objectives. The priorities chosen to guide the University for the next decade were:

- Support graduate study and research to maintain the University's position as the major research center in the province.
- Maintain a strong liberal education program.
- Support regional needs, for example, research into problems in northern Canada and the establishment of programs for francophone Albertans.
- Provide professional programs comparable to any in North America.
- Become involved in more international programs.

The next section of the planning document outlined how the strategy was to be carried out. The University's programs were to be accessible to all who had the ability and the interest to undertake such study. Innovative methods of instruction were to be encouraged, including integration of computer usage in the core curriculum; library services were to be computerized; and experimental courses encouraged. The University's priorities for computer facilities and services were outlined, with specialization to take place in areas where it had a natural competitive advantage, and other technologies were to be acquired from other organizations. The planning document also outlined how the physical facilities would be utilized and how funds would be allocated.

Source: "The Next Decade and Beyond: A Plan for the Future," University of Alberta brochure, Edmonton, Alberta, Canada, March, 1986.

Figure 1.5   *Some characteristics of strategic management in not-for-profit organizations.*

CHARACTERISTICS	LIKELY EFFECTS
Objectives and expectations • May be multiple service objectives and expectations. • May be multiple influences on policy. • Expectations of funding bodies very influential.	• Complicates strategic planning. • High incidence of political lobbying. • Difficulties in delegating/decentralizing responsibilities and decision making.
Market and users • Beneficiaries of service not necessarily contributors of revenue/resources.	• Service satisfaction not measured readily in financial terms.
Resources • High proportion from government or sponsors. • Received in advance of services. • May be multiple sources of funding.	• Influence from funding bodies may be high. • May be emphasis on financial or resource efficiency rather than service effectiveness. • Strategies may be addressed to sponsors as much as clients.

1.4 SUMMARY

This chapter set out to explain the focus, concept and scope of this book and to propose a framework for approaching the subject. The hope is that by this stage readers will have some understanding of the kinds of problems with which the text is concerned. Later the book sets out to amplify the different elements of strategic management identified and outlined in this chapter. However, before proceeding to this, the next chapter looks at how strategy formulation occurs in practice so that readers can place the discussion in the remainder of the book in the context of managerial practice.

References

1. From D.J. Hickson, Richard J. Butler, David Cray, Geoffrey R. Mallory, and David C. Wilson, *Top Decisions: Strategic Decision Making in Organizations*, (Oxford: Basil Blackwell Publisher, 1986), p. 28.

2. These reasons for the complexity of strategic management are based on the explanations given by Gerry Johnson, *Strategic Change in the Management Process*, (Oxford: Basil Blackwell Publisher, 1987), pp. 5–6.

3. We have chosen not to provide a definition as such of what is meant by strategy, preferring to discuss the characteristics of strategic decisions as a means of explanation. A useful analysis of alternative definitions can be found in C.W. Hofer and D. Schendel, *Strategy Formulation: Analytical Concepts*, (St. Paul, Minnesota: West Publishing Co., 1978), pp. 16–20.

4. A useful distinction is made by R.N. Anthony and J. Dearden, *Management Control Systems*, (Homewood, Illinois: Richard D. Irwin Inc., 1976), between operational levels of management and strategic levels. They identify three levels of management activity:

   i) Strategic planning is the process of deciding on the goals of the organization, on changes in these goals, on the resources used to attain these goals and on the policies that are to govern the acquisition, use, and disposition of these resources.
   ii) Management control is the process by which managers assure that resources are obtained and used effectively and efficiently in the accomplishment of the organization's goals.
   iii) Operational control is the process of assuring that specific tasks are carried out effectively and efficiently.

   While we recognize that the majority of managers are engaged in the third level of activity for most of their time, the first two levels are clearly of great importance and this book is mainly concerned with these levels.

5. See for example, W.F. Glueck, *Strategic Management and Business Policy*, 3rd Edition, (New York: McGraw–Hill, 1988), or Arthur A. Thompson, Jr. and A.J. Strickland III, *Strategic Management: Tasks of the General Manager*, 3rd Edition, (Plano, Texas: Business Publications Inc., 1986).

6. For a detailed discussion see J–C Spender, "Strategy Making in Business" which is a doctoral thesis from the Manchester Business School (1980). Spender's views are also summarized in P. Grinyer and J–C Spender, *Turnaround: Managerial Recipes for Strategic Success*, (London: Associated Business Press, 1978). Also see Grinyer and Spender, "Recipes, Crises and Adaptation in Mature Businesses," *International Studies of Management and Organization*, Vol. IX, No.3, (1979), p. 113.

7. One of the most stimulating papers which addresses the problems arising from an over-constrained view of the scope of a business is that by Theodore Levitt, "Marketing Myopia," *Harvard Business Review*, July–Aug, (1960).

8. Peter F. Drucker, *Management: Tasks, Responsibilities, Practices*, (New York: Harper and Row Publishers, 1974), pp. 649–54.

9. Chapter 18 in G. Steiner and J. Miner, *Management Policy and Strategy* (New York: Macmillan

Publishing Co., Inc., 1977), discusses aspects of strategy in not-for-profit organizations. An interesting and brief discussion of the problems and differences in the non-commercial sector can also be found in an article by M.L. Hatten, "Strategic Management in Not-for-Profit Organizations," *Strategic Management Journal*, April-June, (1982).

10. An interesting discussion of strategy in government departments can be found in H. Tendam, "Strategic Management in a Government Agency," *Long Range Planning*, Volume 19, Number 4, (1986), pp. 78–86.

11. This discussion on strategy in not-for-profit organizations is based on Chapter 11 of T.L. Wheelan and J.D. Hunger, *Strategic Management*, Second Edition, (London: Addison-Wesley Publishers Ltd., 1978).

Recommended Key Readings

For a general discussion of the concept of strategy, refer to the following:

Andrews, Kenneth R. *The Concept of Corporate Strategy*. Homewood, Illinois: Richard D. Irwin, 1984.

Berg, Norman A. *General Management: An Analytical Approach*. Homewood, Illinois: Richard D. Irwin, 1987.

Schendel, Dan E. and Charles W. Hofer, eds. *Strategic Management: New View of Business Policy and Planning*. Boston: Little, Brown & Company, 1979.

For more information on strategic management in small businesses, refer to small business management textbooks, or the following articles:

Gibb, Allan and Mike Scott. "Strategic Awareness, Personal Commitment and the Process of Planning in the Small Business." *Journal of Management Studies*, 22:6, (November, 1985), pp. 597–631.

de Kluyver, C.A. and M. McNally. "Developing a Corporate Planning Model for a Small Company." *Long Range Planning*, 15:1, (1982), pp. 97–106.

Some sources of information on strategic management in not-for-profit organizations are:

Grayson, Leslie E. and Curtis J. Tompkins. *Management of Public Sector and Nonprofit Organizations*. Reston, Virginia: Reston Publishing Co., 1984.

Gruber, Robert E. and Mary Mohr. "Strategic Management for Multiprogram Nonprofit Organizations." *California Management Review*, XXIV:3, (Spring 1982), pp. 15–22.

McLaughlin, Curtis P. *The Management of Non-Profit Organizations*. New York: John Wiley and Sons, Inc., 1986.

Nutt, Paul C. "A Strategic Planning Network for Non-profit Organizations." *Strategic Management Journal*, Vol. 5, (1984), pp. 57–75.

Unterman, Israel and Richard Hart Davis. "The Strategy Gap in Not-for-profits." *Harvard Business Review*, (May-June 1982), pp. 30–40.

For a review of the role and relevance of strategic management to the public sector see:

Bryson, J.M. and W.D. Roering. "Applying Private Sector Strategic Planning in the Public Sector." *Journal of the American Planning Association*, (Winter, 1987).

Montanari, John R. and Jeffrey S. Bracker. "The Strategic Management Process at the Public Planning Unit Level." *Strategic Management Journal*, Vol. 7, (1986), pp. 251–265.

Ruffat, Jean. "Strategic Management of Public and Non-Market Corporations." *Long Range Planning*, Vol. 16, (1983), pp. 74–84.

Chapter 2
STRATEGIC DECISION MAKING IN PRACTICE

2.1 INTRODUCTION

In Chapter 1, the idea of corporate strategy was introduced, as were the elements of strategic management — strategic analysis, strategic choice and strategy implementation. It is important to emphasize that these elements are parts of a model, the purpose of which is to help readers think about strategic problems and formulate strategy. It is also important, however, to understand that the model does not necessarily describe how strategies followed by organizations *actually* come about. There now exists a good deal of evidence about just how this does occur, so before going on to examine the elements of the model in more detail in Parts II, III and IV, it is important to have a clearer understanding of the process of strategic decision making in practice. This chapter sets out to provide a basis for that understanding and its content will be developed further in Chapters 5 and 11 in particular.

The first part of the chapter is concerned with the *nature of strategic change*, i.e., the ways in which strategic changes are observed to come about in organizations. The conclusion reached is that strategic changes may take different forms but that, typically, they do not occur as major, sudden changes in direction but as more gradual, "incremental developments," with only occasional more "global" change.

The second part of the chapter is concerned with *how managers make strategic decisions*. Here the focus is on the process of decision making: how a strategic problem is recognized and defined; how a decision to take a course of action is actually made. It appears that a neat and rational process is not necessarily employed by managers and that some of the aspects of the strategic management model outlined in Chapter 1 may not be apparent in the processes actually employed. Rather, strategy needs to be understood as an outcome of the social, political and cultural processes of management in organizations. In this sense planning processes may more sensibly be seen as contributing to, rather than accounting for, strategic decisions.

In the final part of the chapter there is a discussion of what can be learned from the practice of strategic decision making in terms of *implications for the study of strategy*. It is, however, important to sound something of a warning: just because managers behave in particular ways does not mean these are the "right" ways or the most sensible ways. It is important to assess what is "good practice" and build on that. The approach taken in this book is that readers will be able to assess a good deal better for themselves which of the techniques and concepts in the rest of the book are most useful if they have an understanding of strategic decision making as it happens.

2.2 THE NATURE OF STRATEGIC CHANGE

Strategic changes are often conceived of as sudden major changes. However, there is increasing evidence to show that the strategic development of organizations is better described in terms of continuity. There is a tendency towards "momentum" of strategy;[1] once an organization has adopted a particular strategy then it tends to develop from that strategy and within it rather than reversing its direction. The result is that fundamental changes in strategy in organizations are relatively rare; they do take place but are usually infrequent and may be of a dramatic nature. Henry Mintzberg's historical studies of organizations [2] over many decades showed that "global" change did take place but was infrequent. Typically, organizations changed *incrementally*, during which time strategies formed gradually; or through *piecemeal change* during which some strategies changed and others remained constant; there were periods of *continuity* during which established strategy remained unchanged; and also periods of *flux* in which strategies did change but in no very clear direction. Figure 2.1 illustrates these patterns.

Figure 2.1   *Patterns of strategic change.*

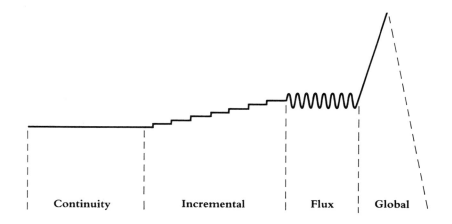

| Continuity | Incremental | Flux | Global |

On the whole, then, strategies of organizations tend not to change dramatically from year to year, perhaps even for very many years. One strategic move may well grow out of the existing mainstream strategy, which in itself, gradually changes. Over time, then, the organization may develop a quite significant shift in strategy, but gradually. Illustration 2.1 shows how this might occur. In many respects, from a management point of view such gradual, incremental change makes a lot of sense. No organization could function efficiently if it were to undergo major revisions of strategy very frequently: and, in any case, it is unlikely that the environment would change so rapidly that this would be necessary. Incremental change, might, therefore be seen as an adaptive process to a continually changing environment; indeed we will see that this is the view held by some writers on the management of strategy, and by many managers themselves. There are, however, dangers here. Environmental change may not always be gradual enough for incremental change to keep pace: if such incremental strategic change lags behind environmental change then the organization may get out of line with its environment and, in time, need more fundamental, or global, strategic change to occur. Mintzberg's work seems to suggest that this is so; global change tends to occur at times of crisis in organizations, typically when performance has declined significantly.

Conceiving of an organization's strategy in terms of such patterns of change means it is important to be careful about just what is meant by strategy. Typically, strategy is written about as though it is developed by managers in an *intended*, planned fashion. This may be so but it should be recognized that strategies may also come about in other ways. There may be *emergent* strategies which come about, or are realized without the explicit intention of managers but which result from the flow of more operational, day-to-day decision making. [3] It may also be that the strategies managers do advocate explicitly are not put into effect: these are *unrealized* strategies.

These distinctions raise the point as to whether or not strategy should be thought of as that which managers say they are following (or think they should be following), or that which is actually being implemented by the business over time. They may well be the same, but it is also possible that they may not. This issue is discussed further at the end of the chapter.

2.2.1 INCREMENTAL STRATEGIC MANAGEMENT

In the late 1950s, Lindblom [4] suggested that rational planning models of strategic choice were unrealistic. He argued that, given the complexity of organizations and the environments in which they operate, managers cannot consider all possible strategic options in terms of all possible futures and evaluate these against preset unambiguous objectives. This is particularly so in an organizational context in which there are likely to be conflicting views, values and power bases. Rather, choice of strategy is made by comparing options and considering which would seem to give the best outcome and be most possible to implement. Lindblom called this strategy building through "successive limited comparisons." The implication is that those options most approximating past decisions are likely to

---

ILLUSTRATION 2.1   *Incremental Strategic Change at Hewlett-Packard Co.*

The strategy followed by Hewlett-Packard has changed markedly in the last decade, not by huge strategic leaps but incrementally.

Hewlett-Packard (H–P) is a supplier of electronic test and measurement instruments, and computer products. Its traditional business strength was in instruments like oscilloscopes for industrial testing and these still account for about one third of the company's business. Computer products are now a greater portion of H–P's business and it is the third largest maker of minicomputers after IBM and Control Equipment Corporation.

Started in 1939, H–P had grown rapidly and by 1980 there were about 50 divisions producing and marketing about 9,000 products. Each had its own manufacturing and marketing departments and formed a loosely knit federation of highly autonomous divisions. This structure encouraged entrepreneurial spirit and participatory management was practiced. H–P pioneered such management techniques as flextime, no layoff policy, and open door management in the US.

John Young became President and Chief Executive in 1978 and he recognized that strategic change was necessary. The company still had reasonable earnings and was not desperately seeking remedies to a crisis situation. But, the environment in which the company operated was changing, and the market was becoming more competitive. Customers for computers were looking for complete systems instead of continuing the helter-skelter computerization of the past. Instruments had become more sophisticated and incorporated computers. No longer was the company selling to engineers, its main customer in the past, but to less technically oriented managers as well. The company's organization prevented the cooperation necessary to respond to the new market, and this had lead to delays in the development and marketing of such products as workstations, software, and desktop computers.

The strategic change necessary was substantial, but was not imposed on the organization all at once. Young was sensitive to the advantages of H–P's culture and did not want to risk losing the informality and camaraderie existing in the organization. The structural changes announced in 1984 were referred to as "drastic" and "far-reaching" by the business press. However, the restructuring had been contemplated for some time and had been cautiously approached. The following are some of the incremental changes preceding the 1984 restructuring:

- Coordinating groups, *ad hoc* committees and task forces were used to introduce cooperation among divisions who had been very autonomous. These groups gathered information and encouraged communication.

- In 1980, a recruitment program beefed up research and development by hiring outsiders. This was a way of getting new ideas and approaches into the company.

- In 1981, a program management approach was used to develop the HP9000 computer because the project required the cooperation of ten H–P divisions.

- In 1982, a new division within the Computer Marketing Group focused on "applications marketing" and supplying sales support for software products originating in different H–P divisions. This move was designed to sensitize the divisions to "customer related concerns."

- In 1983, a "group" team was put together to develop the "Spectrum" computer. This set an example for the major restructuring to come. An Information Technology Group was established to help divisions learn how to cooperate on projects.

These moves lead to the restructuring in 1984 when the company was organized into groupings related to the needs of the market. The customer groupings were office/administrative products, engineering products, and factory floor/automation products with a marketing section including all salespeople to avoid the overlapping and duplicated efforts of the past. This transformation at H–P has been described in several ways, including: from a "products" to a "customer/marketing" orientation; from an instrument company to a computer colossus; from a decentralized to a centralized company; and from an engineering run company to a "management" one.

Young was aware of the need for the incremental approach. It is reported that his style is to build consensus, not to be authoritarian. He moved cautiously, being careful not to disrupt H–P's tradition of participatory management and was committed to a hands off approach that involved coaching others to find solutions to problems. Finally, Young installed new reporting and performance measuring systems to further develop links and cooperation throughout the company. After four years of strategic change, H–P was in a position to respond in a coordinated manner to the increasingly competitive market.

Source: "Can John Young Redesign Hewlett-Packard?" *Business Week*, (December 6, 1982), pp. 72–8; "Mettle Testing Time for John Young," *Fortune*, (April 19, 1985), pp. 241–4; "Hewlett-Packard: Continuing the Search for Excellence," *Business Marketing*, (November 1985), pp. 74 and 76.

be those looked upon most favorably because they build on the experience of the organization and its managers. The decision will then be put into operation and, in effect, tested in action before being developed further.

This position is similar in many respects to that argued by Quinn. [5] His study of nine major multinational businesses concluded that the management process could best be described as *logical incrementalism*. By this he meant the following:

1. Managers have a view of where they want the organization to be in years to come and try to move towards this position in an evolutionary way. They do this by attempting to

ensure the success and development of a strong, secure but flexible core business, but also by continually experimenting with "side bet" ventures.

2. Effective managers accept the uncertainty of their environment because they realize that they cannot do away with this uncertainty by trying to "know" factually about how the environment will change: rather, they seek to become highly sensitive to environmental signals through constant environmental scanning. They also manage uncertainty by testing changes in strategy in small-scale steps.

3. They also try to encourage experimentation in the organization: indeed, there is a reluctance to specify precise objectives too early as this might stifle ideas and prevent the desired sort of experimentation. There is also recognition that such experiments cannot be expected to be the sole responsibility of top management — that they should be encouraged to emerge from lower levels, or "subsystems" in the organization.

4. Such a process is seen by managers to have significant benefits. Continual testing and gradual strategy implementation provide improved quality of information for decision making and enable better sequencing of the elements of major decisions. There is also a stimulation of managerial flexibility and creativity and, since change is always likely to be gradual, it is more likely possible to create and develop a commitment to change throughout the organization. Such processes also take into account the political nature of organizational life since smaller changes are less likely to face the same amount of resistance as major changes. It is also more possible to accommodate the variety of resource demands and political ambitions of different groupings — or coalitions — in the organization (see Chapter 5).

If management process is incremental, the idea of a neat sequential model of strategy has to be questioned. The idea that the implementation of strategy somehow follows a choice, which in turn has followed analysis, does not hold. Rather, strategy is here seen to be worked through in action. In a sense, the implementation of strategy is the continual testing of the suitability of a strategy to the circumstances of the organization.[6]

This view of strategy making as a process bears similarity to the descriptions managers themselves often give of how strategies come about in their organizations. Illustration 2.2 provides some examples of managers talking about the strategic decision making process in their organization. It is essentially a "logical incremental" view. They see themselves as "strategists" continually adapting to their environment while not "rocking the boat" too much so as to maintain efficiency and performance, and to keep the various stakeholders in the organization — shareholders, other management departments and the employers, for example, — content. Quinn argues that: "Good managers are aware of this process, and they consciously intervene in it. They use it to improve the information available for decisions and to build the psychological identification essential to successful strategies . . . properly managed, it is a conscious, purposeful, proactive, executive practice."[7]

ILLUSTRATION 2.2   *A Logical Incrementalist View of Strategic Management*

Managers often see themselves managing adaptively; continually changing strategy to keep in line with the environment, while maintaining efficiency and keeping stakeholders happy.

1. We tend to test a number of different approaches on a small scale with only limited or local company identification. If one approach works, we'll test it further and amplify its use; if another bombs, we try to keep it from being used again. . . . then along comes another issue and we start all over again. Gradually the successful approaches merge into a pattern of actions which becomes our strategy.

2. I begin wide-ranging discussions with people inside and outside the corporation. From these a pattern eventually emerges. It's like fitting together a jigsaw puzzle. At first the vague outline of an approach appears like the sail of a ship in a puzzle. Then suddenly the rest of the puzzle becomes quite clear. You wonder why you didn't see it all along.

3. We had no particularly entrenched ideas as to where we were . . . so there was an infinite amount of flexibility. One thing we decided was that we wanted to keep this appeal — it might not bring us an enormous leap forward, but as long as we can keep adjusting our merchandise mix and image satisfactorily, we can keep a fair share of the market.

4. The real strength of the company is to be able to follow these peripheral excursions into whatever . . . one has to keep thrusting in these directions; they are little tentacles going out, testing the water.

5. We haven't stood still in the past and I can't see with our present set up that we shall stand still in the future; but what I really mean is that it is a path of evolution rather than revolution. Some companies get a successful formula and stick to that rigidly because that is what they know — for example [company x] did not really adapt to change, so they had to make what was a revolution. We hopefully have changed gradually and that's what I think we should do. We are always looking for fresh openings without going off at a tangent.

Source: Extracts 1 and 2 from J. B. Quinn, *Strategies for Change*, (Homewood, Illinois: Richard D. Irwin Inc., 1980); extracts 3, 4 and 5 from G. Johnson, *Strategic Change and the Management Process*, (Oxford: Basil Blackwell Publisher, 1987).

Figure 2.2 *A notional pattern of incremental change (the environment changes gradually and organization strategy develops incrementally in line with it).*

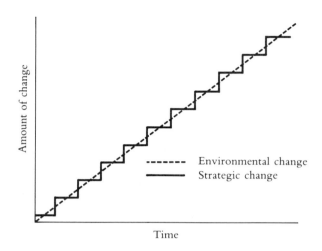

Time

Source: G. Johnson, *Strategic Change and the Management Process,* Oxford: Basil Blackwell Publisher, 1987.

Quinn also suggests that the various decisions in the incremental process should not be seen as entirely separate. Because the subsystems of the organization are in a continual state of interplay with each other, the managers of each will know what the others are doing and will be able to interpret each other's actions and requirements. They are, in effect, learning from each other about the feasibility of a course of action in terms of resource management and its internal political acceptability. Moreover, the formulation of strategy in this way means that the implications of the strategy are continually being tested out. This continual readjustment does, of course, make a lot of sense if the environment is considered to be a continually changing influence on the organization. It is a process through which the organization keeps itself in line with such change, as shown notionally in Figure 2.2.

2.2.2 PLANNING AND STRATEGIC MANAGEMENT

Where within all this, then, is the relevance and role of the "planning process?" The words strategy and planning have become so inextricably associated that it becomes necessary to define the role and forms of planning more clearly. This necessity stems from a common confusion between planning as a formalized activity, often known as corporate planning within an organization, and planning as a more generalized term for what managers do when making strategic decisions.[8]

Planning, in the sense of analyzing situations, considering the outcomes of proposals and thinking through the sequence of actions required to put change into effect, is part of the job of a manager anyway: so, as far as strategic decisions are concerned, planning is not just the task of a corporate planner. Indeed, given an incremental process of strategic change, planning at the managerial level may be a more significant influence than planning at the corporate level.

It is also important to be clear about the role of corporate planning in an organization. There is little evidence to support the idea that corporate planning as an activity, or corporate planners as managers in organizations, are actually responsible for strategic decisions being made.[9] Rather, the role of corporate planning appears to be to contribute to the strategic management process in three main ways:[10]

1. Assisting in the adaption of the organization to its environment by means of monitoring changes in the environment, formulating environmental and strategic scenarios and acting in a consultancy capacity to parts of the organization wishing to examine the implications of environmental change. In this sense, corporate planning is carrying out a strategic analysis function.

2. Providing an integration role in an organization by acting as a communication channel between, for example, a corporate head office and its divisions.

3. Providing a control mechanism to monitor the performance of parts of the organization (e.g. divisions) against strategic priorities. Here corporate planning has a role in the implementation of strategy.

The picture emerges of corporate planning as an aid to, rather than as the means of, strategic decision making.

It should also be clear that planning, whether in the form of corporate planning or as a task of individual managers, may occur within an incremental process of change just as it may when global change occurs. In an incremental context, planning may take the form of the planning of decisions within parts of the organization dealing with strategic issues which help form overall strategy. However, there is some evidence that formal planning may contribute more to fundamental shifts in strategy originating at a corporate level. For example, in his study of the different patterns of strategy formulation, Mintzberg[11] found that "intended" strategy (by which he meant the sort of formalized planning for change of strategy often associated traditionally with strategic planning) tended to occur most often where there was global change.

Planning, then, is the responsibility of managers and is an important aspect of strategic management: and strategic management is not the property of a corporate planning department but the responsibility of managers and just as much part of incremental change as it is of more global change.[12]

2.3 HOW STRATEGIC DECISIONS ARE MADE

"Logical incrementalism" can be thought of as a rational, but action oriented, process of strategic management. It includes the idea that managers consciously and logically seek to manage strategy, and that strategy comes about through such management logic. Other research, however, emphasizes the "organizational action" dimension of strategic management a good deal more. This research [13] has sought to understand more fully the processes which actually occur in organizations and give rise to strategic decisions. Four stages can be used to describe such decision processes:

1. *Problem awareness:* the recognition that "something is amiss," that a state of affairs exists which needs remedying;

2. *Problem diagnosis:* the collection of information about, and examination of the circumstances of, the problem and the definition of the problem;

3. *The development of solutions:* the generation of possible solutions to the problem;

4. *The selection of a solution:* the means by which a decision about what is to be done is reached.

These stages are amplified in the following discussion and illustrated in Figure 2.3 and Illustration 2.3.

2.3.1 PROBLEM AWARENESS

Awareness of a strategic problem typically occurs at an individual level. It is individuals who are likely to get a "gut feeling" that something is wrong: and these may not be managers of course; they might well be salespeople, office staff or machine operators. This awareness is likely to develop through a period of what Lyles[14] calls "incubation" in which managers sense various kinds of stimuli which confirm and define a developing picture of the problem. These stimuli are what Norburn[15] calls "signals" or "ear twitchers" and appear to be primarily of three types. First, there are internal performance measurements such as levels of turnover or profit performance. Second, there is customer reaction particularly to the quality and price of services or products. And third, there are changes in the environment, particularly in terms of competitive action, technological change and economic conditions. Together these signals create a picture of the extent to which an organization's circumstances deviate from what is normally to be expected. This deviation may not be from a specified set of performance criteria, such as profit measures, but could well be a perceived divergence from a normal trading pattern or a change from a typical customer response, for example.

This accumulation of stimuli eventually reaches a point where the amount of evidence is such that the presence of a problem cannot be ignored at an organizational level. This "triggering point" is likely to be reached when the formal information systems of the organization begin to highlight the problem; perhaps the variance against budget becomes undeniable or a number of sales areas consistently report dropping sales. It is at

Figure 2.3   *A model of the strategic decision process.*

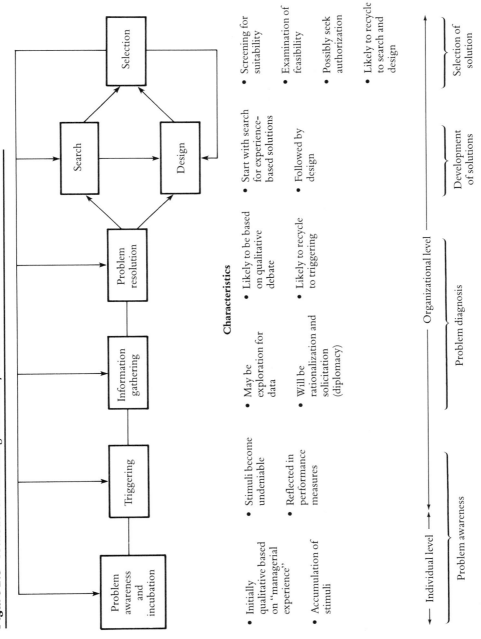

ILLUSTRATION 2.3 *Toxicem's decision to reduce energy costs*

Toxicem (a pseudonym), a chemical company facing rising energy costs, decided to generate in-plant electricity to reduce costs. The decision illustrates the iterative nature of the decision process, and the role of triggering and diplomacy.

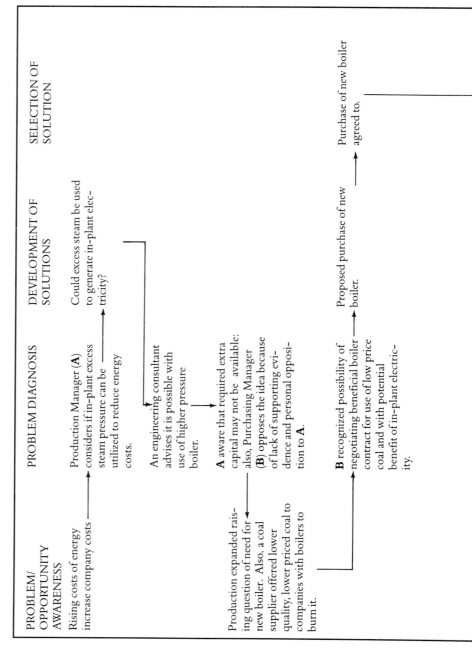

PROBLEM/
OPPORTUNITY
AWARENESS

PROBLEM DIAGNOSIS

DEVELOPMENT OF
SOLUTIONS

SELECTION OF
SOLUTION

Rising costs of energy increase company costs

Production Manager (**A**) considers if in-plant excess steam pressure can be utilized to reduce energy costs.

Could excess steam be used to generate in-plant electricity?

An engineering consultant advises it is possible with use of higher pressure boiler.

A aware that required extra capital may not be available: also, Purchasing Manager (**B**) opposes the idea because of lack of supporting evidence and personal opposition to **A**.

Production expanded raising question of need for new boiler. Also, a coal supplier offered lower quality, lower priced coal to companies with boilers to burn it.

B recognized possibility of negotiating beneficial boiler contract for use of low price coal and with potential benefit of in-plant electricity.

Proposed purchase of new boiler.

Purchase of new boiler agreed to.

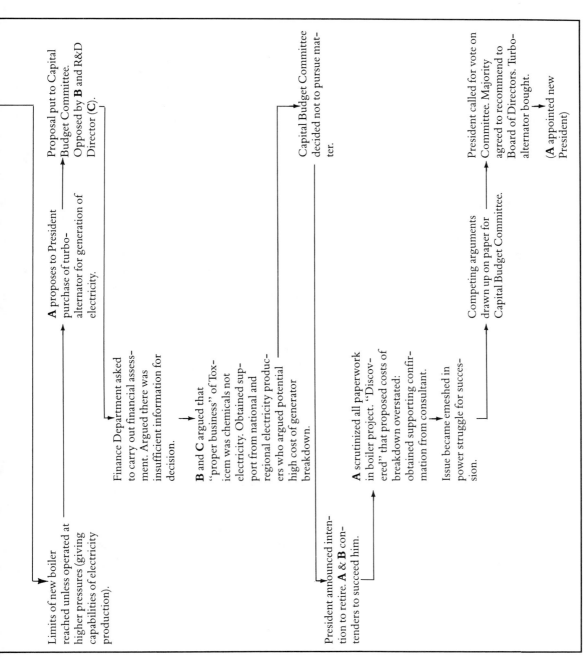

Source: Adapted from the Toxicem case in Chapter 1 of D.J. Hickson *et al.*, *Top Decisions*, Oxford: Basil Blackwell Publisher, 1986.

this point that more organized activity takes over from individual consideration of the problem.

The importance of this first stage of the individual's role in problem recognition needs to be emphasized. There is evidence to suggest that successful business performance is associated with management's ability to sense its environment.[16] This does not mean that the company necessarily needs to have complex or sophisticated means of achieving this sensitivity but rather that managers respond to or take into account a wide range of influences and have an internally consistent view of these influences.

2.3.2 PROBLEM DIAGNOSIS

At the organizational level, problem diagnosis may involve information gathering and problem resolution (or definition).

Information gathering could take the form of:

1. Exploration for information to determine more clearly the facts about the problem. Such information is likely to be sought and gathered on a verbal and informal basis[17] and this method seems to be used in companies with more senior management. What these managers are doing, in effect, is building up a picture of the strategic position of their organization through environmental sensing. There is little evidence of extensive formalized systematic environmental analysis.

2. The rationalization of information and stimuli to do with the problem so as to clarify the picture of the problem. This is a process likely to draw heavily on existing managerial experience. Information generated from the more formalized environmental analysis in this process is likely to be used to post-rationalize or justify managers' emerging views of the situation.

3. A process of "diplomacy" to establish what peer groups or those with power in the organization think about the problem and to gather political support for individuals' views of the problem.

The resolution (or definition) of what constitutes the nature of the problem may prove difficult. There is likely to be an attempt, through debate and discussion, to get some sort of organizational view, or consensus, on the problem to be tackled. In effect, the resolution of the nature of the problem also comes about through a process of diplomacy and is likely to take shape in terms of both collective managerial experience and the political processes in the organization. Some organizations may also find difficulty in proceeding beyond this stage and find that the process reverts to information gathering or the triggering of a different problem.

Overall, it needs to be emphasized that, in practice, formal analysis tends to play much less of a role than might be suggested in some management texts. Rather, problem diagnosis tends to be rooted in managerial experience and different views tend to be resolved through social and political processes.

2.3.3 THE DEVELOPMENT OF SOLUTIONS

Mintzberg[18] shows how the choice of solution is likely to have two stages; the first is the development of possible solutions and the second is the selection between them.

Managers will first search for ready-made solutions to the problems which have been triggered. This will first occur through *memory search*, in which the manager seeks for known, existing or tried solutions, or *passive search* which entails waiting for possible solutions to be suggested. Only if these methods are unsuccessful will the manager move on to more active searches, calling upon personal experience as a starting point. There will likely be a number of these searches before any attempt is made to *design* a solution. (By design is meant the custom-made building of a strategy to handle the problem at hand.) In either case the process of choice tends to be iterative. Managers begin with a rather vague idea of a possible solution and gradually refine it by recycling it through selection routines (see below) back into problem identification or through further search routines. The process is developmental, based on debate and discussion within the organization and, again, the collective management wisdom and experience in the organization. There is little evidence that such a process is highly structured or that there is a clear set of options neatly set down, or clear criteria against which to analyze the choices available.[19] Again, as with the process of problem diagnosis, the importance of what might loosely be called managerial experience and its role within an essentially social and political process is evident.

2.3.4 THE SELECTION OF A SOLUTION

As has been seen, the process of developing solutions may overlap with the processes of selecting solutions. These somewhat arbitrary categorizations for the purposes of description should perhaps be regarded as part of the same process in which a limited number of potential solutions gradually are reduced until one or more emerges. This may occur in a number of ways.

Through "screening," managers eliminate that which they consider not to be feasible. However, the predominant criterion for assessing feasibility is not formal analysis but managerial judgment followed by political bargaining. Formal analysis is the least observed of these three approaches. The use of analytical techniques in organizations should therefore be seen, again, within an essentially social and political process. It should also be realized that analysis is not the only means by which insights into problems or solutions can be obtained. For example, Quinn suggests that successful managers actively use bargaining processes in order to challenge prevailing strategic inclinations and generate information from other parts of the organization to help in making decisions.

It should be remembered that the whole process is likely to be taking place below the most senior levels of management, so referring possible solutions to some higher level may be required. Another way of selecting between possibilities is to refer the choice to this more senior level of management — to seek *authorization*. Typically, though not always, authorization is sought for a completed solution after screening has taken place. This raises the question as to whether or not it is sensible to view this referral as a sort of checking of an incrementally generated strategic solution against some overall strategy. It would certainly be in line with Mintzberg's view that while most strategic decisions emanate from decisions within management subsystems, it is the role of leadership to maintain some sort of general direction. If this view is taken then the process of authorization can be thought of as the matching of one strategic decision against an overall, more generalized, strategy or mission of the organization.

These findings are, in general, borne out by David Hickson and his colleagues[20] in a study of 150 major decisions in 30 different public and private sector organizations in the UK. The study identified three broad types of decision-making process:

1. *Sporadic* processes characterized by many delays and impediments, many sources of influence and information on decisions and, therefore, protracted personal interaction and informal negotiation.

2. *Fluid* processes in which there are fewer delays and sources of influence, and more formal channels of communication which take rather less time.

3. *Constricted* processes in which information sources are more readily available and decisions can be made within groups or by individuals without extensive reference to others in the organization. This might be the case in a business with a dominant chief executive, or where there is an issue relating primarily to one part of an organization.

Over time all three types of process are likely to be found in most organizations. However, there seems to be some bias towards sporadic decision making in manufacturing industries where decision making tends to be more decentralized and subject to many conflicting interests, in comparison with service industries, which are rather more characterized by fluid processes and face rather less complexity. Government sector organizations tend to be characterized by more sporadic decision processes largely because of committee procedures, external intervention and the need to arrive at a politically acceptable consensus.

2.4 STRATEGY FORMULATION AS A CULTURAL PROCESS

Traditionally, strategy has been viewed as the response of an organization to its environment. The environment changes and management rethinks and adjusts strategy as necessary. However, the organization has severe limitations when making such readjustments. The constraints given most attention by writers have been constraints in the environment itself which hinder change (competitive action, government legislation, economic forces and so on) and internal organizational resource constraints (a lack of finance or competent management, for example).

This view omits a major influence on strategy formulation, namely the strategy makers themselves. It is too simple to think of strategy as a response to the environment for it is evident that, faced with similar environments, organizations will respond differently: as has been seen, the response is likely to be influenced by the past experience of the managers and by the wider social and political processes in the organization. These social processes of strategy formulation have received much attention in the work of those writers and researchers[21] who have sought to understand how some businesses seem to perform consistently so much better than others — the so-called "excellent" companies. The general conclusion these writers come to is that processes of strategic management need to be understood as an essentially cultural process.

In this book, "organizational culture" is taken to mean "the deeper level of basic *assumptions and beliefs* which are shared by members of an organization, which operate unconsciously, and define in a basic 'taken for granted' fashion an organization's view of itself and its environment."[22] Further, culture includes the ways members of the organization behave towards each other, the rituals and routines of organizational life, the stories told of organizational history, the type of language and expression commonly used, and the organizational "symbols" such as logos, organization charts, status symbols, policies on rewards and incentives, and so on:[23] in short, "the way we do things around here."[24]

2.4.1 CULTURE AND STRATEGY

There is now a growing understanding that the strategy of an enterprise, its structure, the sort of people who hold power, its control systems, and the way it operates, tend to reflect the culture of that organization. The work of Miles and Snow[25] illustrates this. They point out that there are organizations in which the prevailing beliefs are essentially conservative, where low-risk strategies, secure markets, and well tried potential solutions are valued: they call these organizations *defenders*. In contrast, there are organizations in which the dominant beliefs are more to do with innovation and breaking new ground. Here management tends to go for higher risk strategies and new opportunities. Miles and Snow call these *prospector*-type organizations. The different beliefs and assumptions held by these two different types of operations are also reflected more widely.[26] For example, organizational stories in defenders are typically about historical stability and consensus whereas in prospector organizations they are about growth and change with tales of dissension rather than consensus. The routines in these two types of organizations are also different; prospector organizations tend to have less rigid approaches to decision making and planning, for example, with less of an emphasis on formal relationships between people and groups.

The point is that prospectors and defenders do not behave in the same way even within similar environments. The strategies such organizations follow are better accounted for by their prevailing beliefs than by the environmental stimuli. For example, faced with a declining market demand, the defender is likely to follow a strategy of concentration on the market niche in which it specializes and a tighter control of costs, while the prospector searches for opportunities to obtain new markets or increase market share. In turn, in defender type organizations, conservative approaches and an emphasis on efficiency tend to be institutionalized by a dominance over time of managers with personally conservative ideologies, often from managerial functions which emphasize control and efficiency — notably accountants and production management.

2.4.2 THE RECIPE AND THE CULTURAL WEB

The set of beliefs and assumptions which forms part of the culture of an organization has variously been called an interpretative scheme,[27] a paradigm,[28] and a recipe.[29] Here the word recipe[30] is used. The recipe is the set of beliefs and assumptions held relatively commonly throughout the organization; taken for granted in that organization, but discernible to the outside observer in the stories of organizational history and explanations of events. The recipe makes sense of the situation managers find themselves in and provides a basis for formulating strategy. Illustration 2.4 gives examples of such recipes.

It is not suggested that the beliefs and assumptions which make up the recipe are necessarily identical for everyone in the organization — though there is evidence to suggest that in some organizations it is particularly uniform.[31] Nor is it suggested that it is a static set of beliefs over time — though it is quite likely that it will evolve gradually rather than change suddenly. What it does represent, however, is the collective managerial experience seen to be so important in the formulation of strategy. Managers cannot reinvent their world afresh for all circumstances they face or decisions they make. The recipe, containing the experience gathered over years, can be applied to a given situation, providing relevant information for assessing the need for change, a likely course of action, and the likelihood of success of that course of action.

ILLUSTRATION 2.4 *Examples of Recipes*

The recipe for success in an industry represents managers' views of "how to succeed" in their business environment and key strategic considerations. The examples below were selected to illustrate possible recipes that could be held about two very different industries.

Industry: Forest Products such as pulp, paper, and lumber.
Examples of Firms: Georgia Pacific Corporation
                   International Paper Co.
                   MacMillan Bloedel Ltd.
The following are views and perceptions that managers might hold about how to run a successful forest products firm:

- A superior raw material position is critical to obtain a competitive advantage.

- Low processing costs are critical as prices are established on commodity markets.

- Input costs (materials, labor, fuel) relative to other areas must be constantly monitored.
- Sales are subject to commodity demand which is cyclical.
- Growth is based upon acquiring more raw materials and/or the ability to integrate vertically.
- Additional value added is desirable.
- Vertical balance from raw materials through to processing is necessary.

Industry: Personal Consumer Products such as toothpaste and soap.
Examples of Firms: Colgate-Palmolive
                     Procter and Gamble
                     Unilever

The following are views and perceptions that managers might hold about how to run a successful consumer products firm:

- Strong and aggressive advertising and promotional activities are critical.
- Constant introduction of new or repackaged products is necessary.
- Development of a proprietary, or differentiated, product is important.
- Recognition of market segmentation and the matching of products to markets is necessary.
- Continuous monitoring of the market is necessary as market preferences are constantly shifting and competitors are always developing new products and introducing different marketing activites.
- Growth is possible through exploitation of market opportunites for current products and development of related products.

Managers in these two industries hold quite different recipes if success is to be achieved.

The forest products firms have to focus on production processes and cost controls. If economies of scale are to be achieved, it is important to maintain a balance in the volume of output at all stages in the production process. A firm's production costs, relative to those of competitors, domestic or foreign, are a critical consideration. Such companies are very dependent on markets they are unable to influence because commodity prices are established worldwide. It is not possible to differentiate products through promotional activities.

This contrasts dramatically with personal consumer products. Marketing is the focus for competition in this industry. It is very important to differentiate products, usually through advertising or packaging. Customers number in the millions and their preferences shift and can be influenced. The development of new products is important if the firm hopes to grow. Innovative process technology might be important for some products if the techniques can be kept secret and/or patented.

The relationship and distinction between the recipe and organizational strategy need to be made clear. Figure 2.4 helps to do this. Environmental forces and organizational capabilities do not in themselves create organizational strategy: it is people who create strategy. The mechanism by which this is done is through the recipe. The forces at work in the environment, and the organization's capabilities in coping with these, are made sense of through the assumptions and beliefs called the recipe and in this way strategy is formulated. The strategies managers advocate and those which emerge through the social and political processes previously described are, then, typically configured within the bounds of this recipe. However, environmental forces and organizational capabilities, while having this indirect influence on strategy formulation, nonetheless do impact on organizational performance much more directly. For example, for firms in the forest products industry cited in Illustration 2.4, it is critical that managers appreciate the cyclical nature of the industry.

Figure 2.4   *The role of the recipe in strategy formulation.*

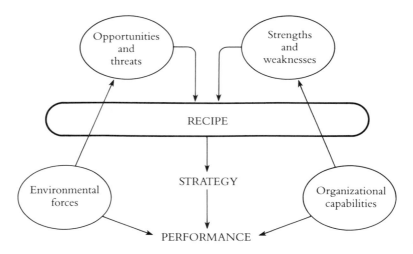

During the mid-1970s, the industry experienced rapid growth in capacity and demand with strong prices. By the 1980s, a downturn had occurred in the industry which left firms with excess capacity and oversupplied markets. Operating costs had increased and the high level of debt required to finance expansion became a burden as interest rates rose. It took some time for the firms to adjust to the changing environment and to lower operating costs in line with falling prices. This had adverse impact on the performance of forest industry firms and eventually forced a reappraisal of the firms' strategies, in particular strategic implementation. This potential difference between actual influences and managerial perceptions of influences on the organization can give rise to significant problems — and is an issue returned to later.

The recipe may, then, be a very conservative influence on strategy. This is the more so since, as has been seen, the links between the recipe itself and "the way we do things around here" are likely to be close. This is shown in Figure 2.5. For example, the link between the power structure in the organization and the core set of beliefs held by managers in that organization is likely to be strong. The recipe represents the formula for success which is taken for granted in the business and likely to have grown up over years; the most powerful groupings within the business are likely to have derived their very power from association with this set of beliefs and their ability to put them into operation.[32] For example, the consumer products firm, Colgate-Palmolive, mentioned in Illustration 2.4, was a marginal performer until a turnaround was initiated by the CEO after it was learned that Sir James Goldsmith, a major shareholder, was about to take action to revitalize the company. The recipe for success was altered when the CEO's perception of what had to be done to turn the company around was reinforced by an outsider with similar perceptions. In this case, the manager had realized that the existing recipe and its cultural underpinnings were no longer appropriate for formulating a strategy.

The recipe is also likely to be associated with the control systems, routines, and rituals of the organization which will tend to preserve the status quo: and here the sorts of myths and stories and the types of language used will tend to reflect and support the existing core beliefs. The point is that the recipe is not just a set of beliefs and assumptions; rather it is embedded in an organizational-specific cultural web which legitimizes and preserves the assumptions and beliefs in the organization. This is shown in Illustration 2.5.

Figure 2.5   *The cultural web of an organization.*

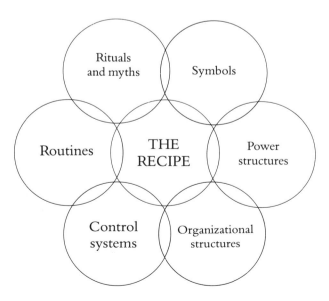

2.4.3 A Cultural View of Patterns of Strategic Change

Faced with pressures for change, managers will likely deal with the situation in ways which protect the recipe from challenge. This raises difficulties when managing strategic change, for it may be that the action required is outside the scope of the recipe and the constraints of the cultural web and that members of the organization would be required to change substantially their core beliefs or "the way we do things around here." Desirable as this may be, the evidence is that it does not occur easily.[33] Managers are much more likely to attempt to deal with the situation by searching for what they can understand and cope with in terms of the existing recipe. In other words, they will attempt to minimize the extent to which they are faced with ambiguity and uncertainty by looking for that which is familiar. Figure 2.6 illustrates how this might occur. Faced with a stimulus for action, in this case declining performance, managers are first likely to seek means of improving the implementation of existing strategy, perhaps through the tightening of controls. In effect,

---

ILLUSTRATION 2.5   *The Cultural Web of The British Columbia Buildings Corporation*

The British Columbia Buildings Corporation (BCBC) was created through a Provincial Act in June 30, 1976. The mandate of the Crown corporation (government owned), which essentially replaced the former Ministry of Public Works, was "to identify the short- and long-term accommodation service requirements of the British Columbia Government, and to satisfy those requirements in a responsive and cost-effective manner."

The introduction of a "user-pay" system for client organizations within government was met with a mixture of enthusiasm and skepticism. The so-called new "cowboy" top executives, some of whom had been hired from the "oil patch", saw it as an opportunity to "do it right" while there was skepticism from those who would now be accountable to BCBC, and who had seen many programs come and go.

By 1987, under the direction of CEO Peter Dolezal and his five vice presidents: J. Robinson (Real Estate); B. Wilson (Planning & Client Services); J. Davies (Development); A. Kemp (Property Management); and D. Truss (Administration & CFO), the Corporation was managing a growth in portfolio of 29% with less than 50% of the previous staffing levels under the old Ministry. They had substantively achieved their goal of operating with a "private sector mentality," but most surprising of all, they had done it with high morale, high productivity, and a downsizing imperative which saw not a single person laid off. The secret to much of the success of this public sector organization has been the willingness of the Corporation, acting as a monopoly, to use competitive market standards as a measure of effectiveness and to respond with corrective measures when they fall short.

The diagram below summarizes the cultural web of BCBC.

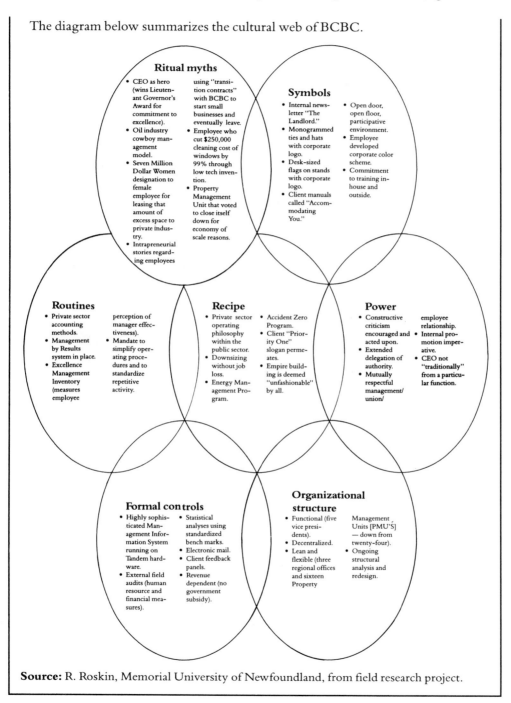

Ritual myths

- CEO as hero (wins Lieutenant Governor's Award for commitment to excellence).
- Oil industry cowboy management model.
- Seven Million Dollar Women designation to female employee for leasing that amount of excess space to private industry.
- Intrapreneurial stories regarding employees using "transition contracts" with BCBC to start small businesses and eventually leave.
- Employee who cut $250,000 cleaning cost of windows by 99% through low tech invention.
- Property Management Unit that voted to close itself down for economy of scale reasons.

Symbols

- Internal newsletter "The Landlord."
- Monogrammed ties and hats with corporate logo.
- Desk-sized flags on stands with corporate logo.
- Client manuals called "Accommodating You."
- Open door, open floor, participative environment.
- Employee developed corporate color scheme.
- Commitment to training in-house and outside.

Routines

- Private sector accounting methods.
- Management by Results system in place.
- Excellence Management Inventory (measures employee perception of manager effectiveness).
- Mandate to simplify operating procedures and to standardize repetitive activity.

Recipe

- Private sector operating philosophy within the public sector.
- Downsizing without job loss.
- Energy Management Program.
- Accident Zero Program.
- Client "Priority One" slogan permeates.
- Empire building is deemed "unfashionable" by all.

Power

- Constructive criticism encouraged and acted upon.
- Extended delegation of authority.
- Mutually respectful management/union/employee relationship.
- Internal promotion imperative.
- CEO not "traditionally" from a particular function.

Formal controls

- Highly sophisticated Management Information System running on Tandem hardware.
- External field audits (human resource and financial measures).
- Statistical analyses using standardized bench marks.
- Electronic mail.
- Client feedback panels.
- Revenue dependent (no government subsidy).

Organizational structure

- Functional (five vice presidents).
- Decentralized.
- Lean and flexible (three regional offices and sixteen Property Management Units [PMU'S] — down from twenty-four).
- Ongoing structural analysis and redesign.

Source: R. Roskin, Memorial University of Newfoundland, from field research project.

they will tighten up their accepted way of operating. If this is not effective, then a change of strategy may occur, but, nevertheless, a change in line with the existing recipe. For example, managers may seek to extend the market for their product but retain the same views about the range of products they produce, the main virtues of the products, the nature of what remains as the main market, and how they should go about operating in that market. There would be no change to the recipe itself and there would not likely be any until this attempt to reconstruct strategy in the image of the existing recipe also failed. What would happen would be the predominant application of the familiar and an attempt to avoid or reduce uncertainty or ambiguity.

This is, in effect, an alternative explanation for the observed phenomenon of incrementalism; some writers have accounted for incrementalism not as a logical phenomenon but as a phenomenon rooted in the belief systems of organizations. However, the outcome of processes of decision making of this kind is not likely to be the careful, logical, adaptive

Figure 2.6   *Dynamics of recipe change.*

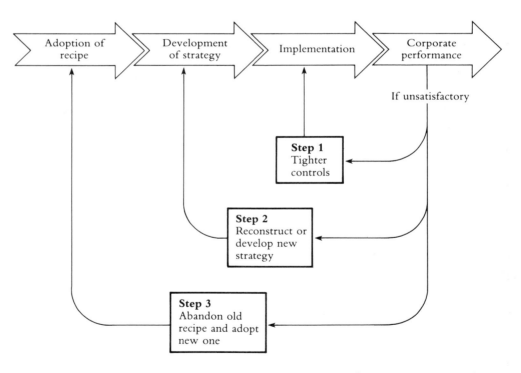

Source: P. Grinyer and J.C. Spender, *Turnaround: Managerial Recipes for Strategic Success*, London: Associated Business Press, 1979, p. 203.

strategy making in line with environmental change shown in Figure 2.2. Rather, it is likely to be an adaptation in line with the perceived management wisdom as enshrined in the recipe. Nonetheless, the forces in the environment will have an effect on performance. Over time this may well give rise to the sort of drift shown in Figure 2.7 in which the organization's strategy gradually, if imperceptibly, moves away from the environmental forces at work in the marketplace. This pattern of drift is made more difficult to detect and reverse because, not only are changes being made in strategy — albeit within the parameters of the recipe — but, since such changes are the application of the familiar, they may achieve some short term improvement in performance, thus tending to legitimize the action taken. The recipe is, then, a virtually inevitable feature of organizational life which, at best, can be thought of as encapsulating the distinctive competences of organization[34] or, on the other hand, as a conservative influence likely to prevent change and result in the kind of strategic momentum noted earlier.

As will be argued later in this book, the important conclusions would appear to be that there is a need for the strategist to understand what beliefs and assumptions comprise the recipe, what mechanisms in the cultural web preserve it, and how the recipe can be challenged sufficiently to prevent an inability to achieve strategic change.

Figure 2.7   *Incremental strategic change and strategic drift.*

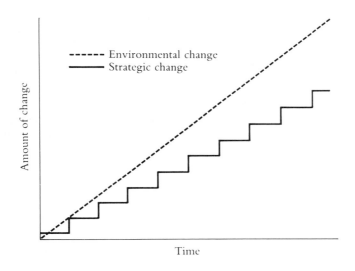

The environment changes gradually but organization strategy fails to develop in line with it. Strategy moves imperceptibly away from environmental "reality."

2.5 A SUMMARY OF IMPLICATIONS FOR THE STUDY OF STRATEGY

This chapter has dealt with the processes of strategic management as they are to be found in organizations. The chapter is therefore descriptive not prescriptive. There is no suggestion here that, because such processes exist, this is how strategy *should* be managed. However, it is important to understand the reality of strategy making in organizations not least because those who seek to influence the strategy of organizations must do so within that reality. There is little point in formulating strategies, which may be elegant analytically, without having an understanding of the processes actually at work. Moreover, it is this book's intention that an understanding of the subject should build on this reality and, wherever possible, relate an essentially analytical approach to the real world of managers.

In this concluding section of the chapter, the basic lessons of this chapter are briefly summarized and related to what follows in the rest of the book.

2.5.1 A SUMMARY OF THE KEY POINTS

1. It is important to distinguish between the *intended* strategy of managers — that which they say the organization will follow — and the *realized* strategy of an organization — that which it is actually following. This is particularly important when considering how relevant current strategy is to a changing environment: it may be more useful to consider the relevance of realized strategy than intended strategy.

2. Strategy usually evolves incrementally: strategic change tends to occur as a continual process of relatively small adjustments to existing strategy through activity within the subsystems of an organization.

3. However, there is likely to be an overall strategic direction, a strategic momentum, a change in which is often associated with an organization getting out of line with a changing environment (strategic drift) and eventually reaching a point of crisis.

4. Formal planning (e.g., in the sense of corporate planning) is important as an aid to analyzing strategic positions and thinking through options, but is not normally a vehicle for the formulation of strategy.

5. The way in which managers assess the need for strategic change is through an essentially qualitative assessment of signals which accumulate from inside and outside the organization.

6. The definition of strategic problems and choice of strategies by managers are not so much reliant on dispassionate analysis of data but, (a) on perceptions of what powerful individuals in the organization see as the problems, and (b) on the manager's reconciliation of the circumstances of the situation with past experience and the received wisdom encapsulated in the core assumptions and beliefs of the organization, known as the recipe.

7. The cultural web of an organization — its political structures, routines, and rituals and symbols are likely to exert a preserving and legitimizing influence on the core beliefs and

assumptions that comprise the recipe and hence make strategic change the more difficult to achieve.

2.5.2 THE IMPLICATIONS FOR STRATEGIC MANAGEMENT

There is no reason to discard the more traditional frameworks for considering strategic issues. For the strategist, building up a clear picture of the strategic position of the organization through some sort of analysis is vital; deciding what strategies are more or less sensible can be aided by techniques of analysis and evaluation; and the logical planning of implementation is also important. However, all of this has to take place in such a way as to address the reality of strategic management as a social, political and cultural phenomenon. The approach in this book has been influenced strongly by this dual need of the strategist: some of the ways in which this need may be addressed can usefully be spelled out at this stage.

As has been stated in Chapter 1, the idea of a purely sequential model of strategic management has been rejected. The headings of strategic analysis, choice and implementation are a useful structure for the book, and for thinking about the problems of strategy, but readers are urged to regard these aspects of strategic management as interdependent and an influence on one another.

This chapter has highlighted the substantial influence of the beliefs and assumptions of managers within a cultural setting. If the strategist is to have an influence on the formulation of strategy and is to consider sensibly the ability of the organization to implement that strategy, it is important that these cultural aspects of the organization be explicitly understood. Without such an understanding, strategy making has little relevance to organizational reality. For this reason emphasis is placed in this book on the importance of understanding the nature of the beliefs and assumptions of managers and the cultural and political context in which they exist. This is regarded as an integral part of the process of strategic analysis and, in Chapter 5, there are sections on how an analysis of such systems may be usefully undertaken. It is also regarded as a factor to be considered in strategy evaluation and is therefore considered again in Chapter 7 when the notion of "cultural fit" is discussed.

Moreover, it is recognized that it is the political and cultural barriers to change which may well provide the major stumbling blocks to the implementation of strategic change. Chapter 11, therefore, comes back to the processes of strategic management with a view to examining how strategy and strategic change can be implemented within the cultural context of the organization. In Chapter 11, it is argued that while the formulation of strategy may well benefit from the sort of rational and analytical approach traditional in the subject, and that it is necessary to plan logically the allocation of resources, managing the acceptance of strategic change is essentially a cultural process and needs to be considered as such and implemented as a culture change process. Chapter 11 considers how this might be achieved. It is also argued in Chapter 11 that leadership in organizations needs to be seen quite clearly as a task which requires that rational and analytical aspects of management *and* cultural aspects be harnessed in order to implement strategic change.

While the reality of judgment and the prevalence of bargaining processes in organizations are accepted, the book also contains examples of, and references to, many techniques of quantitative and qualitative analysis. The value of such analytical approaches is not to be diminished. Not only do they provide an essential tool for managers to conceive of strategic problems and analyze possible solutions, they also provide means whereby the "taken for granted" wisdom of the organization and assumed courses of action can be challenged.

The overall aim is, then, to provide a framework for strategy and strategic management which usefully combines the rigor of analysis with the reality of the processes of management.

References

1. The idea of strategy "momentum" is discussed fully in D. Miller and P. Friesen, "Momentum and Revolution in Organizational Adaptation," the *Academy of Management Journal*, Volume 23, No. 4 (1980), pp. 591-614.

2. These generalized patterns of strategy development are based on those discussed by Henry Mintzberg in "Patterns of Strategy Formation," *Management Science*, (May 1978), pp. 934-48, although his own categorization is a good deal more complex than the one used in this book.

3. Terms such as "deliberate," "realized," and so on, are again those used by Henry Mintzberg, (see reference 2).

4. Lindblom's paper "The Science of Muddling Through," *Public Administration Review*, Volume 19, (Spring 1959), pp. 79-88 is one of the earliest which criticizes an over-rational view of strategy formation and argues for an incremental perspective within a social and political context.

5. J.B. Quinn's research involved the examination of strategic change in companies and has been published in *Strategies for Change*, (Homewood, Illinois: Richard D. Irwin Inc., 1980).

6. The term "unfolding rationality" is used by Lou Pondy in explaining incrementalism in a paper entitled "The Union of Rationality and Intuition in Management Action," in S. Srivasta, ed., *The Executive Mind*, (San Francisco: Jossey-Bass, Inc., Publishers, 1983).

7. See *Strategies for Change* (reference 5), p.58.

8. In "What is Planning Anyway?," *Strategic Management Journal*, Vol. 2 (1981), pp. 139-324 Henry Mintzberg suggests that planning has taken on different meanings for managers. Planning may mean any of the following: future thinking, integrated decision making, formalized procedures of planning, (which is what Mintzberg suggests is assumed in most of the literature), and planning as programming (for example, budgeting). He makes the point that these different meanings are relevant to the management task and it is often not entirely clear what is being referred to when the word planning is used.

9. This is borne out in much of the research into strategic decision making and corporate planning. For example see Quinn, *Strategies for Change* above; H. Mintzberg, O. Raisinghani and A. Theoret, "The Structure of Unstructured Decision Processes," *Administrative Science*

Quarterly, Vol. 21 (1976), pp. 246-75; W.K. Hall, "Strategic Planning Models: Are Top Managers Really Finding Them Useful?," *Journal of Business Policy*, Vol. 3, No. 2,(1973), pp. 33–42.

10. The role of corporate planning is based on the research findings in the doctoral dissertation of H. Bahrami entitled "Design of Corporate Planning Systems," University of Aston, October 1981. This research was conducted in 14 large, mainly multinational, UK-based firms.

11. Henry Mintzberg, "Patterns of Strategy Formation," *Management Science*, pp. 934-48.

12. Writers who advocate a step-by-step, formalized planning approach as a basis for thinking about strategic management, recognize the importance of the less formalized management aspect. For example, G. Steiner and J. Miner in *Management Policy and Strategy*, (New York: Macmillan Publishing Co., Inc., 1977), p.92 say: "The formal system (of planning) should help managers to sharpen their intuitive anticipatory inputs into the planning process. At the very least, the formal system should give managers more time for reflective thinking . . . But formal planning cannot be really effective unless managers at all levels inject their judgments and intuition into the planning process."

13. For a summary of "organizational action" explanations of strategic management see Chapter 2, Gerry Johnson, *Strategic Change and the Management Process*, (Oxford: Basil Blackwell Publisher, 1987).

14. For a thorough discussion of the problem awareness and diagnosis stages of the decision-making process, see M.A. Lyles, "Formulating Strategic Problems: Empirical Analysis and Model Development," *Strategic Management Journal*, Vol. 2, (1981), pp. 61-75.

15. The presence and nature of these signals are confirmed and discussed in D. Norburn and P. Grinyer, "Directors Without Direction," *Journal of General Management*, Vol. 1, No. 2, (1973-4), pp. 37–48.

16. This proposition is supported by the research of P. Grinyer and D. Norburn (reference 15), J.B. Quinn (reference 5), and D. Miller and P. Friesen, "Archetypes of Strategy Formulation," *Management Science*, Vol. 24, No. 9, (1978), pp. 921–33.

17. Researchers who have examined environmental influences on strategy would broadly agree with this. See, for example, P. Grinyer and D. Norburn, "Directors Without Direction," F. Aguilar, *Scanning the Business Environment* (New York: Macmillan Publishing Co., Inc., 1967); H. Mintzberg, *et al*, "The Structure of Unstructured Decision Processes," *Administrative Science Quarterly*, pp. 246-75

18. This discussion is based on the findings detailed in Mintzberg, *et al*, "The Structure of Unstructured Decision Processes," pp. 246-75.

19. Fahey confirms the absence of the establishment of clear options or clear criteria of evaluation in his study "On Strategic Management Decision Processes," *Strategic Management Journal*, Volume 2, (1981), pp. 43-60.

20. The discussion on sporadic, fluid and constricted processes of decision making is based on the work by David Hickson and his colleagues at Bradford Management Centre published in the book *Top Decisions: Strategic Decision Making in Organizations*, (Oxford: Basil Blackwell Publisher, 1986).

21. There have now been a number of writers who have attempted to study excellence in organizations. This began early in the 1980s with T.J. Peters and R.H. Waterman, Jr., *In Search of*

Excellence, (New York: Harper and Row Publishers, 1982), but has also included studies such as Rosabath Moss Kanter, *The Change Masters*, (New York: Simon and Shuster, 1983), and has included replications of such studies in different parts of the world; for example see D. Clutter-buck and W. Goldsmith, *The Winning Streak*, for a UK study and K. Inkson *et al.*, *Theory K; The Key to Excellence in New Zealand Management*, (Auckland: David Bateman Limited, 1986.)

22.   Edgar Schein, *Organizational Culture and Leadership*, (San Francisco: Jossey-Bass, Publishers, Inc., 1985), p. 6.

23.   The approach in this book, in common with some other writers, is that culture can be understood not just as a set of beliefs and assumptions, but also as the behavior patterns, language, and social devices such as rituals and control systems. This view is generally known as a "cultural adaptationist" view of culture and is expressed more fully by Roger Keesing in "Theories of Culture," *The Annual Review of Anthropology*, Volume 3, (1974), pp. 73-79.

24.   The expression "the way we do things around here" as an explanation of culture was coined by Terrence E. Deal and Allan A. Kennedy, *Corporate Cultures; The Rites and Rituals of Corporate Life*, (Reading, Mass.: Addison-Wesley, Publishers Ltd., 1982).

25.   This section is based on the work of Raymond E. Miles and Charles C. Snow, *Organizational Strategy, Structure and Process*, (New York: McGraw-Hill, 1978).

26.   A.D. Meyer worked with Miles and Snow on their research and separately published findings on the different cultures of defenders and prospectors. This can be found in "How Ideologies Supplement Formal Structures and Shape Response to Environments," *Journal of Management Studies*, Vol. 19, No. 1, (1982), pp. 45-61.

27.   The term "interpretative schemes" is used by J.M. Bartunek in "Changing Interpretative Schemes and Organizational Re-Structuring the Examples of a Religious Order," *Administrative Science Quarterly*, Vol. 29, (1984), pp. 355-72.

28.   The term "paradigm" is used by Jeffrey Pfeffer in "Management as Symbolic Action; the Creation and Maintenance of Organization Paradigms," in a book of readings edited by L.L. Cummings, and B.M. Staw, *Research in Organizational Behavior*," (Greenwich, Connecticut: J.A.I. Press, 1981), pp. 1-15. It is also a term used by A. Sheldon in "Organizational Paradigms, a Theory of Organizational Change," *Organizational Dynamics*, Vol. 8, No. 3, (1980), pp. 61-71, and by Gerry Johnson, *Strategic Change and the Management Process*, (Oxford: Basil Blackwell Publisher, 1987).

29.   The term "recipe" is used by J. Spender in his doctoral thesis "Strategy Making in Business," PhD Thesis, School of Business, University of Management, 1980. It was also a term used by Peter Grinyer and J-C Spender in "Recipes, Crises and Adaptation in Mature Businesses," *International Studies of Management and Organization*, Vol. 9, (1979), pp. 113-23, and in *Turnaround: Managerial Recipes for Strategic Success; The Fall and Rise of the Newton Chambers Group*, (London: Associated Business Press, 1979). Both Grinyer and Spender did use the term to signify those beliefs and assumptions held at an industry rather than organizational level.

30.   Although we use the term recipe in this volume it is used in an organization specific sense. We have chosen to retain the use of the word recipe rather than "paradigm," largely for purposes of continuity, since it was used in the first edition.

31. The word "clans" was used by W.G. Ouchi in "Markets Bureaucracies and Plans," *Administrative Science Quarterly*, Vol. 25, (1980), pp. 129-41, to refer to organizations with particularly homogeneous sets of beliefs and assumptions.

32. A number of writers and researchers have pointed to the links between the locus of power in organizations and the perceived ability of such powerful individuals or groups to reduce uncertainty. See D.J. Hickson *et al.*, "A Strategic Contingencies Theory of Intra-Organizational Power," *Administrative Science Quarterly*, Vol. 16, No. 2, (1970), pp. 216-29; D.C. Hambrick, "Environment, Strategy and Power Within Top Management Teams," *Administrative Science Quarterly*, Vol. 26, (1981), pp. 253-76. Since the recipe is, in effect, the "perceived wisdom" of how to operate successfully in the organization, it is likely that those most associated with the recipe will be the most powerful in the organization; although he uses the term paradigm Johnson also makes this point (see reference 13).

33. Certainly C. Argyris vividly illustrates the extent to which "theories-in-use" as a code of behavior are very resistant to change and challenge [see *Organizational Learning: A Theory of Action Perspective*, (London: Addison-Wesley, Publishers Ltd., 1978).]

34. Both S.A. Lippman and R.P. Rumelt, "Uncertain Imitability; An Analysis of Inter-firm Differences in Efficiency under Competition," *Bell Journal of Economics*, Vol. 13, No. 2, (1982), pp. 418-38 and R.R. Nelson and S.G. Winter, *An Evolutionary Theory of Economic Change*, (Cambridge, Mass.: Harvard University Press, 1982), point out that the routines of organizations can provide distinctive competences upon which organizations can build in order to achieve competitive advantage.

Recommended Key Readings

For an examination of how strategic decisions are made in private and public sector organizations: D.J. Hickson, R.J. Butler, D. Cray, G.R. Mallory and D.C. Wilson. *Top Decisions*. Oxford: Basil Blackwell Publisher, 1986.

Gordon Donaldson and Jay W. Lorsch. *Decision Making at the Top: The Shaping of Strategic Direction*. New York: Basic Books, 1983.

Liam Fahey, "On Strategic Management Decision Processes." *Strategic Management Journal*, Vol. 2, (1981), pp. 43-60.

D. B. Jemison, "Organizational vs. Environmental Sources of Influence in Strategic Decision Making," *Strategic Management Journal*, Vol. 2, (1981), pp. 77-90.

On incremental strategic change: J.B. Quinn. *Strategies for Change - Logical Incrementalism*. (Homewood, Illinois: Richard D. Irwin Inc., 1980.)

On cultural influences on strategy: R.E. Miles and C.C. Snow. *Organizational Strategy, Structure and Process*. (New York: McGraw-Hill, 1978.)

For a detailed historical examination of strategic change processes in organizations see Gerry Johnson. *Strategic Change and the Management Process*. (Oxford: Basil Blackwell Publisher, 1987); some general conclusions from this are discussed in Gerry Johnson "Re-Thinking Incrementalism." *Strategic Management Journal*, Vol. 9, No.1, January-February 1988, pp. 75-91.

Part II

Part II
STRATEGIC ANALYSIS

The first part of this book has shown that an organization needs to adjust strategy as circumstances within and around it change. To effect change successfully, managers need to form a view of the key influences on their choice of strategy. Strategic analysis is concerned with providing an understanding of the strategic situation an organization faces. Such an analysis provides the background against which sensible future choices may be made and also provides some useful insights into the difficulties of implementing strategic change. Readers should remember, however, that this relationship between analysis, choice and implementation is not a simple one in practice and, therefore, strategic analysis should not be viewed as a one time exercise which precedes choice and implementation. Strategic analysis should be a process of becoming better informed about an organization's situation, and in some circumstances this can only be gained by implementing changes (perhaps on a limited scale). Indeed, the process of strategic choice and strategy implementation described in Parts III and IV will constantly challenge the validity of the strategic analysis as well as build upon the analysis.

Analyzing an organization's situation can be a very complex task and, for convenience, it is helpful to divide the analysis into the different types of influence on strategy described in Chapter 1. The structure of this part of the book follows this division:

- Chapter 3 is concerned with the influence of the environment on an organization. The challenge is to make sense of this complexity so as to understand the key variables affecting the performance of the organization and how well the organization is positioned in terms of such influences.

- Chapter 4 looks at the resources an organization possesses in an attempt to understand the organization's strategic capability. These resources will include plant, people and their skills, finance, and systems. The need is to understand how the configuration of such resources (an organization's value chain) influences strategic capability.

- Chapter 5 shows how the culture of an organization might be understood as an influence on strategy. It also examines how individuals and groups can influence the development of strategy in terms of their own interests or expectations. The importance of assessing the bases and configurations of power is also discussed. The objectives of organizations are seen as an outcome of political and cultural processes rather than as preordained targets.

Although this part of the book is divided into three chapters it should be remembered that there are very strong links between these various influences on strategy. For example, environmental pressures for change may be constrained by the resources available to make changes or the organizational culture which may cause resistance to change. The relative importance of the various influences will change over time and show marked differences from one organization to another. A good strategic analysis must provide an understanding of all these issues.

Chapter 3
ANALYZING THE ENVIRONMENT

3.1 INTRODUCTION

Strategists, faced with the need to understand the effects of the environment, are dealing with a difficult problem. The formulation of strategy is concerned with matching the capabilities of an organization to its environment. But the notion of the environment encapsulates many different influences, and the difficulty is understanding this diversity in a way which can contribute to strategic decision making. The danger is the adoption of a balance sheet approach which consists of listing all conceivable environmental influences in an attempt to identify opportunities and threats. It is relatively easy to see that an organization might have a whole range of things going for it and a range going against it: long lists can be generated for most organizations. However, if environmental analysis consists of this alone the limitations are significant. No overall picture emerges of what are the really important influences on the organization. What is more, there is the danger that environmental influences will be dealt with in a piecemeal way instead of in terms of fundamental strategic responses.

In practice, managers cope with the range of influences by evolving, over time, accepted wisdom about their industry, its environment, and sensible responses to different situations. This was discussed in Chapter 2. This chapter, however, takes a rather more analytical approach and provides a series of steps to enable an assessment of the environment to take place. It is necessary to see the role of each step in relation to the others, so they are briefly introduced here and summarized in Figure 3.1.

1. A first step is likely to involve some sort of *auditing of environmental influences*. Here the aim is to identify which of the many different sorts of environmental influences have affected the organization's development or performance in the past and to consider which ones may in the future.

2. Second, it is useful to take an initial view of the *nature of the environment* of the

Figure 3.1 *Steps in environmental analysis.*

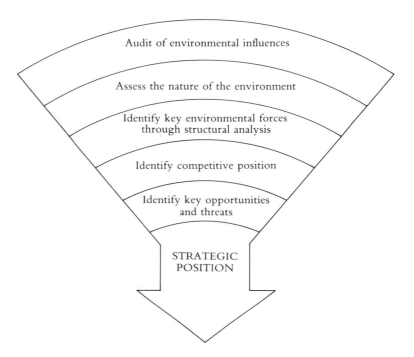

organization in terms of how uncertain it is. Is it relatively static or does it show signs of change, and in what ways? This initial view helps in deciding what focus the rest of the analysis is to take. If the organization is in a fairly simple/static environment then detailed, systematic historical analysis may be very helpful. If the environment is in a dynamic state or shows signs of becoming so, then a future oriented perspective is more sensible. This initial view may also highlight some environmental considerations to be examined in more detail later. For example, it may become clear that there are particular aspects of the environment which are changing: it will be necessary to consider whether or not these changes are strategically significant.

3. The third step moves the focus towards an explicit consideration of individual environmental influences. The general understanding already begun can be much enhanced by a *structural analysis* which aims to identify the key forces at work in the competitive environment and why they are significant.

From these steps should emerge a view of the really important developments taking place around the organization. It may be that there are relatively few of outstanding significance: or it could be that there are many interconnected developments. What matters is that there should be an attempt to understand why these are of strategic significance.

4. The fourth step is to analyze the organization's *competitive position*; that is, how it stands in relation to those other organizations competing for the same resources, or the same customers. This may be done in a number of ways but this chapter concentrates on (a) strategic group analysis, which seeks to map competitors in terms of similarities and dissimilarities of the strategies they follow and (b) market share analysis, which seeks to map out the relative power of an organization within its market.

5. The final step is to relate this understanding of the environment more specifically to the organization. Here there is a need to ask to what extent the forces identified are *opportunities or threats* (or indeed both). This can be done by considering the extent to which the organization's strategy and structure are matched or mismatched to developments in the environment. What this analysis seeks to provide is a picture of environmental influences clear enough to provide an understanding of opportunities which can be built on and threats which have to be overcome or circumvented. Such a picture is important for strategic evaluation.

3.2 AUDITING ENVIRONMENTAL INFLUENCES ON ORGANIZATIONS

Illustration 3.1 shows some of the environmental influences important to organizations. The illustration is not intended to provide an exhaustive list but does serve to give examples of ways in which strategies of organizations are affected by the environment and also indicates some of the ways organizations seek to handle aspects of their environment.

It would be possible to devote the whole of this chapter — indeed of the book — to a discussion of the ways in which different sorts of environmental influences affect organizations.[1] This is not done here because the chapter is primarily concerned with how to understand the strategic importance of the influences rather than to provide a catalogue of influences. It is also important to appreciate that over time different environmental forces will be more, or less, important. For example, the concern about oil prices of the mid 1970s and the accelerating inflation which followed, gave way at the end of the decade to concern about the effects of recession and the cost of capital. It is also the case that key environmental issues for one organization may not be the same for another. A multinational corporation might primarily be concerned with government relations, since it may be operating plants or subsidiaries within many different countries with quite different systems of government and government attitudes. A small business would likely be very concerned by the shutdown of a plant employing a large portion of its customers. A retailer, on the other hand, may be primarily concerned with customer tastes and behavior. A computer manufacturer is likely to be concerned with the technical environment which leads to innovation and perhaps obsolescence of his own equipment. The point is that there is unlikely to be a definitive set of environmental issues especially important for all organizations over time.

ILLUSTRATION 3.1   *Examples of environmental influences*

The following are examples of ways in which organizations interact with aspects of the environment.

Economic Environment

- Changes in exchange rates have a major impact on firms involved in exporting and/or importing and multinationals.
- Fluctuations in commodity prices lead to major changes in operations, for example declining sugar prices lower raw materials costs in the food industry.
- European, Japanese, Canadian, and other firms are making large investments in the US.

Capital markets

- In Canada and the US, financial institutions such as banks, savings and loans, insurance companies, and brokerage firms who, in the past, each provided different services to clients, are beginning to offer comprehensive financial services in "one stop" financial institutions.
- The use of new forms of financial securities, stripped bonds, junk bonds, non-voting shares, and dequity has increased. Drexel, Wall Street's fourth largest investment bank, has attempted to secure a large portion of the junk bond business.
- Technology and deregulation of the financial industry permit worldwide, around the clock, transactions.

Demographics

- About 40% of all families have two incomes, increasing disposable income.
- Two demographic groups in the population, yuppies (with more income to invest) and the older, greying citizens (with savings to invest) increase the opportunites in personal finance counselling services.
- A declining baby population has led Johnson and Johnson to advertise the use of their baby powder for adults.

Economic forecasting

Financial policy

Demographic forecasting

The Enterprise

Environmental   sensing   and

Socio-cultural

- Consumer fitness and health consciousness has required distillers to develop new "light" products and to market them more effectively.
- Busy career women and working mothers do less home sewing for themselves and/or family than previous generations of women, leading to a decline in the demand for fabrics. Retailers of sewing fabrics are experiencing declining sales and are fighting for remaining market share.
- Smoking is becoming less socially acceptable having implications for the tobacco industry but also for any business that must separate smoking and non-smoking employees and customers.

Ecology

- Increasing concern in Canada and the Northeastern states about acid rain may lead to tighter pollution controls on some industries.
- In 1986, the US courts ruled that the Environmental Protection Agency had the right to fly over and take photographs of a chemical plant without a warrant.
- A United Nations Commission report highlighted the continued degradation of the world's soil, air, water, and forests.

Labor Markets

- Organized labor (AFL–CIO) has targeted private sector clerical workers as possible members now that there has been a decline in members from heavy industries.
- Some companies are creating pools of "contingent" workers employed as needed rather than hiring regular employees who work traditional 40 hour weeks.
- Profit sharing plans (ESOPs) are increasing in popularity as an approach to motivating employees and increasing productivity.

Competitors

- General Electric Co. obtained near monopoly control of the market for some jet airplane engines when a competitor and former market leader, Pratt and Whitney, cancelled plans to develop a comparable fuel efficient engine.
- Department stores have had to reassess their target markets and merchandise selection as specialty stores and junior department stores eroded their market share.
- Until recently AT&T in the US and Telecom Canada had a monopoly on telephone long distance services. Now competitors are allowed to provide such services.

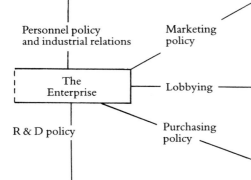

Personnel policy and industrial relations

Marketing policy

The Enterprise

Lobbying

R & D policy

Purchasing policy

Government

- Increasing protectionism represents opportunities for some firms, and lost opportunities for others.
- Deregulation of the transportation industry has increased competition.
- In Canada, the government is proposing to ban the advertising of tobacco products.
- The Federal Trade Commission blocked Coca Cola Co.'s buyout of Dr. Pepper Co. and PepsiCo Inc.'s purchase of Seven-up Co.

Technology

- Robots, or "steel collar" workers, initially used in automotive plants, are now more sophisticated and are being utilized in a variety of industries including electronics and candy and textile manufacture.
- Several companies are attempting to commercialize "neural-net" computers, that is, computers that "think."
- A technology breakthrough that reduces the loss of electricity when it is transmitted long distances may reduce energy costs to users.

Supplies

- Just in time (JIT) and other inventory systems place different demands on suppliers.
- Some US firms now contract foreign manufacturers to produce all or most of their products with only final assembly and packaging being done in the US.
- In Canada, reforestation has become a priority as supplies of wood are reduced and are located further from mills.
- Some Canadian industries are at a disadvantage when competing on international markets as they are forced to purchase Canadian produced raw materials at higher prices (grain required in brewing) or to pay higher prices on imported materials because of tariffs and import quotas (fabrics required by the fashion industry).

While it is not possible to identify a definitive list of environmental influences of greatest importance in all circumstances, it is useful to consider as a starting point just what influences in the wider environment have been particularly important in the past. Also, the extent to which changes presently occurring may make some influences more or less significant in the future for the organization and its competitors should be considered. Figure 3.2 is designed to help with such an audit by providing a summary of some of the questions to ask about likely key forces at work in the wider environment.[2] Later in the chapter there is a consideration of how the more specific competitive forces at work in the environment are likely to affect the organization.

The ability to sense changes in the environment is important because perceived changes in environmental influence signal the possible need for changes in strategy: they provide opportunities and warn of threats. The evidence is that organizations more adept at sensing environmental changes perform better than those not as skilled.[3] The problem of coping with environmental influences affecting the organization has two aspects. The first is understanding the extent to which environmental changes will affect strategy: this is a matter of analysis and will be dealt with in this chapter. The second is relating these changes to the capability of the organization to cope with such changes. This will be introduced at the end of this chapter and taken up again in the following chapter. However,

Figure 3.2   *An audit of environmental influences.*

---

1. **What general environmental factors are affecting the organization?**

2. **Which of these are the most important at the present time? In the next few years?**

Economic factors:
Business cycles • GNP trends • Interest rates • money supply • inflation • unemployment • disposable income • energy availability and cost.

Technological:
Government spending on research • government and industry focus of technological effort • new discoveries/ developments • speed of technology transfer • rates of obsolescence.

Socio-cultural factors:
Population demographics • income distribution • social mobility • life-style changes • attitudes to work and leisure • consumerism • levels of education.

Political/legal:
Anti-trust legislation • environmental protection laws • taxation policy • foreign trade regulations • employment law • government stability.

it is important to stress that techniques of analysis are, in themselves, no guarantee that organizations will be able to respond to change. The extent to which an organization will be successful in sensing and adapting to change will depend largely on its flexibility and sensitivity which, in turn, depend on the quality of its management, its organizational culture and its structure. These aspects of change will be dealt with in Chapters 10 and 11.

3.3 UNDERSTANDING THE NATURE OF THE ENVIRONMENT

Strategic decisions are, by their very nature, made in situations of uncertainty. Uncertainty is a problem for managers to cope with and in practice, managers cope with it through the mechanism of the recipe, the employment of organizational routines and the reliance on organizational culture discussed in Chapter 2. However, it is also possible to make sense of uncertain conditions through analysis. Strategic analysis is an attempt to reduce the many environmental influences to a pattern which can be readily understood and acted upon. To do this it makes sense to begin by asking: (a) Just how uncertain is the environment? (b) What are the reasons for that uncertainty? (c) How should the uncertainty be dealt with?

Environmental uncertainty increases the more environmental conditions are dynamic or the more they are complex.[4] The degree of dynamism in the environment has to do with the rate and frequency of change. Many organizations find themselves in a more dynamic environment than they have previously experienced. The idea of complexity perhaps needs a little more explanation. Complexity may result in different ways, for example:

- Complexity may result from the sheer *diversity* of environmental influences faced by an organization. A multinational company operating in many different countries is an example of this. While it could be that few of the influences are in themselves changing rapidly, the sheer number of influences the organization has to cope with increases uncertainty.

- Complexity may also arise because of the amount of *knowledge* required to handle environmental influences. An extreme example of this would be a space agency like NASA. The environmental variables it is having to deal with are enormously complex just in terms of gaining knowledge about them.

- A third way in which complexity may increase is if the different environmental influences are, in themselves, interconnected.[5] Suppose influences such as raw material supplies, exchange rates, political changes, and consumer spending are not independent of each other but related one to another: then it is much more difficult to understand influence patterns than if they are unconnected.

Lowest uncertainty exists where conditions are static and simple. As environmental influences become more dynamic or more complex, uncertainty increases. Figure 3.3

Figure 3.3   *Growing uncertainty according to the nature of the environment.*

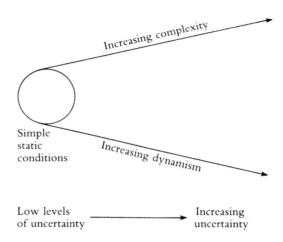

summarizes this. The significance as far as this chapter is concerned is that differences in the nature of the environment call for different approaches to understanding and responding to the environment.

3.3.1 UNDERSTANDING SIMPLE/STATIC CONDITIONS

In simple/static conditions, an organization is faced with an environment not too difficult to understand and not undergoing significant change. Raw material suppliers and some mass manufacturing companies are, perhaps, examples. Here technical processes are relatively straightforward, competition and markets may be fixed over time and there may well be few markets. If change does occur, it is likely to be fairly predictable. Lawyers certainly used to consider themselves in this situation, limited by professional regulation which minimized competition, with no lack of demand and able to command high earnings. In such circumstances it makes sense to analyze the environment on a historical basis: a historical pattern, once identified, might well be expected to continue over time, or at least be sensibly refined systematically. In fact, there is evidence that in static conditions, environmental scanning is likely to be a more continuous, systematic exercise than in dynamic situations where it is more intermittent:[6] since there is more likelihood of being able to use the past as a predictor of the future it is worth investing management time in systematic auditing of environmental influences over time.

In situations of relatively low complexity it may also be possible to identify some predictors of key environmental influences. For example, in government agencies, demographic data such as birth rates might be used as lead indicators to determine the required provision of schooling. Another example of such a predictor might be the way in which sales of consumer durables were thought to be dependent on real income. Since, historically, sales seemed to be related to movements in real income, some analysts thought it possible to predict a rise or decline in market demand according to changes in real income. The danger is that the influence of real income may not always be unconnected with other influences: and a company which relied on real income as a predictor in the consumer durables industry might have been misled. The possibility of inflation might persuade customers to offset future decline in the purchasing power of their savings by bringing forward purchases of consumer durables.

3.3.2 UNDERSTANDING DYNAMIC CONDITIONS

In dynamic conditions the environment shows signs of major change. For example, organizations faced with technological advances, more sophisticated consumers and an internationalization of markets, find that they can no longer make decisions based on the assumption that what has happened in the past will continue. The recording industry provides an example of very dynamic conditions. There is a possibility that vinyl records and tapes will be preempted by the compact disc (CD). Furthermore, the digital audio tape (DAT), yet another technological advance developed in Japan, could threaten records, tapes and CDs.

There is evidence that as dynamic conditions increase, the interpretation of these conditions becomes more inspirational.[7] Managers sensibly address themselves to considering the environment of the future, not just of the past. There are, however, more structured ways of trying to understand and deal with the future. Some form of the scenario planning approach might be employed, for example. This could involve identifying possible major future changes by a method such as the Delphi technique[8] and based on these projections, building alternative scenarios[9] for the future. In effect, the analyst would construct possible alternative futures. These scenarios might then be considered in terms of the likely behavior of suppliers, competitors and consumers so that an overall state of possible competitive environments is built up. It is then possible to carry out strategic analysis based on each of the different scenarios, evolve different strategies for different possible futures, and monitor environmental change to see which of the scenarios — and hence which of the contingency strategies — is likely to be most appropriate. (Scenario planning is also discussed in Chapter 8 when the evaluation of strategic options is considered.)

There are dangers of course. Both a reliance on individuals' sensitivity to trends and the more formal approach of scenario and contingency planning suffer from the risk of myopic perception and response. It is sometimes difficult to get managers to develop scenarios and responses markedly different from those already familiar to them — a problem of recipes again. Another danger is that possible scenarios cease to be thought of as possibilities and start to be thought of as real. Managers may build inflexible strategies and organizational structures around mere possibilities rather than regarding the scenarios as conceptions around which to consider future strategic options and creating the flexibility in strategy and structure to allow speedy responses to environmental change as it actually occurs.

3.3.3 Understanding Complex Conditions

Organizations in complex situations are faced with environmental influences difficult to comprehend. They may, of course, also face dynamic conditions. With the growth and application of more and more sophisticated technology, in particular, there is an increasing move to this condition of greatest uncertainty. The computer industry, airlines, and the electronics industry are all in, or moving into, this dynamic/complex situation. Furthermore, a multinational may, as a corporate body, be in a complex condition because of its diversity but find that different operating companies face varying degrees of complexity and dynamism.

How, then, do organizations facing complexity cope with their conditions? There are both organizational and information processing approaches. Complexity as a result of diversity might be dealt with by ensuring that different parts of the organization responsible for different aspects of diversity are separate and given the resources and authority to handle their own part of the environment.[10] Where high knowledge requirements are important it may also be that those with specialist knowledge in the organization become very powerful because they are relied on, not only to make operational decisions, but are trusted to present information in such a way that a sensible strategic decision can be made: or indeed, they themselves become responsible for the strategic decisions. As an information processing approach, there may be an attempt to model the complexity. This may be done through a financial model, for example, which seeks to simulate the effects on an organization of different evironmental conditions (see also Chapter 8). In its extreme form there may be an attempt to model the environment itself. The major banks draw on models of the economy, for example. However, for most organizations facing complexity, organizational responses are probably more common than extensive model-building.

3.3.4 The Nature of the Environment — The Use of the Perspective

Table 3.1 summarizes the discussion on understanding the nature of the environment: the approach has both conceptual and practical uses. The key points are these:

- If the organization's environmental situation is fairly static and simple, then a detailed analysis of past environmental influences may be very sensible.
- The more the situation becomes dynamic the more a focus on the future is essential, perhaps through some exercise such as scenario building.
- The more complex the environment becomes then, in terms of information processing, the more it may be necessary to move towards more sophisticated techniques such as model-building and simulation.
- In both dynamic and complex conditions there are organizational responses for coping with environmental conditions. It is therefore important to remember the significance of examining the suitability of the organization's structure (discussed in Chapter 10) and management systems (Chapter 11) as part of the strategic analysis. It may be that many of the organization's problems arise from a structure or control system not suited to its environment.

Table 3.1   *Handling different environmental conditions.*

	Conditions		
	Simple/static	*Dynamic*	*Complex*
Aims	Achieve thorough historical understanding of the environment	Understand the future rather than rely on the past	Reduce complexity
Methods	Analysis of past influences and their effect on organizational performance Forecasting based on past trends/influences	Managers' sensitivity to change Techniques such as scenario planning, contingency planning, sensitivity testing	Specialist attention to elements of complexity Model-building
Dangers	The advent of unexpected or unpredicted change	Management myopia Inflexible organizational structures	Unsuitable organizational structure or control systems

3.4 STRUCTURAL ANALYSIS OF THE COMPETITIVE ENVIRONMENT

Whichever approach to analysis outlined above is taken, the aim is to gain a "picture" of the environment which provides a useful basis for constructing strategy. The difficulty, of course, is that the number of influences, and the degree of their relevance for any given organization is, potentially, very great. There is a need for some framework of analysis which provides a structure for conceiving of environmental influences.

A useful guide on the necessary sort of considerations for this is provided by Michael Porter.[11] The following section draws on the approach he proposes and is summarized in Figure 3.4. It is essentially a structured means of examining the competitive environment of an organization so as to provide a clear understanding of the forces at work. Although designed primarily with commercial organizations in mind, it is of value to most organizations facing strategic problems. Illustration 3.2 is a brief structural analysis of the North American hotel industry. It highlights how relatively easy entry into an industry leads to a competitive environment. It might usefully be referred to in conjunction with this section of the chapter.

Porter argues that "competition in an industry is rooted in its underlying economics, and competitive forces exist that go well beyond the established combatants in a particular industry."[12] The task of the strategist is to determine which of these forces are of greatest importance to the organization and which can be influenced by the strategic decisions of management. There are four key forces to be considered.

ILLUSTRATION 3.2   *Environmental Structural Analysis of the Hotel Industry*

A structural analysis highlights the competitive forces at work in the environment thereby providing management with a basis for strategic evaluation.

This is a brief summary of the structure of the hotel, or accommodation, industry. Four key sources of competitive forces are examined.

Threat of Entry — Entry into the industry is relatively easy and the number of rooms has increased about four times in the past decade. Restored downtown hotels are reentering the market, and foreign chains are interested in the North American market. All-suite hotels providing separate sleeping and working areas plus kitchen facilities and complimentary breakfasts are opening in many cities. Investors have been eager to finance hotel building. There appear to be few economies of scale except with reservations systems, advertising, and supply purchasing.

The Power of Buyers and Suppliers — Overcapacity in the industry has lead to discounting especially for corporate customers and tour operators. As competition exists in all segments of the industry, customers usually have a choice of accommodation but do not exert concentrated market power. There are a large number of suppliers for most items giving hotel operators modest buying power with some having integrated backward.

The Threat of Substitutes — Only token competition is possible from substitutes such as Bed and Breakfast operators, the use of recreational vehicles by holidayers, camping, and corporate-owned or rented apartments in some locations.

The Rivalry Among Existing Competitors — Competition is intense in all segments, from luxury to budget accommodations. Some hotels offer different classes of rooms, regular or executive, with the latter having additional amenities or services. Hotel chains such as Holiday Inns, Marriott, and Ramada are entering the budget market by opening hotels or acquiring hotels and operating them under different names. National advertising and nationwide reservations systems are keys to obtaining a market share for chains or franchises. Independents rely on convenience of location. Fancy amenities are constantly being introduced even in budget chains. Competitive innovations include frequent guest programs, striking architectural features, exercise facilities, walk-in closets, and theme restaurants.

Competition in the industry has been spurred on by investors (insurers, pension funds, real estate syndicators) willing to finance the construction of hotels to be operated for a management fee by firms such as Hilton, Hyatt, Marriott, and Sheraton. Budget chains are also expanding, examples being Motel 6, Econo Lodges, Days Inns, and Thrifty Scot Motels in the U.S. and Venture and Relax Inns in Canada. Industry analysts are predicting some relignment in the industry through takeovers or mergers, and by the failure of some chains. The environment of the hotel industry is a very dynamic one, and any firm in the industry has to monitor developments constantly.

Source: "Vacancy Signs Are Lit, But More New Hotels Are on the Way," *Business Week*, (March 17, 1986), pp. 78–9; "Cheap Dreams: The Budget Inn Boom," *Business Week*, (July 14, 1986), pp. 76–7; and "Glitzy Resorts and Suburban Hotels: Hyatt Breaks New Ground," *Business Week*, (May 4, 1987), pp. 100–01.

Figure 3.4 *A model for structural analysis.*

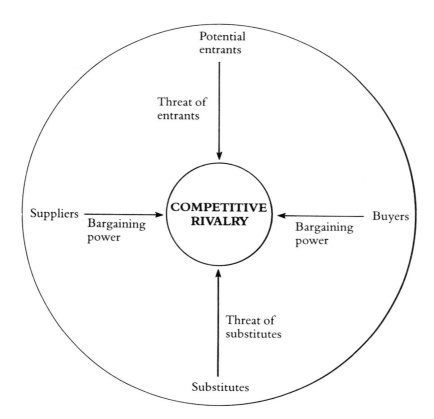

Source: M.E. Porter, *Competitive Strategy,* New York: Free Press, 1980, p.4. Copyright © by The Free Press, a division of Macmillan Publishing Co., Inc. Reprinted with permission.

3.4.1 The Threat of Entry

Threat of entry will depend on the extent to which there are *barriers to entry* which most typically are:

- *Economies of scale.* These will differ by industry. The really important question is not what the optimum scale of operation is, but how damaging it is to operate below that level. For example, in the machine tool industry the optimum scale of production is theoretically very high but the cost of producing at half that level is relatively low: for producers of nylon, on the other hand, it has been shown that the optimum scale of production is much lower but the cost of producing at half that level is high.[13] The problem in analyzing the significance of this is that economies of scale are difficult to assess precisely, as indeed are the costs of producing below optimum levels of scale. However, some sensible and quite basic questions can be asked. For example, how large is the market and how many competitors are already there? If the market opportunity is small then it is likely to be more difficult to achieve adequate levels of scale than if it is large. In a given market is there any indication that profitability is linked to scale? For example, is there a major producer who is profitable and smaller competitors who are not?

- *The capital requirement of entry.* This is linked to economies of scale. For savings and loans and trust companies to compete fully with banks in the handling of day to day personal financing, they would have to create the facility to process cheques, involving enormous capital expenditure to set up a clearing system.

- *Access to distribution channels.* One of the major barriers to entry is the availability of profitable channels of distribution. For example, to market a new food product, such as potato chips, one of the barriers to entry is the ability to distribute the product to the many outlets retailing this type of product. It is difficult to displace existing products on supermarket shelves unless the firm is willing to drastically reduce price, spend huge amounts on promotion and selling activities, or pay high rebates to the supermarkets. In the case of a new food product, the market is also likely to be difficult to enter if there are only a few distributors in an area, or if the food business is dominated by a few distributors or supermarket chains.

- *Cost disadvantages independent of size.* The learning, or experience, obtained in producing a product leads to improvements in product and process design which reduce costs. To a large extent these have to do with early entry into a market and the experience so gained. This phenomenon is usually known as the "experience curve" and is dealt with in the next chapter.

- *Legislation or government action.* Deregulation in certain sectors of the economy has meant that many managers who in the past had operated in protected environments found themselves facing increased competition, or experiencing competition for the first time. Long distance telephone services are now available from several companies, not just the telephone company. The airlines and the trucking industry are much more competitive because deregulation has reduced barriers to entry and removed other regulations which constrained competition. In Canada, the government's removal of import quotas on shoes has resulted in more competition for Canadian shoe manufacturers.

- *Differentiation.* By differentiation is meant the provision of a product or service regarded by the user as meaningfully different from competition; its importance will be discussed more fully in Chapter 6. However, here it is important to point out that organizations able to achieve strategies of differentiation provide for themselves very real barriers to competitive entry.

  Differentiation can be achieved in many ways including through advertising, a superior production process, a unique distribution system, or the creation of an image or reputation. Unusual quality is associated with Smirnoff vodka and Chivas Regal scotch. Mercedes-Benz cars are perceived as being excellently engineered prestigious products. Maytag appliances have a reputation for quality and reliability and Cross writing instruments have an image of distinctiveness. The idea of differentiation is not peculiar to the private sector. For example, universities and colleges have sought to differentiate the courses and qualifications they offer; and museums, art galleries or exhibition centers have sought to differentiate themselves from competitors through the services they offer, the architecture of buildings or featured special exhibitions.

These barriers to entry differ by industry, therefore it is impossible to generalize about which are more important than others. What is important is that the analyst should establish (a) which barriers, if any, exist; (b) to what extent they are likely to prevent entry in the particular environment concerned; and (c) the organization's position in all this — whether it is trying to prevent entrants or attempting to gain entry.

3.4.2 THE POWER OF BUYERS AND SUPPLIERS

The next two forces can be considered together because they have similar effects on the competitive environment. Buyers and suppliers influence margins: the greater their power the more likely it is that margins will be low. It is important, then, to assess the power of buyers and suppliers and any likely changes. There are useful indicators of the extent of this power which can be used by the analyst.

Supplier power is likely to be high when:
- there is a concentration of suppliers rather than a fragmented source of supply.
- the switching costs from one supplier to another in the industry are high; perhaps because a manufacturer's processes are dependent on the specialist products of a supplier, or a product is clearly differentiated.
- there is the possibility of the supplier integrating forward if they do not obtain the prices, and hence the margins, they seek.
- the supplier's customers are of little importance to the supplier, in which case the supplier is not likely to regard the long term future of the customers as of particular importance.

Buyer power is likely to be high:

- when there is a concentration of buyers, particularly if the volume purchases of the buyers is high.
- when there are alternative sources of supply, perhaps because the product required is undifferentiated between suppliers or, as for many public sector operations in the 1980s, when deregulation of markets spawns new competitors.
- if the component or material cost is a high percentage of their total cost, buyers will be likely to "shop around" to get the best price and therefore "squeeze" the suppliers.
- where there is a threat of backward integration by the buyer if satisfactory prices or suppliers cannot be obtained.

The problem of constructing strategies which will maintain or provide power along the supplier-buyer channel can be critical for competitive success or efficiency. For example, municipalities, having realized that their historically fragmented mode of buying reduced buying power, sought to increase this by forming buying groups. The converse is also the case of course; it might also be possible for a supplier to seek out market segments with less powerful buyers, or differentiate products so that buyers become more dependent on that product.

3.4.3 THE THREAT OF SUBSTITUTES

The next force Porter identifies is the threat of substitutes. The question here is to what extent an organization can legitimately regard itself as operating in a discrete market with a limited number of like competitors, as opposed to having as potential competitors a wider range of substitute products. The threat may take different forms. There could be substitution of one product for another — the calculator for the slide rule is an extreme example, or sugar substitutes for sugar. A substitute may hold down or depress margins: for example, the producers of natural fabrics found that the advent of man-made fibers depressed prices and margins. It may be that competitors need to be thought of as those competing for discretionary expenditure: for example, furniture manufacturers or retailers need to understand that they compete for available household expenditure with suppliers of televisions, VCRs, microwave ovens, cars and holidays.

The issues that arise are: To what extent is there a danger that substitutes may encroach on the organization's activities? What steps can be taken to minimize the risk of such substitution, perhaps through differentiation or low cost profiles? And, more positively, is there the possibility that one's own products could find new markets as substitutes for some other product?

3.4.4 THE EXTENT OF COMPETITIVE RIVALRY

Competitors will also be concerned with the degree of rivalry between those in their own industry. How intense is this competition? What is it based upon? Is it likely to increase or decrease in intensity? How can it be reduced? All these questions need to be thought about in the process of strategic analysis. The degree of rivalry is likely to be based on the following:

- The extent to which competitors in the industry are *in balance*. Whatever their number, where competitors are of roughly equal size there is the danger of intense competition as one competitor attempts to gain dominance over another. Conversely, the most stable markets tend to be those with dominant organizations within them.

- A market in *slow growth* — particularly one entering its maturity stage and where competitors are keen to establish themselves as market leaders — is likely to be highly competitive.

- *High fixed costs* in an industry, perhaps through high capital intensity[14] or high costs of storage, are likely to result in competitors cutting prices to obtain the turnover required. This can result in price wars and very low margin operations.

- If the addition of *extra capacity is in large increments* then the competitor making such an addition is likely to create at least short-term over-capacity and increased competition.

- Again, the importance of *product differentiation* is clear. If a product or service is not differentiated then there is little to stop customers from switching between competitors, which in turn raises the degree of rivalry between them. This is sometimes referred to as a commodity market situation.

- Where there are *high exit barriers* to an industry, there is again likely to be the persistence of excess capacity and, consequently, increased competition. Exit barriers might be high for a variety of reasons: a high investment in nontransferable fixed assets such as specialist plant, the cost of lay-offs, or the reliance on one product to be credible within a market sector even if the product itself makes heavy losses.

Illustration 3.3 outlines why competitive rivalry has increased recently in the North American fast food business.

3.5 IDENTIFYING THE ORGANIZATION'S COMPETITIVE POSITION

All organizations — business, government or not-for-profit — are in a competitive position. That is, they are competing either for customers or, perhaps in the case of government services, for resources. It is therefore important that they understand the nature of their competitive position. This may be achieved in a number of ways. First, the kind of audit of environmental influences outlined in Section 3.2 above, is likely to provide indications of key factors which will affect competitors in an industry. These can be used to examine the extent to which such competitors are likely to be able to respond effectively to such influences. Illustration 3.4 provides an example of a competitive assessment of full line department stores and the situation they faced in the general merchandise retailing business.

ILLUSTRATION 3.3   *Increasing Competition in The Fast Foods Industry*

The fast food industy is an example of a sector where increasing competition requires strategists to constantly reassess the environment.

Fast food firms have expanded rapidly and now sell not only the traditional hamburger but a wide range of foods like fish, sandwiches, salads, pizza, and ethnic dishes. In North America, there is now a fast food outlet for every 700 persons. Sales have leveled off and slow industry growth is anticipated. These factors have led to a very competitive environment.

Indications of the competitiveness in the industry include the rate of new product introduction and the focus on advertising. A host of new products has been introduced by expanding menus and the startup of new firms specializing in non-hamburger fast foods. New products include: breakfasts, salads, baked potatoes, fish, and chicken. New fast food firms provide Mexican, Italian, Oriental, and other ethnic dishes.

Advertising is key to attracting and retaining customers. Customers are fickle and will switch from one outlet to another and from one food type to another. Product differentiation is difficult to achieve. The major fast food firms have huge advertising budgets; advertising campaigns and approaches are constantly changing in an effort to attract customers.

The fast food industry is comprised largely of firms with thousands of individual outlets, often organized through franchise arrangements. Size is important in order to achieve purchasing and marketing economies of scale through national advertising. Standardized procedures and well-developed management control mechanisms are necessary to insure that all of a firm's outlets provide consistent quality and service. Although McDonald's is the largest firm in the industry, it does not dominate and constantly monitors the environment in order to maintain its position.

The large, well-known fast food firms which compete against each other on a national basis also face competition from local and regional independent fast food operations. In addition, the industry is pressured by grocery stores catering to the same customers by selling hot, take-out food, and family restaurants which have positioned themselves between the limited menu fast food outlet and the pricier, up-scale restaurant.

Since the industry is facing a period of slow growth, individual firms will have to take market share from competitors in order to grow. Another opportunity for the large franchise chains will be to enter the small town markets, or to replace the institutional caterers by establishing specialized restaurants in hospitals and office buildings, and on college campuses and military bases. International expansion is another opportunity but a challenging one as North American eating habits may not be as acceptable in other cultures.

Source: "The Fast Food Industry Is Slowing Down," *Business Week*, (May 18, 1987), pp. 50–1; David Baines, "A&W's Recovery Recipe Blends Old and New," *Financial Times of Canada*, (August 10, 1987), p. 11.

While such an approach can be used to build up a picture of competitors, it is, however also useful to be able to consider competitive positions in terms of a more general framework of analysis. This section explains three such frameworks: life cycle models, the notion of strategic groups and the importance of market power in considering market structures.

3.5.1 LIFE CYCLE MODELS AND THE NATURE OF MARKETS

The idea of the *life cycle*[15] is perhaps the most common basis for conceiving of the ways forces in the environment affect an organization in competitive terms. The notion here is that conditions in the marketplace, primarily growth stages and maturity of markets, will fundamentally affect market conditions and competitive behavior. For example, in situations of market growth an organization might expect to achieve its own growth through growth in the marketplace; this is clearly different from situations where markets are mature and where market growth has plateaued. Here growth for an organization has to be achieved by taking market share from competitors. This is an altogether different task and will likely require quite different strategies.

An example from the not-for-profit sector illustrates what happens when an organization enters the decline stage of the life cycle model. Charitable organizations established to prevent the spread of tuberculosis (a communicable disease caused by infection with the tubercle bacillus) and to help victims receive treatment, found that their services were no longer needed as the disease was virtually eliminated in Canada and the United States. Some of these organizations refocused their strategies and efforts on related diseases and illnesses associated with the lungs and the respiratory system. In effect, these not-for-profit organizations positioned themselves on a different life cycle.

Whether it be private sector industry or not-for-profit organizations, understanding the extent to which the market (for sales or resources) is growing is important for formulating strategy. Moreover, competitors face similar circumstances, and the strategies being adopted by those competitors will also suffer according to the nature of the market. The life cycle model provides one useful basis for conceiving of such competitive influences. Figure 3.5 summarizes some of the conditions to be expected at different stages in the life cycle. (The idea of the life cycle is also useful in the evaluation of strategies and will be discussed again in Chapter 7.)

ILLUSTRATION 3.4   *Competition in General Merchandise Retailing*

The environment in general merchandise retailing has changed in the last two decades and the traditional full line department store has faced increased competition from discount retailers and specialty stores.

General merchandise retailing is big business — approximately $170 billion of sales annually in the U.S. and $16 billion in Canada. The full line department stores (FLDS) have lost 10% of their market share in the last 20 years largely to chain and independent specialty stores but also to junior or discount department stores. Some FLDS have closed stores, for example, Gimbel's and Ohrbach's in downtown New York, while others have been reduced in size, sold, merged, or acquired by competitors.

The following table summarizes the characteristics of the three categories of general merchandisers:

Full Line Department Stores

Examples:	In US	Dayton Hudson	In Canada	Eaton's
		Sears, Roebuck		The Hudson's Bay
		Federated Stores		Company

Market Focus — Broad merchandise base in multiple levels of fashion/quality. Appealed to a wide range of consumer tastes in the middle and up-scale categories.
Competitive Emphasis — Feature wide range of merchandise to supply a wide range of consumer tastes, i.e., providing choice. Merchandise backed up with personal and support services. Reputation for value. Well known names.
Aspects of Implementation — Traditionally, decentralized (at store level) purchasing but now more centralized. Decentralized authority over operations. Usually store level management involved in local strategic inputs.

Junior Department Stores

Examples:	In US	K-Mart	In Canada	Woolco
		Wal-Mart		Zellers
		Woolworth		

Market Focus — Lower reaches of fashion/quality and lower prices.
Competitive Emphasis — Narrower range of assortments with focus on functional needs and standard products. Feature excellent price-value relationship. Convenience of location. Few personal services.
Aspects of Implementation — Mass merchandising based on economies of scale in purchasing. Centralized purchasing and control of all operations, including selection, pricing, promotion, and store layout. Minimum of personal and support services.

Specialty Stores

Examples:	In US	Lord and Taylor	In Canada	Birks Jewellers
		Benetton		Tip Top Tailors
		Toys 'R' Us		

Market Focus — Confined by choice to narrow scope on fashion and quality dimensions. Located in variety of "niches" ranging from high to low fashion and prices, with selected merchandise correlated to target customer group.
Competitive Emphasis — Excellent selection with narrowly defined niche. Good personal service. Conveniently located often near FLDS.

Aspects of Implementation — Centralization of authority in head offices. Stores operated on a "formula" with standardized merchandise and promotional programs. Economies of scale in purchasing with volume obtained through multiple stores.

The FLDS were caught in the middle between the junior department and the specialty stores, losing sales to both. In the 1980s, retailers had to become increasingly focused in their merchandise mix and be more concerned with projecting a sharp image to customers. Costs had to be kept in check and price ranges monitored carefully. FLDS experienced problems in all these areas. Also, local preferences became less important as national brand advertising tended to create nationwide fashion trends. No longer could FLDS be all things to all people as consumers become less homogeneous as a result of the proliferation of lifestyles and the stratification of incomes.

The changes in the environment have not gone unnoticed by the FLDS. Responses have included the following:

- Increasing productivity by selling more from less space, improving warehousing and distribution, remodelling old stores, and leasing space to others.

- Centralizing buying operations.

- Purchasing or establishing specialty store chains and discount department stores.

- "Boutiquing," i.e., separating the big stores into a conglomeration of individual specialty stores.

- Designing premium price store brands which are now exclusive goods, not lower cost alternatives to national brands.

- Scaling down range of merchandise, e.g., dropping furniture, large appliances, and carpeting but adding gourmet foods and restaurants.

- Restoring personal services, traditionally a strong asset.

The nature of the FLDS's competitive position changed and they initially failed to respond adequately. Only recently have they faced the reality of the environment and begun to formulate and implement new strategies.

Source: Ellen Roseman, "Retail Giants Slipping in Service, Share of Market," *The Globe and Mail* (Toronto), July 12, 1984, p. 12; "Specialty Stores Still Gaining Share," *The Financial Times of Canada*, November 4, 1985, p. 4; Francis Phillips, "Big Stores Fight Back," *The Financial Post*, February 8, 1986, pp. 1–2; "Department Stores Facing Bleak Future," *The Globe and Mail*, (Toronto), June 24, 1986, p. B10; "How Department Stores Plan to Get The Registers Ringing Again," *Business Week*, (November 18, 1985), pp. 66–70; "How Three Master Merchants Fell From Grace (Dayton Hudson, Sears, Best Products)," *Business Week*, (March 16, 1987), pp. 38–40; "David Farrell's Iron Hand Has Built a Powerhouse (May Department Stores)," *Business Week* (July 7, 1986), pp. 75–6; "How They're Knocking the Rust off Two Old Chains (Woolworth, K Mart)," *Business Week*, (September 8, 1986), pp. 44–48.

Figure 3.5   *The life cycle model.*

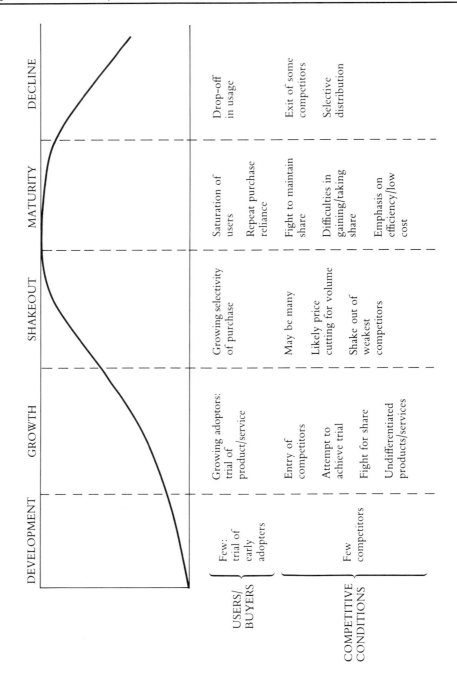

3.5.2 STRATEGIC GROUP ANALYSIS[16]

The strategic analyst must determine the nature of the competition the organization faces. In particular, who are the most direct competitors and on what basis is competition likely to take place? Given this understanding it is then possible to gauge the extent to which strategy is appropriate in the competitive circumstances. The concept of the "industry" as a whole is not a particularly helpful place to begin because the boundaries of an industry can be very unclear and are not likely to provide any precise delineation of competition. In a given industry there may be many companies each with different interests and different bases of competition. There is a need for some intermediate mapping of the bases of competition between the individual firm and the industry level.

Strategic group analysis is one means of providing this intermediate level of analysis. The idea is to identify more finely defined groupings of organizations so that each grouping represents those with similar strategic characteristics, following similar strategies or competing on similar bases. Porter argues that such groups can usually be identified using two or at the most three sets of key characteristics as a basis of competition. In the commercial printing industry (see Illustration 3.5), the strategic map positions firms providing printing services on two dimensions, degree of specialization and production technology. Strategic groupings can be based on a variety of dimensions which will vary by industry. For example, price/quality and product line would be appropriate for retailing. A strategic map such as the one in Illustration 3.5 is a very useful device[17] for clarifying the bases and groupings of competition.

A number of writers have provided checklists analysts can use to assess company characteristics, to establish the extent to which such characteristics differentiate between the companies and help identify strategic groupings. These characteristics are summarized in Figure 3.6.[18] Which of these characteristics are particularly relevant in terms of a given organization or industry is a matter for identification according to the history and development of that industry, identification of the forces at work in the environment (see Sections 3.2 and 3.4 above), the sort of competitive activities of the firms being studied, and so on. The analyst tries to establish these characteristics which most differentiate firms or groupings of firms from others.

This sort of analysis is useful for all organizations which seek to understand competition: its use is not restricted to commercial operations only. For example, universities or hospitals might sensibly identify nearest and furthest competition in such a way. Moreover, analysis of this kind is likely to yield a better understanding of the competitive characteristics of competitors. It also allows the analyst to ask how likely or possible it is for his organization to move from one strategic group to another. Mobility between groups involves considering the extent to which there are real barriers to entry between one group and another in terms of how they compete (see 3.4.1 above). For example, in the brewing industry while it is difficult for a local or regional brewer (such as Anchor in California, Old New York in New York, and Boulder in Colorado) to become a national operator (such as Schlitz, Pabst, Miller, Anheuser-Busch), not least because of the capital investment required, it is also difficult for the national operator, concerned with maintaining national brands, to compete with the local brewer providing well-established and often preferred local brands.

ILLUSTRATION 3.5   *Strategic Groups in the Commercial Printing Industry*

The structure of the commercial printing industry can be understood in terms of the strategic groupings of firms with similar characteristics.

The commercial printing industry is very competitive and firms within the industry attempt to align themselves so that they are insulated against the worst competitive forces. Commercial printers can compete in many ways, including: the breadth of their product line; catering to different target markets; their cost structure and thus their pricing; by serving particular geographic areas; the extent of the value-added to their product; the degree of ancillary services provided customers; and the amount of financial leverage possessed.

The map below plots four groups of commerical printers on two dimensions or bases of competition, degree of specialization and production technology.

Strategic Groups in the Commercial Printing Industry

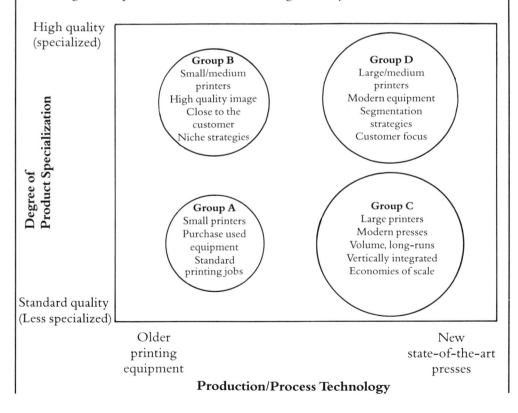

Group A is made up of small shops which use old technology and perform standard printing jobs. This group of printers is vulnerable in that they are not usually strong financially, and are being squeezed by in-plant printing and "quick" printers on the one hand and low cost specialty printers on the other. Firms in this group are caught in the middle as they lack market share (note smaller circle) and are not profitable.

Group B printers are also small, but may be medium-sized, and use old technology but they have been able to specialize, enabling them to produce high quality products. They pay more attention to marketing than Group A printers and as they are more profitable are better able to upgrade their equipment.

Group C printers are large and have the financial strength to obtain high technology equipment. They are low cost producers due to long runs and volume printing. They are often so large that they can bargain with paper suppliers.

Group D firms are medium to large printers who use modern production technology and serve specialized markets. These printers can be profitable but are vulnerable to competition from smaller printers anxious for business. On the whole they are well-positioned to face the competitive rivalry of the industry.

Strategic group maps should not be viewed as being a static representation of an industry. In the commercial printing industry, Group A firms will attempt to specialize and upgrade equipment. Group B printers will attempt to grow at the expense of Group D printers. Printers in Group C will continue to maintain technologically advanced production methods to improve performance and will attempt to increase their marketing skills. Printers in Groups C and D will most likely challenge each other for business.

Source: Richard S. Clark, "Strategy for Printing Profits: How Strategic Groups Compete," *Canadian Printer & Publisher*, (June 1985), pp. 47–50; and Richard S. Clark, "Building a Better Business Plan," *CA Magazine*, (November 1986), pp. 44–54.

3.5.3 MARKET STRUCTURES AND MARKET POWER

As will be seen in the next chapter, the extent to which a competitor has greater market share than another is an important aspect of the capability of that competitor. Market share is, in effect, a measure of market power[19] and it is important to gain an understanding of both the structure of a market and the relative power of competitors within that structure. One way of doing this is to break down the market according to the segments in that market and examine market shares within those segments.

The extent to which an organization has located and exploited a clear market segment is likely to affect its vulnerability to substitutes, its bargaining power with regard to suppliers and buyers, the threat of entry into its market area and the degree of rivalry it faces. Moreover, as will be seen in Chapter 6, it has important implications for considering

Figure 3.6 *Some characteristics for identifying strategic groups.*

It is useful to consider the extent to which organizations *differ* in terms of **characteristics** such as:

- Extent of **product (or service) diversity**
- Extent of **geographic coverage**
- Number of **market segments served**
- **Distribution channels** used
- Extent (number) of **branding**
- Marketing effort (e.g., advertising spread, size of sales force etc.)
- Extent of **vertical integration**
- Product or service **quality**
- **Technological leadership** (a leader or follower)
- **R & D capability** (extent of innovation in product or process)
- **Cost position** (e.g., extent of investment in cost reduction)
- **Utilization of capacity**
- **Pricing policy**
- Degree of **leveraging**
- **Ownership structure** (separate company or relationship with parent)
- Relationship to **influence groups** (e.g., government, lenders)
- **Size** of organization

Source: M.E. Porter, *Competitive Strategy,* New York: Free Press, 1980 and John McGee and Howard Thomas, "Strategic Groups: Theory, Research and Taxonomy," *Strategic Management Journal,* Vol. 7, No. 2, (1986), pp. 141–60.

strategic options. Segmentation is an important concept for the strategist and warrants some attention.

It may be possible to identify how a market may be segmented and which competitors are concentrating on which segments in a quantitative way by establishing the values of market segment and competitor shares by segment; or a more qualitative approach may be sensible. In either case, what is needed is a breakdown of the market into the segments which are important from a strategic point of view. The importance could arise for a number of reasons: for example, because certain segments are more competitive than others; or because by segmenting the market in a particular way new opportunities for product differentiation emerge; or because some segments are growing and others are not; or some segments are much bigger than others.

It is also important to remember that a market can be segmented in various ways: and each different basis of segmentation could give rise to a different assessment of environmental opportunities. Suppose that Table 3.2 represents the structure of a market worth

$100 million, and suppose that all the companies involved are manufacturing much the same sort of basic product. If company C thinks of its markets in overall terms, then it would consider itself to be fairly weak. But suppose the segments shown in the table are based on different customer types: then immediately it is clear that company C is relatively strong in one part of the market — Segment IV — and this could substantially affect the strategic opportunities open to it depending on the opportunities and threats in that segment.

Again, by looking at the market segmentation in Table 3.2 other implications about the competitive environment emerge. Segments I and II are the largest where the competitive battle is at its fiercest. Companies A and B are concentrating on these segments with company D running behind. Company C specializes in Segment IV which it dominates. But what of Segments III and V which are growing? They account for $25 million and no one is really concentrating on them. Even as simple a model as this raises questions about the strategic positions of the various firms and the possible limitations and opportunities they have. Company D, with say, a 25% share of I ($10 million), a 10% share of II ($2.5 million) and a 10 % share of III ($1.5 million), has a turnover of $14 million and is probably having to operate at low margins to try to compete in I and II. Is there an opportunity to concentrate on dominating III and V, achieving perhaps a 40% share of each and sales of $10 million at higher margins? Companies A and B, of course, are probably more concerned with retaining their dominance of I and II respectively. Again, this simple segmentation exercise might point out an opportunity in V which A and B had not previously considered.

The relationship between market share (and power) and strategic choice will be discussed again in Chapters 6 and 7.

Table 3.2 *Competitor analysis by market segment.*

Segment	Size $m	Competitor positions			
		A	B	C	D
I	40	Dominant	Weak		No. 2
II	25	No. 2	Dominant		Weak
III	15	Weak		Weak	Weak
IV	10			Dominant specialist	
V	10 (growing)	No one specializing (all weak)			
Total market	100				

3.6 SWOT ANALYSIS

If the forces at work in the environment and likely future changes in that environment are identified, then there are bases for considering the sorts of opportunities and threats which might exist for the organization. However, a word of warning is needed here. Opportunities and threats cannot be "absolute." As was said in Chapter 1, considering a strategic situation is an iterative problem: what might at first appear to be an opportunity may not be so when considered against the resources of the organization (Chapter 4), its culture or expectations of stakeholders (Chapter 5), the strategies available (Chapters 6 and 7) or the feasibility of implementing the strategy (Part IV). However, at the risk of oversimplification, the idea of strategy formulation is to construct a strategy which will take advantage of the opportunities and overcome or circumvent the threats. Given that it is not necessarily very clear what environmental changes constitute opportunities and what constitute threats how can the problem be considered? And how can potentially dangerous preconceptions be challenged?

The analysis outlined here is one approach. The aim is to identify the extent to which the current strategy of an organization and its more specific strengths and weaknesses are relevant to, and capable of, dealing with the changes taking place in the business environment. Moreover, the aim is to do this in such a way as to isolate the key opportunities and threats while at the same time identifying key aspects of organizational capability which provide strengths or indicate weaknesses in dealing with those environmental changes. SWOT therefore stands for strengths, weaknesses, opportunities and threats, but rather than just listing these in terms of managers' perceptions, the idea is to undertake a somewhat more structured analysis so that the findings yielded will contribute to the formulation of strategy. Although what follows is somewhat crude as an analytical device, it has proved in practical application to be a helpful means of achieving these aims.

The procedure can be undertaken in a number of steps, and for the purposes of this description it is assumed that a group of managers is working on the problem of strategic analysis.

1. The managers would first identify the current or prevailing strategy or strategies the organization is following. This would not necessarily be the strategy as advocated or published, but the realized strategy (see chapter 2) of the organization. This in itself might be problematic; managers do not always agree on the strategy they are following even though they are busily putting it into operation: so this debate, in itself, is often very important.

2. Managers should then identify the key changes in the organization's environment following the sorts of procedures outlined in this chapter. It is helpful to first do this individually and then to pool individual views and attempt to reach a group view. The aim should be to arrive at a list of key changes or influences on the organization. While there is no fixed number to be agreed upon, it is helpful if the list does not exceed seven or eight key points.

3. The managers then do the same in terms of the resource profile of the organization. Following the procedures to be outlined in the next chapter (Chapter 4), they try to identify

the key capabilities, or strengths, and key limitations (weaknesses) of the organization. They might do this individually first and then pool their views to provide a consolidated list. Again, it is useful to keep the total list to no more than ten points. Also the managers should attempt to avoid overgeneralizing their views and try to keep to quite specific points: a statement such as "poor management" means very little and could be interpreted in any number of ways. If they really mean that the organization has, historically, not been good at motivating change in the organization, then that is a more specific and useful point.

4. The group then has a list of key environmental issues against which they can establish the relevance and significance of the current strategy or strategies and the strengths and weaknesses of the organization. Illustration 3.6 gives an example of the type of list drawn up by one company undertaking this exercise.

5. The managers then need to examine the statements one against another. They can do this by taking each statement in the left hand column in turn, examining it in terms of the key environmental issues and "scoring" either a + (or a weighted + +) or a – (or a – –). As follows:

a) Mark + if there would be a benefit to the organization, i.e.,

+ a strength would enable the organization to take advantage or counteract a problem from an environmental change.

+ a weakness would be offset by the environmental change.

b) Mark – if there would be an adverse effect on the organization, i.e.,

– a strength would be reduced by the environmental change.

– a weakness would prevent the organization from overcoming the problems associated with an environmental change or would be accentuated by that change.

When this procedure is completed, the analysis will look something like the completed Illustration 3.6. What this yields is a much clearer view of the extent to which the environmental changes and influences provide opportunities or threats given current strategies and organizational capabilities. For example, Illustration 3.6 shows that the major opportunities for the organization are the increasing "casual" eating habits of customers. The manager also found that they were reasonably well placed to deal with an industry-wide problem of overcapacity. However, other environmental issues seem to be rather limited in opportunity and there are major threats in terms of the growing concentration of retailers, the trend to "healthier eating," and competitors' market power. The maturation of the market could be an opportunity or threat as could other issues, depending on the extent to which the organization can utilize and develop the strength in funds availability and its distribution network, and overcome the main weaknesses it has.

Illustration 3.6 also shows that some of what the managers originally conceived of as strengths seem to be more neutral when examined against the key environmental issues. They may be strengths as far as the history of the organization is concerned, but do not seem to be so relevant (indeed some are actually scored negatively) in terms of the way the organization's environment is developing. Similarly, an analysis of perceived weaknesses

ILLUSTRATION 3.6 *A SWOT Analysis*

Examining environmental influencs in terms of current strategies and organizational strengths and weaknesses can yield useful insights into key environmental impacts and key isues of current strategy.

A manufacturer of chocolate products undertook such an exercise and the results are illustrated below.

Key Issues in The Environment	Overcapacity in industry	Growing retail concentration	Health lobby/healthier eating	Increased "casual" eating	Low growth in market	Aging population	Competitors' market power	+	–
Current strategies									
Rationalization	+	–	0	0	+	0	+	2	1
Gain market share	– / +	+	–	+ / –	– / +	0	–	4	5
Main strengths									
Availability of funds	+	+	+	+	+	+	+	8	0
R&D/technology/innovation	+	0	–	+	+	–	–	3	3
Known brands	0	–	–	+	+	+	–	3	3
Extensive distribution	+	+	0	+	+	0	+	5	0
Good labor relations	+	+	0	0	+	0	+	4	0
Main weaknesses									
Subsid. B. low share	–	–	–	+	–	–	–	1	6
Few brand leaders	–	– / +	0	0	–	0	–	1	4
Too traditional	–	–	–	–	–	0	–	–	6
Over-wide product range	+	–	–	+	–	+	–	3	4
Information systems	–	–	0	0	–	0	–	0	5
+	7	5	2	7	7	3	4		
–	5	8	5	1	6	2	8		

shows that their importance varies. The analysis also shows the extent to which the current strategies address the issue of a changing environment and comes to the view that they do so only partially, raising important questions in particular about the pursuit of market share in current mainline chocolate products.

A SWOT analysis therefore provides a mechanism for systematically thinking through the extent to which the organization can cope with its environment. However, the analysis requires both an understanding of the environment and the resource capabilities of that organization. It is this which is the subject of the next chapter.

3.7 SUMMARY

This chapter has provided a step-by-step approach to analyzing the complexity and uncertainty of the organization's environment and its effect on the organization. It started with identifying a problem the analyst faces; the influences of the environment are so many and varied that trying to understand its effects can reduce the strategist to a rather unhelpful listing exercise. The approach proposed here starts with an identification of the many different forces at work in the environment but seeks to analyze these in terms of their impact on the organization and its competitive position. The aim of such analyses is to move towards an explicit understanding of:

1. The environmental influences which have most affected the organization and its performance.
2. The extent to which competitors are similarly or differently affected by environmental forces; and therefore the organization's competitive position.
3. The specific opportunities and threats for the future development of strategy.

References

1. There are books which do review environmental influences on organizations. For example see books one and two of M. Glew, M. Watts and R. Wells, *The Business Organization and Its Environment*, (London: Heinemann Educational Books International Limited, 1979) and L. Fahey and V.K. Narayanan, *Macroenvironmental Analyses for Strategic Management*, (St. Paul, Minn.: West Publishing Co., 1986).

2. For an example of a more detailed and more systematic approach to environmental auditing for strategic purposes see George Steiner, *Strategic Planning: What Every Manager Must Know*, (New York: Macmillan Publishing Co., Inc., 1979).

3. D. Norburn's work supports this and is summarized in "Directors Without Direction," *Journal of General Management*, Vol. 1, No. 2, (1973-74), pp. 37–48. Also D. Miller and P. Friesen, "Strategy Making in Context: Ten Empirical Archetypes," *Journal of Management Studies*, Vol. 14, No. 3, (1977) support this assertion.

4. R. Duncan's research on which this classification is based can be found in "Characteristics of Organizational Environments and Perceived Environmental Uncertainty," *Administrative Science Quarterly*, (1972), pp. 313-27.

5. This notion of interconnectedness was put forward by F.E. Emery and E.L. Trist in "The Causal Texture of Organizational Environments," *Human Relations*, Vol. 18, (1985). The idea has been developed in the context of the implications on uncertainty by R.H. Miles in *Macro-Organizational Behavior*, (Santa Monica, California: Goodyear Publishing Company, 1980), pp. 200-09.

6. L. Fahey and W. King summarize a survey carried out in 12 large business organizations in the US which shows that it is firms in stable environments which tend to have regular and continuous scanning mechanisms. Firms in less stable conditions tend to have more irregular (*ad hoc*, reactive, crisis initiated, etc.) scanning mechanisms. This survey is outlined in "Environmental Scanning for Corporate Planning," *Business Horizons*, Vol. 20, No. 4 (August 1977), pp. 61–71.

7. The term "inspirational" is used by J.D. Thompson and A. Tuden in "Strategies, Structures and Processes of Organization Decision," J.D. Thompson, ed., *Comparative Studies in Administration*, (Pittsburgh: University of Pittsburgh Press, 1958). They argue that as dynamic conditions increase, managers cease to be as reliant on understanding what has gone before and become more concerned with sensing what they expect will happen.

8. For a useful guide on the Delphi method see F.J. Parente and J.K. Anderson-Parente, "Delphi Inquiry Systems," in G. Wright and P. Ayton, eds., *Judgmental Forecasting*, (New York: John Wiley and Sons, Inc., 1987).

9. For an example of method and an illustration of the use of scenarios in global economic forecasting see D. Norse, "Scenario Analysis in Interfutures," *Futures*, Vol. 11, No. 5, (1979), pp. 412–22. For a brief discussion of the role of scenario analysis see R.D. Zentner, "Scenarios, Past, Present and Future," *Long Range Planning*, Vol. 15, No. 3, (1982), pp. 12–20.

10. Breaking up the organization into different parts to cope with such diversity is sometimes called "differentiation", a term coined by P. Lawrence and J. Lorsch in *Organization and Environment*, (Homewood, Illinois: Richard D. Irwin Inc., 1969), to describe this aspect of organizational design. This aspect of organizational structure will be returned to in Chapter 10.

11. See M.E. Porter, *Competitive Strategy: Techniques for Analyzing Industries and Competitors*, (New York: Free Press, 1980).

12. This quotation is taken from M.E. Porter, "How Competitive Forces Shape Strategy," *Harvard Business Review*, (March-April, 1979), pp. 137–45, which is a useful summary of his approach.

13. For a discussion of these differences in economies of scale by industry see C. Pratten: "Economies of Scale in Manufacturing Industries" *Department of Applied Economics Occasional Papers, No. 28*, (Oxford: Cambridge University Press: 1971).

14. High capital intensity has been shown to be a major cause of rivalry since, to maintain utilization of plant, competitors will reduce prices (and margins) to achieve volume. This is discussed more fully in Chapter 7 of this book and in S. Schoeffler, "Capital-Intensive Technology vs ROI: A Strategic Assessment," *Management Review*, (September 1978), pp. 81–4.

15. A good discussion of the relevance of the idea of life cycle is to be found in Peter Doyle, "The Realities of the Product Life Cycle," *Quarterly Review of Marketing*, (Summer, 1976).

16. The term "strategic groups" was used initially by Michael S. Hunt in his doctoral dissertation, "Competition in the Major Home Appliance Industry, 1960-70," (Harvard University, 1972), and is now commonly used in writings on competitive strategy.

17. Porter discusses the value of strategic maps as an analytical tool on pp. 152-5 of *Competitive Strategy: Techniques for Analyzing Industries and Competitors*.

18. The characteristics listed in Figure 3.6 are based on those discussed by Porter (see reference 17) and by J. McGee and H. Thomas "Strategic Groups; Theory, Research and Taxonomy," *Strategic Management Journal*, Volume 7, (1986), pp. 141-60. The latter paper, in particular, provides a very useful review of the sorts of strategic group analyses which have been undertaken and a good many other references readers can follow up.

19. The relationship between market share and the strategic position in organizations is taken up again in Chapter 4 when the idea of the experience curve is discussed. See P. Conley, "Experience Curves as a Planning Tool," available from the Boston Consulting Group as a pamphlet, and B. Hedley, "Strategy and the Business Portfolio," *Long Range Planning*, Vol. 10, (Feb. 1977), pp. 9–15. In Chapter 7, the importance of market share is discussed in terms of the PIMS data, the basic findings of which are available in PIMS Letters available from the Strategic Planning Institute, Haymarket, London.

Recommended Key Readings

M.E. Porter. *Competitive Strategy: Techniques for Analyzing Industries and Competitors*. New York: Free Press, 1980. Essential reading for those who are faced with the structural analysis of an organizational environment.

L. Fahey and V.K. Narayanan. *Macroenvironmental Analysis for Strategic Management*. St. Paul, Minn: West Publishing Co., 1986, is a sound structural approach to analyzing the strategic effects of environmental influences on organizations.

For more thorough treatment of techniques of forecasting for management purposes the following are useful:

S. Makridakis and S. Wheelwright. *The Handbook of Forecasting: A Manager's Guide*. New York: John Wiley and Sons, Inc., 1987, or *Forecasting Methods for Management*. New York: John Wiley and Sons, Inc., 1985.

Chapter 4
ANALYZING RESOURCES

4.1 INTRODUCTION

The previous chapter emphasized the importance of *matching* the organization's strategies to the environment within which the organization is operating. However, any individual organization must also pursue strategies it is *capable* of sustaining. This chapter is concerned with understanding an organization's *strategic capability* and how resource analysis can contribute to this understanding.

In the private sector, strategic capability is crucially linked to the competitive position of an organization and its ability to sustain competitive advantage. In the public sector, capability is concerned with the extent to which the organization is able to fulfil its expected role within acceptable financial limits and without undue overlap with other providers.

In order to understand strategic capability, it will be necessary to consider organizations at various levels of detail. Certainly, there are broad issues of resource capability relevant to the organization as a whole. It will be seen that these are largely concerned with the overall *balance* of resources. However, the capability of any organization is fundamentally determined by the *separate* activities the organization undertakes in designing, producing, marketing, delivering and supporting its products or services. Gaining an understanding of these various activities and the *linkages* between them is crucial when assessing strategic capability.

This concern about an organization's resource profile is not limited to strategic analysis. It will be a key determinant during strategic choice, helping to identify directions which best match the organization's strategic capabilities (where possible). Equally, the need for detailed resource planning and deployment is a key ingredient for successful implementation of new strategies. These two further aspects of resources will be discussed in Chapters 8 and 9 respectively. Illustration 4.1. shows the importance strategists place on various resources to obtain company performance.

An organization's resources are not confined to those it "owns." Strategic capability is strongly influenced by resources outside the organization which are an integral part of the

---

ILLUSTRATION 4.1   *Resource Strengths*

Strategists, that is, managers, perceive different resources as strengths in the formulation of a firm's strategy.

"Business strategies directed to fulfillment of ambitious financial objectives will be successful only if the people responsible for implementing them are highly capable and properly motivated. Thus, we seek people with superior potential and work closely with them to encourage their development."
Masco Corporation, *1985 Annual Report*, p. 11.

"Despite the challenge of finding the funds to support rapid growth over the years, we have maintained a strong balance sheet and strong banking support. Our asset base is diverse and we maintain a reasonable balance between liquidity and economic risk."
Federal Industries Limited *Strategic Plan.*

"An integral part of maintaining our record as a unique growth company is the planning and development of new products."
Masco Corporation, *1984 Annual Report*, p. 10.

"Behind our store formats is an infrastructure of efficient warehousing and distribution services, a highly sophisticated data processing capability, and a private brand program clearly superior to any with which we compete."
Loblaw Companies Limited, *Annual Report*, p. 4.

"The company employs 19,200 professional engineers and scientists and 5,800 supporting technical personnel. Thus, one out of five Rockwell employees is involved in pursuing the technological advances necessary for our four core businesses to strengthen their leadership position."
Rockwell International, *1985 Annual Report*, p. 5.

"Business is nothing more than people, and it's characterized by a lack of leadership, not a shortage of capital. Anybody can buy assets, but you need people to form a team and spark each others imaginations."
Michael Blair, President of Enfield Corp., quoted in *The Financial Post*, Feb. 23, 1987.

"CAM–NET management places a premium on the company's ability to keep abreast of the technological revolution in telecommunications. The Company's philosophy holds that the only way to maximize CAM–NET's growth is to anticipate each successive wave of Canadian deregulation by building up its capabilities in advance."
Growth Stock Review, February 1987.

"One of the major strengths at Greyhound is our ability to view the company objectively. Management's job is to see the company not as it is . . . but as it can become!"
Greyhound Corporation advertisement, *Business Week*, March 9, 1987, p. 18.

chain between the product or service design, through production and marketing, to the use of the product or service by consumers. Section 4.2. will introduce this important concept of the *value chain* and the way in which it affects strategic capability and the competitive performance of an organization.

The most successful organizations have a consistent resource "theme" running through the value chain. For example, if an organization chooses to compete largely through cost leadership, this should be found in *many* aspects, from procurement to targeting markets and customer support. Importantly, this cost competition will also be sustained by the special *linkages* which are developed within the value chain or with suppliers, channels or customers.

Before reviewing methods which can be used to analyze an organization's resource position, it is necessary to understand how the various analyses will contribute to the overall assessment of strategic capability. These analytical methods can be grouped under four headings, as summarized in Fig. 4.1.

Figure 4.1   *Methods of analyzing resources.*

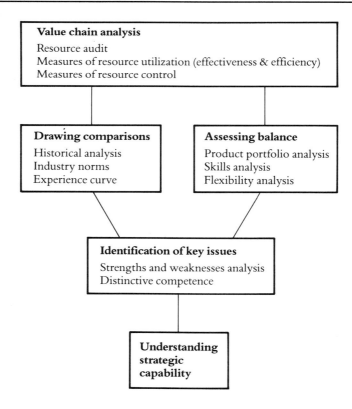

1. *Data analysis.* A resource analysis needs to build on a bank of data, much of which will be in quantitative form (the data base). If the strategic capability of an organization is to be understood this analysis must go beyond a simple listing of resources. It must assess resources in relation to the organization's strategic purpose and in addition to a *resource audit*, data will be needed on how resources have been *utilized* and *controlled*. The concept of the value chain will be used as a way of relating resources to strategic capability and providing this data base. It should be remembered that in terms of understanding the strategic capability of an organization, these data are of little value unless subjected to further analysis. This is an important observation, particularly in relation to the use of financial data in resource analysis. Many managers are capable of producing a wide variety of financial ratios and performance indicators but fail to extract any strategic significance from them.

2. *Comparison.* The strategic capability of an organization is better understood in relation to how the resource base has changed historically and the relationship of this to company performance. The concept of the value chain emphasizes the importance of competitor comparisons when assessing capability. Additionally, the concept of the experience curve can be helpful in understanding the relative standing of an organization's products in their markets compared to the competition.

3. *Balance.* Very often an organization's strategic capability is impaired, not because of problems with any individual resource area, but because the balance of these resources is inappropriate. Two quite different examples of balance are: (1) a firm has too many new products whose introduction is costly, creating cash flow problems, and (2) a company has a top management team expert in financial matters but lacking knowledge and understanding of the manufacturing aspects of the business.

4. *Identification of key issues.* It has already been mentioned that resource analysis must be capable of identifying those issues of particular strategic importance in any given situation. Value chain analysis is centrally concerned with this relationship. However, it is usually important to make an overall assessment of key issues affecting strategic capabilities *after* the various analyses discussed in this chapter.

4.2 VALUE CHAIN ANALYSIS

4.2.1 THE VALUE SYSTEM

Understanding strategic capability through resource analysis can easily degenerate into a listing of an organization's resources and a failure to identify how the particular resource profile of the organization contributes to its strategic performance. *Value chain analysis*[1] is helpful for placing resource analysis in this strategic context. This section introduces readers to the value system to provide a background against which the later discussions should be set. There are important links to future chapters of the book since an understanding of the value system is also crucial to strategic choice (Chapter 7) and resource planning during implementation (Chapter 9).

An organization's strategic capability is ultimately judged by the consumers or users of the products or services of the organization. The extent to which these products/ services are *valued* by consumers/users is determined by the way the various activities required to design, produce, market, deliver and support the product are performed. These strategically important *value activities* need to be analyzed and understood when assessing an organization's strategic capability. However, it will be seen below that the analysis must consider some important issues:

- The concept of *value* relates to how the ultimate consumer/user views the organization's product/service *in relation to competitive offerings*. An analysis of resources must establish *how* this competitive difference is achieved within the value system.

- Many of the value activities will be performed *outside* the organization (e.g. by suppliers, channels or customers). It is essential that the organization's own *value chain* is seen in this wider context (see Figure 4.2).

- The *linkages* and relationships between the various value activities are often the basis on which competitive advantage is achieved. This also applies to linkages between the value chain of an organization and those of suppliers, channels, and customers.

Figure 4.2   *The value system.*

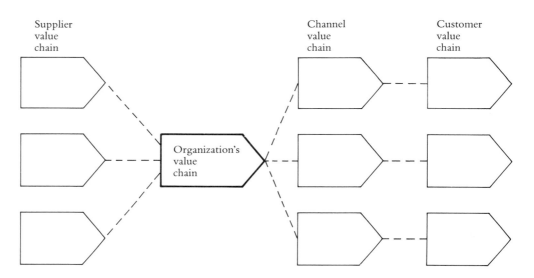

Source: M.E. Porter, *Competitive Advantage: Creating and Sustaining Superior Performance*, New York: Free Press, 1985. Used with permission of The Free Press, a Division of Macmillan, Inc. Copyright © 1985 Michael E. Porter.

4.2.2 Value Chain Activities

Figure 4.3 is a schematic representation of the value chain showing its constituent parts. The *primary* activities of the organization are grouped into five main areas; inbound logistics, operations, outbound logistics, marketing and sales, and service.

- *Inbound logistics* are the activities concerned with receiving, storing and distributing the inputs to the product/service. This includes materials handling, inventory control, and transport.

- *Operations* transform these various inputs into the final product or service. For example, machining, packaging, assembly, and testing.

- *Outbound logistics* collect, store and distribute the product to customers. For tangible products this could be warehousing, materials handling, and transport, in the case of services it may be more concerned with arrangements for bringing customers *to* the service if it is at a fixed location (e.g. entertainment events).

- *Marketing and sales* provide the means whereby consumers/users are made aware of the product/service and are able to purchase it. This would include sales administration, advertising, selling, and promotional activities. In government agencies, communication networks which help users access a particular service are often important.

Figure 4.3   *The value chain.*

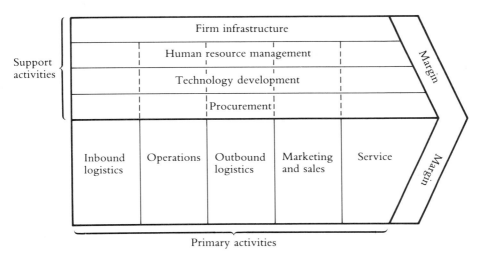

Primary activities

Source: M.E. Porter, *Competitive Advantage: Creating and Sustaining Superior Performance,* New York: Free Press, 1985. Used with permission of The Free Press, a Division of Macmillan, Inc. Copyright © 1985 Michael E. Porter.

- *Service* is all those activities which enhance or maintain the value of a product/service such as installation, repair, training, and spare parts.

Each of these groups of primary activities will be linked to support activities. These can be divided, for convenience, into four areas:

- *Procurement* refers to the *process* for acquiring the various resource inputs to the primary activities (not to the resources themselves). As such, it occurs in many parts of the organization.
- *Technology development.* All value activities have a "technology" even if it is simply "know-how." The key technologies may be concerned directly with the product (e.g. R&D, product design) or with processes (e.g. process development) or with a particular resource (e.g. raw materials improvements).
- *Human resource management.* This is a particularly important area which transcends all primary activities. It is concerned with those activities involved in recruiting, training, developing and rewarding people within the organization.
- *Management systems.* Systems designed to plan, organize work and activities, direct people, and control operations, are crucially important to an organization's strategic capability in all primary activities.

4.2.3 THE RESOURCE AUDIT[2]

Simply listing all the activities an organization performs is not an adequate basis on which to analyze the value chain. Although the analysis does need to be comprehensive it is crucial to isolate those value activities which are strategically distinct and on which the organization's strategic capability is built — in contrast to other activities which may be necessary but are not the means through which the organization's products/services sustain their distinctive value in the eyes of consumers/users.

Referring back to Figure 4.3, it should be clear that the resources an organization possesses itself, or those which exist within its wider value system, will be dispersed among the various primary activities. Additionally, the support activities will be crucially important in marshalling those resources and using them to good strategic purpose. Table 4.1 plots these various resources onto the value chain to provide a checklist of resources to be assessed in an analysis.[3] It should be noted that within each activity different *types* of resources are identified:

- *Physical resources.* An assessment of a company's physical resources must stretch beyond a mere listing of the number of machines or the production capacity, and ask questions about the nature of these resources, such as age, condition, capability, and location of each resource.
- *Human resources.* The analysis of human resources must examine a number of relevant questions. An assessment of the number and types of different skills within an organization is clearly important but other factors such as the adaptability of human resources

Table 4.1 *A checklist for resource auditing.*

Support activities	Primary activities				
	Inbound logistics	*Operations*	*Outbound logistics*	*Marketing and sales*	*Service*
Procurement	Transport Warehousing Capital	Machines Consumables	Transport Warehousing	Product/service Patents/licenses Brand names Market research	Franchisees Credit facilities
Technology development	Know-how Design Technology transfer (in)	Process development	Shipments	Network of contacts Information systems	Fault diagnosis
Human resource management	Recruitment Supplier examination Shareholders Creditor relations	Team spirit Job satisfaction Subcontractors	Subcontractors	Agents Sales force Distributors Merchandisers Goodwill	After-sales staff Reputation Maintenance staff
Management systems	Purchasing systems Vehicle scheduling Materials handling	Production planning Quality control Cash management Stock control Facilities layout	Delivery scheduling	Order processing Debtor control	Customer service system

must not be overlooked. For example, if a company is likely to face a period of difficulty or retrenchment it is important to know how able the people are to cope with a situation where some of the traditional boundaries and demarcation lines will have to change to ensure economic survival. As with physical resources, the location of key human resources could be important. A multinational company may be concerned that all its skilled operatives are in high wage countries making it difficult to compete on world markets.

- *Financial resources.* This would include the sources and uses of money within the value chain such as obtaining capital, managing cash, the control of debtors and creditors, and the management of relationships with suppliers of money (shareholders, bankers and creditors).

- *Intangibles*. One mistake which can be made in a resource analysis is to overlook the importance of intangible resources. There should be no doubt that these intangibles have a value since when businesses are sold part of their value is "goodwill." In some businesses, particularly services such as lawyers, retail shops, and the catering industry, goodwill could represent the major asset of the company and may result from brand names, good contacts, company image, or reputation. Illustration 4.2 describes a company whose reputation is very important to its expansion plans.

4.2.4 RESOURCE UTILIZATION

One of the key aspects of value chain analysis is the recognition that organizations are much more than a random collection of machines, money and people. These resources are of no value unless organized into *systems* which enable good products or services to be produced in a way which ensures that they are valued by the final consumer/user. In other words, *value activities* and the linkages between them are more important than resources *per se*. A resource analysis must therefore proceed beyond a simple audit of resources to an assessment of how those resources have been utilized. This is related to the decisions which have been made about the linkages between value activities and also between the value chains of suppliers, channels or customers. The measures of resource utilization discussed below would need to be applied in that broader context. It is the planning of these linkages which can provide either distinctive cost advantages *or* become the basis on which the organization's products/services are differentiated from competitive offerings. Whereas competitors can often imitate the separate activities of an organization, it is more difficult to copy linkages within and between value chains. Illustration 4.3 shows one example of this.

Any of the following types of linkages may help sustain competitive advantage:

1.   It has already been mentioned that the primary activities within the value chain will be linked to support activities (see Figure 4.3). Any one of these linkages could provide advantage. For example, an organization may have a unique system for procuring materials or for sales order processing.

2.   There will be important links *between* the primary activities. In particular, important choices will have been made about these relationships and how they influence overall value and strategic capability. For example, a decision to hold high levels of finished inventory may ease production scheduling problems and provide for a faster response time to the customer. However, it will probably add to the overall cost of operations. An assessment needs to be made as to whether the added value of inventory is greater than the added cost.

3.   In many organizations, there are possibilities that the same strategic outcome can be achieved in different ways. For example, the quality image of a movie theater may be sustained through its careful selection of films or the technical excellence of its equipment,

---

ILLUSTRATION 4.2   *"Cartier" — Building a Strategy on a Reputation*

Cartier has a well-established name in luxury goods which proved to be an invaluable resource when the company decided to expand.

Cartier was a leading jeweler to the monarchy, the nobility, the rich and the famous, and has been the crown jeweler to 21 royal families. It's very high priced jewelry was sold from three boutiques in Paris, London, and New York. Now the company wants to use its reputation as a supplier of exquisite jewelry to increase sales to a billion dollars by 1990 from about $400 million in 1985.

This will require selling more luxury goods to a broader clientele. New stores will be opened, such as twelve boutiques and five full-line jewelry stores in the US. Several new products will be introduced including silverware, china, crystal, and bath products. The firm has the world licenses for Yves Saint Laurent and Ferrari jewelry and accessories. Cartier wants to expand its clientele to include new millionaires and yuppies with money to spend on luxury goods.

Critics claim that this new strategy will destroy the Cartier name by running down the firm's reputation and alienating old clients. Cartier responds that its products will be of premium quality and that it will be careful not to associate the Cartier name with inferior merchandise.

Observers of the luxury goods market caution that the strategists at Cartier will have to be very careful not to over-leverage the firm's name and reputation for the sake of growth. Basing a strategy on a reputation which took years to acquire is not without some risk.

Source: "For Today's Cartier, Snob Appeal is Not Enough," *Business Week*, (December 16, 1985), pp. 80–1.

---

or the general ambience of the cinema. It is important to understand which of these aspects is *actually* valued by consumers/users and plan the utilization of resources accordingly.

Linkages to the value activities undertaken in supplier organizations can also be a key source of competitive advantage. For example, a publisher may be able to persuade (or help) its authors to provide manuscripts on computer discs compatible with typesetting facilities, hence reducing the work needed in book production.

4. An analysis should also assess the extent to which *suboptimization* is occurring within the overall value system. For example, the organization may reduce its own in-house finished goods inventory and find that distribution channels are carrying unduly high inventories, forcing up costs which are then reflected in mark-up and hence the relative competitiveness of the products in retail outlets.

ILLUSTRATION 4.3   *Value Chain Example — Canadian Tire Corp.*

Canadian Tire's ability to compete in Canadian retailing was determined by a cost based competitive strategy which was sustained throughout the value chain.

Linkages Throughout the Value Chain — Canadian Tire Corp.

Support Activities	INBOUND LOGISTICS	OPERATIONS	OUTBOUND LOGISTICS	MARKETING & SALES	SERVICE
MANAGEMENT SYSTEMS	Purchasing system	Inventory control Dealer recruitment & training		Corporate coordination of advertising	Franchise dealer network
HUMAN RESOURCE MANAGEMENT	Good supplier relations	Profit sharing			Dealer association
TECHNOLOGY DEVELOPMENT	Fully automated warehousing	Inventory control computerized	Computerized check-outs tied to inventory system	Computerized market information system	
PROCUREMENT	Private brands Volume purchases Independent suppliers	Inventory management programs for dealers	Truck and container hauling operation	Discount coupons Catalogues Flyers	Automotive parts remanufacturing plant Credit card operation
OTHER	Assembling merchandise items	Management of retail outlets	Multiple locations	Merchandising activities	Auto service centers Gasoline stations Pit stop lubrication centers

Primary Activities

Canadian Tire is one of the largest and most successful retailers in Canada. Sales exceed $2.4 billion from over 400 stores selling a selection of automotive, sporting goods, hardware, housewares, and electronics products. The company assembles the merchandise from independent suppliers who provide national brands but also private branded products manufactured to exacting specifications. The merchandise is delivered to automated warehouses with computerized inventory systems and is distributed to the stores through the company's own long haul operation. The stores are operated by independent dealers under a franchise type of arrangement. These dealers are carefully selected and trained and then provided with assistance in operating and managing the stores. Employees participate in fringe benefit plans, a profit sharing scheme, and training programs. Computer systems manage inventory levels which are controlled by a "just-in-time" merchandise delivery system. Marketing is coordinated from corporate headquarters but regional differences are taken into account. The company regularly surveys customers to monitor whether or not they still perceive that Canadian Tire always has merchandise of value available at the lowest prices. A computerized strategic information network gathers comprehensive market information to use in planning and as feedback to dealers.

The productivity of a firm's manufacturing process can often be improved. An example is provided by the use of Kanban, or "just in time," a system of supplying parts and materials just at the moment they are needed in the factory production process so that parts and materials are instantly put to use. Such a system requires the cooperation of suppliers to insure that arrival of parts and materials is coordinated with the production process. There are many advantages to such a system. Kanban reduces capital investment by increasing capacity in plants of the same, or even reduced, size. Savings occur in reduced cost of work-in-process, lower direct labor costs, and better quality control. Kanban has been widely used in Japan for some time and is now being introduced in many North American plants.

5. It will be seen in Chapters 7 and 8 that one of the crucial strategic decisions for an organization is the extent to which it should specialize or diversify its activities. Within the organization's own industry, this means deciding which value activities should be entirely within its own value chain; which should be undertaken on a "tried basis" (e.g., subcontracting, dealers), and which should be entirely within another organization's value chain (i.e., deciding demarcation lines). During strategic analysis it is important to establish the organization's current position in relation to this issue and its impact on strategic capability.

Overall, it needs to be emphasized that the greater the number of linkages within the organization's value chain or between the value chain of an organization and its suppliers, distributors or customers, the more difficult it will be for competitors to imitate their activities.

In assessing how resource utilization influences strategic capability it is helpful to distinguish between two separate measures of utilization — *efficiency and effectiveness*. These relate directly to discussions in later chapters on how organizations choose strategies which will ensure competitive advantage. *Efficiency* is a critically important measure for those organizations which either choose, or are required, to compete on the basis of cost competitiveness. This would also apply to many government services. In contrast, *effectiveness* is a key measure for organizations who choose to differentiate themselves from competitors by sustaining products/services which are valued for their uniqueness (in one way or other). These measures will now be considered in a little more detail.

Efficiency

Efficiency is concerned with how "well" resources have been utilized irrespective of the purpose for which they were deployed. Efficiency can be assessed by analyzing the current configuration of the organization's value chain and applying a number of different measures: (See Table 4.2.)

1. *Profitability* is a broad measure of efficiency for commercial organizations, particularly if it is related to the amount of capital being used to run the business.[4] Other financial

Table 4.2   *Some measures of resource utilization.*

Resource area	Efficiency	Effectiveness
Physical resources		
• Buildings	Capacity utilization	Match between production/ marketing resources and nature of work
• Plant & machinery	Capacity utilization, unit costs Job design, layout, materials flow	
• Financial	Profitability, use of working capital	Capital structure
• Materials	Yield	Suitability of materials
• Products	Damage (e.g., in transit)	Match between product and market need
• Marketing and distribution	Sales per area Sales per outlet	Choice of channels Choice of advertising method
Human resources	Labor productivity Relative size of departments	Allocation of jobs to people Duplication of effort
Intangibles	N/A	Exploitation of image, brand name, market information, research knowledge, etc. Consumer complaints level

measures are concerned with the utilization of specific resources contributing to this overall picture (e.g. inventory turnover, times interest earned).

2. *Labor productivity* is a measure of how efficiently human resources are being used. To some extent it combines an assessment of both efficiency and effectiveness since poor allocation of people to jobs (effectiveness) would also result in low productivity. Often productivity can be improved by attention to linkages within the value system. For example, the sales force of an organization may be used on an agency basis to sell a complimentary range of products. In other cases, productivity improvements may have occurred due to the rationalization of certain value activities between the organization and a supplier (e.g. where manufacturers package items ready for display removing the need for unpacking and re-packaging).

3. *Yield* can be a very important measure of efficiency in industries where raw materials or energy are a major element of cost. The efficiency of the cutting department in a clothes manufacturing company will be assessed in this way and could determine the cost competitiveness of the company. Again, improvements may be achieved by proper planning *through* the value chain. For example, wastage through handling damage or deterioration of perishable goods may well be reduced by attention to transportation and storing arrangements with suppliers and channels.

4. *Capacity utilization* is often a prime measure of efficiency for organizations whose major cost is overhead. This is particularly important in many service industries, such as theaters or fast food outlets, where there is often little extra cost attached to satisfying additional customers. During the 1980s, the need to sustain high levels of capacity utilization became so critical to cost-structure and competitiveness that many organizations decided to subcontract certain of their activities. This also occurred in government services as budgets tightened.

5. *Working capital* utilization can reveal much about the way in which the financial resources are used strategically. An assessment needs to be made of how well the company has managed to achieve an appropriate balance between the *risk* it runs from operating at low levels of working capital and the inefficiency of having too much capital. Some organizations choose to change the balance of their working capital by factoring out certain aspects, such as debtors, in return for cash. In other words, they re-define the boundaries of the organization's value chain in order to maintain efficiency.

6. *Production systems.* Understanding the various aspects of a company's production system such as job design, layout, and materials flow are important when assessing a company's efficiency in production terms. It may be found, for example, that excessive costs have been incurred through unnecessary handling and transportation of materials during manufacture or that the company could take advantage of new operational methods. Many public sector services have found that efficiency can be improved if emphasis is switched from one value activity to another. For example, in a library, an up-to-date "self-help" computer system can avoid the need for a larger staff to help readers locate books.

Effectiveness

A full understanding of a company's use of resources also requires an analysis of the effectiveness with which resources have been used. The effectiveness of an organization can be critically influenced by the ability to get all parts of the value chain working in harmony — including those key activities within the value chains of suppliers, channels, or customers. This is a key task for management and is largely concerned with developing and sustaining common attitudes and culture among all of those in the value chain so that people see the purpose of the products/services in similar ways and agree on which value activities are critical to success. Much of the misunderstanding and friction between suppliers and buyers stems from differences in attitudes and perceptions of these issues. There are a number of different measures of effectiveness: (See Table 4.2.)

1. *Use of people.* There are many situations where people may be used ineffectively. For example, an engineering design team may be designing for lowest cost while the organization is actually competing based on uniqueness of product.

2. *Use of capital.* An analysis of changes in a company's long-term funding (capital structure) may give useful insights. A company may be foregoing the opportunity of additional long-term funds (loans or share issues) and as a result may have difficulty carrying out necessary investment programs. Sometimes the opposite is true, a company may be too highly leveraged[5] for the realities of the markets in which it is operating. Many companies have found that when general levels of profitability are low and interest rates high, the conventional wisdom of using leveraging to improve profitability is impossible to achieve. Organizations which have grown by a series of mergers and takeovers are particularly astute at putting together packages of finance (money and share options) which are regarded as attractive by the shareholders of the organizations being taken over.

3. *Use of marketing and distribution resources.* The effectiveness with which a sales force is being used can often be judged by assessing the volume of sales each salesperson produces. However, expenditure on other items such as advertising or distribution may be more difficult to assess. Companies very often use rules of thumb, for example, a percentage of sales to be spent on advertising; or attempt more rigorous and expensive analysis, such as advertising effectiveness research. A crucial judgment when analyzing the value chain is whether the marketing effort could have been delivered more effectively in a different way. For example, would agents have been better than an in-house sales force?

4. *Use of research knowledge.* The assessment of how effectively research knowledge is used is equally problematic. Tangible measures are available, such as the number of product and process changes developed internally or the competitive advantage gained from technical improvements which resulted in better quality or lower cost. Companies are increasingly trying to cope with their worries about underutilization of the R&D resource by providing better links with the commercial function and by improving monitoring and control arrangements. During the 1980s, many companies looked more seriously at the possibilities of *technology transfer*[6] instead of developing new technology

themselves. For example, the automobile industry saw developments of this kind when General Motors attempted to speed up technological advances by acquiring electronic firms such as Electronic Data Systems Corp. and Hughes Aircraft Co.

5. *Use of production systems.* Poor utilization of resources may result from the choice of an inappropriate system of production. For example, a hotel may have designed its production systems to cope with the normal summer trade when families stay at the hotel. However, these systems are most ineffective in coping with large conferences used as "fill-in" during the winter months. A production system needs to be geared to the basis on which the organization competes. Where cost competitiveness is crucial, highly integrated production systems may be essential. However, more flexible systems will be required if quality of service (e.g. delivery time) is the main competitive weapon.

6. *Exploitation of intangible assets* such as image, brand name, or market information is another measure of effectiveness. The extent to which the images of celebrities such as TV personalities have been exploited is an example of the effective use of an intangible asset.

4.2.5 CONTROL OF RESOURCES

The last criterion against which a company's resource capability needs to be assessed is the extent to which the resources have been properly controlled. Table 4.3 identifies some controls which should be investigated. There could be situations where good quality resources have been deployed in the right way and used efficiently, but still performance is poor as the resources are poorly controlled.

The way in which linkages within the value chain and with the value chains of suppliers, channels, or customers are controlled can also be crucial. Very often the financial control systems of an organization will tend to discourage such linkages because they do not fit the compartmentalized system of resource control. The following illustrates some important aspects of resource control:

1. *Control of key personnel.* Sometimes certain individuals or departments operate in ways not conducive to the smooth functioning of the company as a whole. This can be a particular problem with creative and professional people within organizations who often have their own views on what their jobs should entail. It is often desirable for creative people to be *outside* the organization (e.g. freelance broadcasters in radio and TV) while continuing to be a key resource within the value chain.

2. *Costing.* This is an area where small, fast-growing, organizations often fall down. The management knows what resources are needed to establish the company in the market and how to deploy those resources to good effect. However, they are often unaware of how their method of operating will influence costs and revenue and hence the profitability of the company. In other words, they do not understand how they should exert control over their resources. In many large organizations, and particularly in the public sector, there is often a confusion between cost-effectiveness and cost minimization. As a result, the organization becomes obsessed with cost-cutting while failing to realize that this creates a

Table 4.3   *Aspects of resource control.*

Resource area	*Typical controls to investigate*
Physical resources	
• Buildings	Security, maintenance
• Plant, machinery	Production control Maintenance system
• Financial	Costing system Budgets Investment appraisal
• Materials	Supplier control (quantity, quality and cost) Control of inventory
• Products	Inventory control Quality control Losses (e.g., theft)
Human resources	Control of key personnel Leadership Working agreements Control of outlets (e.g., distributors)
Intangibles	Control of image (e.g., public relations) Industrial relations climate Control of vital information

downward spiral, leading to a product/service valued less by consumers/users, creating a worsening cost structure as demand falls and so on.

3. *Quality of materials.* In certain industries, the quality of the finished product is highly dependent on the quality of certain materials or components which are purchased from suppliers. A car will not function properly if its tires, battery, or carburetor are defective. All these items will normally be bought in their finished form from suppliers. Any difficulties the car manufacturer experiences with customer complaints can be traced back to how control was exerted over these important supplies. In the context of the value chain, there are different ways this might be achieved. For example, by establishing rigid quality *specifications*, by inspecting the suppliers quality control *systems*, or by *inspecting* incoming supplies. The relative cost and effectiveness of these alternatives is an important consideration. In many cases, it is absolutely vital to place the responsibility for control of quality on the suppliers, as seen in Illustration 4.4.

4. *Marketing outlets.* Many manufacturers fail to exert sufficient control over how their outlets present and sell their goods. Retail outlets may sell 5,000 to 10,000 different

---

ILLUSTRATION 4.4   *Quality-drive at IBM*

If an organization embarks upon a new strategy which involves improving quality, changes are required through the value chain, from the final inspection staff back to the suppliers. The example below describes how quality was improved at an IBM plant in the UK. It is typical of quality drives in the plants of many North American companies around the world.

Long-term quality improvement cannot normally be achieved by *adding-on* a better quality control system to an otherwise unchanged operation. At IBM's Havant plant it was decided that quality improvement meant changes in most parts of the operation. The decision to start the quality drive came in 1980, not because of worries about declining quality, but based on the knowledge that competitors (particularly the Japanese) were setting and achieving higher standards, giving them real competitive advantage.

One particular electromechanical product illustrated this process of quality improvement very well. Too many products were reaching the testing stage from the subassembly and final assembly processes with major defects. This was leading to overall poor quality and delivery performance. The immediate problem appeared to be variable performance between individual operators — but this problem was soon solved by discussion and some training. It was then apparent that problems were often due to inadequacies in the manufacturing or support services rather than assembly. Representatives from engineering and other support services were progressively drawn into the improvement process. These service groups started to focus on defining more realistic parameters for their own quality performance. The next effect was that buyers and procurement engineers improved the quality of purchased parts. This drew external suppliers into the improvement chain.

Major improvements in quality were caused by making quality a key strategic goal for everyone and two other powerful forces. The first was called "service pressure" which occurred when one part of the organization made a specific request for the removal of service problems which were preventing quality improvement. The second was peer pressure, or the embarrassment factor, which happened when some groups were visibly achieving better results than others.

The results were impressive — the output quality of the plant (measured by failures at installation or within warranty) was improved five-fold in a four year period through this "rolling-back" of quality improvement within the organization and its supply chain.

Source: *Management Today*, (April 1986).

products including many products in direct competition with each other. Monitoring and controlling the marketing efforts of outlets is important, but often difficult. Again, different approaches are possible ranging from the direct ownership of outlets (i.e. bringing distribution into the organization's own value chain); appointment of approved dealers; the provision of customer training; and the use of merchandising teams.

5. *Stock and production control.* On occasion, a company's poor performance can be traced to poor control of stock or the system of production. A poor delivery record often results from ill-developed production control systems which rely on high "buffer" inventory between the various steps in production.

6. *Control of losses.* Most companies face the problem of losses due, for example, to theft. Retailers are particularly vulnerable in this respect and euphemistically refer to these losses as "shrinkage." Poor company performance may be attributed to lack of control in this area. However, organizations face a real dilemma since the introduction of more stringent controls and checks could be counterproductive by reducing the "value" of the service in the eyes of consumers. This is a problem shared by retail outlets, and many government services such as libraries and sports centers.

7. *Control of intangibles.* The company's ability to control its image through public relations activities is one example of this. The industrial relations record can indicate how well "team spirit" or organizational culture are controlled. In some cases, the control of vital information which could be of commercial benefit to competitors would be particularly important to monitor.

The importance of control during the implementation of strategy will be given full consideration in Chapter 11. At this stage it is hoped that readers have recognized that in order to understand the strategic importance of a company's resources it is necessary to look at how resources are utilized and controlled as well as the intrinsic nature of those resources.

4.2.6 FINANCIAL ANALYSIS

Financial analysis is used at all stages of resource analysis, not only as part of value chain analysis. It will be seen later in the chapter, for example, that the forecasting of the cash requirements for different activities will be an important measure of how well an organization's resources are balanced (portfolio analysis). Also, financial measures such as profitability, leveraging, and liquidity will be used to compare the performance of a company with its competitors, as a means of analyzing the company's resource position.

Financial analysis is included as a separate section here for the sake of clarity and because many managers are uncertain about the contribution financial analyses can make to understanding an organization's strategic capability. Financial ratio analysis can be very useful but is also potentially very misleading if not interpreted in the context of the overall resource analysis.[7] When using financial analyses[8] as part of resource analysis the following issues need to be kept in mind:

1. Financial ratios (such as, inventory turnover, sales margins, leveraging), are of no

importance in themselves. However, the *implications* of these ratios are critical. These may not emerge until some sensible basis of comparison is established (see below). Even then a word of warning is necessary. It may be that an organization is successfully differentiating itself from its competitors by extra spending in selected areas (e.g. advertising). Provided this results in value (possibly through price or market share) this may well be a defensible spending pattern.

2.   Only certain value activities will be of critical strategic importance to an organization. The financial analyses relating to those activities will be particularly useful. For example, rate of inventory turnover may be important to a supermarket operation, unit profit margins to a specialty store, or sales volume to a capital intensive manufacturer.

3.   The key value activities will change over time and so should the key financial measures to monitor. For example, during the introduction of a new product, the key factor may be to establish *sales volume*; once established, *profit/unit* might be most important; during decline, *cash-flow* may be essential to support the introduction of the next generation of products. In addition to published financial data, the management would normally have access to more financial information (such as cost data) which would help provide a fairly comprehensive analysis of many of the resource *utilization* and *control* issues raised above. Figure 4.4 summarizes some of the ways financial ratios can be helpful for understanding an organization's resources from the point of view of strategic capability.

4.3 COMPARATIVE ANALYSIS

The preceding two sections have paid considerable attention to the concept of the value chain and the ways it can be used to assess strategic capability. Value chain analysis encourages managers to take a critical look at their organization's resources with the purpose of understanding how particular value activities and the linkages between activities help the organization sustain its competitive advantage within its "industry." However, it is also valuable to assess how the value chain has changed and developed historically, since this gives insights into how (and perhaps why) the organization has chosen, or been forced, to shift its resource base.

In addition, the work of the Boston Consulting Group (BCG) on the *experience curve* of organizations is valuable in understanding how cost structure and competitiveness might be related to the nature of an organization's markets and its relative position within them.

This section discusses these different bases of comparison: the historical, the Industry Norm, and the Experience Curve, as valuable means of improving the understanding of an organization's strategic capability.

4.3.1 HISTORICAL ANALYSIS

Historical analysis looks at the deployment of the resources of a business in comparison with previous years, in order to identify any significant changes in the overall levels of resources. Typically, financial ratios will be used as well, and the identification of any

Figure 4.4 *Financial ratios and resource analysis.*

FINANCIAL RATIO	USED TO ASSESS
1. Return on capital	Overall measure of performance
2. Cost structure	
Sales profitability	Sales performance
Gross margin	Direct costs
Sales expenses Overheads Labor	1. Indirect cost 2. Value of expenditure 1. Labor productivity 2. Relation to "value"
Materials	1. Purchasing policies 2. Quality of materials 3. Relation to "value"
Dividends	Power of shareholders
Interest	Capital structure (see below)
3. Asset turnover	
Fixed assets	Capital intensity
Inventory	1. Cash tied up 2. Delivery performance 3. Risk of write-offs
Debtors	1. Cash tied up 2. Use of credit 3. Risk of bad debts
(Creditors)	Choice of suppliers
4. Liquidity	Short term risk
5. Capital structure (leveraging)	1. Long term risk 2. Using available resources

significant variations in the proportions of resources devoted to different activities will be made. Although this seems like a fairly straightforward analysis to perform, it can reveal trends which might not otherwise be apparent. For example, a manufacturing company which owns its own retail outlets may find that because of the relatively favorable climate for retailing there has been a slow drift of the business away from the traditional base of manufacturing. It is only when a comparison of the deployment of resources is made with the situation five years before that the significance of this slow drift becomes apparent. In some cases, companies have been prompted to reassess where the major thrust of their business should be in the future. In other words, they have redefined the boundaries of their value chain slowly over time.

4.3.2 COMPARISON WITH INDUSTRY NORMS

Historical analysis can normally be improved significantly by an additional comparison with similar factors analyzed for the industry as a whole. This helps to put the company's resources and performance into perspective and reflects the fact that it is the relative position of a company which matters in determining its performance. The danger of industry norm analysis is that the company may overlook the fact that the whole industry is performing badly and is losing out competitively to other countries with better resources or even other industries which can satisfy customers' needs in different ways.

If an industry comparison is performed, therefore, it is wise to make some assessment of how the company's resources compare with those in other countries and industries. This can often be done by looking at a few of the more important measures of resource utilization, such as inventory turnover or yield from raw materials. However, readers are reminded of the preceding discussion concerning the importance of establishing and maintaining a distinctive *value chain* for an organization. A comparison of similar *value activities* between organizations can be extremely valuable if the strategic context is not forgotten. For example, a straight comparison of resource deployment between two competitive companies (say in terms of an analysis of cost structures), may reveal quite different situations in the labor cost as percentage of total cost. The *conclusions* drawn from this, however, depend on circumstances. If the firms are competing head-on largely on the basis of price, then differentials in labor costs will be of crucial importance. In contrast, the additional use of staff by one organization may be essential for the special services provided which differentiate that organization from its competitor. For this reason some authors[9] give more emphasis to undertaking a parallel resource analysis of major competitors rather than trying to establish the "norm" within the industry. Although in principle this approach is of considerable value, keeping detailed profiles of competitors' resources may prove very difficult and expensive.

Illustration 4.5 provides two examples of businesses which have departed from industry norms and, as a result, have established value chains different from competitors.

4.3.3 THE EXPERIENCE CURVE

The idea of the experience curve results from the work of the Boston Consulting Group (BCG), a worldwide business consultancy operation that has conducted studies of company performance showing a direct and consistent relationship between aggregate growth in volume of production and declining cost of production.[10] It should also be pointed out, however, that they claim their findings to be as relevant to service organizations as they are to manufacturing businesses. The concept is useful both in strategic

---

ILLUSTRATION 4.5   *Caution With Industry Comparisons: Two Examples*

It is necessary to be very cautious when making comparisons between company performance and industry norms. The company that behaves differently might just be developing a unique value chain which might result in a very successful strategy.

Louisiana-Pacific Corp.
It appears that Louisiana-Pacific does some things differently than others in the forest products industry. Some examples are:

- Between 1975 and 1985, competitors bought huge timber acreages while Louisiana-Pacific did not.

- In 1986, Louisiana-Pacific began acquiring land at a time when others had stopped doing so. The company was able to purchase timberland acreage at the lowest prices in 20 years.

- The industry experienced a major strike and while competitors settled with the unions, Louisiana-Pacific held out. The union was eliminated and the company's costs of production were cut.

- About 40% of American waferboard (a plywood substitute) is produced by Louisiana-Pacific. The product is profitable, but competitors are threatening to expand into the business. Louisiana-Pacific is already thinking of developing higher profit products (such as house siding) from waferboard. Companies which appear to be deviants from industry norms should not be dismissed. A company with a different approach, such as Louisiana-Pacific, just might have something going for it.

The Flower Industry and George R. Heublein
The fresh flower industry is very fragmented. The flowers are grown by many small producers in many parts of North America and are also obtained from overseas. Several distributors wholesale the flowers to tens of thousands of small, independently operated, floral retailers.

The sales of this industry, which includes fresh cut flowers, houseplants, bulbs, and related products, are estimated to be $7 billion per year. Three quarters of the sales are to the "occasion" market, that is, flowers for occasions such as weddings, anniversaries, birthdays, funerals, and special holidays. Supermarkets saw a market opportunity and have recently entered the fresh flower business. Although demand for flowers has increased, a North American still only purchases one half the amount of flowers a European does.

George R. Heublein also sees an opportunity in the flower business but his strategy is new to the industry. He has acquired, or plans to acquire, businesses in all stages of the distribution channel — greenhouses, bulb farms, distributors, and retail outlets. This "vertical integration" is a first for the industry and appears to make sense.

Quality and reliability of supply will be controlled and a large retail chain will give a national presence for marketing purposes. Heublein has, in effect, lengthened the value chain with this new approach to operating in the flower business.

Source: "Louisiana-Pacific's Harry Merlo: "The Logger Who Blazes His Own Trail", *Business Week*, (December 22, 1986), pp. 63–4; "Planting the Seeds of a Blossoming Business, *Business Week*, (June 1, 1987), p. 82.

analysis and choice. For convenience, the underlying principles behind the experience curve will be introduced here though much of this is relevant to later discussions — particularly in Chapter 7. The premise of the BCG findings is that in any market segment of an industry, price levels tend to be very similar for similar products. Therefore, what makes one company more profitable than the next must be the levels of its costs. Hence, the experience curve is a particularly relevant analysis for organizations competing on the basis of cost leadership.

The BCG attempted to unearth the key determinants of low levels of cost. Their arguments can be summarized as follows:

1. The relationship between unit costs and total units produced over time resembles that shown in Figure 4.5. The BCG calls this curve the experience curve.

2. Some of the reasons for this relationship suggested by the BCG are:
   (a) *The learning function.* Anyone doing a job learns to do it better over time, and given increased experience, labor costs should in fact decline by about 10 – 15% each time cumulative experience doubles.
   (b) *Specialization.* As scale of production increases so it becomes possible to split jobs

Figure 4.5 *The experience curve.*

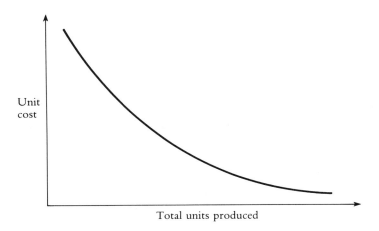

into more and more specialist jobs. "Doing half as much but twice as often equals the same amount of effort but twice the experience with the task.

(c) *Scale*. The capital costs required to finance additional capacity diminish as that capacity grows.

3. Since cost is, in general, a function of experience, then cost is also a function of market share. If this is true then the importance of gaining and holding market share becomes very significant indeed. This is what was referred to as "market power" in Chapter 3.

4. Market share does not necessarily relate to the overall market. If a product is differentiated so that it is competing in a definable, relevant market segment, then it is the market share of that segment which is important.

The overall implication of the BCG's findings is that successful companies make their profits from products in which they dominate their market segment. This view has become a very strong influence on many companies' choices of strategy.

However, it should also be noted that there have been some significant reservations voiced about the value of the experience curve ideas: a) because some of the key variables such as market growth and share are not always easy to be precise about; and b) because there is a risk that managers will interpret the conclusions too simplistically, by failing to recognize the opportunities afforded by market segmentation or product differentation, for example.[11]

The use of experience curve analysis is confined to a *qualitative comparison* of an organization's resource *vis-à-vis* its competitors particularly in relation to cost efficiency, but can prove very valuable for that purpose. It can be extremely useful in clarifying the key determinants of competitiveness in conjunction with a more detailed assessment of the value chain for each business unit.

4.4 ASSESSING THE BALANCE OF RESOURCES

Value chain analysis, which has been the continuing theme of the previous sections, is an extremely powerful analytical approach when applied at the level of individual business or service units. It helps to identify the key value activities and important linkages between these activities and between the value chains of suppliers, channels, and customers. However, in many organizations, there is an additional resource issue which is of equal, and complementary, importance, namely, the extent to which the organization's resources are *balanced as a whole*. Three important aspects of such an analysis would be:

- The extent to which the various activities and resources of the organization complement each other. *Portfolio analysis* is particularly useful in analyzing this issue.

- The degree of balance of the *people* within the organization in terms of both individual skills and personality types.

- Whether the *degree of flexibility* in the organization's resources is appropriate for the level of uncertainty in the environment and the degree of risk the company is prepared to take.

4.4.1 Portfolio Analysis

The concept of the experience curve (discussed above) underlines the important relationship between market dominance and profitability.

In order to dominate a market, a company must normally gain that dominance when the market is in the growth stage of the product life cycle. In a state of maturity, a market is likely to be stable with customer loyalties fairly fixed. It is therefore more difficult to gain share. But if all competitors in the growth stage are trying to gain market share, competition will be fierce: therefore, only those companies prepared to invest in order to gain share will achieve dominance. This might well mean that a company following the principles suggested by the BCG will need to price low and spend high amounts on advertising and selling in order to dominate. Such a strategy is one of high risk unless such low margin activity is financed by higher profit earning products. This leads to the idea of a balanced product mix. The BCG have suggested the model of the product portfolio or the growth share matrix as a tool for considering product strategy. This product portfolio is shown as Figure 4.6.

The matrix combines market growth rate and market share and thus directly relates to the idea of the experience curve:

- A *star* is a product (or business) which has a high market share in a growing market. The company may be spending heavily to gain that share but the experience curve effect will mean that costs are reducing over time and hopefully at a faster rate than the competition. The product (or business) could, then, be self-financing.
- The *question mark* (or problem child) is also in a growing market but does not have a high market share. Its parent company may be spending heavily to increase market share but, if it is, it is unlikely to be getting sufficient cost reductions to offset such investment because the experience gained is less than for a star and costs will be reducing less quickly.

Figure 4.6 *The product portfolio.*

		Market share	
		High	Low
Market growth rate	High	Star	Question mark (or Problem child)
	Low	Cash cow	Dog

- The *cash cow* is a product (or business) with high market share in a mature market. Because growth is low and market conditions more stable, the need for heavy marketing investment is less. But high market share means that experience in relation to low share competition continues to grow and relative costs reduce. The cash cow is thus a cash provider.

- *Dogs* have low share in static or declining markets and are thus the worst of all combinations. They are often a cash drain and use up a disproportionate amount of company time and resources.

Portfolio analysis can also contribute to strategic evaluation, as will be seen in Chapter 7. In the context of resource analysis, it is particularly useful in as much as it raises some important questions about resources. For example:

- Is the mix of products, services or businesses balanced across the organization? The idea of a portfolio of interests emphasizes the importance of having areas of activity which provide security and funds (cash cows) and others which provide for the future of the business (stars and question marks).

- Drucker[12] has long emphasized the importance of reviewing activities to ensure that the appropriate amount of management, physical, and financial resources is being allocated to the activities: management should not provide excessive resources to dogs while starving question marks and thus reducing the chance of turning them into stars.

- Does the balance of a company's products/markets match the resources available to the company? A company particularly good at development and design may not match the analysis of product/market position which indicates a predominance of mature products in static markets. This may suggest the need to move funds from the development area to promotion or market development.

Although portfolio analysis was developed in the context of private sector business, the resource lessons are similar in government services. For example, the funding of new ventures/services is often achieved informally by using resources from well-established areas (particularly staff time). There are some classic dogs in the portfolios of most government departments — the question is whether there is the political will to kill some of them off, releasing resources for other purposes.

4.4.2 SKILLS ANALYSIS

Organizations must possess the necessary balance of skills needed to run a business successfully. Companies need the capability to manage their production and marketing systems as well as to control the financial and personnel aspects properly. Belbin[13] has looked at another aspect of the balance of human resources, namely the extent to which management teams contain an adequate balance of personality types to operate effectively. Some of the more common personality types needed within an effective team are identified in Figure 4.7.

Figure 4.7 *Personality types for the effective team.*

Chairman/team leader
Stable, dominant, extrovert
Concentrates on objectives
Does not originate ideas
Focuses people on what they do
  best

Plant
Dominant, high IQ, introvert
A "scatterer of seeds"; originates
  ideas
Misses out on detail
Trustful but easily offended

Resource investigator
Stable, dominant, extrovert
Sociable
Contacts with outside world
Salesperson/diplomat/liaison
  officer
Not original thinker

Shaper
Anxious, dominant, extrovert
Emotional, impulsive
Quick to challenge and respond to
  challenge
Unites ideas, objectives and
  possibilities
Competitive
Intolerant of ambiguity and
  vagueness

Company worker
Stable, controlled
Practical organizer
Can be inflexible but likely to
  adapt to established systems
Not an innovator

Monitor evaluation
High IQ, stable introvert
Measured analyses not innovation
Unambitious and lacking
  enthusiasm
Solid, dependable

Team worker
Stable, extrovert, low dominance
Concerned with individual's needs
Builds on others' ideas
Cools things down

Finisher
Anxious, introvert
Worries over what will go wrong
Permanent sense of urgency
Preoccupied with order
Concerned with "following
  through"

Source: R.M. Belbin, *Management Teams: Why They Succeed or Fail,* London: Heinemann
Educational Books International Limited, 1981 and R.M. Belbin *et al.,* "Building
Effective Management Teams," *Journal of General Management,* Vol. 3, No. 3, (1976).

4.4.3 FLEXIBILITY ANALYSIS

Another issue which needs to be assessed is the extent to which an organization's resources are flexible and adaptable. It is important to assess how far flexibility is balanced with the uncertainty faced by the organization; flexibility has no strategic significance without an understanding of this uncertainty. A manufacturing company facing a highly volatile raw materials market may choose to spread its sources of supply despite the fact that this could prove more costly. In contrast, it may be happy to have a highly inflexible, high volume mass production system since it is trading in a stable market and this system of production ensures a highly competitive cost structure.

A flexibility analysis need be no more sophisticated than a simple listing of the major areas of uncertainty and the extent to which the company's resources are geared to cope with each of these. Table 4.4 illustrates a typical analysis which seeks to compare the major areas of uncertainty faced by a company with the degree of flexibility in the related resource areas.

Table 4.4   *Flexibility analysis — an example.*

Major areas of uncertainty	Flexibility		Comments
	Required	*Actual flexibility (at present)*	
1. Demand for product A	Capacity (possibility + 20%) or Inventories	Overtime could cover Low	Probably OK
2. Price of raw materials from present supplier	New suppliers New materials	None known at present Production system cannot cope	Problem area Seek information on new suppliers
3. Major customer may go bankrupt	Replacement customer	No leads	Sound out potential customers
4. Long term loan may not be renewed next year	Other sources of capital	Good image on stock market	New share issue looks favorable
5. Chief design engineer may retire	Design capability for products presently in development	Deputy not suitable Chief may agree to part-time "consultancy" arrangement	Training and/or recruitment needs urgent attention

4.5 IDENTIFICATION OF KEY ISSUES

The last major aspect of resource analysis is the identification of the key issues arising from previous analyses. It is only at this stage of the analysis that a sensible assessment can be made of the major *strengths and weaknesses* of an organization and the strategic importance of these (see Illustration 4.6). The resource analysis starts to be useful as a basis against which to judge future courses of action. There are several assessments which can be made:

1. SWOT[14] analysis has already been referred to in Chapter 3. This can be a very useful way of summarizing many of the previous analyses and combining them with the key issues from the environmental analysis. One of the benefits of using *value chain* analysis is that it should help avoid some of the common pitfalls of SWOT analysis. In particular the analysis must be clear on:

(i)   The reasons *why* particular activities or resources are identified as strengths or weaknesses.

(ii) The fact that value activities are more important than resources *per se*. In other words, it is the use to which resources are being put which is critical.

(iii) The *linkages* between various value activities are likely to be the key strength (or weakness) of the organization. This would include linkages with the value chains of suppliers, channels, and customers.

2. A strengths and weaknesses analysis can be particularly powerful if it incorporates a comparison with competitors. This can be done using the concept of distinctive competence. *Distinctive competence*[15] is concerned with identifying those particular strengths which give the company an edge over its competitors and those areas of particular weakness which are to be avoided. This may require a parallel analysis of competitors' resources as previously mentioned. A supermarket's distinctive strength might be found in its layout and display and control systems which allow for high volume trading at minimal cost. Its particular weakness would be its inability to provide advice to customers. This analysis would help in assessing how viable a move into new product areas might be, such as do-it-yourself products or furniture. Illustration 4.7 provides some examples of distinctive competences.

This is, of course, the main reason why there has been so much emphasis on value chain analysis in this chapter. It is an ideal way of understanding the distinctive competence of an organization particularly when a comparison is made of the value chains of major competitors.

It should be noted that some authors have argued that it is more useful to develop resource analyses specifically designed to detect the onset of important strategic phases in a company's development. In particular, Argenti[16] has concentrated on the identification of companies likely to go bankrupt. Although others[17] have not given the same degree of emphasis to resources, there is general recognition that poor resources, badly managed, can be a significant contributing factor to company failure.

ILLUSTRATION 4.6   *Strengths and Weaknesses at Avon Products Inc.*

The development of a strategic plan to turn Avon Products Inc. around (the company was facing declining profits and a threatening environment), brought into sharp focus the strengths and weaknesses of the company.

Avon Products Inc. was the world's leading manufacturer of beauty products, health care items, and fashion jewelry with about 12% of the North American market. For almost 100 years, the company grew by merely adding more representatives to its door-to-door sales force. But, in 1980, profits declined and the environment had changed in a manner threatening to the company.

Avon had lost touch with its customers mainly because they had changed: they had more disposable income than in the past; they were changing their discretionary buying patterns; they were entering the workforce in increasing numbers; and they had less discretionary time. The number of sales representatives was declining, and it was becoming more difficult for representatives to find customers at home. In addition, the competition was increasing and becoming stronger.

In 1984, Avon developed a corporate strategy to stabilize their direct-selling business and to explore alternative selling approaches. The objectives included: increasing sales 10% yearly, increasing earnings per share by 14%, and achieving a 20% return on equity by 1988.

The environment for the company presented some opportunities, but also contained some threats. The opportunities included: increased sales made possible by segmentation of the market; new sales systems which could be used; and growth in the health care business with an aging population. On the other hand, threats in the environment included: home-direct selling was less attractive as a channel of distribution; competition was increasing; direct mail as a selling system was easy to enter but difficult to be successful in; cosmetics, fragrances, and toiletries were mature markets; and there was increased risk to international operations.

Given the circumstances, it was important to identify Avon's strengths and weaknesses in order to ascertain whether or not the strategy could be successfully implemented.

Strengths:
Position in industry
- largest market share
- has been very successful
- good reputation and Avon name well-known

Financial
- debt is less that 30% of capitalization
- only one third of assets are fixed

- borrowing capacity of $500 million
- financial control system in place

Marketing
- unique direct selling system in industry
- ability to manage direct selling system
- good product development and marketing
- new product introduction easy

Production
- low cost manufacturer
- massive manufacturing capacity

Weaknesses:

Position in industry
- beauty image being eroded
- discount policy has hurt image

Planning
- no formal planning system

Financial
- some international operations losing money
- declining profitability of beauty products

Marketing
- dependence on direct selling for 70% of sales and profits
- no market segmentation
- low level of advertising

Sales force
- commissions may be too low
- part-time sales force not as productive
- sales force needs more training
- declining in numbers

Products
- no brand loyalty
- styling of jewelry products too traditional
- giftware products too expensive

By 1987, it appeared that the company's strategy was successful having built on resource strengths and overcoming resource weaknesses.

Source: John Thackray, "Planning an Avon Turnaround," *Planning Review*, (January 1985), pp. 6–11; Hicks Waldron, "Putting a New Face on Avon," *Planning Review*, (July 1985), pp. 18–23; "Big Names Are Opening Doors For Avon," *Business Week*, (June 1, 1987), pp. 96–7.

ILLUSTRATION 4.7   *Examples of Distinctive Competences*

Sometimes there is some aspect of a company's strategy that provides it with a competitive advantage over other companies in the industry. This advantage, or distinctive competence, often explains the company's superior performance. Three examples are provided below.

Harlequin Enterprises is the world's largest publisher of romantic fiction. The romantic novels produced by Harlequin are done to a "formula" that varies only slightly depending on the series: "Harlequin Romance," "Harlequin Presents," "Harlequin Temptation," "Harlequin American Romance," "Harlequin Romantic Intrigue," and "Harlequin Superromance." They are all well written, are the same length, have similar cover designs, and have standardized plots. The novels are widely marketed in many retail outlets and in countries around the world. Harlequin has built up excellent editorial skills in the area of romantic novels through the control of the quality of writing and the extreme consistency of the product in addition to the accurate targeting of the product in the market.

Hechinger Co., a do-it-yourself (DIY) hardware retailer in the Eastern and Midwestern states, is doing better than other companies in the same industry, including such large competitors as Scotty's, Lowe's, Home Depot, and Payless Cashways. While competitors emphasize sales to professional carpenters, plumbers, and contractors, Hechinger aims exclusively at the DIY market. There are two reasons for this market focus: higher margins are obtained on these sales, and sales are less dependent on the new housing starts cycle. The company also builds large stores with complete selections so that customers need only make "one stop" for all home and garden items.

Hasbro Inc. is now the largest US manufacturer of toys, larger than such well-known toymakers as Fisher-Price, Mattel, Coleco, and Tonka. Sales in the toy industry are usually based upon "hits" or "fads" doing well, for example, Coleco's Cabbage Patch dolls. Hasbro has been able to defy the industry's boom-and-bust cycles resulting from these "hits" by competing in all toy market segments (preschool, boys, girls, stuffed, and games). Hasbro's "hits" have been in all segments resulting in a leveling out of fluctuations in sales and increasing profits. The company also attempts to market fewer faddish toys and chooses instead ones that have some staying power, for example, the G.I. Joe doll. The company begins by marketing to the parents of newborns with the goal of retaining them as customers as their children grow up.

Source: "Harlequin Bash Honors 35 Years of 'Fulfillment' Between the Lines," *The Financial Post*, (October 27, 1984), p. 12; "Patched up: Harlequin Woos Back Silhouette, While its Parent Courts a Long-term Strategy," *Canadian Business*, (November 1984), pp. 13–14 and 19; "Hechinger's: Nobody Does it Better In Do-It-Yourself," *Business Week*, (May 5, 1986), p. 96; "How Hasbro Became King of the Toymakers," *Business Week*, (September 22, 1986), pp. 90–2.

4.6 SUMMARY

Resource analysis is an important means of assessing an organization's *strategic capability* which in turn is necessary if sensible choices for future strategy are to be made. Traditionally, much of the discussion of resource analysis has centered around the idea of strengths and weaknesses.

The concept of the value chain is particularly useful in understanding an organization's strategic capability since it concentrates on value activities and the linkages between activities rather than simply resources *per se*. This underlines the fact that capability is strongly related to the way in which resources are deployed and controlled. It has also been emphasized that a resource analysis must not be confined to those resources an organization owns. Often it is the linkages between the value chains of suppliers, channels, and customers which are the cornerstone of an organization's capability, and which prevent imitation by competitors.

Perhaps the most crucial issue in the chapter has been the contention that strategic capability is best understood in relation to other (competitive) organizations. Finding the the distinctive competence of the organization in relation to competitors or other providers is vital in a resource analysis.

Equally, it should be remembered that resource capability is only one piece of the puzzle. The strategic importance of the environment has been discussed in Chapter 3. The next chapter considers the third ingredient, namely the extent to which an organization's culture and power structure can influence strategy.

References

1. An extensive discussion of the value chain concept and its application can be found in Michael Porter's book *Competitive Advantage* (New York: Free Press, 1985). The concept is introduced in Chapter 2 of the book.

2. There are a number of papers and standard texts which include traditional resource audits, for example, C.W. Hofer and D. Schendel, *Strategy Formulation: Analytical Concepts*,(St. Paul, Minnesota: West Publishing Co., 1978), p. 149, and R.B. Buchelle, "How to Evaluate a Firm," *California Management Review*, (Fall, 1962), pp. 5–16, look at resource analysis within functional areas. The latter provides extensive checklists. T.G. Whelan and J.D. Hunger, "Using the Strategic Audit," *SAM Advanced Management Journal,* Vol. 52, No. 1, (Winter, 1987), pp. 4–12, extend the audit to management processes too.

3. Chapters 4 and 8 in R.G. Murdick, R.H. Eckhouse, R.C. Moor and T.N. Zummerer, *Business Policy: A Framework for Analysis,* 2nd edition, (Columbus Ohio: Grid Publishers, Inc., 1976), look at strategic analysis from a functional viewpoint and, as such, provide some useful guidelines and checklists for functional resource analysis. However, readers who are unfamiliar with the details of resources in any functional area might consult one of the following:

    P. Kotler, *Marketing Management: Analysis, Planning and Control,* 4th Edition, pp. 652-7 (Englewood Cliffs, N.J.: Prentice-Hall Inc., 1980), for a systematic marketing audit. Kotler's "audit" also reviews the market and competitive situation together with marketing objectives. He also tries to assess aspects of resource utilization and control.

A.G. Cowling and C.J.B. Mailer, *Managing Human Resources*, (London: Edward Arnold Publishers Limited, 1981). Chapter 11 is concerned with personnel planning and illustrates how an analysis of the personnel resources of a company can be undertaken.

R. Wild, *Production and Operations Management,* 3rd Edition, (New York: Holt, Rinehart & Winston Inc., 1984). Chapter 1 is concerned with the nature of operating systems and the role of operations management. Although the text does not specifically list an "operating audit" the discussion gives an understanding of how to analyze and assess a company's operating system.

J.M. Samuels and F.M. Wilkes, *Management of Company Finance*, 3rd Edition, (New York: Van Nostrand Reinhold, 1980). Chapters 5, 7, 8 and 14 give a full picture of the sources and applications of companies' financial resources.

4. J. Sizer, *An Insight into Management Accounting*, 2nd Edition, (London: Pitman Publishing Limited, 1979) is a good source for readers who wish to improve their understanding of profitability measurement.

5. For an explanation of the importance of leveraging see Chapter 5 of *An Insight into Management Accounting* (reference 4 above).

6. For discussions of technology transfer on an international dimension, see W.H. Davidson, "Structure and Performance in International Technology Transfer," *Journal of Management Studies*, Vol. 20, No. 4, (1983), pp. 453–66, and M.G. Harvey, "The Application of Technology Life Cycles to Technology Transfers," *Journal of Business Strategy,* 5(2), (1984), pp. 51–8.

7. D. Beaven, "What the Ratios Saw," *Management Today*, (July, 1982), points out some pitfalls of using ratio analysis too blindly.

8. Chapter 4 in *An Insight into Management Accounting* (see reference 4 above) deals in detail with the value of financial ratio analysis and how such an analysis can be done (with examples). Some authors suggest analyses which can help detect important aspects of strategy. For example, E.I. Altman, *Corporate Bankruptcy in America*, (Lexington, Mass.: Health Lexington, 1971), explains how his "Z-factor" can be used to predict the failure of companies. C.J. Sutton, *Economics and Corporate Strategy*, (Oxford: Cambridge University Press, 1980), Chapter 7, relates analyses to mergers and takeovers.

9. For example, M.E. Porter, *Competitive Advantage*, (New York: Free Press, 1985), argues that strategic capability can only be properly understood by assessing the competitive advantage of individual organizations.

10. Further readings on the BCG models are:
P. Conley, *Experience Curves as a Planning Tool*, available from the Boston Consulting Group as a pamphlet.
B. Hedley, "Strategy and the Business Portfolio," *Long Range Planning*, 10, 1977, pp. 9–15 and J.H. Grant and W.R. King, "Strategic Formulation: Analytical and Normative Models," in D. Schendel and C. Hofer (eds), *Strategic Management: A New View of Business Policy and Planning*, (Boston: Little, Brown and Company, 1979), pp. 104–22.

11. Readers may refer to the following:
S.P. Slatter, "Common Pitfalls in Using the BCG Product Portfolio Matrix," *London Business School Journal*, (Winter, 1980).

R. Wensley, "PIMS and BCG: New Horizons or False Dawn," *Strategic Management Journal*, 3(2), 1982, pp. 147–58.

John Thackeray, "The Corporate Strategy Problem," *Management Today*, (Oct., 1979).

12. P. Drucker, in *Managing for Results,* (London: Pan Books Ltd., 1973) shows how resources can be mismatched with opportunities and how this might be remedied.

13. R.M. Belbin, B.R. Aston and R.D. Mottram, "Building Effective Management Teams," *Journal of General Management*, 3, (1976), pp. 23–29.

14. This idea of SWOT as a commonsense checklist for use in strategic analyses and evaluation has been used by writers on strategy for many years: for example S. Tilles in "Making Strategy Explicit" which was written in 1966 and is reproduced in I. Ansoff, ed., *Business Strategy*, (Harmondsworth: Penguin Books Limited, 1968.)

15. An interesting discussion of distinctive competence can be found in M.A. Hitt and R.D. Ireland, "Corporate Distinctive Competence, Strategy Industry and Performance," *Strategic Management Journal*, Vol. 6, (1985), pp. 273–93.

16. J. Argenti, *Corporate Collapse: Causes and Symptoms*, (New York: McGraw-Hill, 1976), is based on research into a number of major British companies (most notably Rolls Royce prior to the 1971 collapse).

17. See, for example, Chapter 2 in S. Slatter, *Corporate Recovery*, (Harmondsworth: Penguin Books, Limited, 1984.)

Recommended Key Readings

M.E. Porter. *Competitive Advantage*. New York: Free Press, 1985, is the seminal text on value chain analysis. Readers should, in particular, refer to Chapters 2 and 3 in the context of this chapter.

Articles on carrying out a resource audit are:

Robert B. Buchelle. "How to Evaluate a Firm." *California Management Review*, (Fall 1962.), pp. 5-17.

Harold W. Henry. "Appraising a Company's Strengths and Weaknesses." *Managerial Planning*, (July-August 1980), pp. 31-6.

G.A. Steiner. *Strategic Planning*. New York: Free Press/Collier Macmillan, 1979, Chapter 8.

Howard H. Stevenson. "Defining Strengths and Weaknesses." *Sloan Management Review*, (Winter 1976), pp. 1-8.

T.L. Wheeler and J.D. Hunger. "Using the Strategic Audit." *SAM Advanced Management Journal*, Vol. 52, No. 1, 1987, pp. 4–12.

To understand the value of financial analysis, readers should refer to texts such as:

E.A. Helfert. *Techniques of Financial Analysis*, Fourth Edition. Homewood, Ill.: Richard D. Irwin Inc., 1978.

J.F. Weston and E. Brigham. *Managerial Finance*. Hinsdale, Ill.: Dryden Press, 1980.

J. Van Horne. *Financial Management and Policy*. Englewood Cliffs, N.J.: Prentice-Hall Inc., 1980.

Chapter 5
EXPECTATIONS, OBJECTIVES, AND POWER

5.1 INTRODUCTION

There is a temptation to look for a neat and tidy way of formulating strategy. Such a method might, apparently, be achieved through the analysis of the organization's environment (Chapter 3) and the extent to which the company's resources, or strategic capability (Chapter 4) are matched with the environment. However, this "economic" analysis of strategy fails to recognize the complex role *people* play in the evolution of strategy, as mentioned in Chapter 2. This chapter looks at how the cultural and political systems of an organization can be analyzed and understood as part of a strategic analysis. This is a recognition that strategy is also a product of what people *want* an organization to do or what they feel the organization should *be like*. There has been a growing awareness of the central importance of these issues in understanding strategy formulation and implementation since the early 1980s.

It should be clear from earlier discussions (Chapter 2) that strategies tend to evolve in organizations within a cultural and political system and that the concept of an objective, value-free, analysis of an organization's strategies (either past or future) is misplaced. Although the analysis of an organization's environment and resource position provides an important background to the strategic choices the organization faces, any changes need to take place within the cultural and political realities of the organization. A strategic analysis must provide a proper understanding of how the social and political situation might affect the viability of different strategies, and Figure 5.1 provides a framework for such an analysis. The figure identifies different "layers" of cultural/political influences on strategy, ranging from broad issues such as the values of society, to very specific influences on strategy such as organizational objectives. Of crucial importance is the need to assess the power structure within and around any organization. It should be remembered that there are multiple connections between these various influences and that the figure is a simplification of reality. These complex interconnections need to be understood. An analysis needs to assess the influence of the following factors on company strategies:

- A number of cultural factors in an *organization's environment* will influence the internal situation. In particular, the values of society at large and the influence of organized groups need to be understood.

- The *nature of the business*, such as market situation and types of products and technology are important influences not only in the direct sense discussed in Chapter 3 but also in the way they affect the expectations of individuals and groups.

- The most pervasive of all these general influences is the organizational *culture* itself. The meaning and importance of culture has already been discussed in Chapter 2 which also explained why culture is a key driving force behind an organization's strategies.

- At a more specific level, individuals will normally have shared expectations with one or more groups of other people within the organization. These shared expectations may be concerned with undertaking the company's tasks and reflect the formal structure of the organization (e.g. departmental expectations.) However, *coalitions* also arise as a result of specific events and can transcend the formal structure.

- Internal groups and individuals are also influenced by their contacts with *external*

Figure 5.1 *Expectations, objectives, and power.*

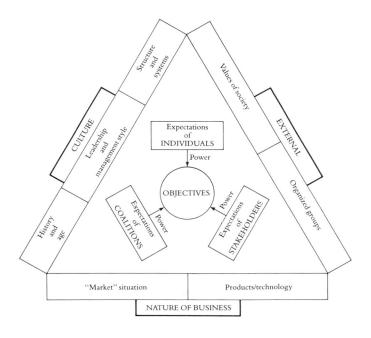

stakeholders — groups which have an interest in the operation of the company such as customers, shareholders, suppliers or unions. For example, sales staff may be pressured by customers to represent their interests within the company.

- Individuals or groups, whether internal or external, cannot influence an organization's strategies unless they have an influencing mechanism. This mechanism is called *power*. The variety of ways power can be derived will be discussed later.

- Organizational *objectives* traditionally have been afforded a central/dominant role in influencing strategy. (i.e. strategy is seen as the means of achieving preordained and unchangeable objectives.) That is not the view taken in this book. While organizations do have objectives which are often valuable in strategy formulation, these should not be regarded as an unchangeable set of expectations. They should be viewed as an important part of the strategic equation, open to amendment and change as strategies develop.

- Objectives tend to emerge as the wishes of the most dominant coalition; usually the management of the organization although there are notable exceptions. However, in pursuing these objectives, the dominant group is very strongly influenced by their reading of the political situation (i.e. their perception of the power structure). For example, they are likely to set aside some of their expectations in order to improve the chance of achieving others.

This chapter is concerned with providing some approaches to analyzing these issues as part of a strategic analysis. Illustration 5.1 discusses many of these factors as they influence a particular company's strategy.

ILLUSTRATION 5.1   *Expectations, Objectives and Power at Hershey*

Expectations, objectives and power have a major impact on strategic management at many companies. An example is provided by Hershey Foods Corporation where values influence stakeholder expectations, impact on corporate objectives, and have power in that they are a driving force providing direction.

Hershey Foods Corporation is a leading manufacturer of candy products with annual sales of over $2 billion. Established in 1893 by Milton Snavely Hershey, the company has been very successful and now is a leader in the candy business. Hershey and Mars each have about one-third of the market with the ten best sellers usually being shared about equally. Other firms, such as Cadbury and Nestle have much smaller market shares. Growth in candy sales is fairly stable and company sales growth depends to a large extent on gaining market share. The industry environment is a very competitive one with advertising being important.

Hershey Foods has a history that still influences operations. Founder Hershey had very strong commitments to a strong work ethic and all-American values. The founder's values included: high moral and religious beliefs; truth, honesty and integrity, thrift, economy and industry; the "do unto others" rule; an emphasis on education; high quality standards; valuing the rewards of doing good for others; and an emphasis on family and community. These values are still important to Hershey Foods Corp. today.

A "values" study was recently conducted to identify the core beliefs of the company. The twelve values identified were condensed to four: people orientation; honesty and integrity; consumer- and quality- consciousness; and results orientation. The survey was conducted by members of management and provided an opportunity to communicate with employees.

The survey has been followed up with actions designed to reinforce the values. Each employee carries a wallet-sized card stating the four values. Management training seminars are used to increase an understanding of the values. An orientation film and house newsletters also focus on the values. Most importantly, Hershey managers believe that the values must be demonstrated or practiced through behavior in addition to being merely communicated.

Hershey managers are also sensitive to areas where these traditional values many be in conflict with employee expectations or changes in society. For example, the values held by individuals cannot be ignored. The company also believes that it must improve its two-way communications with employees, and that some revisions may be required in the reward system structure. The traditional values may be seen as conservative when risk taking and innovation may be necessary for success in the candy business. Hershey has not only made an effort to publicize its values to employees, but has also communicated them to other stakeholders, such as investors, customers, and the communities where the company operates.

The emphasis on values has been incorporated into Hershey's strategy, that is, to become a major food company. Diversification into other food areas is being undertaken to reduce Hershey's vulnerability to the cyclical prices experienced in the markets for chocolate and sugar. Among the acquisitions are Friendly Ice Cream Corp. (restaurants), Cory Coffee Service, a pasta maker, and Y&S Candies. In the candy business, growth is achieved through new products, including some for grownups, and these products make up about 20% of sales.

Hershey's management is aware that its values may not fit with expansion and strategy plans and that it becomes more difficult to transfer these values to acquired companies. Management attempts to instill the values in acquisitions and divisions, but they recognize that there may be another set of values at the plant or division level, and that subsidiaries have their own subcultures. Hershey's values are not arbitrarily imposed, but instead try to complement those already existing.

For Hershey, values represent the basis for operating the business. Other companies might have similar commitment to a culture, philosophy, or mission. At Hershey, values provide a sense of self, or personality, for the company; some coherence for relations with divisions; and a mechanism for interacting with stakeholders.

Source: Steve Lawrence, "Bar Wars: Hershey Bites Mars," *Fortune*, (July 8, 1985), pp. 52–7; Sally J. Blank, "Hershey: A Company Driven by Values," *Management Review*, (November 1986), pp. 31–5.

5.2   GENERAL INFLUENCES ON INDIVIDUALS AND GROUPS

There is a wide variety of factors which can influence the expectations individuals and groups are likely to have of an organization. For convenience, these general influences can be grouped into three categories as shown in Figure 5.2.

When analyzing the significance of these factors on the strategic development of any organization it is important to ask the following questions:

1. *Which* factors inside and outside the organization have most influence on the expectations of groups and individuals within the organization?

2. To *what extent* do current strategies reflect the influence of any one or combination of these factors?

3. How far would these factors help or hinder the *changes* needed to pursue new strategies?

Readers are encouraged to bear these questions in mind when following the text of this section.

5.2.1   EXTERNAL INFLUENCES

Values of Society

Attitudes to work, authority, equality and a whole range of other important issues are constantly shaped and changed by society at large. From the point of view of corporate strategy, it is important to understand this process for two major reasons. Firstly, values of society change and adjust over time and, therefore, policies acceptable twenty years ago may not be so today. There has been an increasing trend for the activities of companies to be constrained by legislation, public opinion, and the media. Secondly, companies which operate internationally have the added problem of coping with the very different standards and expectations of the various countries in which they operate.

Organized Groups

Individuals very often have allegiances to other groups which can influence their attitudes. These allegiances may be highly institutionalized and directly related to their working situation, such as membership in trade unions, or may be more informal and unrelated, such as membership in churches or political groups. Memberships in professional bodies or institutions can be particularly important in organizations with a high proportion of professional staff. Engineering companies, research and development departments, accountancy sections, and many government departments, are all dominated by professional people who very often have strong "professional" views of their role which may not be in accord with the managerial view of how these people can be best used as a resource. At the corporate level, the whole organizational ethos of the company may be influenced by its membership in a trade association or similar body. These bodies may exert influence informally but often seek to impose norms of behavior on member companies through the development of "codes of conduct."

Figure 5.2   *Influences on individuals and groups.*

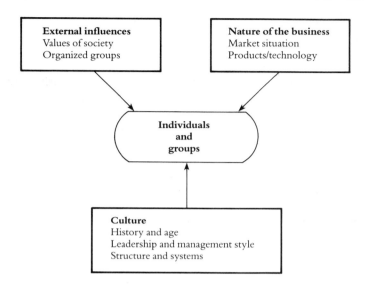

5.2.2   NATURE OF THE BUSINESS

There are a number of issues concerning the nature of a business which will also influence attitudes to company policy. These are much more specific to the particular circumstances of a company but are very often concerned with the market situation and the nature of the products/technology within the company.

Market Situation

Different companies face quite different market conditions and any one company will face different conditions as time goes on. This is most clearly shown by the difference between recession and boom. As a result of this, the attitudes of people within the company will also change, often quite markedly, as external conditions change. Policy decisions which can be made in companies facing a highly competitive and depressed market would meet considerable resistance in other companies which face less stringent conditions. During the 1980s, companies, and even whole industries, were subjected to massive changes in scale, working practices, and product/market strategy. The steel and chemical industries provide examples. Steel mills have been downsized, or even closed, and workers have accepted concessions in wages and working conditions to save jobs. Many chemical companies were formerly the suppliers of chemicals in bulk to companies which then did further processing. They are now producing and marketing specialty chemical products themselves.

People are also influenced by the position of the company in relation to the life cycle of its products and/or markets. People who have only known a company during a period of rapid growth may have developed expectations which will be totally inappropriate when its products enter the stage of maturity.

Products/Technology

Technology influences attitudes in two main ways. First, technology may put a constraint on the way in which the company is able to operate and survive in a competitive environment and therefore dictate methods of operating and the tasks people perform. The impact of production line work in the automobile industry on the attitudes and antagonisms which had built up within the car companies has received much discussion.[1] Second, technology changes the mix of skills required by companies which, in turn, may change company culture. If a company has developed for a long time with little outside influence, individuals and groups may become very introspective. A change in technology may necessitate the company "buying-in" outside help and, as a result, introducing new attitudes to the company which can have a profound influence on the way people view future policy.

Illustration 5.2 provides two examples of companies where the "nature of the business" has changed and has affected corporate policies.

ILLUSTRATION 5.2   *Examples of Changes in the "Nature of the Business"*

External environmental changes can have profound effects on the management and employees of companies. The two examples below illustrate the impact when the "nature of the business" changes.

American Telephone and Telegraph Co. (AT&T)

The culture existing during most of the company's first one hundred years of operation was based upon the fact that it was a monopoly regulated by government. Managers were molded to excel in this monopolistic and regulated environment, and the company operated as a hierarchical functional organization. Managers had a high sense of mission, that is, a commitment to service, but within a structured environment that provided security. All this started changing in the early 1980s when AT&T was broken up into a smaller AT&T and seven regional operating companies.

Deregulation, divestiture, and increasing competition made old structures and the approach to conducting business obsolete. New organizational structures, new ways of assigning work, and new attitudes towards how employees thought about their work were required. Managerial levels were reduced and some decentralization of decision making occurred, broadening the responsibilities of managers. Managers were provided with opportunities for innovation which had not previously been available, and there was a new emphasis on teamwork and risk taking. Decision making was faster. Consideration was given to various incentive pay and profit sharing plans.

The new companies were now to operate as competitive enterprises supplying information systems. In the past the culture was based on a commitment to service and employee loyalty. These previous strengths were replaced by an emphasis on market forces and cost competitiveness. The new companies became quite different places in which to work.

Aluminum Co. of America (Alcoa) and the Alcan Aluminum Ltd. (Alcan)

These two aluminum companies, one American and one Canadian, have recently experienced the most drastic change in their history. The consumption of aluminum peaked in 1980 and these companies have been facing reduced demand as other materials are substituted for aluminum and as competition increased from low-cost foreign ingot producers. In the past, increasing demand allowed producers to establish prices but now prices are market driven. Industry analysts claim that Alcan's style and culture have tolerated mediocre performance since the company has only earned nine percent on equity for the past 30 years.

Alcoa and Alcan are thinking and acting differently now. Both are trying to find new ways to add value to the products they sell but at a time when other producers are doing the same. Mills are being modernized in a effort to make the companies low cost producers. Both companies are attempting to diversify within the aluminum business by developing new products which will allow them to move into more profitable custom-made and fabricated products. Alcoa has doubled its R & D expenditures and wants to transform itself from a "metals" company to a "space age" materials producer. The new products Alcoa is thinking about include aluminum hydrids, ceramics, composite alloys, powders, and plastics for industries such as aerospace and packaging.

Both companies are attempting to grow by nuturing new businesses within their corporate structures rather than through large acquisitions. Objectives and expectations have changed for these companies and industry analysts wonder if they have the mind sets to become the entrepreneurial companies required by the changes in the nature of the aluminum business.

Source: James E. Olson and Thomas A. Cooper, "CEOs on Strategy: Two Companies, Two Strategies (AT&T and Bank of America)," *Journal of Business Strategy*, Vol. 8, No. 1, (Summer 1987), pp. 51–7; "Can Jim Olson's Grand Design Get AT&T Going?," *Business Week*, (December 22, 1986), pp. 48–9; Bud Jorgensen, "Cost Savings Start to Pay Off for Alcan," *The Globe and Mail* (Toronto), January 31, 1987, B1; "Alcoa: Recycling Itself to Become a Pioneer in New Materials," *Business Week*, (February 9, 1987), pp. 56–7; Alan D. Gray, "New Improved Alcan Looks Beyond Aluminum," *Financial Times of Canada*, (May 4, 1987), p. 11; Harvey Enchin, "Alcan Sets Sweeping Changes in Bid to Regain Its Lost Lustre," *The Globe and Mail* (Toronto), July 6, 1987, B1 and B11.

5.2.3   Organizational Culture

It should be clear from the discussions in Chapter 2 that an understanding of the *processes* of policy making in organizations cannot be achieved without paying attention to the issue of *organizational culture*. It is equally important when analyzing the strategic position of an organization to assess how this culture has influenced the development of the organization and the strategies it has pursued. Chapter 2 suggested that a useful analysis of culture can be achieved by examining the *cultural web* of factors within an organization which preserve and sustain the core beliefs, or the recipe. This section suggests how the elements of this cultural web might be analyzed. This is important for two reasons in relation to later parts of the book. First, this kind of analysis provides the background against which an assessment of future strategic choices can be made (Chapter 7), both for options which might be possible within the current recipe and for those which would require more significant change. Second, where the recipe would need to be changed it also provides a background against which to assess how change might be achieved (Chapter 11).

To simplify the discussion in this section, different facets of the cultural web will be discussed in order to build up an analysis of the influence of culture on strategy. However, it must be remembered that the subtle interrelationships between these various facets are of greatest importance and readers should *not* regard the following discussions as a series of unrelated issues. The impact of the cultural web on an organization can be analyzed by looking at the following sorts of issues (see Figure 5.3).

History and Age (Tradition)

The *stories, rituals and symbolic behavior* in an organization provide valuable insights into the core beliefs of that organization — the recipe — and can contribute to strategic analysis.[2] These factors are a product of the history and age of the organization since they arise and develop over time through the experiences of individuals and groups undertaking the day-to-day tasks of the organization. The stories and myths distill the essence of the company's past strategies and instill particular types of behavior in those individuals and groups currently within the organization. The attitudes of outsiders towards that organization are also affected by the company's traditions.

Stinchcombe[3] found in his research that the way companies were organized and managed bore a strong relationship to the era in which that particular industry had its foundations. For example, pre-Industrial Revolution industries, such as farming or construction, still retain many of the features associated with craft industries despite modern methods of operation. History can be a considerable problem when culture has developed in a way which threatens the survival of the organization in the light of a changing environment — such as new technologies and competitors. The staffing at docks was greatly reduced with the introduction of containers requiring less labor intensive activity. Mature industries, such as steel and coal mining, are experiencing difficulty adjusting to competitors with modern, more efficient plants.

In analyzing the impact of this history on an organization's strategy — both past and

Figure 5.3 *Analyzing the impact of the cultural web on strategy: a checklist.*

Aspects of cultural web	Some useful questions
A. Stories and myths	1. What **core beliefs** do the stories reflect? 2. How **strongly held** are these beliefs by power holders? 3. How **pervasive** are the beliefs (through the levels)? 4. How do beliefs relate to **strengths** and **weaknesses**? 5. Who are the **heroes**? 6. Do the heroes **conform** to or **challenge** the beliefs?
B. Rituals and symbols	1. What **behavior** is expected and rewarded (e.g., risk taking)? 2. What **language** is used to describe the organization and its activities? 3. What is the dominant **attitude** towards each stakeholder group?
C. Leadership and management style	1. What are the **core beliefs** of the leadership? 2. What aspects are stressed in public (e.g., annual reports)? 3. How do they regard structures (e.g., centralist or devolutionist)? 4. What **type** of strategy is favored (e.g., defensive or speculative)? 5. What attributes are sought in **new recruits**?
D. Structure and systems	1. Do structures/systems encourage **collaboration** or **competition**? 2. What aspects of strategy are most closely **monitored** and **controlled**? 3. What **kind of training** is given?

future — there are a number of questions to consider. The answers should give a clearer understanding of the organization's core beliefs. (See Figure 5.3.) These questions range from whether the stories and myths are predominantly concerned with success or failure, change or stability, to what type of language is used within the organization.

Leadership and Management Style

In later chapters, it will be seen how important the leadership[4] of an organization is in terms of shaping and changing culture in order to ensure survival and success. Accordingly, it is important during strategic analysis to establish how previous and current leadership has contributed to the organization's culture.

Miles and Snow,[5] whose findings were discussed in Chapter 2, categorize organizations into three basic types in terms of how they behave strategically (see Table 5.1). When undertaking a strategic analysis, this categorization provides a means of assessing the dominant culture of the organization. By reviewing the types of systems and the historical choices of strategy, the analyst can distinguish between a defender and a prospector organization and, hence, judge the extent to which new strategies might fit the current recipe. In the context of the current discussion on leadership, the central dilemma for organizations should now be clear. On one hand, a cohesive culture almost demands, and

Table 5.1 *Different types of organization culture and their influences on policy making.*

Organization type	Characteristics of policy making		
	Dominant objectives	*Preferred strategies*	*Planning and control systems*
1. Defenders	Desire for a secure and stable niche in market	Specialization: cost-efficient production; marketing emphasises price and service to defend current business; tendency to vertical integration	Centralized, detailed control Emphasis on cost efficiency Extensive use of formal planning
2. Prospectors	Location and exploitation of new product and market opportunities	Growth through product and market development (often in spurts) Constant monitoring of environmental change Multiple technologies	Emphasis on flexibility, decentralized control, use of *ad hoc* measurements
3. Analyzers	Desire to match new ventures to present shape of business	Steady growth through market penetration Exploitation of applied research Followers in the market	Very complicated Coordinating roles between functions (e.g., product managers) Intensive planning

Source: R.E. Miles and C.C. Snow, *Organizational Strategy, Structure and Process*, New York: McGraw-Hill, 1978.

often produces, "cloning" within the organization — where more and more like-minded individuals are selected into key leadership roles or become "socialized" into the organization's dominant beliefs and approaches. On the other hand, the dangers of blindly following this recipe are apparent. This issue is discussed more fully in Chapter 11 which looks at how culture can be managed and changed.

Structure and Systems

The *structure* and *systems* of an organization are also an important part of the cultural web and as such, influence how individuals and groups perceive the organization's strategies. Chapters 10 and 11 will discuss how the design and management of structure and systems is crucial to the successful implementation of strategy. However, at this stage it is worthwhile to briefly highlight ways in which structure and systems contribute to culture (see Figure 5.3). For example, an organization structured and managed as a series of separate and competitive units is unlikely to have a cohesive culture at the level of these subunits, making collaborative ventures (between units) difficult. Indeed, in many such organizations the systems of control and reward are likely to have developed in a way which encourages and supports competitive (rather than collaborative) behavior. It is not surprising, therefore, that individuals and groups are likely to favor strategies which can be pursued in a devolved rather than an integrated way.[6]

A close look at the control systems of the organization can be very instructive about which aspects are most closely monitored. Government development agencies established to attract and assist industry sometimes are so obsessed with the "stewardship of funds" that they forget the purpose they are to serve. Bureaucratic procedures and conservative attitudes by staff prevent many applicants for assistance from being successful. The training programs of organizations can be useful pointers to core beliefs. For example, some organizations only have training in the "technical" skills of the job while others place more emphasis on the development of general skills and attitudes.

Illustration 5.3 provides an example of how one corporation expresses its organizational culture.

5.3   COALITIONS AND STAKEHOLDERS

Although individuals may have a wide variety of personal aspirations, most organizations have groups whose members hold identifiably shared expectations. These groups can be formally identified as *stakeholders* (e.g. managers, lenders, unions, shareholders, customers).

However, a better understanding will emerge if *coalitions*[7] (of common expectations) are identified. It will be seen in the following sections that coalitions tend to arise as a result of events rather than from being enshrined in the formal systems of the organization. Coalitions may occur within departments, geographic locations, different levels in the hierarchy, and different age groups. Most individuals will "belong" to more than one such coalition. In order to obtain any influence in decision making, individuals will need to

---

ILLUSTRATION 5.3   *Organizational Culture at Magna International Inc.*

The organizational culture of a company can be expressed in many different ways. Magna designs, develops and manufactures a diverse line of automotive components and systems for sale primarily to original equipment manufacturers from over 70 plants in North America. By studying the "Corporate Constitution" below, an analyst can obtain valuable information on the core beliefs of the company.

Magna's Corporate Constitution

Board of Directors
Magna believes that outside directors provide independent counsel and discipline. A majority of Magna's Board of Directors will be outsiders.

Employee Equity and Profit Participation
Ten per cent of Magna's profit before tax will be allocated to employees. These funds will be used for the purchase of Magna shares in trust for employees and for cash distributions to employees, recognizing both performance and length of service.

Shareholder Profit Participation
Magna will distribute, on average, 20 per cent of its annual net profit to its shareholders.

Management Profit Participation
In order to obtain a long term contractual commitment from management, the Company provides a compensation arrangement which, in addition to a base salary comparable to industry standards, allows for the distribution to corporate management of up to 6 per cent of Magna's profit before tax.

Research and Technology Development
Magna will allocate 7 per cent of its profit before tax for research and technology development to ensure the long term viability of the Company.

Social Responsibility
The Company will contribute a maximum of 2 per cent of its profit before tax to charitable, cultural, educational and political institutions to support the basic fabric of society.

Minimum Profit Performance
Management has an obligation to produce a profit. If Magna does not generate a minimum after-tax return of 4 per cent on share capital for two consecutive years, Class A shareholders, voting as a Class, will have the right to elect additional directors.

Major Investments
In the event that more than 20 per cent of Magna's equity is to be committed to a new unrelated business, Class A and Class B shareholders will have the right

to approve such an investment with each class voting separately.

Constitutional Amendments
Any change to Magna's Corporate Constitution will require the approval of the
Class A and Class B shareholders with each class voting separately.

Source: Magna International Inc., *Annual Report*, 1985, p. 3.

identify themselves with the aims and ideals of these coalitions. Political parties, of course, represent this process in operation quite clearly, but readers need to recognize that a similar process occurs in virtually every organization. Similarly, external stakeholder groups will attempt to influence strategy, to a greater or lesser extent, through their links with internal groups or individuals.

5.3.1 CONFLICTS OF EXPECTATIONS

Since the expectations of groups are likely to differ, it is quite normal for conflict to exist within organizations regarding the importance and/or desirability of many aspects of strategy. This section considers some typical expectations and how they might conflict. The main points are summarized in Figure 5.4. In many different circumstances, a compromise will need to be reached between expectations which cannot all be achieved simultaneously. These can vary from the conflict between growth and profitability; growth and control/independence; cost efficiency and jobs; volume/mass provision versus quality/specialization, through to the problems of sub-optimization where the development of one part of an organization may be at the expense of another.

What emerges is the need to understand the expectations of different groups and weigh these in terms of the power they exercise. For example, financial institutions such as

Figure 5.4 Some common conflicts of expectations.

1. In order to grow, short term profitability, cash flow and pay levels may need to be sacrificed.

2. When family businesses grow, the owners may lose control if they need to appoint professional managers.

3. New developments may require additional funding through share issue or loans. In either case financial independence may be sacrificed.

4. Public ownership of shares will require more openness and accountability from the management.

5. Cost efficiency through capital investment can mean job losses.

6. Extending into mass markets may require decline in quality standards.

7. In public services a common conflict is between mass provision and specialist services (e.g. preventative dentistry or heart transplant).

8. In public services savings in one area (e.g. social security benefits) may result in increases elsewhere (e.g. school meals, medical care).

banks may not hold shares in a company but may well have a direct interest through the funds they loan. The bank's main expectation is to achieve a secure return on their investment in terms of interest and a company with high borrowings may well discover that meeting the bank's expectation becomes a dominant requirement.

Municipal or local governments are excellent examples of the kind of influence a variety of stakeholder groups with differing expectations can have on the strategy to be followed. The electorate is able to influence the situation by allocating power to political parties. They in turn are subject to their own internal pressures from groups with differing expectations and must reconcile their policies with the views of other parties and the administrators in local government departments. An example of a corporation attempting to build coalitions with various stakeholders is given in Illustration 5.4.

It is useful when analyzing the strategic importance of expectations within a company to look for one of three commonly occurring situations:

1. *Where the parts are more important than the whole.* This is illustrated in some large corporations where authority is decentralized and the divisions are independent of corporate headquarters. In such cases, the employees and management identify with their own units more so than with the corporation.

2. *Where the whole is more important than the parts.* This is often seen in family companies where the maintenance of a strong family identity is often achieved at the expense of the efficient running of the various parts of the company. Some large organizations such as Shell and IBM put a great deal of effort into sustaining identity with the company as a whole.

3. *Where external influences are very important.* This is best typified by many voluntary organizations whose members have strong demands on their time from other sources (home and work), or in organizations in which professionals such as doctors, lawyers or scientists, play an important part and view the maintenance of external codes of practice or standards to be of overriding importance.[8] The way in which the organization operates is dominated by these outside influences.

Such an analysis is important since it contributes significantly to the understanding of an organization's core beliefs and its strategic position which will be necessary when assessing future strategies. For those who wish to effect strategic change, it provides valuable insight into the circumstances in which change would be effected, particularly when linked to an assessment of the power structure of the organization (see below).

5.3.2 IDENTIFYING COALITIONS

It is one thing to talk about coalitions and the way they influence a company's strategies, but it can often, in practice, be quite difficult to identify coalitions. There is always the danger of concentrating too heavily on the formal structure of an organization as a basis for identifying coalitions since this can be the easiest place to look for the divisions in expectations mentioned previously. It is, however, essential to unearth "informal" coalitions and assess their importance.

ILLUSTRATION 5.4   *Building Coalitions at Manville Corporation*

In 1982, Manville Corp. filed for reorganization under Chapter 11 of the Bankruptcy Code in order to defend itself from mounting claims by asbestosis victims. By 1986, the company was emerging from Chapter 11 bankruptcy and W. Thomas Stephens became the chief executive. One of the challenges confronting Stephens was the rebuilding of ties with employees, customers, investors, and other stakeholders.

The following are some of the actions taken by management at Manville to create new coalitions with stakeholders to put the problems experienced by the company behind it and to begin rebuilding the business:

Employees — Stevens visited several of the company's plants and held talks with small groups of Manville employees. A series of seminars was held for employees in Washington, D.C. on asbestos related problems and some proposed legislation regarding future compensation.

Managers — Stephens planned to push decision making down to the lower levels in the firm which would help restore management's credibility with employees.

Customers — a new marketing campaign was initiated to restore the company's credibility. A multimillion dollar fund was established to deal with any product claims from purchasers of Manville roofing and insulation products.

Creditors — The company's creditors had to be convinced that the company's final reorganization plan was in their interest.

Shareholders — The company's shareholders were concerned that the plan diluted their stockholdings and had to be reassured of the financial viability of the plan.

The Public (including victims) — full page advertisements were placed in 21 newspapers across the country explaining the company's position and reasons for the reorganization.

The coalition building which took place at Manville was done under somewhat drastic circumstances. Nevertheless, it is an example of deliberate efforts by a strategist to accommodate various stakeholders.

Source: Marcia Bishop, "Bankruptcy as a Business Strategy: The Manville Experience," *Planning Review*, (March 1985), pp. 12–17; "Now Comes the Hard Part for Manville," *Business Week*, (July 7, 1986), pp. 76–7.

Other problems in this kind of analysis are that individuals will tend to belong to more than one coalition and that coalitions will line up in different groupings depending on the issue at hand. For example, marketing and production departments could well be united in the face of proposals to drop certain product lines while being in fierce opposition regarding plans to buy-in new items to the product range. Specific events often trigger the formation of coalitions. For this reason it is helpful to speculate on the *degree of unity or diversity* between the various coalitions when they are faced with a number of possible future events. This is also a tool for strategic evaluation. Nevertheless, this process can be very helpful during strategic analysis by uncovering potential alliances or rifts which may be significant in thinking about future strategic choices.

Pfeffer[9] provides a very interesting example of how such an analysis can be undertaken. Table 5.2 shows a typical analysis in the case of a company which operated on two sites (Omaha and St. Louis). The various coalitions and external stakeholders are identified and the table is used to map-out their expected reactions to a variety of possible changes. Several useful points emerge from this analysis:

- There will always be some events over which the majority of coalitions can unite. Such solidarity tends to occur during the early stages of development of new companies or

Table 5.2   *The attitudes of various coalitions towards possible future changes.*

Possible changes	A	B (internal coalitions)						C (external stakeholders)			
	Whole company	1 Market. dept.	2 Prod. dept.	3 Omaha plant	4 St. Louis plant	5 Grads.	6 Clerical staff	1 Suppl. A	2 Cust. X	3 Shr.hdr. M	4 Local comm.
1. Sell out to competitor	–	–	–	–	–	–	–	0	–	0	–
2. Introduce computerized systems	+	+	?	+	0	+	–	0	+	+	0
3. Close St. Louis plant	?	+	–	+	–	0	0	0	+	0	–
4. Develop new Far East markets	?	?	–	+	–	0	0	+	–	+	0
5. Sub-contract production	?	+	–	–	–	0	0	–	0	–	–

Note: + = support; 0 = neutral; – = oppose; ? = divided opinion.

when survival is threatened by such events as a possible takeover by a major competitor.

- New coalitions may become important in certain of the situations envisaged. For example, the proposal to close the St. Louis plant would meet resistance not only from the employees there but also from any local support they were able to muster. Equally, computerization would be resisted by clerical staff who had hitherto never been viewed as a cohesive group.

- In some cases there would be *divided views* within one of the coalitions. For example, the export section of the marketing department might be delighted by plans to expand sales in the Far East but not so their American-based counterparts. Thus, these would need to be viewed as separate coalitions in such circumstances.

- At this stage it is important to identify potential alliances between coalitions regarding any of these future options. In this example, a particularly significant observation is that the possibility of closing the St. Louis plant could well see an alliance between the Omaha plant and the marketing department with strong support from the major customer X. In any such move, the St. Louis plant could only rely on production staff and local community action; others seem to be broadly indifferent.

5.4 POWER

The previous section was concerned with analyzing how expectations are "structured" within and around any organization. Such an analysis is only useful alongside a parallel analysis of the power individuals or groups possess. Power is the mechanism by which expectations are able to influence policy and is an important part of the cultural web. In most organizations power will be unequally shared between the various coalitions or stakeholders. In other words, policy making tends to be dominated by one group, usually the management of the company.[10] Before proceeding it should be understood what is meant here by power.[11] In particular, a distinction needs to be drawn between the power people or groups apparently have as a result of their positions within the organization and the power they actually possess due to other reasons. For the purposes of strategic analysis, power is best understood as *the extent to which individuals or groups are able to persuade, induce or coerce others into following certain courses of action.* This is the mechanism by which people holding one set of expectations will dominate policy making or seek compromise with others. An analysis of power must, therefore, begin by an assessment of the sources of power.

5.4.1 SOURCES OF POWER WITHIN ORGANIZATIONS

Power within companies can be derived in a variety of ways, any of which may provide an avenue whereby the expectations of an individual or group may influence company policy. The following are the normally recognized sources of power: (See Figure 5.5.)

1. *Hierarchy* provides people with formal power over others and is one method by which senior managers influence policy. In particular, if strategic decision making is confined to top management it can give them considerable power. However, it is important to remember that this type of power has very limited effect if used in isolation. Many industrial disputes illustrate the impotence of management if they rely only on formal power.

2. *Influence* can be an important source of power and may arise from personal qualities (the charismatic leader) or because a high level of *consensus* exists within the group or company (i.e. people are willing to support the prevailing viewpoint). Indeed, there is strong support for the view that the most important task managers have is to shape the culture of the organization to suit their strategy.[12] It is important to recognize, however, that the extent to which an individual or group can use their influence is determined by a number of other factors. For example, access to channels of communication (the media) is an essential requirement. In many situations, prior commitments to principles or specific courses of action can give individuals influence. Some of these principles may be quite central to the organization's mission. For example, a new CEO may be committed to computerization of a company's operations regardless of the consequences for employment.

3. *Control of strategic resources* is a major source of power within companies. It should be remembered that the relative importance of different resources will change over time and hence power derived in this way can show dramatic changes. The power of organized labor is most potent when demand for output is high and labor supply short. The decline in the earnings of steel workers between 1970 and 1980 is evidence of the erosion of this source of power. Within any one company, the extent to which the various departments are seen as powerful will vary with the company's circumstances. Design or R&D departments may be powerful in companies developing new products or processes, whereas marketing people may dominate companies primarily concerned with developing new markets.

4. *Knowledge/skills.* The logical extension of the previous point is that individuals can derive power from their specialist knowledge or skills. Certain individuals may be viewed as irreplaceable to the company, and some will jealously guard this privileged position by creating a mystique around their particular job. This can be a risky personal strategy since others in the organization may be spurred to acquire these skills or to devise methods of bypassing them. The power of many organizations' computer specialists was threatened by the advent of microcomputers which provided others within organizations with a means of bypassing those specialists.

5. *Control of the environment.* Most people know that events in the company's environment are likely to influence company performance. However, some groups will have significantly more knowledge of, contact with, and influence over, the environment than others. This can become a source of power within the company, since these groups are able to reduce the uncertainty experienced by others.[13] It is probably for this reason that financial and marketing managers have traditionally been seen as dominant in policy determination while production managers have taken a back seat.[14] This source of power

Figure 5.5   *Sources of power.*

A. **Within organizations**	B. **For external stakeholders**
1. Hierarchy (formal power) (e.g., autocratic decision making)	1. Control of strategic resources (e.g., materials, labor, money)
2. Influence (informal power) (e.g., charismatic leadership)	2. Involvement in strategic implementation (e.g., distribution outlets, agents)
3. Control of strategic resources (e.g., strategic products coal)	3. Possession of knowledge (skills) (e.g., subcontractors)
4. Possession of knowledge/skills (e.g., computer specialists)	4. Through internal links (e.g., informal influence)
5. Control of the environment (e.g., negotiating skills)	
6. Involvement in strategic implementation (e.g., by exercising discretion)	

becomes most important when the environment is hostile or unpredictable. Then most of the factions will unite behind those who are seen to be best able to protect the company, despite the fact that the "medicine" doled out might represent a denial of many of their expectations.

6. *Exercising discretion.* This is a very often overlooked but most significant source of power within all organizations. Individuals derive power because they are involved in the company's decision processes by the very nature of their jobs. The execution of strategy, by its very complexity, cannot be controlled in all its minutest detail by one person or group and hence many other people within the company will need to interpret and execute particular parts of that policy and, in doing so, will use their own personal discretion. This is a major source of power for middle management in organizations. The extent to which discretion is allowed to influence policy is obviously related to the types of control systems within the organization. These will be discussed in Chapter 11.

5.4.2 Sources of Power for External Stakeholders

As with internal groups, those outside the organization may have a number of sources of power to help them influence the organization's strategies. These are summarized in Figure 5.5.

1. *Resource dependence* is the most common source of power. For example, major suppliers, banks and shareholders all derive power from this source. The short term survival of the company may be critically dependent on one or more of these stakeholders. As discussed in Section 3.4.2 of Chapter 3, the power buyers or suppliers exercise over an organization is also likely to depend on the extent to which they are able to exercise control over resource provision or acquisition.

2. *Involvement in implementation* through linkages between value chains can be an important source of power for suppliers, channels, and buyers as mentioned in Chapters 3 and 4. One of the major changes since the 1960s in many industries has been the extent to which power has shifted from the manufacturing sector to the distribution sector. The greater knowledge distribution companies have of trends in consumer tastes allows them to dictate terms to manufacturers rather than simply being outlets for goods designed and planned by manufacturing companies.

3. *Knowledge and skills* critical to the success of the company may be a source of power. A subcontractor for example, may derive power in this way, if it performs a vital activity in the company's value chain.

4. *Internal links* can provide a way for external stakeholders to influence company strategy. This is determined by the policy-making processes within the organization. At one extreme, a highly authoritarian organization is likely to be hostile to any attempts by outside stakeholders to be formally involved in formulation of strategy, and therefore any influence on policy must be derived in other ways. In contrast, some organizations, actively seek to involve a wide variety of stakeholders in strategic decision making. *Industrial democracy*[15] is concerned with the extent to which stakeholders *can* be formally involved in policy making.

5.4.3 METHODS OF ASSESSING POWER

Since there are many different sources of power and influence, and each is also dependent upon circumstances, some managers find this type of political analysis quite bewildering. However, it is important to incorporate a political analysis into any strategic analysis and this section provides readers with some simple guidelines on how this can be done.

The analysis will, once again, rely heavily on Pfeffer[16] who argues that the best way to cope with this complex situation is by stepping back from the detail and looking for *indicators of power*. For simplicity, there are four major indicators of power:

1. The *status* of the individual or group. One measure of status might be position within the hierarchy, but others are equally important, for example, an individual's salary, or job grades of groups. Equally, the reputation a group or individual holds with others will be relevant.

2. The *claim on resources* as measured by the size of a department's budget, or the number of employees within that group. In particular, trends in the proportion of resources claimed by that group may be a useful indicator of the extent to which their power is waxing or

waning. The least powerful groups invariably see their resources eroded by the more powerful. A useful comparison can be made with similar groups in comparable organizations.

3. *Representation in powerful positions*. The best example of this is the composition of the board of directors and their particular specialisms. The weakness of the production function may be caused by lack of representation at board level. Within less hierarchical organizations, representation on important committees could be a measure of power, although a simple "head-count" in this type of analysis would overlook the extent to which the individuals are influential. Here individual status should be taken into consideration.

4. *Symbols of power*. Internal division of power may be indicated in a variety of ways. Such physical symbols as the size and location of people's offices, whether they have a secretary, carpets, a private telephone, or newspapers delivered each morning, are all important clues. Whether individuals are addressed by their first or last names, even the way they dress, may be symbols of power. In more bureaucratic organizations, the existence of "distribution lists" for internal memoranda and other information can give useful clues to the power structure. Surprisingly, these lists do not always neatly reflect the formal hierarchical structure and may provide pointers as to who really is viewed as powerful within the organization.

None of these four indicators of power by itself is likely to fully uncover the structure of power within a company. However, by looking at all four it may be possible to identify which people or groups appear to have power, based on a number of these measures. Table 5.3 illustrates how such an analysis might be performed to assess the relative power of the marketing and production departments, and the Omaha and St. Louis plants, using the previous example (Table 5.2). It is clear that the marketing department is seen as powerful by all measures and the production department universally weak. Equally, the Omaha plant looks particularly powerful in relation to St. Louis.

Along with this internal assessment of power, a similar analysis of the power held by *external stakeholders* needs to be carried out. The indicators of power are slightly different.

1. The *status* of an external party, such as a supplier, is usually indicated by the way the party is discussed among company employees and whether they respond quickly to the supplier's demands.

2. *Resource dependence* can often be measured directly. For example, the proportion of a company's business tied up with any one customer, or a similar dependence on suppliers, can normally be easily measured. Perhaps the key indicator is the ease with which that supplier, financier or customer could be replaced at short notice.

3. *Negotiating arrangements*. Whether external parties are treated at arms length or are actively involved in negotiations with the company can be significant. For example, a customer who is invited to negotiate over the price of a contract is in a more powerful position than a similar company given a fixed price on a take-it-or-leave-it basis.

Table 5.3 *Assessing the relative power of coalitions.*

1.   Internal coalitions

Indicators of power†	1 Marketing dept. ★	2 Production★	3 Omaha plant★	4 St. Louis plant★
A. *Status*				
1. Position in hierarchy (closeness to board)	H	L	H	M
2. Salary of top manager	H	L	H	L
3. Average grade of staff	H	M	H	L
B. *Claim on resources*				
1. Number of staff	M	H	M	M
2. Size of similar company	H	L	H	L
3. Budget as % of total	H	M	H	L
C. *Representation*				
1. Number of directors	H	None	M	None
2. Most influential directors	H	None	M	None
D. *Symbols*				
1. Quality of accommodation	H	L	M	M
2. Support services	H	L	H	L

2.   External stakeholders

Indicators of power†	Supplier A★	Customer X★	Shareholder M★
1. Status	H	H	L
2. Resource dependence	L	H	H
3. Negotiating arrangements	M	H	L
4. Symbols	H	H	L

★ These are examples — the list will clearly vary from one situation to another.
† H = high; M = medium; L = low

4. *Symbols* are equally valuable clues. These include whether the management team wines and dines certain customers or suppliers, or the level of person in the company who deals with a particular supplier. The care and attention paid to correspondence with outsiders will tend to differ from one party to another.

Again, no single measure will give a full understanding of the extent of the power held by external groups, but the combined analysis will be very useful. Part 2 of Table 5.3 illustrates how an analysis of the power of external stakeholders can be performed (using the data from Table 5.2).

This extended example has been used to illustrate how an analysis of both the expectations and power structures in an organization can be undertaken as part of a strategic analysis. To gain maximum benefit from this type of analysis, readers need to look for a combination of strongly held expectations and the power to exercise them. For example, customer X may well pose a significant problem for a strategy of entering new Far East markets — the company may lose X's business on which they are highly dependent. Furthermore, the survival of the St. Louis plant looks even more precarious when this analysis of power is added to the previous assessment of the attitudes of coalitions. Not only does St. Louis appear to be isolated (see the previous analysis) but the most powerful groups (marketing and customer X) would welcome closure. In contrast, both St. Louis and its major potential ally (production), have little power themselves.

5.5 ORGANIZATIONAL OBJECTIVES

Many, if not all, organizations will have formally stated objectives. However, ideas that objectives are somehow "given" in formulating strategy, that they are received by the organization in the same way as environmental change, or that they *exist* like plant and equipment, are obviously fallacious. Objectives are set by somebody or some group of individuals. Referring back to Figure 5.1, it can be seen that organizational objectives result from the expectations of individuals and groups within and around the organization together with the power these separate groups have in influencing the overall objectives of the organization. So, organizational objectives tend to be shaped by those who have most power — normally the management of the organization.

However, this dominant coalition is likely to be influenced by the expectations of other stakeholders, and in particular the power they perceive these groups to have when objectives are being formulated. Some stakeholder groups do not seek to impose objectives as such on an organization but they do insist on imposing constraints. A municipal government may not have the power or desire to impose any objectives as such on a company in its area: it can, however, impose constraints on such matters as pollution control and planning permission. The influence of the stock market on companies may be regarded as a constraint: if a company does not perform to expectations then it is likely to suffer a reduction in share price. The Federal government may argue that it is not its intention to influence the policies of private companies but may impose sanctions if that company defies a trading embargo for example. Given that objectives arise out of these differences of expectations, it is unwise to regard objectives as permanent or preordained.[17] They are a product of the sort of cultural and political processes discussed above and should be regarded as such in the analysis and formulation of strategy.

Illustration 5.5 shows the kinds of formal objectives stated by companies. Just a brief glance shows that there are differences in their content and in the extent to which they are specific. They all have two things in common: they express in some way desired ends to be achieved and they are all expressed as formal organizational aims. However, they are different types of statements about desired ends. These differences can be thought of as a hierarchy of objectives.[18] Objective 1 is an expression of what might be called *mission*; 2 and 3 are expressions of *corporate objectives*; and 4 and 5 are expressions of *unit objectives*. The following discussion is summarized in Table 5.4.

ILLUSTRATION 5.5   *Examples of Objectives*

An organization's objectives are of different kinds and vary in the extent to which they are specific.

1. Mission
"To achieve an international reputation for excellence by providing products and services to the energy and resource industries and to invest principally in energy-related assets in North America."
ATCO Limited, *Annual Report*, 1982.

2. Corporate: Open
"To strive for excellence and competitive differentiation as opposed to imitating others and accepting how things were done in the past without question."
Revelstoke Companies Ltd., *Annual Report*, 1986.

3. Corporate: Closed
"Earn, as a company, 10 percent after-tax profit margin on sales and 20 percent after-tax return on shareholders' equity."
Masco Corporation, *Annual Report*, 1985.

4. Unit: Open
"Pursue opportunities outside traditional regulated utility activities in the Union Gas Limited franchise area."
Unicorp Canada Corporation, *Annual Report*, 1986.

5. Unit: Closed
"Increase Unicorp's ownership in Mark Resources Inc. to over 50 percent."
Unicorp Canada Corporation, *Annual Report*, 1986.

Table 5.4   *The nature of objectives.*

Types of objectives	Common characteristics	
1. Mission	General Visionary Central and overriding Often unwritten	Open
2. Corporate	Often expressed financially Express stakeholder expectations Formulated by senior management	Open or closed
3. Unit	Specific to units of organization Operational Often multiple	Open or closed

5.5.1 MISSION

The mission of an organization is the most generalized sort of objective and can be thought of as an expression of its *raison d'être*. Richards,[19] writing on objectives, calls mission the "master strategy" and says it is "a visionary projection of the central and overriding concepts on which the organization is based." He goes on to say that it "should not focus on what the firm is doing in terms of products and markets currently served, but rather the services and utility within the firm." However, if there is substantial disagreement within the organization about its mission, this may well give rise to real problems in resolving the strategic direction of the organization.

5.5.2 CORPORATE OBJECTIVES

Corporate objectives and unit objectives are distinguished in this chapter because, within organizations, there are different "levels" of objectives with different characteristics. *Corporate objectives* are often expressed in *financial* terms. They could be the expression of desired sales or profit levels or rates of growth, or dividend levels, or share valuations. Increasingly, however, organizations have corporate objectives of a non-financial nature, such as employee welfare or technological advance, but it is rare for these to be unaccompanied by financial objectives. They are frequently formal *statements of stakeholder expectations*. Traditionally, this may have meant the shareholders, so the corporate objective may have been a statement about the required return to shareholders. However, since it is now becoming increasingly recognized that stakeholders might also be employees, customers, suppliers, the local community and so on, there could be formal statements of objectives to be met on their behalf.

Corporate objectives are usually formulated by senior members of the Board of Directors and top management. They are more likely to be handed down to lower levels of management than to be formulated by such lower levels. In a divisionalized company, for example, corporate objectives may be set by the board at head office and then translated into divisional objectives which become financial targets for the division.

5.5.3 UNIT OBJECTIVES

Unit objectives are here distinguished from corporate objectives insofar as they are likely to have the following sorts of characteristics:

- They relate to the individual units of the organization. For example, they may be the objectives of a division or of one company within a conglomerate. In the case of government organizations, the unit could be a department of a municipality or a toll bridge in a regional transportation authority.

- They may be financial objectives stated in much the same way as corporate objectives, but at a unit level. A corporate objective of a given growth in profit after tax might be translated into an objective for each business unit. Unit objectives are likely to be more operational in nature than corporate objectives. In this sense, they are to do with the planning of operational activity, which is discussed in the next section.

- Multiple objectives might well be more common at the unit level than at the corporate level. This is likely to be the case if objectives are conceived of in operational terms since the operations of a business are multi-faceted.

5.5.4 THE PRECISION OF OBJECTIVES

Illustration 5.5 may be looked at in another way. Some objectives (numbers 3 and 5) can be measured: it is possible to say they can be achieved at some future time. These are "closed" objectives. Others (numbers 1, 2 and 4) are objectives that can never be achieved since they will always persist. They are like the individual who might say his aim is to make more money; he can always make more money no matter how much he makes. These are "open" objectives.

Many writers[20] have argued that objectives are not helpful unless they are capable of being measured and achieved (i.e. unless they are closed). This view is not taken here. Open statements may in fact be just as helpful as closed statements. For example, mission should be a very important influence on strategy: it may concentrate people's perception of their operation on the needs of customers and the utility of the service, for example, and at the same time set the boundaries within which they see the business developing. But statements of mission are very difficult to make in closed terms. The role of this sort of objective is very much to do with focusing strategy rather than deciding when it has been "achieved." In addition, there may be some important objectives which are difficult to

---

ILLUSTRATION 5.6   *The Use of Objectives at Counsel Trustco Corporation*

Counsel is a Canadian financial management company operating in three areas: financial services, real estate and health care. The company used objectives in a logical way, that is, as the bases for evaluating performance. In its annual report, Counsel states the previous year's objectives along with an indication of whether or not the objectives were achieved. An example of this is given below. The objectives for the next year are also included in the report.

1985 Performance Against Objectives

1.   *Profitability:* **To earn a consolidated pre-tax profit of $5.4 million in Counsel Trust, including $2.2 million from trust company operations and $3.2 million from real estate operations.**
     Pre-tax earnings generated from trust company operations were $2.2 million and from real estate operations were $3.4 million.

2.   *Capitalization:* **To raise a minimum of $10 million in additional capital.**
     Total capital raised was $16.5 million. A share issue produced $12.5 million and the amalgamation with Termguard raised $4 million.

3.   *Growth:* **To achieve asset growth in Counsel Trust of $150 million at a minimum spread of 175 basis points.**
     Counsel Trust achieved asset growth of $144 million and maintained a 175 basis point spread.

4.   *Productivity:* **To increase productivity in counsel Trust by 57% measured by assets per employee.**
     A 42% productivity gain was realized — measured by growth in assets managed per employee.

5.   *Mortgage Arrears:* **To reduce mortgages 30 days or more in arrears, including foreclosed mortgages, to 3% of total mortgages.**
     Mortgage arrears as at December 31, 1985 were 6.16% and 4.67% as at March 31, 1986. Significant mortgage arrears were acquired through the Termguard amalgamation.

6.   *Corporate Strategies:* **To define strategies for (i) spread business (ii) savings business and (iii) mortgage business.**
     Strategies for the spread business are in place. Savings business strategies are in place and include a direct market strategy which is now in the planning stages. A mortgage business strategy is partially completed.

7.   *Organizational Effectiveness:* **To implement stage II of Counsel Trust's human resources program successfully as measured by less than 12% turnover and by having 10% more employees rated Counsel Standard (our term for above average).**
     The employee turnover rate was 21% in 1985, compared to 44% in 1984. Forty-six percent more employees were rated Counsel Standard this year.

8.   *Computer System:* **To improve corporate efficiency by ensuring that (i) user up-time averages more than 90% between 8:30 a.m. and 5:30 p.m. each business day and (ii) all modifications are completed on time and on budget.**
     This objective was achieved.

9.   *Guaranteed Mortgage Certificates:* **To successfully launch GMC Investors Corporation such that the corporation meets its first year budget.**
     Launch of this new financial product was delayed until later in the year by the regulatory process. As a result, the first year budget for the product was not met.

10. *Counsel Properties Inc:* **To become fully operational by year end including acquisition and development of income-producing properties.**
     This objective was achieved.

11. *Pension Fund Management:* **to earn a minimum of $1.2 million in revenue through pension fund management and consulting.**
     Revenue for the year totalled $923,000.

Source: Counsel Trustco Corporation, *Annual Report*, 1985.

quantify or express in measurable terms. An objective such as "to be a leader in technology" may be highly relevant in today's technological environment, but may become absurd if it has to be expressed in some measurable way. Illustration 5.6 shows how one organization used its objectives to evaluate performance.

There are times when specific objectives must be met. These are times when immediate or urgent action is required, such as in a crisis or at times of major (usually strategic) transitions when it is essential for management to focus on a limited number of priority requirements. An extreme example would be in a *turnaround* situation. If the choice is between going out of business and surviving, then there is no room for latitude through vaguely stated requirements.

It is also helpful to have closed objectives for planning purposes. Here the objective becomes a target to be achieved. Suppose a company is seeking to develop and launch new products, for example. It is helpful in this case for managers to have some yardstick, of profitability perhaps, against which to judge the success of the new venture.

5.6 SOCIAL RESPONSIBILITY[21]

While the dominant objectives of commercial organizations are invariably expressed in terms of financial performance, it should be clear from discussions in this chapter that organizations never pursue a single objective to the exclusion of all other considerations.

In the past twenty years or so there has been an increasing acceptance by management of the diversity of stakeholder interests and expectations to be accommodated. This has given rise to the notion of *social responsibility*, by which is meant the acceptance by management of organizational responsibilities of a social nature wider than the legal minimum it is bound to fulfill. A wide variety of issues[22] can be considered to fall under this broad heading. These issues are summarized in Figure 5.6.

How organizations respond to these issues varies considerably and may be summarized in Table 5.5. There are four broad groupings of response, each of which may give rise to conflicts of objectives and policy.[23]

1. At one extreme there are organizations which largely conform to Milton Friedman's maxim that "the business of business is business," and that the "only social responsibility of business is to increase its profit."[24] (See categories 1 to 3 in Table 5.5.) The holders of these beliefs argue that not only is it not the duty of business to be concerned about social issues but that in doing so they would detract from the primary way in which they should be contributing to society, that is by operating economically efficient businesses. Social responsibility, they argue, is the domain of government which should prescribe, through legislation, the constraints society chooses to impose on business in their pursuit of economic efficiency. Expecting companies to exercise these duties can, in extreme cases, undermine the authority of government and give business organizations even more

Figure 5.6 *Some questions of social responsibility.*

Should organizations be responsible for...

Employee welfare
. . . providing medical care, assistance with mortgages, extended sickness leave, assistance for dependents, etc.?

Working conditions
. . . enhanced working surroundings, social and sporting clubs, above minimum safety standards, etc.?

Job design
. . . designing jobs to the increased satisfaction of workers rather than economic efficiency?

Internal aspects

Pollution
. . . reducing pollution below legal standards if competitors are not doing so?

Product safety
. . . danger arising from the careless use of product by consumers?

Marketing practices
. . . curtailing advertising which promotes products which harm health (e.g., tobacco and candy)?

Employment
. . . positive discrimination in favor of minorities?

Community activity
. . . sponsoring local events and supporting local good works?

External aspects

power. Somewhat paradoxically, however, it is often devotees of this school of thought who most resent government "interference" in business affairs.

2. The next group is represented in categories 4 to 7 in Table 5.5. Here social responsibility is exercised in a careful, selective way and usually justified in terms of economic common sense. Sponsorship and welfare provision would be rationalized as sensible expenditures akin to any other form of investment or promotion expenditure. Many companies recognize that this careful attention to aspects of social responsibility could be in the long term interests of the company. For example, the avoidance of "shady" marketing practices will prevent the need for yet more legislation in that area. They argue that if managers wish to maintain discretion, in the long run, over issues such as marketing practices, they are wise to operate responsibly in the short term. Within this group lie companies which would agree with an industrial journalist[25] who, when asked why some companies behave more responsibly than others replied "because some companies are smarter than others!" They

Table 5.5   *Social responsibility, ten roles of the firm.*

Role	Behavior and attitude		
	Economic	*Social*	*Political*
1. *Profit maximizer*	Profit dominates	Regarded as an impediment to profit	Actively avoids involvement with political system
2. *Profit satisfier*	Growth dominates	Reacts against societal and social pressures as incursions	Avoids interaction with political system
3. *Defender of free enterprise*	The business of business is business	Reacts against social component as being not within firm's proper scope	Stands up for "free enterprise"
4. *The lone wolf*	Prime emphasis on profit	Voluntarily but unilaterally assumes responsibility	Avoids involvement unless cornered
5. *Societally engaged*	Prime emphasis on profit	Interactively engaged	Engaged only in negotiation of the rules of the game
6. *Societally progressive*	Prime emphasis on profit	Interactively engaged	Positively involved in formulation of national industrial policies
7. *Global actor*	Prime emphasis on profit	Interactively engaged	Assumes a responsibility to foster a balance between national and international economic policies
8. *Developer of society*	Financial self-sufficiency	Produces changes in the lives of people through innovation	Positively involved with emphasis on planned development of social infrastructures
9. *Social servant*	Secondary to societal obligations	Provides essential but non-economic goods and services	Positively involved in formation of national industrial policies with emphasis on social matters
10. *Employment provider*	Subsidized operation	Provides jobs	Subsidized and supported by government

Source: *Facing Realities — The European Societal Strategy Project — Summary Report*, produced jointly by the European Foundation for Management Development and the European Institute for Advanced Studies in Management, 1981, p. 14.

would argue that management ignores social influences at their peril and that "smarter" companies are those which recognize and cope with these issues in policy making. The conflicts of responsibility which arise here are, for example, between pollution control and job provision. Extra costs of pollution control could mean uncompetitive costs and thus threaten plant closure and loss of jobs.

3. The third category is the "progressive" organization which regards a wide variety of social responsibility issues as an important influence on policy making. (See category 8 in Table 5.5.) The Quaker companies of the last century are a good example and, to a considerable extent, the attitudes of these companies have remained more progressive than others into this century. Companies in this category might argue that they would retain uneconomic units to preserve jobs and would avoid manufacturing "anti-social" products.

Illustration 5.7 lists one company's involvements in the community as an indication of its social responsibility.

ILLUSTRATION 5.7   *Social Responsibility at Imasco Limited*

Some corporations report their involvement in socially responsive activities in annual reports. The statement below is for Imasco Limited, a major Canadian consumer products and services corporation with operations in Canada and the United States. Imasco's wholly-owned operations include Imperial Tobacco, Imasco USA (Hardee's restaurants), Shoppers Drug Mart Stores, Peoples Drug Stores, The UCS Group (tobacco and gift stores), and Imasco Enterprises (98% ownership of Canada Trustco).

In fiscal 1987 Imasco continued its support for charitable and other worthy causes. Total donations to some 500 Canadian organizations amounted to $1.9 million.

Donations are made for social welfare, aid to the disadvantaged, public health, education, cultural, recreational and youth activities. United appeals and capital campaigns of hospitals and universities make up an important part of the donations budget.

In 1981 Imasco established a $100,000 fund to assist disabled students to attend university in response to the United Nations Declaration of the International Year of the Disabled. Since then the fund has awarded 50 scholarships to 27 students. In 1985 $50,000 was added to the original $100,000 and in fiscal 1986 individual awards were increased from $1,500 to $2,000. In fiscal 1987, a further $50,000 was contributed to the fund.

Job creation initiative

For some time, Imasco has expressed its support for private sector initiatives that contribute practical solutions to the economic and social problems caused by unemployment, especially among young Canadians. To help alleviate this problem Imasco committed $7 million to the Montréal Job Creation Initiative in December 1986. This experimental project is designed to create 1,000 permanent jobs over the next three years.

The idea is to sponsor a project whereby entrepreneurs with viable business plans are provided with physical facilities and administrative assistance to start up new enterprises. A team of small business development specialists will manage the project. One Enterprise Centre opened this spring and a second Centre will open later in the year.

The choice of Montréal as the location of the two Enterprise Centres reflects Imasco's commitment to the community in which Imasco's head office is located and in which our principal division, Imperial Tobacco, has been established since 1912.

Sponsorship of sports and the arts

Imperial Tobacco is one of many companies in Canada that recognize the need to support the search for excellence in sports and in the arts. Through support for a number of sports competitions, exhibitions and artistic events associated with product brand names, Imperial Tobacco makes a major contribution to the development of these pursuits in Canada.

The calendar of sports events begins this year with the Canadian Open Golf Tournament, Glen Abbey, Oakville, Ontario, June 29–July 5. Next will follow the du Maurier Classic for women golfers at the Islesmere Golf Club, Montréal, Québec, July 6–12.

Tennis events begin with the Player's International for men in Montréal, August 8–16, followed by the Player's Challenge for women in Toronto, Ontario, August 15–23.

Two equestrian events will be held again this year; the du Maurier International, Spruce Meadows, Calgary, Alberta, September 12–13, and the du Maurier Cup at the Atlantic Winter Fair, Halifax, Nova Scotia, October 17.

Imperial Tobacco will also sponsor the Player's Challenge Series of motor racing events held across Canada from early June to late September.

The du Maurier Council for the Arts

The du Maurier Council for the Arts was established in 1971, and since then has distributed over $5.6 million to performing arts groups across Canada.

Because of the great success of the du Maurier sponsored tour of the Royal Winnipeg Ballet in 1985–86, a second tour was sponsored from November 1986 to April 1987. This tour consisted of 31 performances in 18 Canadian cities.

Also worth mentioning is the du Maurier Council's three-year commitment of more than $1 million towards the cost of building the du Maurier Theatre Centre at Harbourfront, Toronto.

Imasco USA

Imasco USA recognizes its importance to the communities in which it operates and is involved in local and national charitable organizations. Hardee's is the largest corporate sponsor of the International Special Olympic Games, which will be held this year July 31–August 8, in South Bend, Indiana.

Hardee's has pledged a minimum of US $500,000 to the Games. More than 4,500 athletes will take part.

Shoppers Drug Mart

Shoppers Drug Mart continues to develop programmes designed to promote good health and to alleviate the problems of the handicapped. Shoppers has received awards for its help to senior citizens, and has trained its employees to help the hard of hearing. The company is working with the Canadian National Institute for the Blind to produce prescription labels in braille.

Peoples Drug Stores

Peoples Drug Stores contributed over US $245,000 to charitable causes and pledged a further US $243,000 during the fiscal 1987. Peoples continued its long record of public information and educational programmes with a new series of pamphlets, "Help your Health: you can, we can" in cooperation with the National Council on Patient Information and Education.

Political contributions

Imasco provides financial support for political parties and other organizations which stand behind the principles of a strong private business sector and democratic government.

In accordance with a policy approved by the Board of Directors, the Corporation contributed $108,000 to federal and provincial political parties and other causes in fiscal 1987.

Employee participation and encouragement

The Corporation encourages employees at all levels of the organization to take an active part in community activities and in many cases provides assistance for such involvement. Employees are also encouraged to take up active membership in trade and professional associations which have as their aim education, training and the general betterment of the members' abilities and the advancement of their disciplines. In fiscal 1987 some 540 employees participated through company-paid memberships in 459 associations in Canada and the USA.

Source: Imasco Limited, *Annual Report*, 1987, p. 28.

5.7 SUMMARY

This chapter has analyzed how the expectations of individuals and groups might influence an organization's strategies. It has been necessary to look at the expectations of people both inside and outside the organization (e.g. customers, suppliers, financiers). So, what people *want* an organization to do or to be like can influence strategy provided those individuals or groups have sufficient *power*. This has long been thought of in strategic terms under the label of objectives. However, it is misleading to regard objectives in the traditional way, i.e. being "handed down from on high." Preordained objectives are rarely used in formulating strategy except in a very general sense (e.g. the mission of the organization).

Objectives and, indeed, strategies are better thought of as the product of a complex interplay between the issues discussed in this chapter: the expectations of individuals and groups, the values of society, organized groups, and the dominant culture of the organization. These cultural and political issues pervade the organization's structure and systems, influencing the way people behave and the type of person selected into the organization. Such issues need to be understood and analyzed as an essential background against which strategic change can be planned and effected successfully. This theme will be discussed further in later chapters.

References

1. For example: Huw Beynon, *Working for Ford*, (Harmondsworth: Penguin Books Ltd., 1984). Also Michael Edwardes, *Back from the Brink*, (London: Pan Books Ltd., 1983.)

2. The importance of symbolic behavior is underlined by many authors. For example: see Chapter 16 in T. Peters and N. Austin, *A Passion for Excellence*, (New York: Random House, 1985), and T.C. Dandridge, I. Mitroff, W. Joyce, "Organizational Symbolism: A Topic to Expand Organizational Analysis," *Academy of Management Review*, Vol. 5, (1980), pp. 77-82.

3. A.L. Stinchcombe, "Social Structure and Organizations," in J.D. March, ed., *Handbook of Organizations*, (Chicago, Ill.: Rand McNally, 1965), pp. 142–93.

4. The importance of leadership in shaping culture is underlined by Peters and Austin (ref 2), and E.H. Schein, *Organizational Culture and Leadership*, (San Francisco: Jossey-Bass Publishers, Inc. 1985), among others.

5. R.E. Miles and C.C. Snow, *Organizational Strategy, Structure and Process*, (New York: McGraw-Hill, 1978).

6. M. Kanter, *The Change Masters: Innovation for Productivity in the American Corporation*, (New York: Simon and Schuster, 1983), has called this "segmentalist" structures.

7. A number of writers have influenced how we view coalitions in organizations. The following references should be useful for readers who are interested in pursuing this area: R.M. Cyert and J.G. March, *A Behavioral Theory of the Firm*, (Englewood Cliffs, N.J.: Prentice-Hall Inc., 1964);

D. Katz and R.L. Kahn, *The Social Psychology of Organizations*, (New York: John Wiley and Sons, Inc., 1966); J.D. March and H.A. Simon, *Organizations*, (New York: John Wiley and Sons, Inc., 1967); J.D. Thompson, *Organizations in Action*, New York: McGraw-Hill, 1967); A.M. Pettigrew, "Strategy Formulation as a Political Process," *International Studies of Management and Organization*, Vol. VII, No. 2, (1977) pp. 78–87.

8. For a discussion of the influence of the professional on the values and practices of management see the work of R.H. Hall in "Professionisation and Bureaucratisation," *American Sociological Review*, 1968, pp. 92-104, and *Organizations: Structure and Process*, (Englewood Cliffs, N.J.: Prentice-Hall, 1972). Also, J. Pfeffer, *Power in Organizations*, (London: Pitman Publishing Limited, 1981), p. 157.

9. J. Pfeffer, *Power in Organizations*, pp. 37-43, includes an example concerned with educational planning at New York University which is useful for understanding the approach.

10. R.M. Cyert and J.G. March, *A Behavioral Theory of the Firm*, (reference 7), argue that management is usually the dominant stakeholder and its expectations (often growth) tend to influence strategy most strongly.

11. I.C. Macmillan and P.E. Jones, *Strategy Formulation: Power and Politics*, 2nd Edition, (St. Paul, Minn.: West Publishing Co., 1986), p.14, provide some useful definitions of the words "power," "influence," and "authority." Readers should note that in this book the word "power" is used in a much wider sense than their definition, in fact, much nearer to their definition of "authority." The choice was made since it more closely resembles the normal usage of the word "power." The central point to remember is that formal lines of authority do not always describe the *actual* power structure, a point made by M. Dalton, in *Men who Manage* (New York: John Wiley and Sons, Inc., 1959).

12. See for example T. Peters and N. Austin, *A Passion for Excellence*, (reference 2).

13. See for example: D.J. Hickson *et al.*, "A Strategic Contingency Theory of Intraorganizational Power," *Administrative Science Quarterly*, Vol. 16, No. 2, (1971), pp. 216–29 and D.C. Hambrick, "Environment, Strategy and Power Within Top Management Teams," *Administrative Science Quarterly*, Vol. 26, No. 2, (1981), pp. 253–75.

14. Certainly this was found to be the case by J.M. Godiwalla, W.A. Meinhart, and W.D. Warde, in their research documented in *Corporate Strategy and Functional Management* (New York: Praeger, 1979), though Miles and Snow, see reference 5, do point out that in "defender" type companies, production managers may also exercise considerable influence. T. Hill, *Manufacturing Strategy*, Open University, 1985, cites this as a major shortcoming of UK companies compared to many other economies.

15. *Report of the Committee of Inquiry on Industrial Democracy* (Bullock Report), Chairman: Lord Bullock (HMSO, 1977).

16. J. Pfeffer's (reference 9) Chapter 2 is a most interesting discussion of the problems of and approaches to assessing power in organizations.

17. An interesting account of the variety and differences of the objectives of managers may be found in D. Norburn and P. Grinyer, "Directors Without Direction," *Journal of General Management*, Vol. 1, No. 2, (1973-74), pp. 37–48.

18. The idea of a hierarchy of objectives has been used by many writers. For an early example of its use see C.H. Granger, "Hierachy of Objectives," *Harvard Business Review*, Vol. 42, No. 3, (1964), pp. 63–74.

19. See M. Richards, *Organizational Goal Structures*, (St. Paul, Minnesota: West Publishing Co., 1978).

20. See, for example, I. Ansoff, *Corporate Strategy*, (Harmondsworth: Penguin Books Limited, 1968), p.44. He states, "we define an objective as a measure of efficiency of the resource conversion process. An objective contains three elements: the particular attribute that is chosen as a measure of efficiency, the yardstick or scale by which the attribute is measured and the goal — the particular value on the scale which the firm seeks to attain."

21. For a fuller discussion of the issues of social responsibility see K. Davis, "The Case for and against Business Assumption of Social Responsibilities," *Academy of Management Journal*, Vol. 16 , No 2, (1973), pp. 312–22, also E.K. Morgan, "Social Responsibility and Private Enterprise in Great Britain," *National Westminster Bank Quarterly Review*, (May 1977).

22. See, for example, D. Clutterbuck, *How to be a Good Corporate Citizen: Managers' Guide to Making Social Responsibility Work - and Pay*, (New York: McGraw-Hill, 1981). A brief summary is also given in *International Management*, (May 1981), pp. 38-40.

23. Many of the problems arising from differing conceptions of the social roles of organizations in a changing environment are discussed in the report *Facing Realities* published by the European Societal Strategy Project, 1981.

24. This argument is well-illustrated in an article by Milton Friedman entitled "The Social Responsibility of Business is to Increase its Profits," reported by D.J. McCarthy, R.J. Minichiello, and J.R. Curran in *Business Policy and Strategy*, Third Edition, (Homewood, Illinois: Richard D. Irwin Inc., 1979).

25. These comments were made by F. Wright, Business Editor of the *Morning Telegraph*, Sheffield, on a video documentary entitled "Social Responsibility of Companies," made by K. Scholes and A. Wood and produced by Sheffield City Polytechnic Education Services Department, 1979.

Recommended Key Readings

Readers should be familiar with the political context of organizational decision making. We recommend either I.C. Macmillan. *Strategy Formulation; Political Concepts*. St. Paul, Minnesota: West Publishing Co., 1978, or J. Pfeffer. *Power in Organizations*. London: Pitman Publishing Limited, 1981.

Books which deal usefully with strategy as a product of organizational culture are R.E. Miles and C.C. Snow. *Organizational Strategy, Structure and Process*. New York: McGraw-Hill, 1978, and E.H. Schein. *Organizational Culture and Leadership*. San Francisco: Jossey-Bass Publishers, Inc., 1985.

T. Peters and R. Waterman. *In Search of Excellence*. New York: Harper and Row Publishers, 1982, and T. Peters and N. Austin. *A Passion for Excellence*. New York: Random House, 1984, all stress the critical importance of understanding and managing organizational culture in successful organizations.

A more traditional approach to the idea and use of corporate objectives might be useful. The following will help: I. Ansoff. *Corporate Strategy*. Harmondsworth: Penguin Books Limited, 1968 (Chs. 3 and 4), or chapters on objective setting in books by J. Argenti. *Practical Corporate Planning*. London: George Allen & Unwin Publishers Ltd., 1980, and *Corporate Planning*. London: George Allen & Unwin Publishers Ltd, 1968.

On social responsibility: *Facing Realities: The European Societal Strategy Report* available from the European Institute for Advanced Studies in Management (1981).

Part III   *Part III*   *Part III*   *Part III*   *Part III*

Part III   *Part III*   *Part III*   *Part III*   *Part III*

Part III   *Part III*   *Part III*   **Part III**   *Part III*

Part III   *Part III*   *Part III*   *Part III*   *Part III*

Part III   *Part III*   *Part III*   *Part III*   *Part III*

Part III   *Part III*   *Part III*   *Part III*   *Part III*

Part III   *Part III*   *Part III*   *Part III*   *Part III*

Part III   *Part III*   *Part III*   *Part III*   *Part III*

Part III   *Part III*   *Part III*   *Part III*   *Part III*

Part III
STRATEGIC CHOICE

In many ways strategic choice is the core of corporate strategy. It is concerned with decisions about an organization's future and the way it needs to respond to the many pressures and influences identified in the strategic analysis. In turn, the consideration of future strategy must be mindful of the realities of strategy implementation which can be a significant constraint on strategic choice.

Chapter 2 showed that organizations are continually attempting to readjust to their environment and that one of the major criticisms made of managers concerns their inability or unwillingness to consider the variety of strategic options open to the company. Managers tend to remain bound by their recipes and resistant to change. For this reason, this part of the book presents a systematic way of looking at strategic choice. The steps outlined here help to promote a wider consideration of strategy and the appropriateness and consequences of options available to the organization.

The discussion of strategic choice has been divided into three chapters:

- Chapter 6 looks at the strategic options available to organizations and the reasons why some strategies might be viewed more favorably than others.
- Chapter 7 establishes some general criteria (suitability, feasibility and acceptability) against which strategic options might be judged. It also outlines some approaches to assessing the merits of strategies in terms of both their strategic logic and their cultural fit to the organization.
- Chapter 8 looks at techniques which might be helpful in evaluating specific options within the broad framework developed in Chapters 9 and 10. The chapter also discusses how strategies might be selected for implementation.

Chapter 6
STRATEGIC OPTIONS

6.1 INTRODUCTION

The purpose of this chapter is to identify the various strategic options organizations might pursue. The choice between development options is strongly dependent on the particular circumstances of any one organization and this will be discussed in Chapters 7 and 8.

Much of the discussion of strategic choice has been built around the assumption that organizations are concerned with growth as a major objective. Clearly, if organizations wish to grow, they need to seek out new opportunities. While this justification of strategic choice is undoubtedly relevant to a large number of companies, there are also many organizations which, either by choice or circumstances, would not feature growth as a major objective. In fact, during periods of recession many managers will be mainly concerned with the process of managing the organization through a period of retrenchment.

The approach in this chapter, therefore, is to argue that the process of strategic choice must address itself to a wide variety of different situations. Growth is not the reason for strategic choice being necessary; rather, the need lies in the fact that an organization's internal and external circumstances are constantly changing. Change is an absolute prerequisite for long term survival. The emphasis in this chapter is, therefore, on *development strategies* rather than narrower growth strategies.

In reviewing strategic options it is important to distinguish between three separate aspects of any strategy:

1. The *generic strategy* to be pursued, i.e., the basis on which the organization will compete or sustain excellence.

2. The alternative *directions* in which the organization may choose to develop.

3. The alternative *methods* by which any direction of development might be achieved.

Figure 6.1 illustrates these three aspects and also provides a structure for this chapter. While decisions on generic strategy, direction, and method are not independent of each other, they do benefit from separate discussion. For example, an organization pursuing cost leadership may choose to achieve this by market development. However, this still leaves a further choice as to whether entry to new markets is best achieved by acquisition of companies already operating in those markets, or through the company's own efforts, or jointly with other organizations.

To help readers cope with these various complexities, the chapter follows a step-by-step discussion of strategic options in the following way:

- The generic strategies whereby organizations will compete and survive will first be reviewed. There are important links to the concept of the value chain introduced in Chapter 4.

- Strategic options will then be identified in general categories (such as "product development") without discussion of the various methods through which those options might be undertaken.

- These general categories will be discussed in simple product/market terms — from the perspective of a highly specialized organization attempting to review its options. This is not because the majority of companies are in this situation (research, in fact, shows quite the opposite) but because it helps illustrate universally applicable principles for identifying options.

- The different methods of development will then be discussed — again, in general terms without specific reference to any particular development direction.

Figure 6.1 *Development strategies.*

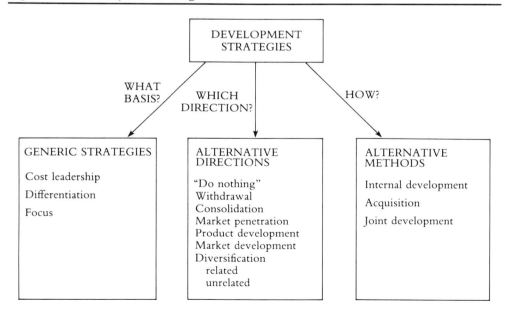

- Chapter 6 will conclude by summarizing the variety of options available to organizations when these aspects are combined. For example, market development by joint development may be achieved by a number of strategies which will be listed.

6.2 GENERIC STRATEGIES

Before considering development directions, it is important to give some thought to the basis on which the organization will compete and/or sustain a superior level of performance. This is what is referred to as choosing the *generic strategy* the organization will follow. This section will review these generic strategies drawing on previous discussions concerning the value chain (Chapter 4) and look forward to the next chapter on the evaluation of strategies.

For commercial organizations, the discussion in this section concerns the establishment of the basis on which a company will build and *sustain competitive advantage*. For public service organizations, it is concerned with the equivalent issue, namely, the basis on which the organization will choose to sustain the quality of its services within agreed budgets. Porter's[1] work is of central importance to this section of the chapter. The purpose of defining the generic strategy of an organization is to ensure that deliberate choices are made about the type of competitive advantage it seeks to attain and the scope within which this will be done (see Figure 6.2). Attempting to be all things to all people is normally a recipe for mediocrity. (Porter calls this "stuck in the middle".)

The figure shows that there are essentially three generic strategies an organization can follow; cost leadership, differentiation and focus. These will now be discussed briefly, and further detailed in Illustrations 6.1 and 6.2.

Figure 6.2   *Three generic strategies.*

COMPETITIVE ADVANTAGE

		Lower Cost	Differentiation
COMPETITIVE SCOPE	Broad Target	1. Cost leadership	2. Differentiation
	Narrow Target	3A. Cost focus	3B. Differentiation focus

Source: M.E. Porter, *Competitive Advantage*, New York: Free Press, 1985, used with permission.

ILLUSTRATION 6.1   *No Frills Vs. Frills: Cost Leadership Vs. Differentiation*

The concepts of cost leadership and differentiation can be illustrated by using examples based on companies which cut frills, or extras, to the minimum, in order to compete, or companies which offer frills to customers as a way of competing. An example of each approach is given below.

Food Lion Inc.

Food Lion is a supermarket chain operating 430 stores in the southeastern United States. The company expects sales of about $3 billion in 1987 and has plans for expansion by adding dozens of additional stores. The company is very profitable with a net profit margin of 2.57%, about twice the industry average.

The company operates no-frills stores and follows a low-price strategy which includes selling some commodity goods, such as cereals and pet foods, at cost. The spartan stores only offer the basics and do not have extras such as flower shops and seafood counters, and as a result, cost less to build, ($650,000 versus $1 million for competitors operating similar size, 25,000 square foot stores). It controls costs tightly and its sales expenses are 14% of sales (about two thirds the industry average) and advertising costs are 0.5% of sales (about one fourth the industry average). The company, and its management, go to great lengths to save money and some of the approaches are:

- Inventory costs are kept low by stocking fewer brands and sizes.
- Advertisements are produced in-house and feature Chief Executive Tom E. Smith in television advertising rather than actors. Newspapers advertisements are kept small.
- Waste heat from refrigeration units is used to warm stores.
- Waste, such as bones and fat, is ground up and sold for fertilizer, recouping about $1 million a year.
- Banana crates are recycled as bins for other items.
- Distribution costs are controlled by locating units within 200 miles of warehouses.
- Unions claim that the company's non-unionized employees are paid lower wages.

Food Lion has obtained a competitive advantage by maintaining a cost structure below that of their competitors allowing them to follow a cost leadership strategy.

All-Frills Airlines

Some airlines are catering to business travellers by providing luxury at reasonable prices. Two examples are McClain Airlines Inc. whose main route is Los Angeles to Chicago and MGM Grand Airline whose main route is Los Angeles to New York.

McClain's frills include: Persian-style carpet; glove-leather seats; four abreast seating instead of the usual six; a telephone in every armrest; seven course meals with china, crystal, and silver; and free drinks on board and in private airport lounges. McClain's fares are about the same as full fare economy on other airlines.

MGM Grand offers even more frills. Its 727's will seat 33 versus the usual 120 and private staterooms are available. There is a bar and dining tables. The fares are about equal to first class airfare on other airlines.

Both airlines are attempting to differentiate their service from that available on regularly scheduled airlines. However, this may be difficult to do since competitors can do some of the same things in their first class sections. Also, other airlines have attempted to concentrate on luxury service in the past and have failed. Whether or not the "frills" will differentiate these airlines sufficiently to attract customers is questionable and this strategy based upon differentiation may not work.

Source: "That Roar You Hear is Food Lion," *Business Week*, (August 24, 1987), pp. 65-6; "Welcome Aboard. The Champagne is on Ice," *Business Week*, (January 19, 1987), pp. 61–2; "These Two Airlines Are Doing It Their Way," *Business Week*, (September 21, 1987), pp. 58 and 62.

6.2.1 Cost Leadership

There are many organizations which sustain their competitive advantage through continued attention to their cost structure in comparison to the competition. For example, cost structure often provides an insuperable barrier to entry through economies of scale in production, R&D, or marketing expenditure. Equally, the concept of the experience curve[2] (see Chapter 4) suggested that cost structure improves markedly as organizations become experienced with new technologies and/or markets. If organizations are to successfully sustain cost leadership across their range of activities, they must be clear on how this is to be achieved through the various elements of the value chain. So, for example, a company may gain cost advantage through its access to low cost sources of raw materials (perhaps achieved through backward integration). Sometimes this applies to other important inputs such as people's time. In many "start-up" situations within large organizations, this time may be "loaned" from mainstream activities — or simply not accounted for.

In other organizations, cost advantage is gained within the organization's own operations — perhaps because of its special skills, technologies or systems, or high levels of capacity utilization.

In other circumstances, marketing activities provide the opportunity for cost advantage. So, for example, an organization with an extensive field sales force is better placed to introduce new products through this sales network than is an organization just starting up. Many government services have found it possible to spread their range of activities at little cost simply because the infrastructure is already in place (e.g. new sports activities in leisure centers). There are also many circumstances where cost advantage can be gained through the special linkages between an organization's value chain and that of channels or customers. Porter argues that these linkages are crucial to defending the organization's position against competition.

For example, some notable business successes recently have been organizations which have found cost advantage in new forms of distribution irrespective of "traditional" demarcation lines. For instance, specialty retail outlets selling paint and wallpaper or servicing automobiles have transformed these industries during the 1970s and 1980s.

It should be clear from these few examples that cost leadership, as a generic strategy, could be applied to any of the specific development directions outlined below. Therefore, when thinking through the merits of various strategies, this overview is important. Strategists need to be certain that a strategy of product development or backward integration would actually contribute to the organization's *overall* generic strategy.

6.2.2 DIFFERENTIATION

Cost leadership is not the only way organizations can sustain their competitive advantage or superior performance. A quite different type of generic strategy is that of *differentiation* of the organization's strategies from those of major competitors. The concept of the value chain should remind readers that differentiation is only of strategic importance if it is recognized and *valued* by consumers/users. Differentiation can be achieved in many ways within the value chain or through linkages with the value chains of suppliers, channels or customers. For example, a restaurant may differentiate itself in terms of quality of food, or service or ethnic cuisines. A savings and loan (or trust company) may choose to have longer opening hours than a bank or a dentist may provide special orthodontic treatment. Sometimes, linkages between different activities within an organization's value chain are of the most importance in sustaining advantage — new strategic directions may well provide an opportunity to strengthen these linkages or even become a new basis of differentiation from other providers.

For example, Allegis Corporation claimed to be a "distinctive partnership of companies" catering to travellers. The company owned United Airlines (serving 150 cities), Hilton and Westin Hotels (151 hotels around the world), Hertz Car Rental (4,500 locations in 12 countries), and United Vacations (vacation packages to Hawaii and the Orient). This attempt at establishing linkages and differentiation may not have worked as well as anticipated because, in 1987, divestiture and/or breakup of the corporation were considered.

6.2.3 FOCUS

The discussion so far has assumed that generic strategies will be applied widely in the market. In many cases this is not so and a key ingredient of an organization's strategic success is the way strategy is *focused*[3] at particular parts of the market. Clearly, when combined with either cost leadership or differentiation, there are two different subcategories of a focus strategy. There are, once again, many forms of this particular generic strategy. So, for example, aiming a product or service at a particular buyer group, segment of the product line, or smaller geographical area are all very common (and successful) ways of focusing. However, an organization then needs to determine whether within this smaller part of the total market they will compete through cost leadership or differentiation. The arguments above are then of relevance to this further decision. A local brewery may be able to compete against the nationals in its own local area by sustaining a better cost structure (due to reduced distribution and marketing costs). On the other hand, the local image of the brewery's products may be the basis of competitive advantage — in which case cutting back on local marketing expenditure would be a mistake.

Within government organizations there are often some very difficult decisions concerning the focus of strategies. For example, a public library service could undoubtedly be run more cost efficiently if it were to pull out of low demand areas and put more resources into its popular branch libraries. Similarly, it would undoubtedly find that an extension of its services into audio and videotapes or new forms of public information services would prove popular. However, the extent to which these strategies would be regarded as part of the library's purpose would be hotly debated. In other words, the objectives of an organization usually prescribe some boundaries to the type of generic strategies to be followed.

For multinational corporations[4] it is important to establish whether the differences between countries/markets are best served by separate "national" strategies (i.e. focus) or whether the potential cost advantage of operating as a truly integrated multinational corporation will provide a more successful strategy for the organization. Many organizations pursue what has been called a *multi-focus* strategy which seeks to combine the benefits of global integration with separate national strategies. For example, in the automobile industry, although the production of major components (e.g. an engine) may be concentrated in a few locations, the supply of materials, components and services for production will be organized locally. This usually proves to be the most cost effective way of operating and also provides the necessary control to maintain reliable schedules and short delivery times. These would be extremely difficult to achieve if the supply of every small component was organized globally.

Small companies often follow very focused strategies with great success. This is usually referred to as a *niche*[5] strategy where an organization is so specialized to the needs of a very small part of the market that it is secure against competition from large organizations. Illustration 6.2 describes how one very large corporation has focused most of its activities on one product and how it has been very successful in following this strategy.

In considering the basis on which an organization should operate and compete, that organization is invariably forced to review the underlying justifications for its choice of strategies. This is an important aspect of strategic evaluation and, as such, is an issue which will be given considerable discussion in Chapter 7. This brief introduction to generic strategies will provide a background to those further considerations.

ILLUSTRATION 6.2   A Focused Strategy at Kellogg

Kellogg Co., a manufacturer of breakfast cereals, is among the best performing packaged-food companies and is doing things to make sure that it remains a market leader.

Kellogg's sales are dominated by, and focused on, a core business, breakfast cereals. About 80% of its sales are from this core business and the company, unlike many of its competitors, has resisted extensive diversification. Maintaining leadership in the cereal business has not been easy. Cereal consumption has leveled off with population growth slowing and consumers changing their preferences from sugar-coated cereals to natural ingredients. Kellogg faces competition from General Mills, Quaker Oats, Nabisco Brands, and Post Cereals. Some of these competitors are owned by large conglomerates with the financial resources to be aggressive competitors. The fact that Kellogg is so narrowly focused in the core cereal business has meant that it must react promptly to any competitive developments in the industry.

Kellogg has introduced many new produts, including Crispix, Raisin Squares, and Nutri-Grain. The company has spent heavily on advertising and promotion to support its traditional products, including Corn Flakes and Rice Krispies, and to introduce the new products.

Some of the new products depend on new high technology manufacturing processes. For example, the company guards very carefully how it gets the two distinct grains together in one piece to produce Crispix and how it wraps cereal around a fruit center to produce Raisin Squares. In addition to emphasizing product development and innovative manufacturing processes, Kellogg is paying attention to basic manufacturing functions such as quality control and the development of fewer but more reliable suppliers. Automation is introduced with caution and only after being tested in a experimental plant in London, Ontario.

The company believes that overseas markets for cereals will provide it with the greatest opportunities for growth in the 1990s. Diversification, if undertaken, will follow the same strategy as in the past. New lines will be in related areas and only entered into after a very disciplined evaluation of the appropriateness to Kellogg's core business.

Source: Andre Picard, "Kellogg's Fibre May Pay Off for Investors with Patience," *The Globe and Mail* (Toronto), August 10, 1987, B11; "The Health Craze Has Kellog Feeling G-r-r-reat," *Business Week*, (March 30, 1987), pp. 52-3.

6.3 ALTERNATIVE DIRECTIONS FOR STRATEGY DEVELOPMENT

This section will set out the strategic directions an organization could take. The *methods* for developing alternative directions will be discussed in later sections. Figure 6.3 summarizes the various alternatives.

6.3.1 "DO NOTHING"

It will be seen in Chapter 8 that the evaluation of strategic options requires a useful basis against which to assess the merits of those options. A valuable base is the "do nothing" situation since this helps with the assessment of whether an organization would have sufficient incentive to change from its current activities. "Do nothing" represents the situation whereby a company continues to follow, in broad terms, its current strategies while events around the company change. For example, the "do nothing" situation for a company facing a declining market would entail no major response to this change, such as developing and launching new products. It would, however, allow for the normal operational changes which occur in any business, such as replacing operatives who leave or continuing to advertise at the same level and in the same manner as before.

Figure 6.3   *Alternative directions for development.*

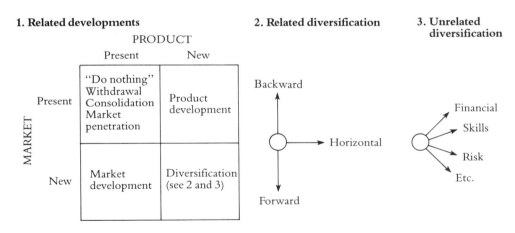

Source: adapted from H. Igor Ansoff, *Corporate Strategy*, Harmondsworth: Penguin Books Limited, 1968, p. 99.

Since most businesses and public service organizations are facing considerable change — both internally and externally — it is rare for "do nothing" to be a viable strategy beyond the very short-term. In this sense, "do nothing" is not really a strategy in the same way as product development or diversification, but is a basis against which these other strategies can be assessed. Nevertheless for *planning purposes*[6] it is helpful to include "do nothing" in the range of options so that it is evaluated with the strategic options under consideration. This provides a discipline in planning which ensures that the "do nothing" situation is not disregarded.

6.3.2 WITHDRAWAL

This is an often overlooked option, although there are many circumstances where complete or partial withdrawal from a market would be the most sensible course of action. Some examples make the point.

- In certain markets the value of a company's products or assets is subject to considerable change over time and a central issue in policy making may be the astute acquisition and disposal of these products, assets, or businesses. This is particularly important for companies operating in markets subject to speculation, such as energy, metals, commodities, land, or property.

- The objective of a small entrepreneur may be to "make his million" and then retire. In these circumstances he may follow policies designed to make the company an attractive proposition to buy rather than being guided by longer term considerations. In family companies this can be a source of considerable conflict between those who hold this view and others who may be more concerned with providing a more stable company for their children to inherit.

- Large, diverse companies may view their subsidiary companies as assets to be bought and sold as part of an overall corporate strategy. This *divestment* or *disinvestment*[7] needs to be carefully planned. The use of disinvestment as a central part of company policy in some multinational companies has proved to be a source of friction between the company and host government.

- During the 1980s, *buy-outs*[8] (either complete or partial) by management and/or employees became quite common. Often they were triggered by the privatization of companies in the government sector.

- Sometimes organizations will partially withdraw from a market by licensing the rights to other organizations. This became common in the government sector where particular services have been privatized.

- The most extreme form of withdrawal is when an organization's position becomes so untenable that voluntary or forced *liquidation* may be the only possible course of action.

In Illustration 6.3, three examples are given of companies which have followed withdrawal strategies. Withdrawal strategies have become much more common in the 1980s as companies attempt to rationalize acquisitions made in earlier years.

ILLUSTRATION 6.3   *Examples of Withdrawal Strategies*

Diversification has been viewed very favorably by many corporations as an approach to growth. However, the approach is not always successful and sometimes leads to problems. The following are three examples of corporations which diversified but later adopted a withdrawal strategy by divesting themselves of some of the acquired companies.

Allegheny International Inc.

Allegheny is a diversified corporation in consumer goods (U.S., Canada and international), technology products, and industrial specialties. Its two most widely known consumer products are Sunbeam appliances and Wilkinson Sword shaving products. The company had diversified extensively through acquisitions, but recently has been attempting to improve performance by divesting many of the acquired firms. The divestments Allegheny has made, or hopes to make, include: in the international consumer businesses: home appliances, printing and packaging, and Wilkinson Sword; in the technology businesses: fire detection and control equipment, computer-controlled welding, aviation products, and semiconductor manufacture; and in the industrial specialties businesses: thermostats, ion-exchange treatments, combustion and pollution control equipment, rings and forgings, and titanium mill products.

Canadian Pacific Ltd.

With revenues of $15 billion, Canadian Pacific (CP) has been one of the largest industrial corporations in Canada. It is a conglomerate with interests in: shipping, trucking, railways, airlines, hotels, real estate, oil and gas, iron and steel, forest products, and mines and minerals. In 1985, management concluded that the diverse business mix was wrong and began to refocus the company in an effort to improve return on equity. CP is concentrating on rail, steel, and resources, and has divested itself of a lead and zinc producer (Cominco) and its airline, Canadian Pacific Airlines.

Greyhound Corp.

During the 1960s and 1970s, Greyhound diversified extensively by acquiring several businesses in consumer products, food services, financial services, transportation services, bus manufacturing, and meat/poultry products. Since 1982, Greyhound has divested itself of several businesses, including: meat packing, computer leasing, knitting supplies, mortgage insurance, and a bus line. Sales peaked in 1982 at about $5 billion, but by 1987 were down to about $2.5 billion. Now that its holdings have been rationalized, the company is seeking acquisition opportunities with the funds generated from the sales of the weak or inappropriate businesses.

These three cases of withdrawal are examples of the "restructuring" occurring in business. Often a company's withdrawal strategy is followed by another period of growth which might even involve acquisitions.

Source: "Why Something's Got to Give at Allegheny International," *Business Week*, (May 19, 1986), pp. 120–2; "Can Greyhound Leave the Dog Days Behind?," *Business Week*, (June 8, 1987), pp. 72–4.

6.3.3 CONSOLIDATION

Consolidation should not be confused with the "do nothing" situation discussed above. The "do nothing" situation exists when a company simply pursues current policies with complete disregard for important changes occurring both outside and inside the company. Consolidation usually implies changes in the specific way the company operates, with the range of products and markets remaining unchanged. Consolidation is equally relevant to growing, static, or declining markets and may take several forms:

1. *Maintaining share in a growing market.* A company operating in markets showing high levels of growth may wish to maintain market share by growing with the market. In fact, the Boston Consulting Group's work[9](see Chapter 4) shows that the pursuit of growth to achieve dominant market share makes strategic sense. The failure to grow in line with the competition is likely to mean that the firm will end up with an uncompetitive cost structure and, when the market reaches maturity, face a very difficult task increasing its market share.

Government services trying to follow any "natural" growth in demand for particular services can face difficult choices. Unless funds can be diverted from other areas then quality of service may decline (e.g. longer waiting lists), "rationing" arrangements may need to be applied, or the service may be withdrawn from particular areas or groups. Other alternatives have also proved necessary such as fund-raising and the introduction of charges or fees.

2. *Consolidation in mature markets.* Different strategic challenges occur in this instance which need to be addressed in different ways. It is common for organizations to *defend* their position by an increased emphasis on *quality* (of product or service), by increased *marketing activity*, or by improving cost structure through productivity gains and/or increasing capital intensity. Any of these can provide barriers to entry for new competitors. How appropriate these approaches will be depends on the basis on which the organization will choose to compete or secure its position (e.g. cost competition or differentiation from competitors). It is interesting to note that the tightening of public funds available to many government services during the 1980s required a major reassessment of quality, marketing and productivity.

3. In *declining markets*,[10] consolidation may require significant changes. For example, strategies may need to be developed to buy up the order book of companies leaving the market; distributors may need to seek new sources of supply; new internal agreements may need to be developed to ensure continuing cost competitiveness in the smaller market. In both public and private sectors, one of the most difficult decisions is whether to reduce capacity, either temporarily (moth-balling) or permanently.

Often during the transition from a mature to a declining market an organization will follow a strategy of *harvesting* (i.e., gaining maximum pay-off from its strong position). This can be done through licensing of technology or distribution rights, leasing of facilities, et cetera. One of the most difficult strategic decisions is how long to *hang-in* with products/ markets which are in short-term decline but where there is some hope of a market recovery. Usually, if *turnaround*[11] cannot be achieved relatively quickly the product/ market may be dropped.

6.3.4 MARKET PENETRATION

The previous section was concerned with options which would maintain a company's market share in its present markets. Opportunities often exist for gaining market share as a deliberate strategy and this is normally referred to as *market penetration*. Much of the previous discussion is relevant to this option since, for example, improving quality or productivity, or increasing marketing activity could all be means of achieving market penetration. Equally, the arguments concerning the long term desirability of obtaining a dominant market share are relevant. However, the ease with which a company can pursue a policy of market penetration will be dependent on the nature of the market and the prevailing competitive position.

When the overall market is growing or can be induced to grow, it may be relatively easy for companies with a small market share, or even new entrants, to gain market share fairly *rapidly*. This is because the absolute level of sales of the established companies may still be growing and indeed, in some instances, those companies may be unable or unwilling to meet the new demand. Import penetration into some industries can be traced back to the early 1970s when companies were unable to supply the peak demand occurring during booms and their customers had to seek alternative sources overseas. Once established with overseas suppliers many users were reluctant to revert to domestic sourcing. When the boom was over the importers held on to their market share. Organizations which have failed to follow the natural growth of a market may need to catch-up at a later date which can often prove more difficult.

In contrast, market penetration in static markets can be much more difficult to achieve. The lessons of the experience curve would, of course, emphasize the difficulty of market penetration in mature markets since the advantageous cost structure of market leaders should prevent the incursions of lower market share competitors. In declining markets it is difficult to generalize the difficulties of pursuing a policy of market penetration. A company determined to confine its interests to one product/market area and unwilling to permit a decline in sales will need to gain market share. If other companies are leaving the market, penetration could prove easy although the wisdom of the strategy may be in some doubt.

Often, market penetration, particularly in mature markets, can only be achieved through collaboration with others. For example, one response to tightening budgets in the government sector has been to reserve part of the available funding to back collaborative ventures — particularly where it is felt that value for money would be increased (e.g., recreational use of school facilities).

6.3.5 PRODUCT DEVELOPMENT

Often companies will feel that consolidation in their present products/markets does not present adequate opportunity and will search for alternatives which build upon the company's present knowledge and skills. In the case of product development, the company will maintain the security of its present markets while changing and developing new products. Some examples will illustrate the many reasons companies might show a preference for product development. Companies in retailing will follow the changing needs of their customers by a continuing policy of introducing new product lines. Sometimes product development is preferred because the company is particularly good at R&D or because it has structured itself around product divisions. When product life cycles are short — as with consumer electronics — product development needs to be a central part of company strategy.

Nevertheless, product development raises uncomfortable dilemmas for firms. New products may be absolutely vital to the future of the firm. The problem is that the process of creating a broad product line is expensive and potentially unprofitable. (The pharmaceuticals industry is a good example.) For these reasons there has been an increased trend towards technology transfer and collaborative ventures. Also, many organizations choose to *renew* the competitiveness of current products through modifications or new marketing approaches.

6.3.6 MARKET DEVELOPMENT

In the case of market development, the organization maintains the security of its present products while venturing into new market areas. Market development can include entering new *market segments*, exploiting *new uses* for the product, or spreading into new *geographical areas*.

Just as companies have good reasons to prefer product development, other companies might have a strong preference for market development. In capital intensive industries, many of a company's assets (money, plant, skilled people) will be specifically devoted to the technology of a particular product. These assets cannot easily be switched to produce any other products. In this situation, the company's distinctive competence lies with the product and not the market and hence the continued exploitation of the product by market development would normally be preferred. Most capital goods companies have developed this way by opening up more and more overseas markets as old markets become saturated. A similar argument applies to organizations whose distinctive competence is in R&D. The rapid worldwide exploitation of microelectronic technology is a good example. Many service industries, such as insurance, banking, and, recently, advertising companies, have been pulled towards globalization — often because some of their major customers are major multinational corporations.

Exporting is an important method of market development. There are a variety of reasons why organizations might want to develop beyond exporting and *internationalize*[12] by locating some of their manufacturing, distribution, or marketing operations overseas. For example, an organization may need to do so for *defensive* reasons — tariff barriers may have been raised or input controls introduced in important overseas markets. There may be operational or logistical reasons which make the international option more favorable, such as changes in the relative costs of labor, transport, or supplies. In contrast, other organizations may be positively seeking international markets to stave off decline in home based demand — for example, in the capital goods industry. The basis on which international expansion could be pursued will be considered more fully below.

Not-for-profit organizations also have often chosen to develop into new markets as the demand for traditional services has moved (particularly due to demographic changes).

Developments have been particularly sought where they would attract significant additional revenue. For example, universities and colleges have developed into new market sectors (e.g. mature students, part-time studies) and also overseas, as the numbers in the traditional age group (18-22 years old) began to fall and public funding remained relatively static.

Examples of product and market development are provided in Illustration 6.4. This Illustration also provides an example of diversification which is discussed in the following section.

ILLUSTRATION 6.4   *Growth Directions at Kodak*

Growth may be achieved in several ways. Eastman Kodak Co. is developing new products for the photography market, is attempting to enter new photography related markets, and is diversifying in several different businesses. This is a marked change for a company that in the past had concentrated on one product area.

Product Development: Kodak has developed and begun to market dozens of new films and has introduced a new line of automatic 35mm cameras. These initiatives are intended to consolidate its dominant position in the film business and to reestablish its position in the camera business.

Market Development: The company is also entering new markets for its products. It has purchased Fox Photo Inc., making Kodak the largest wholesale photo finisher in the US. This purchase also secures a large customer for Kodak photographic paper and chemical products. The company has to reenter the instant photography market after losing a patent case to Polaroid Corp. It has begun to sell faster "minilabs" (one-hour film processing outlets) which use only Kodak paper and chemicals. Additional sales will be sought in foreign markets. By being a sponsor of the 1988 Olympics in Korea, the company hopes to enhance its sales in the fast growing markets of Taiwan, India, and China.

Diversification: Kodak is also attempting to lessen its dependence on the slow growth photography market. Since 1984, the diversification initiatives have included: alkaline and lithium batteries; electronic publishing systems; drug development and manufacture; blood-analysis testing; and optical disk data storage systems. Some of these are more related to the core photography business than others. Most of the diversification has been external, that is, through acquisition rather than by developing the business from scratch.

Eastman Kodak is attempting to grow through related development in new photography products and new markets as well as through diversification.

Source: "Why Kodak is Starting to Click Again," *Business Week*, (February 23, 1987), pp. 134–5 and 138; "Kicking the Single-Product Habit at Kodak," *Business Week*, (December 1, 1986), pp. 36–7.

6.3.7 Diversification

Diversification as a description of strategy is used in different ways by different people. In this chapter, the word will be used in a fairly general way to identify all directions of development which take the organization away from its present products and present market at the same time.[13] However, it is convenient to divide the consideration of diversification into two broad types:

- *Related diversification* represents development beyond the present product and market but still within the broad confines of the "industry" within which the company operates. For example, some footwear manufacturers are distributing their shoes through their own retail chains.
- *Unrelated diversification* is development beyond the present industry into products/ markets which, at face value, bear no clear relationship to the present product/market.

Subsections 6.3.8 and 6.3.9 discuss diversification, its different forms, and the advantages and disadvantages of developing by diversification. It should be remembered, however, that many organizations are already very diverse and may sensibly be needing to ask the reverse question, namely, how far should they specialize their activities. It is not intended to give separate discussion to *specialization* as an alternative since the arguments are simply the reverse of those used in diversification. Readers should bear this in mind when reading the following sections and view them as a discussion of the relative merits of specialization and diversification.

6.3.8 Related Diversification

Referring back to Figure 6.3, it can be seen that although related diversification takes a company beyond its present products and markets, it still keeps the company in areas where it has some knowledge. The new alternatives are within the industry in which the company presently operates. It is important to be clear what is meant by "industry" and to understand some of the terminology commonly used:

- *Industry* refers to all the steps of manufacturing, distribution, and servicing which go into the production and marketing of a company's products, and other products of which they form a part. This is a very broad definition in some cases since, for example, a manufacturer of nylon cloth might be viewed, for this purpose, as being in the same industry as chemical companies, synthetic fiber producers, clothing manufacturers, designers, and retail outlets, to name but a few. In government services the term "industry" is equally relevant and refers to all the activities necessary to design, create, operate, and deliver the services. Readers should note the important link to the concept of the *value chain* introduced in Chapter 4. Essentially, related diversification refers to developments which increase the range of activities within the value chain of the organization. Importantly, it builds linkages which may be unique and a crucial means of sustaining competitive advantage.

- *Backward integration* refers to development into activities concerned with the inputs into the company's present business (i.e. are further back in the value chain). For example, raw materials, machinery, and labor are all important inputs into a manufacturing company.

- *Forward integration* refers to development into activities concerned with a company's outputs (i.e., are further forward in the value chain). Transport, distribution, repairs, and servicing are examples.

- *Vertical integration* is a broader term used to describe either backward or forward integration (or both together).

- *Horizontal integration* refers to development into activities which are either competitive with, or directly complementary to, a company's present activities. A lending library's extension into tourist information services, or video cassette material would be examples.

To simplify reasons why organizations might view related diversification favorably, the case of a manufacturing company can be considered. There are many value activities occurring both before and after the company's own operations which are candidates for related diversification. These are shown in Figure 6.4. Figure 6.5 summarizes the major advantages and disadvantages of such diversifications. Highly diversified companies might see any of these as reasons to increase their degree of specialization. For example, it may be decided that supplies of raw materials have become available from a reliable low-cost source and this provides a good reason to cease the manufacture of those materials within the company. Illustration 6.5 provides an example of related diversification in a services industry.

6.3.9 UNRELATED DIVERSIFICATION

Unrelated diversification refers to options which lie beyond the boundaries of the industry within which the company presently operates. At face value these options may bear no logical relationship to the organization's activities.

Synergy[14] is a commonly quoted reason for unrelated diversification. Synergy can occur in situations where two or more activities or processes complement each other to the extent that their combined effect is greater than the "sum of the parts." Although the success of product and market development strategies can also depend upon synergy, it is a particularly important idea in the case of unrelated diversification. Synergy may result for financial reasons where, for example, one activity generates a short term positive cash flow and another needs such a source of cash. Equally, the good image of a company may be used as a platform to develop into a new line of business which might have proved very difficult without such support. The estimation of the likely benefits synergy can bring can be a method of strategy evaluation and is discussed in Chapter 7.

Other reasons for unrelated diversification may pertain to the aspirations of decision-makers, the opportunity to employ existing underutilized resources in a new field, or the

---

ILLUSTRATION 6.5   *Related Diversification at Ryder*

Ryder System Inc. has diversified from its traditional one-way truck rental business into a "transportation services" company.

Ryder is the largest full-service truck-leasing company in North America and, through internal expansion and dozens of acquisitions, has moved into several related businesses. It is now a major hauler of new cars, the biggest contractor for mass-transit bus systems, and a significant manager of school bus fleets. In addition, it is in the general-freight trucking business. The company now owns 134,000 vehicles and 1,200 repair facilities throughout the country.

Ryder is also diversifying into specialized truck leasing, or the "dedicated-services" business. Ryder contracts with a company to supply trucks and drivers, to handle maintenance, and to plan operations. Although managed by Ryder, the trucks are painted with the client's logo and the drivers wear the client's uniforms. Ryder has over 200 such contracts.

The aviation services operations depart most from the trucking business, but remain in the transportation area. Airlines have begun to contract out the maintenance of aircraft in a effort to free up capital. Ryder has purchased companies doing over $1 billion a year in business overhauling and distributing airplane parts.

Ryder's focus on related diversification in transportation services has enabled it to establish itself as a low cost producer in most areas and to be large enough to influence pricing. This was accomplished in the very competitive environment that developed after the 1980 deregulation of the trucking industry.

Source: "Tony Burns has Ryder's Rivals Eating Dust," *Business Week*, (April 6, 1987), pp. 104–5.

---

desire to move into a different area of activity perhaps because the present one is in decline. These and other reasons are summarized with brief examples in Figure 6.6.

Strategies of diversification raise a number of potential problems as suggested in Figure 6.5. They therefore require organizations to be clear about how the diversified operations will be managed. In particular, there are important decisions concerning the extent to which new activities are integrated with or separated from current operations. These issues will be discussed in Chapter 10.

Illustration 6.3 gave examples of three companies which followed strategies of unrelated diversification. As all three had experienced some difficulties with diversification, it can be assumed that synergy did not exist among the activities, or that management somehow failed to manage the diversified holdings appropriately.

Figure 6.4   *Alternatives open to a manufacturer to develop by related diversification.*

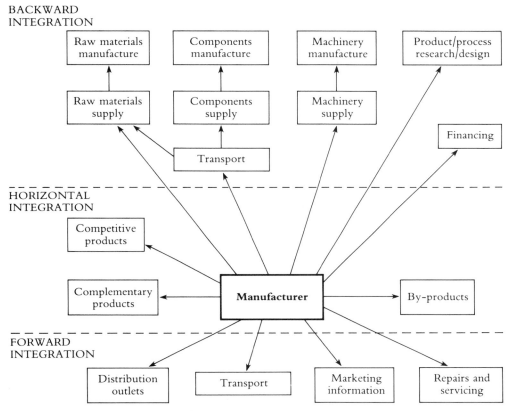

Note: Some companies will manufacture components or semi-finished items. In those cases there will be additional integration opportunities into assembly or finished product manufacture.

6.4 ALTERNATIVE METHODS OF STRATEGY DEVELOPMENT

The previous sections have been concerned with alternative directions in which organizations might develop and the bases on which they could sustain superior performance. However, for each of these alternatives a further choice is also needed, namely, the *method* by which that direction is to be developed. These methods can be divided into three "pure" types: *internal development, acquisition,* and *joint development.*

Figure 6.5   *Some reasons for related diversification.*

A. **Possible advantages**	**Examples / comments**
1. Control of supplies	
• quantity	Clothing manufacturer owns textile plant to secure continuity of supply.
• quality	Components for cars may need to be manufactured by the company.
• price	Printing costs can be reduced if done "in-house".
2. Control of markets	Shoe manufacturer owns a specialty shoe store chain.
3. Access to information	
• technological change	Shoe manufacturers involved in machinery companies to keep abreast of development.
• market trends	Manufacturers concern at being isolated from market trends.
4. Cost savings	Fully integrated steel plants save cost on re-heating and transport.
5. Profit or growth	All sectors of the same industry are not equally profitable at any time.
6. Indirect competition	Manufacturer who owns a raw material supplier may also supply competitors.
7. Spreading risk	Avoids over-reliance on one product/market but builds on related experience.
8. Resource utilization	Manufacturers act as consultants to overseas clients — capitalizing on the know-how.
B. **Possible disadvantages**	
1. Management control	The recipe for success in managing a manufacturing company may not be transferable to a supplier or distribution company.
2. Inefficiencies	In declining industries companies may need to dis-integrate (specialize) as the scale of production declines.

Like most strategic decisions, the choice between these methods is a trade-off between a number of factors, such as cost, speed, and risk. How this trade-off is viewed in any one situation will depend not only on the circumstances of the company but also on the attitudes of those making the decision. This should be apparent since companies within the same industry often have quite different, and long-standing, approaches to development — some always preferring to develop internally, others by acquisition. Before reviewing these alternatives in more detail it is worthwhile looking at the available information about the popularity of these alternatives as methods of development.

Figure 6.6 *Some reasons for unrelated diversification.*

	Reason	Examples/comments
1.	Need to use excess cash or safeguard profit	Buying a tax loss situation.
2.	Personal values or objectives of powerful figures	Personal image locally or nationally may be a strong motive. Many successful businesspeople sink their fortunes into professional sports teams.
3.	Exploiting underutilized resources	Materials are recycled, or manufactured into other products, e.g., coal industry makes building materials from coal waste.
4.	Escape from present business	A company's products may be in decline and unrelated diversification presents the only possible escape.
5.	Spreading risk	Some companies believe that it is good sense not to have all their "eggs in one basket" and so diversify into unrelated areas.
6.	To benefit from synergistic effects	See text.

Both Channon[15] and Sutton[16] provide a detailed picture of the role of acquisition/mergers as a means of strategic development in British industry. Their major conclusions are that development by acquisition tends to go in waves (for example, 1898–1900, 1926–29, 1967–73, and 1985–87), interspersed with long periods where most development (as measured by new investment) occurs internally. Similar patterns of activity have been observed in the United States and other developed countries, particularly in service industries, such as catering or household services, although there has been little written about its extent. The following discussion will attempt to cast some light on the advantages and disadvantages of development internally, by acquisition, or jointly.

6.4.1 INTERNAL DEVELOPMENT

For many organizations, internal development has always been the primary method by which strategy has developed and there are some compelling reasons why this should be so. Very often, particularly with products highly technical in design or method of manufacture, companies will choose to develop new products themselves since the process of development is seen as the best way of acquiring the necessary skills and knowledge to exploit the product and compete successfully in the market place. A parallel argument would apply to the development of new markets by direct involvement. For example, many manufacturers still choose to forgo the use of distributors in export markets since they feel that direct involvement (which they gain from having their own sales force) is of considerable advantage in terms of gaining a full understanding of the market.

Although the final cost of developing new activities internally may be greater than it would by acquiring other companies, the spread of cost may be more favorable and realistic. This is obviously a strong argument in favor of internal development for small companies who simply do not have the resources available, in the short term, to develop in any other way. A related issue is that of minimizing disruption to other activities. The slower rate of change internal development brings usually makes it favorable in this respect.

It is often forgotten that a company may, in reality, have no choice about how new ventures are developed. Companies breaking new ground are not in a position to develop by acquisition or joint development since they are the only ones in the field. This problem is not confined to such extreme situations. On many occasions, organizations which would prefer to develop by acquisition cannot do so since they cannot find a suitable company willing to be bought out. This has been cited as a particular difficulty for foreign companies attempting to enter Japan.[17] Internal development also avoids the often traumatic behavioral problems arising from acquisition.[18] The cultures of the acquiring and acquired companies may be incompatible.

There are also many reasons why companies find it difficult or inappropriate to develop new strategies internally. These reasons will be discussed in the next section since the shortcomings of internal development are very often the reasons for preferring acquisition as a method of development.

6.4.2 Acquisition

Perhaps the most compelling reason to develop by acquisition is the speed with which it allows the company to enter new product/market areas. In some cases, the product and/or market is changing so rapidly that this becomes the only way of successfully entering the market since the process of internal development is too slow by comparison. Another common reason for acquisition is the lack of knowledge or resources to develop certain strategies internally. For example, a company may be acquired for its R&D expertise, its knowledge of property speculation, or its particular type of production system.

The overall cost of developing by acquisition may, in certain circumstances, be particularly advantageous. A company going into liquidation may be a good buy. An extreme example is asset-stripping where the sole motive for the acquisition is short term gain by buying up undervalued assets and disposing of them piecemeal.

The *competitive situation* may influence a company to choose acquisition. In static markets when the market share each company controls is reasonably steady, it is often a difficult proposition for a totally new company to enter the market since their presence would upset this equilibrium. If, however, the new company chooses to enter the market by acquisition, the risk of competitive reaction is reduced. The same arguments also apply when an established supplier in an industry acquires a competitor either for the latter's order book (market share) or to shut down its capacity to help restore a situation where supply/demand is more balanced and trading conditions are more favorable.

Sometimes there are reasons of cost efficiency which would make acquisition more favorable. This cost efficiency could arise from the fact that an established company may already be a long way down the learning curve and may have achieved efficiencies which would be difficult to match quickly by internal development. In the public sector, cost efficiency is usually the stated reason for merging units and/or rationalizing provision.

Many of the problems associated with acquisition have been hinted at in the discussion of internal development. In essence, the overriding problem with acquisition lies in the ability to *integrate* the new company into the activities of the old[19] — an issue which will be given much fuller consideration in later chapters.

6.4.3 JOINT DEVELOPMENT

Joint development of new products/markets has become increasingly popular since the early 1970s. The advantages of joint development can best be illustrated by describing some of the different types of joint development which occur.

1. *Joint ventures*[20] are formal agreements between two or more corporations to form another entity in which all have an equity interest. The strategy is based on the fact that the partners in the joint venture are able to accomplish tasks, or become involved in projects, which likely would be impossible to undertake individually. There are many different circumstances where joint ventures are used. Large civil engineering projects normally require the pooling of several specialist skills, as do major aerospace undertakings. Joint ventures are often used in the opening up of new overseas markets. Partners are sometimes involved to assist in financing a new product, or to provide other resources, such as production, technological, or managerial "know how." Illustration 6.6 describes an example of joint venturing where two companies in a maturing industry are seeking to improve production efficiently by rationalizing their manufacturing plants.

2. *Franchising*[21] is perhaps the best known and most common type of joint development. The details of a franchise agreement can vary considerably but the underlying rationale is the same. The advantages of franchising arise from the fact that each of the parties to the agreement has a particular strength, or interest, in only part of the development process and these two interests are complementary. Perhaps the best known franchising system internationally is the Coca Cola Company. Coca Cola's part in development is its product, its unrivaled brand name, and mass consumer advertising. Franchise holders are responsible for producing, bottling, distributing, and selling Coca Cola (or just some of these activities). By this means, both parties benefit since they are able to use their own limited resources to greater overall effect.

3. *Licensing*[22] arrangements are a form of franchising common in science-based industries, such as chemicals. The R&D department of a chemical company may develop and patent more products than the company is able to manufacture itself. Licenses are, therefore,

---

ILLUSTRATION 6.6   *A Joint Venture in the Tire Industry*

Sometimes environmental circumstances make it logical for companies to participate in a joint venture. An example is provided from the North American tire industry.

The North American tire industry has experienced several major changes. The market has matured and manufacturers have closed 15 plants in the United States since 1979 to eliminate excess capacity. Technological developments have resulted in the production of radial tires which last up to three times longer than previous generation tires. The bias-ply market, once the core of the North American tire industry, has declined to about one fourth of its size ten years ago. Imports are supplying a significant portion of the replacement auto tire market.

It was in this environment that B.F. Goodrich Co. and Uniroyal Inc. decided to merge their tire operations in an equally-owned joint venture to be known as Uniroyal Goodrich Tire Co. Cutbacks to improve efficiency had occurred at both companies and even more economies would be achieved in the joint venture. Five hundred overlapping jobs in manufacturing operations would be eliminated. Uniroyal would benefit from Goodrich's superior rubber-mixing technology and Goodrich would be able to use Uniroyal's tire-curing facilities since its own are not adequate.

The new company would continue to sell Uniroyal and Goodrich brand names and maintain separate sales networks. Some products would be competing against each other and redundant services would be provided by the dealer networks. Nevertheless, the joint venture has created a stronger operation from two of the weakest firms in the industry; one that is more likely to survive in a very competitive, mature industry.

Source: "Uniroyal Goodrich: The New Tough Guy in Tires," *Business Week*, (September 22, 1986), p. 72D.

---

granted to other manufacturers who pay a fee or royalty to the patent holder. Licensing is also used as a means of developing overseas markets without the need to be involved in local manufacture from the US or Canada.

4. *Agents* have been used in joint developments for many years. Many companies develop overseas markets by using local agents not only because of their better local knowledge but also because this is the most cost efficient way to operate. This is particularly true in markets where levels of sales are relatively low and hence do not justify the full time attention of even one sales representative.

The attractiveness of joint ventures could, arguably, increase as environmental change accelerates. For example, given the rate of obsolescence of plant due to technological innovation, it could well be advantageous for a company to consider becoming a marketing and distribution operation working on a joint venture basis with a manufacturer who is more specialized in the necessary field of technology.

6.5 SUMMARY

This chapter has been confined to an identification of the strategic options available to organizations as they develop and change. Before reviewing specific options, it is valuable to establish the *basis* on which the organization will sustain its competitive advantage or excellence. Options have been reviewed in terms of both development *directions* and *methods*. Table 6.1 pulls together both of these facets and provides a summary of the options considered in the chapter.

Table 6.1 *Summary of strategic options.*

Development directions	Development methods		
	Internal	*Acquisition*	*Joint*
1. "Do nothing"	–	–	–
2. Withdraw	Liquidate	Complete sell-out Partial divestment Management buy-out	Licensing Subcontracting
3. Consolidation	Grow with market Increase: quality productivity marketing Capacity reduction/ rationing	Buy and shut down	Technology transfer Subcontracting
4. Market penetration	Increase quality productivity marketing	Buy market share Industry rationalization	Collaboration
5. Product/service development	R&D Modifications Extensions	Buy-in products	Licensing Franchising Joint ventures Lease facilities
6. Market development	Extend sales area Export New segments New uses	Buy competitors	New agents Licensing Joint ventures
7. Backward integration	Switch "focus"	Minority holdings	Technology sharing Exclusive agreements
8. Horizontal integration	New units	Buy subsidiaries	Tied arrangements
9. Forward integration	Create subsidiaries		Franchising Joint ventures
10. Unrelated diversification			

It needs to be recognized that such a listing of options is simply the beginning of the process of strategic choice since the appropriateness of these various options will need to be assessed in the light of an organization's circumstances. The next two chapters will deal with this process of *evaluation* in two stages. Chapter 7 establishes the broad criteria and rationale for matching options with circumstances and Chapter 8 reviews a range of useful evaluation methods for specific options and assesses methods by which organizations actually select strategies to pursue.

References

1. Michael Porter discusses generic strategies in Chapter 2 of *Competitive Strategy*, (New York: Free Press, 1980) and in *Competitive Advantage*, (New York Free Press 1985).

2. P. Conley, *Experience Curves as a Planning Tool*, 1978. (Pamphlet available from the Boston Consulting Group.)

3. Marketing strategy has long acknowledged the importance of market segmentation, a common form of focus strategy. For example, P. Kotler, *Marketing Management*, Fourth Edition, (Englewood Cliffs, N.J.: Prentice-Hall Inc., 1980), Chapter 8.

4. See: Y. Doz, *Strategic Management in Multinational Companies*, (Oxford: Pergamon Press Limited, 1986).

5. P. Modiano and O. Ni-Chionna, "Breaking into the Big Time," *Management Today*, (November 1986) looked at the growth of 16 companies in the UK electronics industry and cite "niche" strategies as a critically important ingredient of their competitive strategy.

6. For example, the "do nothing" situation can be used as a baseline when undertaking financial assessments of strategic options, e.g., through discounted cash flow.

7. S. Slatter, *Corporate Recovery*, (Harmondsworth: Penguin Books Limited, 1984), (Chapter 7) and J. Coyne and M. Wright, eds., *Divestment and Strategic Change*, (Oxford: Philip Allan Publishers Ltd., 1986).

8. See H. Parker, "How to Buy Out", *Management Today*, (January, 1986), pp. 69–71.

9. See references in Chapter 4.

10. M.E. Porter, (see reference 1), Chapter 12. Also, K.R. Harrigan, "Strategies for Declining Industries", DBA dissertation, Harvard University, 1979, on which parts of the chapter are based.

11. See S. Slatter, *Corporate Recovery*, (reference 7).

12. See Y. Doz, *Strategic Management in Multinational Companies* (reference 4).

13. Our use of the term "diversification" is similar to that used by I. Ansoff, *Corporate Strategy*, (Harmondsworth: Penguin Books Limited, 1968). In Chapter 7, Ansoff identifies general reasons why firms might choose diversification as a method of development.

14. The idea of synergy is well explained by I. Ansoff in *Corporate Strategy*. Also, I. Ansoff, *Implanting Strategic Management*, (Englewood Cliffs, N.J.: Prentice-Hall Inc., 1984), pp. 80–4.

15. D.F. Channon, *Strategy and Structure of British Enterprise*, (New York: Macmillan, 1973), based on his research on an analysis of the "Times Top 500" companies in an attempt to replicate earlier studies in the US, notably by Chandler (1962). His findings on the relationship between strategy and structure will be discussed in Chapter 10. At this stage, his observations of how acquisition and merger have been part of the development of UK companies is interesting.

16. C.J. Sutton, *Economics and Corporate Strategy*, (Oxford: Cambridge University Press, 1980). See Chapter 7.

17. J. Capito, "Joining with Japan," *Management Today*, (April, 1983), reviews many of the difficulties foreign companies can face in attempting to acquire Japanese companies. However, he also cites successful examples of such acquisitions.

18. For interesting examples of the turmoil that can result from acquisition see M. Fenton, "Tale of a Takeover," *Management Today*, (September, 1979), pp. 78–81; A. van de Vliet and D. Isaac, "The Mayhem in Mergers," *Management Today*, (Feb. 1986), pp. 38–41; R. Heller, "The Agonies of Agglomeration," *Management Today*, (February, 1986), pp. 42–7.

19. See reference 18.

20. For a comprehensive review of the management of joint ventures, see K.R. Harrigan, *Managing for Joint Venture Success*, (Lexington, Mass: Lexington Books, 1986).

21. See N. Mendelsohn, *Guide to Franchising*, Third Edition, (Oxford: Pergamon Press Limited, 1982), or W.L. Seigel, *Franchising*, (New York: John Wiley and Sons, Inc., 1983).

22. C. Edge, "Britain's Innovation Trap," *Management Today* (November, 1985), pp. 82–7, cites collaborative ventures and technology transfer as important ingredients in the R&D strategies of many companies.

Recommended Key Readings

For an interesting discussion of strategies appropriate to companies in differing market environments see M.E. Porter. *Competitive Strategy*. New York: Free Press, 1980.

Porter (Chapter 2) also reviews the generic strategies available to organizations. This discussion is repeated in M.E. Porter. *Competitive Advantage*. New York: Free Press, 1985.

L.L. Byars. *Strategic Management*. New York: Harper and Row, 1984. Chapter 3 also looks at strategic alternatives.

Chapter 7

Strategy Evaluation: Criteria and Approaches

7.1 INTRODUCTION

The previous chapter has identified a variety of ways organizations may choose to develop. The purpose of this chapter is to discuss some general *approaches* to evaluating these various options. However, it is first necessary to establish the *criteria* against which organizations would "judge" the merits of particular options. These criteria often conflict with each other and evaluation usually requires sensible judgments on how these differing requirements should be weighed.

In order to clarify how organizations might approach these difficult issues of strategic evaluation, the discussion has been divided into two parts. Chapter 7 will look at some general approaches to strategic evaluation. In particular, emphasis will be placed on how an organization's circumstances might dictate the type of strategies it follows. Chapter 8 will look at methods and techniques for evaluation of specific options.

7.2 EVALUATION CRITERIA

A useful way of looking at evaluation criteria is to view them as falling into three categories:

1. Criteria of *suitability* which attempt to measure how far proposed strategies fit the situation identified in the strategic analysis. Does the strategy, for example, capitalize on the company's strengths, overcome or avoid weaknesses, and counter environmental threats?

2. Criteria of *feasibility* which assess how any strategy might work in practice. For example, whether the strategy is achievable in resource terms.

3. Criteria of *acceptability* which assess whether the consequences of proceeding with a strategy are acceptable. For example, will it be profitable or generate the growth expected

by senior management, shareholders, or other stakeholders? One important measure of acceptability is the level of risk involved in any strategy.

The review of evaluation techniques in Chapter 8 will show that different methods tend to focus on one or perhaps two of these criteria. Firstly, however, a little more needs to be said about the evaluation criteria.

7.2.1 Suitability

One of the prime purposes of strategic analysis is to provide a clear picture of the organization and the environment in which it is operating. A useful summary of this situation might include a listing of the major opportunities and threats facing the organization, its particular strengths and weaknesses, and any objectives which have a particularly important influence on policy.[1]

   One important measure of evaluation is the extent to which any strategy addresses the situation described in the strategic analysis. Some authors[2] have referred to this as "consistency." Certain questions need to be asked about any strategic option such as:

- How far does it overcome the *difficulties* identified in the strategic analysis (such as, resource weaknesses or environmental threats)? For example, is the strategy likely to improve the organization's competitive standing, resolve the company's liquidity problems, or decrease dependence on a particular supplier?

- Does it exploit the company's *strengths* and environmental *opportunities*? For example, will the proposed strategy provide appropriate work for skilled craftsmen, help establish the company in new growth sectors of the market, or utilize the present, highly efficient distribution system?

- Does it fit in with the organization's *objectives*? For example, would the strategy entail trading with countries the company would prefer not to, imply loss of control for the owner/manager, or require dropping present products?

7.2.2 Feasibility

An assessment of the feasibility[3] of any strategy is concerned with whether or not it can be implemented. For example, the scale of the proposed changes needs to be achievable in resource terms. As suggested earlier, this process will already have started during the identification of options and will continue through into the process of assessing the details of implementation. However, at the evaluation stage there are a number of fundamental questions to be asked when assessing the feasibility of any strategy:

- Can the strategy be *funded*?

- Is the organization *capable* of performing to the required level (e.g., quality or service level)?

- Can the necessary *market position* be achieved and will the necessary marketing skills be available?

- Can *competitive reactions* be coped with?
- How will the organization ensure that the required *skills* at both managerial and operative levels are available?
- Will the *technology* (both product and process) to compete effectively be available?
- Can the necessary *materials* and services be obtained?

This is not a definitive list but it does illustrate the broad range of questions to be answered. It is also important to consider all of these questions with respect to *timing* of the required changes.

7.2.3 ACCEPTABILITY

The third measure of evaluation is acceptability. This is concerned with an assessment of whether the consequences of proceeding with a strategy are acceptable. This can be a difficult area since acceptability is strongly related to people's expectations. The issue of "acceptable to whom" requires that the analysis be thought through carefully. Some of the questions to help identify the likely consequences of any strategy are:

- What will be the financial performance of the company in *profitability* terms? The parallel in the public sector would be cost/benefit assessment.
- How will the *financial risk* (e.g., liquidity) change?
- What will be the effect on *capital structure* (e.g., leveraging or share ownership)?
- Will any proposed changes be acceptable to the general *expectations* within the organization (e.g., attitudes to greater levels of risk)?
- Will the *function* of any department, group, or individual change significantly?
- Will the company's relationship with outside *stakeholders* (e.g., suppliers, government, unions, customers) need to change?
- Will the strategy be acceptable in the company's *environment* (e.g., will the local community accept higher levels of noise)?
- Will the proposed strategy *fit existing systems* or will it require major changes?

Clearly, a new strategy is unlikely to be the ideal choice for all stakeholders. The management of stakeholder expectations is therefore crucial and will be discussed in Chapter 11.

Illustration 7.1 shows how the criteria of suitability, feasibility, and acceptability can be used to help evaluate a strategic option.

7.3 ASSESSING THE SUITABILITY OF OPTIONS

Chapter 8 will review a variety of methods whereby strategic options can be evaluated — either separately or against each other. However, the sheer number of considerations involved in evaluating a range of options can be quite bewildering. For this reason organizations need to be clear about the types of options which make sense in their particular circumstances. They also need to establish the *rationale*[4] for pursuing one or more of these strategies. It is at this stage — effectively a short-list — where more detailed evaluation is both necessary and practical. Options are only given further consideration (at least in the first instance) if they would appear to suitably address the situation identified in the strategic analysis. Figure 7.1 outlines the approach taken to evaluation in these two chapters.

In Part II of this book there was a continuing emphasis on strategy-making as a process of balancing the (often conflicting) demands of the environment, an organization's resource capability, and the expectations people had of the organization and its development. This same theme is of equal importance during strategic choice.

Good choices of strategy are ones which pay attention to each of these "pressures" from the environment, resources, and expectations. It should be made clear that "proper attention" does not normally mean equal attention. It is usual that one of these factors will be taken as the perspective from which strategies are reviewed, while the other two factors will be regarded as constraints. There is a danger in assuming that a product/ market (environment-led) perspective is the only way to assess strategic options. The dominance of such a viewpoint in the literature is undoubtedly due to the excessive attention paid to strategic development during growth — at the expense of a fuller consideration of a range of different circumstances.

Figure 7.1 *A framework for evaluating strategies.*

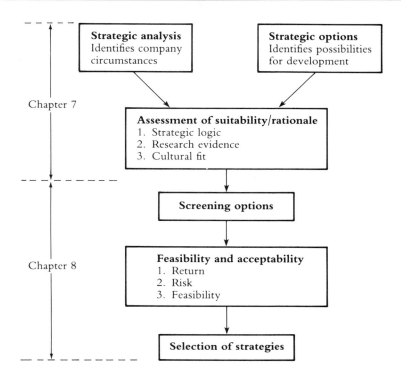

ILLUSTRATION 7.1   *Assessment of the Options: Make or Buy in the Automobile Industry*

A strategic decision many manufacturing companies face is whether or not to make parts and components required in the manufacturing process in-house, or to purchase them from outside suppliers. This decision for the North American automobile industry is examined below using the "suitability," "feasibility," and "acceptability" evaluation criteria discussed in this and the next chapter.

As one aspect of cost-cutting plans, General Motors (GM) Corp., Ford Motor Co., and Chrysler Corp. are reassessing whether or not to manufacture parts and components in-house, or to purchase them from suppliers, referred to as "out-sourcing." GM is the most vertically integrated of the three North American manufacturers; building about 70% of the parts used in its vehicles. Examples of its in-house suppliers include: Hydra-matic Division, automatic transmissions; Delco Moraine Division, brake systems; Rochester Products Division, fuel systems; and Central Foundry Division, castings. Ford and Chrysler are not vertically integrated to any extent. Whereas GM acquires most of its parts and components in-house, Chrysler, for example, obtains about 70% of its parts and components from outside suppliers, but recently has indicated that it might shift some of its parts supply to in-house sources.

There are pros and cons to both methods, and in 1987, the industry was reassessing its position regarding in-house manufacturing versus out-sourcing. In particular, GM was considering assigning more work to outside suppliers. The company is planning to rationalize its parts and components in-house suppliers and also to reduce the size of its parts-making operations which have employed 150,000 workers. The table below summarizes some of the implications GM would have to consider with this change in strategy. The points made here would be similar for other manufacturers.

	Manufacture parts and components in-house	Obtain parts and components by out-sourcing
Suitability	• More reliable supply. • Easier to monitor supply source. • As market preferences change, it is more difficult to shift to new parts needs. • Not always cheaper, but if managed properly, should be cost competitive.	• Flexibility in response to shifting market demands provided by opportunity to "shop" around for parts and ability to change suppliers on short notice. • Cost kept low as auto parts industry very competitive. • May complement efforts to reduce costs.

Feasibility	• Investment required to finance plants and operations. • If plants exist, may have to modernize. • May be difficult to plan and coordinate multiple divisions. • Technology available, but may not be the most recent. • Challenge of balancing parts manufacturing plants output with demands of automobile plant production.	• Adequate suppliers of auto parts exist. • Specialized parts manufacturers involved in R&D and technological advances. • No need to balance plant size and car sales.
Acceptability	• In theory, car divisions can shop around for higher quality and lower prices for parts. • In practice, car divisions often locked into "allied plant" suppliers. • Sometimes in-house contracts are long term and supply parts for the entire manufacturing life of a car model (i.e., committed to same suppliers for long term). • Higher financial risk.	• Supplier might be reluctant to accept strict quality, cost, and delivery specifications. • In order to win contracts, suppliers must compete against artificially low internal division costs. • Capable of weeding out weaker, unsatisfactory suppliers. • Risk of suppliers failing to deliver and to meet JIT demands. • Labor unions in opposition. • May be resistance from divisional management.

Organizations operating in very stable environments may be mainly concerned with *resource utilization* and this will be a more relevant perspective from which to review options (see Table 7.1). The idea of *distinctive competence* discussed in Chapter 4 is seen as the main issue steering company strategy. Product/market opportunities and expectations become constraints on a company attempting to capitalize on this distinctive competence.

For many public service organizations, strategic development centers around the issue of how a *limited resource* should best be used. Usually there are many more demands than can be satisfied. In these circumstances, strategic choice is either dominated by resource capability (i.e., what the organization is best and/or most efficient at providing) or by the expectations of those with the most power who will dictate priorities.

Similarly, there are many other circumstances when the dominant expectations of an organization are the appropriate perspective from which to assess options. New business ventures tend to be dominated by the expectations of the founder, which are not always expressed in product/market terms. The desire to be independent or successful can be very important. A similar situation can recur in an organization at a later date, caused by unexpected or difficult events such as the loss of a major customer or supplier when short term survival, almost at any cost, dominates company strategy. In such a *turnaround* situation, strategic options are assessed primarily by this measure.

In order to provide a properly balanced view of the different approaches to strategic evaluation, the remainder of this chapter will present readers with a variety of approaches reflecting these different perspectives. For convenience, these approaches have been divided into three groups:

1. Approaches which attempt to establish a *strategic logic* linking the nature of the product/market and the resource capability of the organization to the suitability of particular types of strategy.

2. Approaches based on the *research* evidence of how organizational performance is related to choice of strategy.

3. *Cultural fit* approaches where the emphasis is on understanding how well strategies fit the culture and expectations of the organization and the extent of cultural change which would be required to make that strategy work.

Although, in general, each approach might be more or less useful in different circumstances, it must be stressed that essentially they are not alternative approaches. Indeed,

Table 7.1   *Different perspectives for assessing strategic options.*

	Perspectives	*Options concerned with:*	*Constraints*	*Most applicable to situation of:*
1.	Environment (product/market)	Satisfying market opportunities	Resource utilization Expectations	Growth Retrenchment
2.	Resource utilization	Capitalizing on the company's distinctive competence	Environmental opportunities Expectations	Stability Limited resource
3.	Culture/expectations	Meeting the needs of powerful individuals or groups	Environmental opportunities Resource utilization	New companies Turnaround Sudden change Limited resource

readers should feel that strategic evaluation will be improved if a number of approaches are taken since these can provide valuable, and complementary, insights into the appropriateness of various strategies.

7.3.1 STRATEGIC LOGIC

The literature on strategic evaluation has been dominated since the 1950s by rational/ economic assessments of strategic logic. In this section, the discussion will be limited to reviewing a small number of these frameworks indicative of the general approach to strategic evaluation taken by such assessments. Essentially, they are all concerned, in different ways, with matching particular strategic options with an organization's market situation and its relative strategic capabilities. The following four approaches will be briefly reviewed:

1. *Product portfolio analyses* which place emphasis on the nature of the markets (particularly growth rate) and an organization's competitive standing.

2. *Life cycle analyses* which are refinements and extensions of product portfolio analyses and pay more detailed attention to stages in an industry life cycle.

3. *Competitive advantage analyses* which further refine considerations of an organization's ability to sustain its competitive advantage.

4. *Synergy* which is concerned with assessing the value that can be created from a given resource-base — particularly in circumstances where different ventures may be "pulled together" (e.g., mergers or rationalizations).

Although most of the literature is concerned with private sector profit-seeking organizations, the lessons are equally valid in the public sector and the following sections will attempt to interpret the discussion in this context.

Product Portfolio Analyses

Most of the discussion in Chapter 6 was concerned with the analysis of competitive strategies or activities of single organizational units. However, much of the strategic evaluation at the center of large, diverse organizations takes a somewhat different perspective from that at the level of the individual business unit. Literature[5] in the field of corporate strategy draws strong distinctions between the former, called "corporate strategy," and the latter, referred to as "business strategy." In a large and diverse organization, a prime concern for evaluation at the corporate level is to achieve a balanced range (or portfolio) of businesses or activities. The product portfolio concept has already been mentioned in Chapter 6 as a possible justification for unrelated diversification. The idea evolved from the work on experience curves of the Boston Consulting Group (BCG) as described in Chapter 4. Figure 7.2a) illustrates the simple BCG matrix used to indicate where each business activity lies in relation to two factors: market growth rate and market share. It should be remembered that this type of analysis can be used to look at whole businesses (e.g., within a group) or to look at business activities (e.g., products) within any one company. Future options can be plotted onto the matrix in the same way. This matrix can then be used as a guide on a number of important strategic questions relating to the evaluation of future strategies:

- How far will the proposed new strategy improve the company's portfolio of interests? For example, will it help develop business growth areas while removing the dogs that drain cash flow for no long term reward?

- Since stars generally require an investment of funds, will there be sufficient cash cows to provide this necessary investment? This is an important question about the balance of the portfolio. For example, a major reason for company bankruptcies is that a firm may be investing heavily in promotion and stocking policy for products in rapid growth without profitable and well-established products from which it can fund these new ventures.

- In government services[6] it is extremely important to have a balance of activities which matches the range of skills within the organization, otherwise certain groups are badly over-stretched while others remain underemployed.

- Another issue of importance in government services is the political acceptability of the portfolio of activities. Often, the more exciting developments will only be sanctioned if sufficient resources and attention are given to the mundane everyday activities and services.

- There are some situations where dogs may need to be kept since they provide a necessary platform for the successful development of stars or keep competitors' cash cows under threat. A car manufacturer might argue that it needs to be involved in the low profitability bulk market if it wishes to operate in the more specialist, profitable sectors of the market. It is in the former activity that the skill of making cars is learned and improved.

- The long term rationale for product or business development can be highlighted by the matrix. Which strategies are most likely to ensure a move from question marks through to stars and eventually cash cows? In short, is the company likely to dominate its particular markets?

- The matrix can also help in thinking about acquisition strategy. Companies embarking on acquisition programs often forget that the most likely targets for acquisition are not the stars and cash cows of the business world but the question marks or dogs. There may be nothing wrong with acquiring a question mark provided the resources are there to move it towards "star-dom," bearing in mind the real costs and difficulties of acquisition as pointed out in Chapter 6.

There have been a number of refinements and modifications to the original BCG matrix; three of these are illustrated in Figure 7.2 and can be followed up in the references.[7] These matrices can be used in the way described above.

Product portfolio analysis is not a comprehensive evaluation technique. As an evaluation technique, its scope is limited. It is a preliminary step in any evaluation and helps to

Figure 7.2 *Product portfolio matrices.*

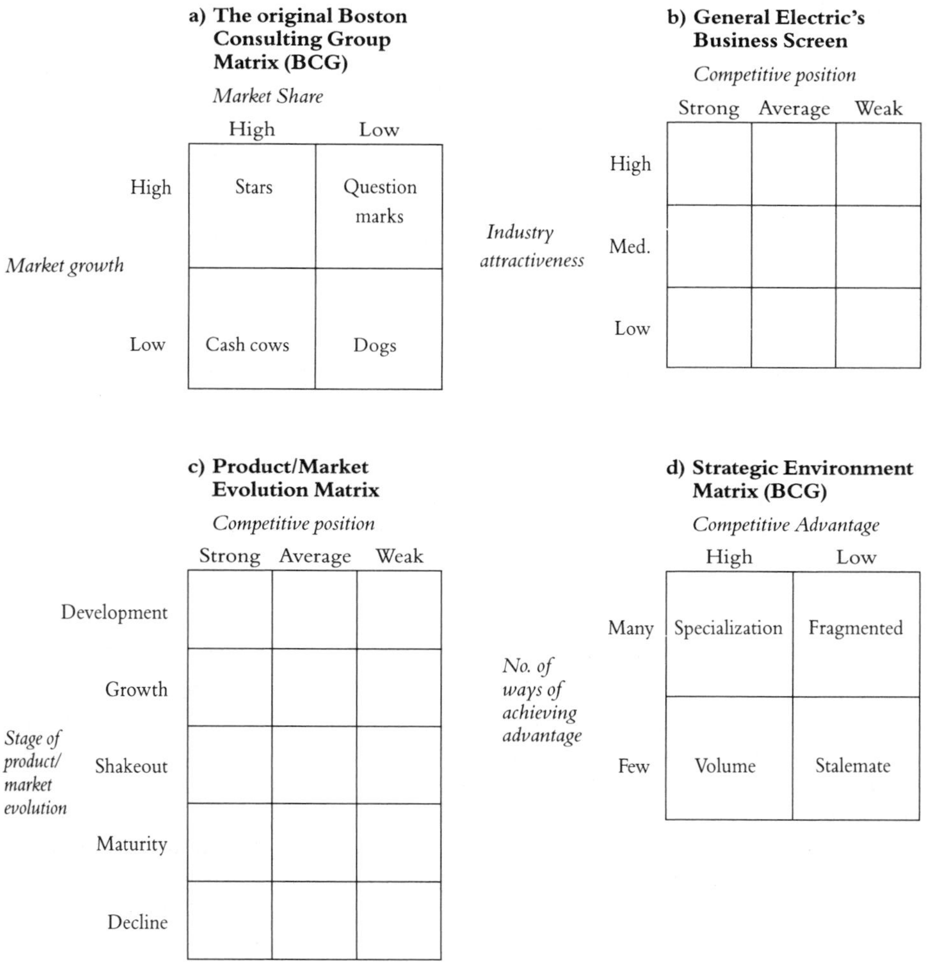

a) The original Boston Consulting Group Matrix (BCG)

Market Share

	High	Low
High	Stars	Question marks
Low	Cash cows	Dogs

Market growth (High / Low, vertical axis)

b) General Electric's Business Screen

Competitive position

	Strong	Average	Weak
High			
Med.			
Low			

Industry attractiveness

c) Product/Market Evolution Matrix

Competitive position

	Strong	Average	Weak
Development			
Growth			
Shakeout			
Maturity			
Decline			

Stage of product/ market evolution

d) Strategic Environment Matrix (BCG)

Competitive Advantage

	High	Low
Many	Specialization	Fragmented
Few	Volume	Stalemate

No. of ways of achieving advantage

Source: Parts a and d from research by the Boston Consulting Group. Part b adapted from *Strategy Formulation: Analytical Concepts,* from Charles Hofer and Dan Schendel, copyright © 1978 by West Publishing Company; all rights reserved. Part c from C. Hofer, *Conceptual Constructs For Formulating Corporate and Business Strategies,* Boston: Intercollegiate Case Clearing House, No. 9-378-754, 1977, p.3, and adapted by C. Hofer and D. Schendel, *Strategy Formulation: Analytical Concepts,* St. Paul, Minn: West Publishing Co., 1978, p.34.

raise questions about the rationale of any strategy. More detailed techniques of evaluation need to be used to assess the overall desirability of any strategy which seems to fit the product portfolio. Readers should also note that some writers have cast doubt on the practical value of the approach.[8]

Life Cycle Analysis

It was mentioned in the previous section that one particular development of the product portfolio concept has been used extensively. This is often referred to as *life cycle analysis* (or product/market evolution analysis as in Figure 7.2). This section will review one such approach as presented and used by the business consultants, Arthur D. Little. [9] Figure 7.3 is a summary of their life cycle portfolio matrix and consists of two dimensions. The market situation is described in four stages — from embryonic to aging, and the competitive position is described in five categories ranging from weak to dominant. The purpose of this matrix is to establish the appropriateness of particular strategies in relation to these two dimensions.

Clearly, if this approach is to provide a strategic logic for the development direction of a specific organization, the crucial issue is to establish where that organization is currently positioned on the matrix:

1. The *position within the life cycle* is determined in relation to eight external factors or "descriptors" of the evolutionary stage of the industry. These are: market growth rate, growth potential, breadth of product lines, number of competitors, spread of market share between these competitors, customer loyalty, entry barriers, and technology. The balance of these factors determines the life cycle stage. So, for example, an embryonic industry is characterized by rapid growth, changes in technology, fragmented market share, and pursuit of new customers. In contrast, aging industries are best described by falling demand, declining number of competitors, and, often a narrow product line.

2. The *competitive position* of the organization within its industry can also be established by looking at the characteristics of each category in Figure 7.3. A *dominant* position is rare in the private sector and usually results from quasi-monopoly. In the public sector it often results from legalized monopoly status (e.g., public utilities). *Strong* organizations can usually follow strategies of their own choice without too much concern about competition. A *favorable* position is where no single competitor stands out but the leaders are better placed (e.g., in retail clothing merchandising). A *tenable* position can usually be maintained by specialization or focus. *Weak* competitors are ones who are too small to survive independently in the long run.

Despite the fact that even such a detailed matrix can suggest that strategic choice is a simplistic and easy affair (which it is not), the A.D. Little matrix can be helpful in guiding strategic choice. Given the wide variety of strategic options discussed in Chapter 6, the main value of this matrix is in narrowing down this range of options to those which are worthy of further consideration given the organization's circumstances. So, for example,

Figure 7.3 *The life cycle portfolio matrix.*

Stages of Industry Maturity

Competitive position	Embryonic	Growth	Mature	Aging
Dominant	Fast grow Start-up	Fast grow Attain cost leadership Renew Defend position	Defend position Attain cost leadership Renew Fast grow	Defend position Focus Renew Grow with industry
Strong	Start-up Differentiate Fast grow	Fast grow Catch-up Attain cost leadership Differentiate	Attain cost leadership Renew, focus Differentiate Grow with industry	Find niche Hold niche Hang-in Grow with industry Harvest
Favorable	Start-up Differentiate Focus Fast grow	Differentiate, focus Catch-up Grow with industry	Harvest, hang-in Find niche, hold niche Renew, turnaround Differentiate, focus Grow with industry	Retrench Turnaround
Tenable	Start-up Grow with industry Focus	Harvest, catch-up Hold niche, hang-in Find niche Turnaround Focus Grow with industry	Harvest Turnaround Find niche Retrench	Divest Retrench
Weak	Find niche Catch-up Grow with industry	Turnaround Retrench	Withdraw Divest	Withdraw

Source: Arthur D. Little.

(referring to Figure 7.3) it is clear that the following general relationships would normally hold good:

1. Where growth is occurring and/or a favorable (or better) competitive position exists, organizations are well placed to follow the *"natural" development* of the market, although this may be achieved in different ways. The extreme case is clearly a dominant organization in an embryonic industry. A company in this position is likely to be creating natural growth through its own efforts and it will seek to defend this position during growth by moving faster than the competition or by cost leadership (through size or experience). Indeed, a dominant company may well be able to defend its position through the whole life cycle of the industry by carefully planned shifts in strategy (for example, through renewing the market strength of a product to avoid competition from innovation).

2. In contrast, weak organizations are unlikely to survive through the life cycle unless they identify and exploit a market niche and, effectively, become a strong supplier within that niche. An important generalization is that as growth declines, organizations will need to be more *selective* in their choice of strategy. This is particularly important if the organization is not in a strong competitive position. Many of the strategies discussed in Chapter 6 allow organizations to be selective and prosper. The concept of *focus* as generic strategy (and niche strategy as an extreme example of focus) is clearly of primary importance. However, in more difficult situations (towards the bottom right hand corner of the matrix), important judgments will need to be made about which product/markets should be pursued and which discontinued. So, a strategy of *retrenchment* would normally be the first step down this route followed if necessary by attempts to *turnaround* the organization's performance or to *divest* parts of the organization or even to *withdraw* entirely from particular products/markets.

3. It is important to recognize that some of the strategic options discussed in Chapter 6 will take on different forms depending on the position on the matrix. For example, a strategy of "market development" for a dominant company would invariably be achieved by the organization's own stimulation of new demand. In contrast, in more mature markets and weaker competitive position, market development would need to be achieved much more selectively by targeting new segments or moving into new markets where the conditions were more favorable (e.g., overseas development).

4. In the public service, the strategy of a state-owned monopoly (such as the Post Office) in an aging market is largely defensive, although its position is protected by its monopoly status. It has been argued that this is necessary since the natural response in an openly competitive situation would be to follow more selective strategies — in particular to reduce levels of service in the unprofitable (rural) areas and concentrate on cost-efficient operations in large cities.

5. It is also interesting to note how many government services have started to refine, prioritize, and differentiate their activities after the long period of growth of the 1960s and 1970s. This was largely achieved by increasing cost efficiency, quality improvements, and discontinuing certain services which were better provided by other bodies.

An example of product portfolio and life cycle analyses as discussed in the two previous sections is given in Illustration 7.2.

Competitive Advantage Analysis

Porter[10] has extended the considerations of the life cycle portfolio by looking at the relationship between the *development stage* of the industry, whether it is in growth, maturity or decline, and the *strategic position* of the individual organization, whether it is a leader or follower within the industry.

It should be noted that the terms "leader" and "follower" are not synonymous with positions of dominance and weakness and hence Porter's analysis provides an additional perspective on the issue of competitive choice. The following provides a resume of the analysis. (See Figure 7.4.)

a) Growth

Much of the traditional literature about strategic development has looked at an industry leader operating in growth markets (or, in the case of a government service, in a position of expanding budgets). Developments in such situations tend to occur by chasing growth as close to current product/market strategies as possible — but inevitably being forced towards increased diversification as growth opportunities dry up. During growth, industry leaders are often compelled to develop the business internally (at least during the early stages) since there are few suitable candidates for acquisition or to work with as partners.

The competitive advantage leaders enjoy during growth stems, for example, from staying ahead of the field by offering unique products or services or through the cost advantage gained from their relative size or experience.

The position for followers in the industry is somewhat different. They may, of course, have entered the industry as a result of the leader(s) being unable (or unwilling) to cope with potential demand. The proliferation of home computer systems in the early 1980s is a good example. Where rapid growth is occurring, the followers may well be able to develop by imitation of the leader's strategy — indeed, the market may be so unsophisticated that it demands imitation. Imitation can be most effective if done at lower cost (e.g., own-brand supplies). Sometimes followers are able to enter the industry through joint ventures with leaders who may be hard-pressed to serve the market alone. Subcontracting is a good example of such a situation, and it can prove to be a low-risk way of gaining experience in the industry. Larger organizations who feel they have missed a major development may well acquire one or more of the smaller follower organizations as a means of catching-up. The major danger for followers during growth is that they may fail to understand that a strategy of imitation, although adequate during growth, can be disastrous as the industry approaches maturity and buyers become more discerning.

b) Maturity

The onset of maturity in any industry (or government service) is usually a very difficult time when expectations need to be adjusted and the strategic role of the organization in the industry given very careful thought.[11] In essence, each organization needs to assess how it can choose a strategic approach which best matches its distinctive competence *vis-*

ILLUSTRATION 7.2   *Product Portfolio and Life Cycle Analyses at Procter & Gamble*

Product portfolio and life cycle analyses are particularly important in multi-product consumer goods companies.

Consumer tastes are constantly changing and it is necessary for consumer goods companies such as Procter & Gamble Co. (P&G) to keep abreast of changes and to adjust product offerings accordingly.

Consumer products illustrate the product life cycle concept very well. New products are always being introduced while others reach maturity and some are withdrawn from the market. It is necessary for P&G to have products in the embryonic, growth, and mature stages of the life cycle and to avoid having too many in the aging stage. This insures that the company will have products distributed in the three quadrants of the BCG portfolio matrix, or in other words, will have products which are cash cows, stars, and question marks, and not too many in the fourth quadrant as dogs. If the company stayed with the same products without introducing new ones, it would most likely end up with a few cash cows and many dogs.

Environmental trends are important in consumer products industries. For example, P&G is monitoring very carefully the current trend of people placing importance on health, or the concern for staying well. This trend is also indicated by the fitness craze and accentuated by the aging population. As a result, P&G has refocused its efforts on health care products and is counting on these products to generate growth, or to create stars.

It is not easy to categorize products, but the following might be one way of looking at some of P&G's products. Their detergent, diaper, and toothpaste products have reached a mature stage and might be considered cash cows. Another group of products are dogs or close to becoming failures, including: Encaprin, a coated aspirin; Duncan Hines cookies which share 13% of the cookie market with three competitors; Norwich aspirin which is not doing well against the market leaders; and a Coca-Cola bottling plant which has been sold.

Through its own R&D and acquisitions, P&G has added some question marks and stars, most of which are in the health care area. In fact, these products have enabled P&G to become the largest US supplier of over-the-counter remedies. Some of P&G's question marks include: a new prescription mouthwash to fight gum disease (which most likely will be available as a non-prescription product also); a drug to reduce osteoporosis called Didronel; a sucrose polyester referred to as olestra, a fat substitute for dieters, that will most likely be used in such P&G products as Crisco, Puritan, and Pringles potato chips.

P&G is also revamping old products and in effect making them into question marks or stars. Question marks might presently include: Metamucil, a natural fiber laxative, which might be sold as an anticholesterol agent; Pepto-Bismol which may be sold as a treatment for ulcers; and Citrus Hill orange juice which will be reintroduced as

Citrus Hill Plus Calcium with the hope that it will become a star. Some revamped products that might be considered as stars are: Pepto-Bismol, the diarrhea remedy to be sold as a cure for overindulgence, and Tartar Control Crest toothpaste which enabled P&G to regain market leadership. In addition, P&G has plans to reinvigorate some of their products in mature stage such as detergents, diapers, and other toothpastes.

P&G is very conscious of the need to balance their portfolio of products to make sure that it has cash cows in the mature stage of the life cycle, but also to have questions marks in the embryonic stage and stars in the growth stage. Products that are considered dogs are either revitalized as new products on a new life cycle or divested.

Source: Jolie Solomon and Carol Hymowitz, "P&G Makes Changes In the Way It Develops And Sells Its Products," *The Wall Street Journal*, August 11, 1987, pp. 1 and 12; "Procter & Gamble Goes on a Health Kick," *Business Week*, June 29, 1987, pp. 90–2.

Figure 7.4 *Competitive strategies for leaders and followers.*

Stage of "industry" development

		Growth	Maturity	Decline
Strategic position of organization	Leader	Keeping ahead of the field	Cost leadership Raise barriers Deter competitors	Redefine scope Divest peripherals Encourage departures
	Follower	Imitation at lower cost Joint ventures	Differentiation Focus	Differentiation New opportunities

Source: M.E. Porter, *Competitive Advantage: Creating and Sustaining Superior Performance,* New York: Free Press, 1985. Used with permission of The Free Press, a Division of Macmillan, Inc. Copyright © 1985 Michael E. Porter.

à-vis competitors. In government services also, a realization that the service cannot hope to be a monopoly supplier with complete "market" coverage will force managers to define the boundaries of their activities and allow others to serve the remaining demand/need. The spate of privatizations within government services (e.g., ancilliary services in hospitals) is an example.

Leaders in an industry may choose to consolidate their position in a number of ways to help them gain competitive advantage by virtue of their leadership:

- By exploiting their superior *cost structure* usually through highly competitive pricing.
- By raising the *structural barriers* — for example, through high levels of marketing expenditure, geographical spread (e.g., globalization[12]), by blocking access to distribution channels or suppliers, or even by encouraging government policies (e.g., new regulations) to make entry more difficult.
- By making it less attractive or more risky for others to challenge the leader's position. This could be done by threatening retaliation, or perhaps by promising to match any offering of the followers. (The "never knowingly undersold" policy of a retail store is a good example.)

The position for followers during maturity is almost the reverse. The most successful strategies of followers occur where they are able to *differentiate* themselves from the leaders. This is usually combined with a quite deliberate strategy of *focusing* on particular parts of the market (segmentation or niche). Readers are reminded of the discussion in Chapter 6 about how this process of differentiation and focus can only be a means to genuine competitive advantage if conceived of throughout the value-chain. Porter[13] provides a very useful framework for identifying the various ways differentation can be achieved effectively by followers and used to their advantage. This is shown in Figure 7.5. The underlying purpose of a follower strategy must be to nullify the competitive advantage of the leader (discussed above) while minimizing the threat of retaliation. The essential messages are:

- Imitation of the leader can only be sustained by pure spending (e.g., price wars) and is unlikely to succeed unless the follower organization has substantial financial resources (e.g., a parent company).
- Followers can compete in the same product/market as a leader by *reconfiguring* part or all of the value chain. For example, they may reduce supply costs by using different sources or outlets, or lower cost marketing methods (e.g., own-label suppliers). However, these differences must be genuinely valuable to customers in some way or other.
- Another alternative is to redefine the competitive scope of the organization in relation to the leader. The best known form of redefinition is to narrow the focus of the organization, i.e. *market segmentation* (or *niche* strategies). So the follower becomes a leader within that segment or niche. Advantage can also be gained by *horizontal integration* (or vice versa) again making the company different from the leader. Real estate firms which provide all the services needed to purchase a new home may

Figure 7.5   *Follower strategies for mature markets.*

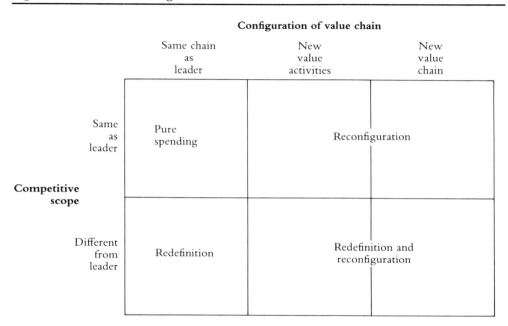

Configuration of value chain

Source: M.E. Porter, *Competitive Advantage: Creating and Sustaining Superior Performance,* New York: Free Press, 1985. Used with permission of The Free Press, a Division of Macmillan, Inc. Copyright © 1985 Michael E. Porter.

compete successfully with the leaders of the separate services (real estate agents, lawyers, insurance companies). *Vertical integration* (or vice versa) may also provide advantage (e.g. the small specialist retailer may provide better after-sales service than the chain store).

Geographical spread on an area by area basis is the route whereby Japanese companies[14] have gradually challenged and displaced the incumbent leaders in other countries (e.g., motorcycles, cars, and consumer electronics). Interestingly enough this globalization process was helped along by a very clear market segmentation (focus) approach. Typically, the Japanese would enter the bottom-end of the market (which was badly defended) and gradually displace the leaders by trading-up from this bridge-head.

c) Decline

Many of the principles concerning competitive strategy in maturity are similar during decline and will not be repeated. However, there are some additional factors specific to decline.[15] The most obvious one is that when demand is reducing, options such as divestment or withdrawal tend to be of pressing concern. Leaders have some difficult decisions to make; in particular the viability of their venture is likely to be threatened unless some other organizations leave the industry. It is quite common for leaders to induce this process by buying competitors and closing down their capacity. In other circumstances (the steel and oil industries and agriculture are good examples), leaders push hard for industry regulation — either voluntary or imposed. Usually, the value chain will have to be reconfigured by the leaders as the economics of the chain shift, as scale is reduced.

For followers, the need to differentiate themselves continues to be of vital importance and it is often the case that the followers (who are more specialist) are the ones who best survive the period of decline. Indeed, decline usually affords some new opportunities as the leaders shed their more peripheral activities. Certainly many of the service elements within organizations are now provided out-of-house by thriving small businesses (e.g., design, advertising, consultancy, research and development work) or through joint ventures.

In recent years, a greater number of "mature" and "declining" industries have become evident. An example of one such industry is given in Illustration 7.3.

Synergy

The previous chapter introduced the concept of synergy[16] as a means of explaining why organizations might choose to take on new activities through market development, diversification, and so on. Synergy was seen as a measure of the extra benefit which could accrue from providing some sort of linkage between two or more activities. The estimation of this extra benefit is an important means of assessing how successful any new strategy might be.

Table 7.2 gives an example of how synergy might be assessed in the case of a single-outlet grocery retailer wishing to increase the overall size of his business. The company wants to assess the degree of synergy between the present business and three alternative methods of development: buying more grocery stores, expanding the product range into alcoholic drinks, and opening a cash and carry wholesaler. The factors identified in the figure are intended to illustrate the possible areas where synergy might occur (use of cash, inventory, premises, or in purchasing, etc). This analysis attempts to assess the contribution of each of these factors towards the relative merits of each option. For example, the fact that the retailer has a good name in the locality should reduce the launch costs of new stores compared with a totally unknown retailer setting up in the area. The detailed assessment of how much these savings might be would then evolve from a consideration of the advertising and promotional campaign details (at a later stage).

The idea of synergy is particularly helpful if it is related to previous discussions about the value chain. In that sense, synergy is a measure of the benefits which can accrue through pursuing linkages between the value chains of two separate activities or businesses. It is often used as an explanation for why a takeover might "make sense." The grocery retailer hopes to gain cost advantage through the increased buying power which would result in the multiple chain strategy. In contrast, strategy two (moving into alcoholic drinks), would seek competitive advantage through differentiation from competitors. Often synergy results from more intangible sources when two or more value chains are

---

ILLUSTRATION 7.3   *"Decline" in the Canadian Tire Industry*

During a period of decline in a mature industry, the firms in the industry have followed quite similar strategies. This illustration outlines what occurred in the Canadian tire industry as demand declined.

The rubber tire is in the mature stage of its life cycle due to several changes in the environment. Tariffs on imported tires were lowered, increasing competition and enabling imported tires to capture 20% of the market. As imported cars increased their share of the market, the original equipment business was reduced by 30%.

Fifty percent of Canadian production is exported to the United States and this is necessary in order to maintain plants with sufficient economies of scale. The market is more difficult as American tariffs have increased and foreign producers are providing increasing competition. Most Canadian tire manufacturing plants are old-fashioned and require modernization. Like most plants in North America, they were designed to manufacture bias–ply tires but, new technology has resulted in the radial tire which now has a very large portion of the market. All the Canadian firms are subsidiaries of foreign, mostly American companies, and all parent companies operate large scale plants in their home countries.

The following are the actions taken by the Canadian companies:

- Uniroyal Tire Ltd. and B.F. Goodrich Canada Inc. formed a joint venture, Uniroyal Goodrich Canada Inc., to rationalize manufacturing operations. As a result of this joint venture, the company has become the leading producer of tires in Canada. (This joint venture was described in Illustration 6.6.)

- Goodyear Canada Inc. has closed its Toronto plant and has rationalized production in plants at Valleyfield, Québec, and Medicine Hat, Alberta. With government assistance, Goodyear Canada will build a new plant in Napanee, Ontario. The closing of the plant in Toronto put 1,550 people out of work. The new plant will employ 400 initially, increasing to 800 when completed in 1992.

- Firestone Canada Inc. has been losing money and has closed a large plant in Hamilton, Ontario.

- Michelin Tire (Canada) Ltd., a leading producer of radial tires owned by French interests, operates three plants in Nova Scotia.

- General Tire Canada Ltd. is a small producer with one plant in Barrie, Ontario.

The industry is not doing well, and most companies have taken defensive actions of some sort. A similar situation exists in the United States where environmental factors have led to the closing of 35 plants in recent years.

Source: Robert English, "Tire Industry's Hope of Future Wearing Thin," *The Financial Post*, February 16, 1987, p. 13; Thomas J. Ensch, "Viewpoint: Tires — a Case for Protection?," *Business Quarterly*, Summer 1985, pp. 49–51; Nino Wischnewski, "Foreign Pressures Tighten Pinch on Canada's 'Marginal' Tire Plants," *The Financial Post*, January 25, 1988, p. 10.

220 Part III Strategic Choice

Table 7.2 *The assessment of synergy for a grocery retailer.*

	Degree of synergy with present activities	Strategy 1 Buy more stores	Strategy 2 Expand into alcoholic drinks	Strategy 3 Open cash and carry wholesaler
1.	Use of cash	Produces profit from idle cash	Produces profit from idle cash	Produces profit from idle cash
2.	Use of premises	None	More turnover/ floor space	None
3.	Use of inventory	Perhaps small gains from moving inventory between stores	None	Reduction of inventory in stores as quick delivery guaranteed
4.	Purchasing	Possible discounts for bulk	None	Reduced prices to stores
5.	Market image	Good name helps launch (i.e., cost of launch reduced)	None	Little

linked. For example, in many acquisitions, the predator company would attempt to impose a tried and tested management recipe in order to transform the financial performance of the companies acquired.

In some industries, companies are forced to seek synergy because their competitors are doing so. The changing face of the financial services industry during the 1980s is a good example. Various financial institutions, such as banks, savings and loans, insurance companies, and brokerage houses, extended into many related services such as insurance, real estate sales, and mutual funds after changes in the legislation governing the industry allowed these practices. Illustration 7.4 describes one company in the financial services industry which appears to be achieving synergy.

Readers should note that the theoretical benefits of synergy are often difficult to accrue in practice — particularly following mergers or acquisitions, as discussed in Chapter 6.[17]

7.3.2 STRATEGY AND PERFORMANCE — RESEARCH EVIDENCE

The analyses in the previous section have attempted to establish a strategic logic, or rationale, to "explain" why some strategies might be more suitable than others. An additional approach to assessing the suitability of options is to review the "research" evidence available on the relationship between the choice of strategy and the performance of organizations. In this context, the continuing work of the Strategic Planning Institute (SPI) through its PIMS data bank is of central importance. This data bank contains the strategy experiences, good or bad, of some 3,000 businesses (both products and services). Each experience is documented in terms of the actions taken by the business (i.e. choice of strategic options), the nature of the market and competitive environment,

---

ILLUSTRATION 7.4   *Achieving Synergy at American Express*

Companies attempt to achieve some form of synergy, if possible, among their various divisions or corporate holdings. This illustration discusses the attempt by American Express to take advantage of synergy in its operations.

Traditionally, the different components of the financial services industry, for example, stockbrokerage, insurance, banking, and credit card companies, were separated by regulation. The deregulation of the industry enabled stockbrokers to sell insurance, insurance salespersons to sell stocks, and banks to act as brokers. One company attempting to take advantage of this opportunity in the environment is American Express (Amex), the credit card issuer with holdings in banking, stockbrokerage, financial planning, and travel services.

Amex's various divisions operated separately until Chief Executive James D. Robinson focused the company on the opportunities provided by synergy relationships. He was concerned with "profit centeritis," a term coined by Robert H. Waterman, co-author of *In Search of Excellence*, to indicate how managers emphasized the performance of their own unit or division and ignored activities requiring cooperation between units of the same company. Robinson advocated cooperation between Amex divisions since the company should be viewed as "one enterprise" and he encouraged cross-selling opportunities. Examples of such cross-selling, or synergistic activites, include:

- Amex's financial planning division sold real estate partnerships syndicated by the stockbrokerage unit.

- The stockbrokerage unit and the overseas banking unit have put together several major financial transactions.

- Life insurance is being sold to Amex cardholders and through the financial planning company.

The reasons for advocating cross-selling were to identify growth possibilities and to establish relationships for even greater cooperative ventures in the future.

However, synergy does not just happen. The Chief Executive must be committed to the concept and must put in place systems to implement it. At Amex, managers were required to identify synergistic projects in their strategic planning and to work with others to make them happen. The progress of these projects was monitored by the director of strategic planning and progress reports made public. The managers were evaluated and rewarded on how well the projects were implemented.

Synergy is one strategic option difficult to achieve. Amex would appear to be an exception.

Source: Monci Jo Williams, "Synergy Works at American Express," *Fortune*, February 16, 1987, pp. 79–80.

and the financial results.[18] Some of the more important PIMS findings, together with other research, will be summarized in this section, for further information readers should follow up the references. There have been other research studies which have sought to clarify the relationship between choice of strategy and organizational performance and they will also be reviewed.

The Importance of Market Share

In the discussion of the strategic environment in Chapter 3, the strategic importance of "market power" was introduced. In understanding the likely impact of the environment on any one organization, market power is a crucial factor to understand. Similarly, when looking at the choices open to organizations in the future, the extent to which they are likely to increase or decrease this market power needs careful assessment.

Much of the research in this area has used market share as a measure of market power and there is clear evidence that market share and profitability are linked. The Boston Consulting Group argues this on the basis of the experience curve and the superior cost structure of market leaders (see Chapter 4) and this assertion is also supported by the findings of the PIMS study, as shown in Figure 7.6. Return on investment (ROI) rises steadily in line with market share.[19]

The PIMS researchers suggest a number of reasons why market share and ROI should be linked[20] and these are largely concerned with the cost benefits market share brings. The purchase to sales ratio differences between high and low market share firms are startling — in simple terms, high market share companies seem to be able to buy more competitively, or produce components more economically in-house. Also, some economies of scale benefit firms with high market shares. For example, marketing costs tend to decline as a percentage of sales with increased share. The indications are also that high market share firms develop strategies of higher price/higher quality than low share competitors. This phenomenon may, in fact, be somewhat circular. High share firms tend to be more profitable, thus providing the cash resources for R&D to improve and differentiate products, thus enhancing their market position and also justifying higher prices which in turn increase profits. It must be remembered that high market share and size are not always the same. There are large firms which do not dominate the markets in which they operate; and there are small firms which dominate segments of markets.

Consolidation Strategies

PIMS research findings provide a useful insight into the likely outcomes of pursuing a wide variety of strategies. Figure 7.7 summarizes some of the findings relating to various types of consolidation strategies discussed in Chapter 6. For example, a common consolidation strategy is the upgrading of product or service *quality*. The evidence is that quality is of very real significance in the improvement of profit performance.[21] The best situation appears to be a combination of high share and high product quality, but even firms with low market shares demonstrate significantly higher profit performance if they have products of superior quality. (In this sense, quality can be a partial substitute for market share in sustaining advantage.)

Figure 7.6   *The relationship between market share and ROI.*

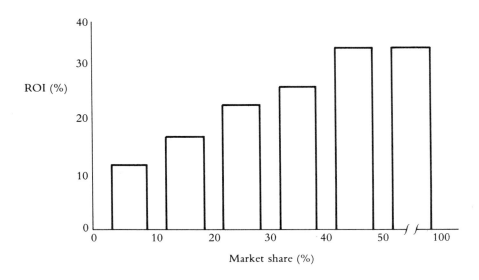

Source: B. T. Gale and B. Branch, "The Dispute About High-Share Businesses," *Pimsletter*, No. 19, The Strategic Planning Institute. Reprinted with the permission of the SPI.

Figure 7.7 suggests that a reliance on increased marketing spending to consolidate an organization's position in its markets does not appear to be a satisfactory way of improving performance. Heavy marketing expenditure (as a percentage of sales) may actually damage ROI for firms with low market shares. This does, of course, pose a problem for a firm trying to improve or maintain its standing within its existing product/market: trying to do so by increasing marketing expenditure is likely to result in reduced profitability. In other words, attempting to "buy market share" is unlikely to be successful.

The combined effect of marketing expenditure and product quality has also been studied. High marketing expenditure is not a substitute for quality:[22] indeed, it appears that high marketing expenditure damages ROI when quality is low (see Figure 7.7). It must be concluded that simply gearing up marketing expenditure as a means of consolidating a company's position is not sufficient.

Another common consolidation strategy is to seek improved productivity through capital investment — for example, by the mechanization of routine tasks. This has become so much a part of accepted "management wisdom" that it might come as something of a shock to learn that there is very little evidence to suggest that increased capital intensity can damage return on investment[23] as shown in Figure 7.7. The reasons for this are important to understand. Managers may expect reduced costs through mechanization and

Figure 7.7 Consolidation strategies — PIMS findings.

a) Quality, market share, and return on investment.

Average ROI (%)	Market share		
	13%	28%	
Low	11	17	23
Average	11	17	26
High	20	26	35

Product quality (rows: Low, Average, High)

Source: R.D. Buzzell, "Product Quality", *Pimsletter*, No. 4, Strategic Planning Institute. Reprinted with the permission of the SPI.

b) Heavy marketing is not profitable for low share business.

ROI (%)	Marketing/sales		
	Low 6%	11%	High
Low	20	13	7
26%	21	19	19
63% High	34	31	34

Relative market share

Source: The Strategic Planning Institute, "A Programme of... The Strategic Planning Institute," 1977. Reprinted with the permission of the SPI.

c) High marketing expenditures hurt profits especially when quality is low.

Average ROI (%)	Marketing/sales		
	Low 6%	11%	High
Low	17	14	5
1%	22	19	18
30% High	32	25	25

Quality

Source: The Strategic Planning Institute, "A Program of... The Strategic Planning Institute," 1977. Reprinted with the permission of the SPI.

d) Investment intensity and ROI.

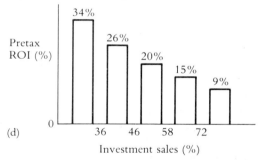

(d)

(Note: "Investment" includes both working capital and fixed capital at net book value. The figures are four-year averages.)

Source: S. Schoeffler, "The Unprofitability of "Modern" Technology and What to do about it," *Pimsletter*, No. 2, The Strategic Planning Institute. Reprinted with the permission of the SPI.

reduced labor input, but assume that revenue will remain constant or rise. However, in capital intensive industries, companies are especially keen to ensure that capacity is fully loaded and may cut prices to keep volume, thus actually reducing overall margins; or undertake uneconomic production runs to keep customers happy; or even raise marketing expenditure to wrestle volume from competition. Since high capital investment is also a barrier to exit, those suffering from low margins are reluctant to get out and they continue to battle on and make the situation worse. Indeed, raising capital intensity in an attempt to improve profit returns is most likely to be successful for companies who already have a strong position in the market, are unlikely to meet fierce price competition, and who are able to make real reductions in layout and production costs.[24] For some of these reasons, many organizations have preferred subcontracting as a means of improving productivity.

Related Developments

Figure 7.8 summarizes some PIMS findings about other types of related developments. It has been argued in the previous section that high market share is very often of strategic advantage to organizations. However, the process of building market share (*market penetration*) is not without its costs[25] as seen in Figure 7.8a). Short term profits are likely to be sacrificed, particularly when a company is trying to build share from a low base. Similarly, *product development* can bring uncomfortable dilemmas to many organizations.[26] New products/services may be absolutely vital to the organization's future. The problem is that these may prove expensive and unprofitable (particularly in the short-run). This is why a balanced portfolio of products is important. Cash cows can fund these developments, and avoid unnecessarily increasing the investment intensity of the company. Product development is likely to require a commitment to high levels of spending on R&D. Figure 7.8b) shows that while high market share companies may benefit in profit terms from relatively high levels of R&D expenditure, companies in a weak market position with high expenditure may suffer badly.

Evidence of this type has convinced many organizations to look seriously at *technology transfer* or acquisition of smaller companies as alternatives to their own R&D efforts. Interestingly enough, the success of many Japanese companies since the late 1950s has built on such an approach.

Figure 7.8c) also confirms that profitability is likely to be depressed by over-rapid rates of new product introductions as organizations debug production, train salespeople, educate customers, and establish new channels.

The following section discusses the performance of companies which diversify. One method of diversifying is to acquire other companies and some of the difficulties encountered with this approach are outlined in Illustration 7.5.

Diversification and Performance

There have been a number of attempts to assess the extent to which diversification is related to performance. Table 7.3 shows two of these studies from the United States[27] and Britain[28] as indicative of the findings. Readers are encouraged to follow up the references[29]

Figure 7.8 *Other related strategies — PIMS findings.*

a) The cost of growth in market share.

The figures in the boxes show the cash flow generated as a % of the investment which has been made. This is greatest when a company already has a high market share which it is consolidating (10%) and lowest where the investment has been used to gain market share from a low starting position (−4%).

Source: Valerie Kijewski, "Market-share Strategy: Beliefs v Actions." *Pimsletter*, No. 9, The Strategic Planning Institute. Reprinted with the permission of the SPI.

Cash flow % investment

Percentage change in market share

Beginning market share

	− 2 Steady	+ 2 Gain
Low	0	− 4
12%	7	2
27%	10	7
High		

b) R&D expenditure, market share and ROI.

Source: S. Schoeffler, "Market Position: Build, Hold or Harvest?" *Pimsletter*, No. 3, The Strategic Planning Institute. Reprinted with the permission of the SPI.

Average ROI (%)

Total R&D/sales

Market share

	1%		3%
	17	14	5
12%	21	24	13
27%	31	32	28

c) New product sales depress profitability.

*Pretax and before financial charges

Source: R. Morrison and D. Tavel, "New Products and Market Position," *Pimsletter*, No. 28. Reprinted with the permission of SPI.

ROI* (%)

New Product Sales (% of total sales)	0.1	3	10	20	%
ROI	22	26	25	22	18

if they would like a full review of the range of research findings on this topic. However, some of the most important conclusions of research findings to date are:

- That more diversified businesses grow faster and that growth tends to be greatest when diversification is of an unrelated nature.

- That related diversifications tend to be more profitable than unrelated. This may not be due to the inherent superiority of related strategies but more likely due to the difficulties of comprehending and coping with the more complex requirements of an unrelated strategy.

- Although a major justification for diversifications is to "add value" through new linkages between value chains of the separate activities, this usually proves to be a disappointment to companies. In other words, the practicalities of achieving these theoretical benefits often elude an organization.

- It is often argued that unrelated diversification can be an important means of spreading the investment risk of shareholders. However, research evidence so far does not show this to be a significant benefit in practice.

Care needs to be taken in interpreting many of these research findings. For example, data bases are not necessarily directly comparable and often come from different countries and different times. So, for example, in Table 7.3, it is possible that the results reflect the trading conditions of the time. Related diversification might be more suited to firms when there are opportunities for expansion in a growing economy. On the other hand, in terms of little or no economic growth, a strategy of concentration on mainline products rather than the spreading of interests might make more sense.

The balance of evidence does warn against unconstrained diversification. As with product development, it is one thing to show that diversified companies can be profitable but it also has to be pointed out that the process of diversification can be very difficult and costly. A firm that follows a strategy of launching new businesses is likely to suffer a major drain on its cash resources. The average length of time it takes to move into profits is eight years and severe losses can be expected for four years.

7.3.3 CULTURAL FIT ANALYSIS

Although establishing the strategic logic of options is very valuable, it is also essential to review those options within the political realities of the organization since this is where they will have to be put into effect. This section is concerned with how options might be assessed in terms of their *cultural fit*. In other words, the extent to which particular types of strategies might be more or less easily assimilated into an organization. This is not to suggest that the culture of an organization should have preeminence in determining strategy. Indeed, one of the key roles of the leadership of organizations is to shape and change culture to better fit preferred strategies.

Perhaps these issues are best understood in terms of the previous discussions (Chapters 2 and 5) about the cultural web of an organization and how it legitimizes and sustains

---

ILLUSTRATION 7.5   *Why Predators May Get Indigestion*

Acquisition needs to be properly planned to avoid post-takeover problems.

Since the mid-1970s, there has been a continuous stream of corporate takeovers and mergers. Acquisitions of a major nature are estimated to number 2,500 to 3,500 per year. Examples of large deals are: General Electric's acquisition of RCA for $6.4 billion; BCI Holdings' acquisition of Beatrice Cos. for $6.2 billion; and Burroughs' $4.7 billion merger with Sperry to form Unisys. Canadian examples are: Dome Petroleum's acquisition of Hudson's Bay Oil and Gas for $4.1 billion; Campeau Corp.'s takeover of Allied Stores for $5.0 billion; and Seagram Co.'s acquisition of 20% of du Pont for $3.1 billion. Everybody seems to be involved as mergers and takeovers are occurring in all industries.

The cover story in the June 3, 1985 issue of *Business Week* was entitled "Do Mergers Really Work? Not Very Often — Which Raises Questions About Merger Mania." The article stated that one half to two thirds of the mergers did not work. Many of the points in the article were summarized in what *Business Week* called "The Seven Deadly Sins in Mergers and Acquisitions:"

- Paying too much.
- Assuming a boom market won't crash.
- Leaping before looking.
- Straying too far afield.
- Swallowing something too big.
- Marrying disparate corporate cultures.
- Counting on key managers staying.

These sins deal with different aspects of strategic management. The price paid and the assessment of the market relate to the acquirer's perception of the environment. Misconceptions of the market result in too much being paid and an overly optimistic estimation of the market leads to incorrect forecasts of future revenues. Irrational thinking, an ego requiring growth, or a rushed decision might encourage a company to make too hasty a decision.

Acquiring businesses outside the acquirer's core area of business is a major strategic decision. This sometimes leads to what some refer to as the "synergy trap" where it is assumed that skills used to run one business are applicable to another. Many companies have learned that synergy thought to exist does not materialize after the merger. Mergers should also be manageable. This is true no manner what the size of the acquiring company. Just because a company is large does not insure that it can successfully merge with another company.

This book emphasizes corporate culture and its importance to strategy. If two companies merge and the two cultures are not comparable, there is likely to be difficulty in integrating operations and even obtaining cooperation. Finally, acquiring companies may experience difficulty if competent managers leave the acquired company. There are now doubts about the interchangeability of managerial skills so it is important to retain managers.

Despite all the problems, mergers are still occurring. According to the *Business Week* article, successful mergers do occur. A merger is more likely to be successful when companies in closely related businesses are involved, when the deal is financed by stock swaps or cash instead of with borrowed money, when a reasonable price is paid, and when management stays around to run the acquisition.

Writers on the subject of mergers stress the importance of integrating the acquired company successfully. Integration should take place at three levels: procedural (accounting systems); physical (physical assets, product lines, production systems, and technology); and cultural. The amount of integration depends on whether or not the acquirer operates as a conglomerate when only procedural integration would be necessary, or undertakes complete absorption when all three are critical. Integration requires an operating plan and involves coordinating, monitoring and controlling activities as well as resolving conflicts. Deliberate efforts at integration are necessary as it is unlikely to occur otherwise.

Source: "Do Mergers Really Work? Not Very Often — Which Raises Questions About Merger Mania," *Business Week*, June 3, 1985, pp. 88–100.

---

the recipe of the organization. On the whole, organizations will seek out strategies which can be delivered without unduly challenging the recipe — managers find such strategies easiest to comprehend and pursue. However, the key judgment is whether or not such strategies are suitable in the face of the organization's current situation — particularly if significant environmental change has occurred. The analyses outlined in the previous sections will give strong indications of whether or not the organization's recipe does require some fundamental change if the organization is to survive and prosper.

Whether the recipe change is required or not, the assessment of strategic options in terms of cultural fit is valuable. If the organization is developing within the current recipe, these analyses help to identify those strategies which would be most easily assimilated. In contrast, if the recipe will need to change, the analyses help to establish how culture will need to adapt to embrace new types of strategy. This will be valuable analysis when planning implementation (see Chapter 11). Illustration 7.6 describes an example of cultural fit which may not be appropriate given the circumstances in which the company finds itself.

One of the key determinants of how culture might influence strategic choice is, again, the life cycle stage of an organization. Schein[30] provides a very valuable discussion of this relationship between life cycle, culture, and strategy which will be summarized here, and

Table 7.3 *Financial consequences of product strategies.*

USA 1960–1969†	Company product strategy★			
	Single product	Dominant product	Related products	Unrelated products
Sales growth (% p.a.)	7.2	8.0	9.1	14.2
Earnings growth (% p.a.)	4.8	8.0	9.4	13.9
Earnings growth per share (% p.a.)	3.9	6.0	7.6	7.9
P/E	14.6	15.7	19.2	15.8
Return on investment (%)	10.8	9.6	11.5	9.5
Return on equity (%)	13.2	11.6	13.6	11.9

UK 1970–1980‡	Company product strategy★			
	Single product	Dominant product	Related products	Unrelated products
Sales growth (% p.a.)	1.0	1.5	1.3	2.1
Profit growth before interest & tax (% p.a.)	0.09	0.75	0.67	1.31
Share growth (capital value % p.a.)	–3.65	–3.54	–3.58	–3.44
Return on capital employed (%)	18.1	19.1	16.9	16.7

★These product groups describe strategies which are progressively more diversified. So, for example, the "dominant product" situation refers to companies which have 70% or more of their sales in one product area and "related" to companies with less than 70% in one product area. Highest profit returns were found for related strategies where diversification remained associated with core skills of the business (termed "related constrained").

Source: †From: Richard P. Rumelt, *Strategy, Structure and Economic Performance*, Boston, Mass.: Division of Research, Harvard Business School, 1974 (Table 3-1, p. 91). Used with permission.
‡R. Reed and G. Luffman, "Diversification: the Growing Confusion," *Strategic Management Journal*, Vol. 7, No. 1, 1986, pp. 29–35.

ILLUSTRATION 7.6 *Polaroid's Strategy and Cultural Fit*

There may have been a need for a recipe change at Polaroid Corp. However, corporate culture may be preventing managers from assessing the environment appropriately.

One half of Polaroid Corp.'s $1.3 billion sales is instant photography equipment and film. The company and its managers continue to be committed to instant photography despite some major competitive threats.

Amateur photographers, the main customers for instant photography, appear to have lost interest in the product. There are several reasons for this: the quality of prints has been poor; the cost high (double the cost of printing a 35 mm film); and the camera is bulky. Moreover, the 35 mm cameras now available are much more convenient and easier to use than earlier models. Instant photography products now have to compete against the "one hour processing" available for conventional film. In the past five years, the sales of instant cameras have declined while the sales of 35 mm cameras have grown rapidly.

Despite these threats in the environment, Polaroid managers have decided to stay in instant photography and have introduced a new camera, the Spectra. According to industry analysts, the new camera does improve the quality of prints, but the cost is still high and the portability of the camera not greatly improved. Management talent at Polaroid comes from within the company and it appears that they are still committed to a segment of the photography market that may be in permanent decline.

Counterarguments from Polaroid are that the market has been down because no new products were available and Spectra corrects that situation. Moreover, Eastman Kodak Co. has withdrawn from the instant photography market after losing a patent infringement suit, leaving Poloroid the only manaufacturer. It is also agreed that Polaroid has little choice but to continue in the instant photography market as attempts at diversification have not been very successful.

Polaroid's recipe for strategy was influenced by its cultural web which includes the personal preferences of managers for instant photography. The commitment to instant photography was consistent with the company's previous recipe and was the easiest to follow. The question now is whether or not the cultural web allowed Polaroid's managers to appropriately assess the realities of the environment. It appears that the company's corporate culture has resulted in a strategy inconsistent with the environment.

Source: Brian Dumaine, "How Polaroid Flashed Back," *Fortune*, February 16, 1987, pp. 72–3 and 76; "Polaroid's Spectra May Be Losing Its Flash," *Business Week*, June 29, 1987, p. 31; "Is Polaroid Playing to a Market that Just Isn't There?," *Business Week*, April 7, 1986, pp. 82–3.

can be usefully linked to the life cycle models discussed in Section 7.3.1 above. A combination of these two perspectives on different stages in the life cycle can prove valuable in establishing options which fit both the strategic logic and the cultural situation. The key points of the ensuing discussion are summarized in Table 7.4.

Embryonic Stage

The culture of an organization in its embryonic stage is shaped by the founders. When the organization survives, these personal beliefs become strongly embedded in the organization and shape subsequent developments. In other words, these core beliefs hold the organization together and become a key part of its distinctive competence. Organizations will typically seek out developments which fit this culture. So, for example, an organization founded to exploit a particular technological expertise will tend to seek further developments to fit this self-image of a technology driven organization. They will favor product or process development when often the economic logic would suggest they would be better advised to seek additional markets to exploit their current assets. Not only do they not possess these "marketing" skills but they also do not *see* the organization in that way — they are excited by the technology and this pervades the way the organization is managed and the strategic choices it makes.

The strength and cohesion of culture in embryonic organizations has also frustrated the attempts of agencies established to help and advise small businesses on their development. The internal culture often rejects the concept of outside "help" even when it might make "economic" sense.

Table 7.4 *Culture, the life cycle, and strategic choices.*

Life cycle stage	Key cultural features	Implications to strategic choice
1. Embryonic	1. Cohesive culture 2. Founders dominant 3. Outside help not valued	1. Try to repeat successes 2. Related developments favored
2. Growth	1. Cultural cohesion less 2. Mismatched and tensions arise	1. Diversification often possible 2. Vulnerability to takeover 3. Structural change needed for new developments 4. New developments need protection
3. Maturity	1. Culture institutionalized 2. Culture breeds inertia 3. Strategic logic may be rejected	1. Related developments favored 2. Incrementalism favored
4. Decline	1. Culture becomes a defense	1. Readjustment necessary but difficult 2. Divestment may prove necessary

Growth

The growth phase of organizations involves a variety of cultural changes in different circumstances. However, there are some commonly occurring situations which illustrate how cultural developments dictate strategic choice:

- The cohesiveness of culture seen in the embryonic stage tends to dissipate (to a greater or lesser degree) into subcultures each of which may favor different kinds of development. It is at this stage, therefore, that the historical base of the company may be less of a guide to the choices that may be made. Indeed it may well be that adequate resources are available to pursue more than one strategy — hence some degree of diversification may be sanctioned in order to keep the peace.

- The growth phase also marks the introduction of significant numbers of new people into the organization and the emergence of a middle management. This, in turn, can reinforce the diversity of expectations within the organization and the diffusion of a single dominant culture and preference for one type of strategy.

- Some organizations in growing markets face uncomfortable dilemmas. The strategic logic may dictate that they should follow the natural growth in the market or risk being uncompetitive once growth starts to ease. However, growth may challenge many of the other beliefs of the organization, such as the desire to maintain a "family" atmosphere and approach.

- Many organizations, and particularly government services, decide that development strategies requiring growth are difficult to foster and deliver within the confines of a predominantly low-risk bureaucratic culture. Therefore, they either reject such developments or decide to develop them in a protected way. This issue will be given more discussion in Chapter 11.

Maturity

By the time organizations reach maturity, their culture tends to have been institutionalized to the extent that people tend not to be aware of it or even find it difficult to understand culture as a meaningful concept. It is only when some crisis threatens the organization that the strength of the culture becomes apparent. As a general rule, mature organizations are likely to favor developments which minimize change and are evolutionary. This, of course, is why incremental (as against global) change is so commonly found within organizations. However, whereas incremental developments may be easier from the cultural point of view, they may well prove wholly inadequate if environmental circumstances are deteriorating rapidly as mentioned above.

Decline

To a large extent the issues of cultural fit during decline are a natural extension of those faced during maturity. A cohesive culture may be seen as a key defence against a hostile environment. Organizations face very difficult decisions concerning retrenchment, divestment, and withdrawal from products/markets ingrained in the culture of the organization. Sometimes this readjustment of an organization's strategies can take many years, particularly when the external image of the organization reinforces this dominant internal situation. In some situations the difficulties of readjustment can be so great that the organization's owners choose to sell out to another organization which may then be able to instigate radical changes.

7.4 SUMMARY

This chapter has reviewed how the *suitability* of various strategic options might be analysed. This is an important process since it requires managers to be explicit about the underlying *rationale* behind particular strategies and to try to understand why these strategies might succeed or fail. Rather than provide a single framework for an analysis of suitability, it has been suggested that a variety of different perspectives is more helpful. This relates to the central theme of this book, namely, that strategic development within organizations is subject to a variety of different influences which, for convenience, have been grouped under three headings — the environment, resources, and expectations/culture.

The extent to which different types of strategies might suit the circumstances of an organization has been reviewed in relation to these various factors. It has been seen that one common threat is the life cycle stage of an organization which affects both the strategic logic of various options and the cultural climate in which strategic developments are taking place.

The next chapter considers strategic evaluation at a more detailed level where assessments concerning the feasibility and acceptability of *specific* strategies need to be sharpened.

References

1. See Chapter 4 for a discussion of SWOT analysis.

2. The idea of consistency of strategy was used by S. Tilles, "How to Evaluate Corporate Strategy," *Harvard Business Review*, Jul.-Aug. 1963, pp. 175–85, to describe the efficiency of policies with respect to the environment." He also referred to the extent to which strategy was appropriate in terms of resources available. These ideas of consistency and appropriateness are encapsulated in the term "suitability" used in this book.

3. The term "feasibility" has much the same meaning as Tilles' (see reference 2 above) criterion of "workability," i.e., is there a likelihood that the strategy can be made to work?

4. This idea that establishing the underlying rationale is an important preliminary analysis is similar to Rumelt's idea of the "strategic frame" discussed in Chapter 2. Rumelt describes this step as follows: "Before one can decide whether or not a given strategy will work some indication that the right issues are being worked on is needed." See, "Evaluation of Strategy: Theory and Models," in D.E. Schendel and C.W. Hofer, eds., *Strategic Management*, (Boston, Mass.: Little Brown and Co., 1979), pp. 196–217.

5. For example, C.W. Hofer and D. Schendel, *Strategy Formulation: Analytical Concepts*, (St. Paul, Minn.: West Publishing Co., 1978) structure their chapters around this distinction between "corporate level" and "business level" strategies.

6. R. Gruber and M. Mohr, "Strategic Management for Multi-program Non-profit Organizations," *California Management Review*, Spring 1982, pp. 15–22.

7. Hofer and Schendel (reference 5) provide a good review of portfolio matrices. Also: "The Strategic Environments Matrix-BCG's New Tool," *Financial Times*, November 20, 1981.

8. Reservations about the use of the Boston Consulting Group's concepts and proposals are to be found in S. Slatter, "Common Pitfalls in Using the BCG Product Portfolio Matrix," *London Business School Journal*, Winter 1980.

9. The techniques built around the life cycle concept described in this chapter have been developed and explained by the consultants Arthur D. Little in a series of booklets, the first of which was *A System of Managing Diversity* by R. V. L. Wright, published in 1974 by Arthur D. Little.

10. M.E. Porter, *Competitive Advantage*, (New York: Free Press, 1985).

11. M.E. Porter, *Competitive Strategy*, (New York: Free Press, 1980), discusses the special problems associated with the onset of industry maturity.

12. S. Segal-Horn, *Strategic Issues in the Globalization of Service Industries*, EIASM Workshop, Brussels, May 1987.

13. See reference 10 for a discussion of how followers in an industry might compete through differentiation.

14. Y. Doz, *Strategic Management in Multi-National Companies*, (Oxford: Pergamon Press Limited, 1986), p. 155.

15. M.E. Porter, *Competitive Strategy*, Chapter 12, reviews strategies for declining industries.

16. See I. Ansoff, *Implanting Strategic Management*, (Englewood Cliffs, N.J.: Prentice-Hall, 1984), pp. 80–4 for a discussion of synergy.

17. See A. van de Vliet and D. Isaac, "The Mayhem in Mergers," *Management Today*, Feb. 1986, pp. 38–41, and R. Heller, "The Agonies of Agglomeration," *Management Today*, Feb. 1986, pp. 42–7.

18. The PIMS data are collected from organizations which subscribe to the services offered by the Strategic Planning Institute. The data shown here are aggregate data, but subscribing organizations are able to access data more specific to their industry sector and use them to analyse their performance relative to that industry sector.

19. These data are further discussed in B.T. Gale, "Planning for Profit," *Planning Review*, January 1978.

20. See R.D. Buzzell *et al.*, "Market Share — a Key to Profitability," *Harvard Business Review*, Jan-Feb. 1975, pp. 97–106.

21. This is discussed in one of the major articles describing the PIMS findings, S. Schoeffler, R.D. Buzzell and D.F. Heany, "Impact of Strategic Planning on Profit Performance," *Harvard Business Review*, Mar-Apr. 1974, pp. 137–45.

22. See reference 21.

23. For a more thorough discussion of the impact on profit performance of capital intensity see S.

Schoeffler, "Captial-Intensive Technology-vs-ROI; A Strategic Assessment," *Management Review*, September 1978. Also S. Schoeffler, "The Unprofitability of Modern Technology," *Pimsletter* No. 2, 1984, pp. 8–14.

24. This is dealt with in another article dealing with the issue of capital intensity, B.T. Gale, "Can More Capital Buy Higher Productivity," *Harvard Business Review*, Jul.-Aug. 1980, pp. 78–86. Also, *Make Ready for Success* (NEDO: 1981) — a report on the UK printing industry between 1974 and 1981 — draws similar conclusions.

25. V. Kijewski, "Market Share Strategy: Beliefs vs. Actions," *Pimsletter* No. 9, 1983.

26. S. Schoeffler, "Market Position: Build, Hold or Harvest?" *Pimsletter* No. 3, 1984 and R. Morrison and D. Tavel, "New Products and Market Position," *Pimsletter* No. 28, 1982.

27. These findings are from the work of R. Rumelt, *Strategy, Structure and Economic Performance* (Cambridge, Mass: Harvard University Press, 1974) and are also summarized in an article by Bruce Scott "The Industrial State: Old Myths and New Realities," *Harvard Business Review*, March/April 1973, pp. 133–48. Readers should be careful about drawing fine distinctions between Rumelt's categories since the sample size of 100 is small and such distinctions would not be statistically significant.

28. R. Reed and G. Luffman, "Diversification: the Growing Confusion," *Strategic Management Journal*, Vol.7, 1986, pp. 29–35. Their results were derived from inflation adjusted data for British industry over the period 1970 to 1980. The top 1000 UK companies were used to produce a sample of 349 who had not changed their product market base over the ten years. The sample included manufacturing and service companies. Significant deletions from the top 100 included non-British companies, those subject to takeover or liquidation during the period, financial institutions, non-public companies and those which government owned or controlled.

29. H.K. Christensen and C.A. Montgomery, "Corporate Economic Performance: Diversification Strategy versus Market Structure," *Strategic Management Journal*, Vol. 2. No.4, 1981, pp. 327–43.
R.A. Bettis, Performance Differences in Related and Unrelated Diversified Firms, *Strategic Management Journal*, No. 4, 1981, 379–93.
R.P. Rumelt, "Diversification Strategy and Profitability," *Strategic Management Journal*, No. 4, 1982, pp. 359–69.
P.H. Grinyer *et al.*, "Strategy, Structure, the Environment and Financial Performance in 48 UK Companies," *Academy of Management Journal*, Vol. 23, No. 4, 1980, pp. 193–220.
C.A. Montgomery, "Product — Market Diversification and Market Power," *Academy of Management Journal*, Vol. 28, No. 4, 1985, pp. 789–98.

30. E. Schein, *Organization Culture and Leadership*, (San Francisco: Jossey-Bass Publishers, Ltd., 1985).

Recommended Key Readings

In Part III of *Competitive Advantage*. New York: Free Press, 1985, M.E. Porter reviews the rationale behind generic competitive advantage in different industry environments.

C.W. Hofer and D. Schendel. *Strategy Formulation: Analytical Concepts*. St. Paul Minn.: West Publishing Co., 1978, provide a useful review of portfolio analyses in Chapter 4.

The work of the PIMS project and many of the findings are summarized in R.D. Buzzell and B.T. Gale. *The PIMS Principles: Linking Strategy to Performance*. New York: Macmillan, 1987.

E. Schein. *Organization Culture and Leadership*. San Francisco: Jossey-Bass Publishers, Ltd., 1985, relates culture, life cycle, and strategic choices.

Chapter 8
STRATEGY EVALUATION: TECHNIQUES

8.1 INTRODUCTION

The previous chapter introduced criteria for strategy evaluation (suitability, feasibility, and acceptability) and also considered how the suitability of particular *types* of strategy might be established in terms of their strategic "logic," the cultural fit with the organization, and the research evidence available linking the choice of strategy to organizational performance.

This chapter is concerned with how *specific* options can be evaluated against this background and considers the following:

- The *screening* of options prior to more detailed analyses of specific strategies.
- Methods of assessing the acceptability and feasibility of specific options against different measures:
  - The *return* a strategy is expected to produce for the costs it would incur.
  - The degree of *risk* a strategy would imply.
  - The extent to which the strategy appears *feasible*.
- A critical review of how organizations *select* future strategies.

Readers are referred back to Figure 7.1 as a reminder of how these various aspects of evaluation relate to each other.

8.2 SCREENING OPTIONS

One of the benefits which should emerge from the assessments of suitability discussed in Chapter 7 is an understanding of the underlying *rationale* behind particular types of strategies — reasons why such strategies might work. However, within these broad types there will still be many *specific* strategies an organization could follow, and the process of evaluation normally requires a narrowing down of these various options before a detailed assessment can be undertaken. This is not to suggest that options "eliminated" at this stage will not be given further consideration later. This section begins by reviewing the basis on which specific strategies can be assessed — whether options are to be judged on an absolute basis, against each other, or against the "do nothing" situation (introduced in Chapter 6).

The section then outlines three contrasting approaches to the screening of options:

1. *Scoring* methods which rank options against a set of predetermined factors concerning the organization's strategic situation. The extent to which specific options fit these criteria determines their position in this "league table."

2. *Decision trees* which also assess specific options against a list of key strategic factors. However, here, options are ranked by progressively eliminating others.

3. *Scenarios* attempt to match specific options with a range of possible future outcomes and are particularly useful where a high degree of uncertainty exists (say in the environment as discussed in Chapter 3). Scenarios are a means of keeping many more options under consideration.

8.2.1 BASES FOR COMPARISON

Many of the following methods of evaluation are only valuable if the analysis of any given strategy has some appropriate basis for comparison. Chapter 4 has already discussed the importance of establishing an appropriate basis for comparison (in assessing strategic capability).

There are problems in only using absolute measures or industry norms as bases for comparison. These measures assume that options are independent of each other, and more importantly, do not address a central problem in strategic evaluation, namely the need to identify the incentive to change from the present strategy to a different one. Since strategic evaluation is concerned with assessing whether or not companies should change their present activities, it is often helpful to use the "do nothing" situation as a basis for comparison since this helps assess the company's incentive to change from present strategies. The "do nothing" situation (introduced in Chapter 6) is the likely outcome if the organization were to continue with current strategies disregarding any changes occurring in the environment or resource position of the company. The easiest way to incorporate the "do nothing" situation into an evaluation is to include it as a strategy option to be evaluated with the others, as will be seen in the later discussions. However, it must be remembered that "do nothing" is not an option *per se* — it merely provides a valuable baseline for assessing the incentive to change.

A useful technique incorporating this approach is *gap analysis*[1] which can be used to identify the extent to which existing strategies will fail to meet performance objectives in the future.

Figure 8.1 outlines the analysis for a single product/single market situation. Of course, this is a highly simplified example and readers must bear in mind that like any other

Figure 8.1 *Gap analysis.*

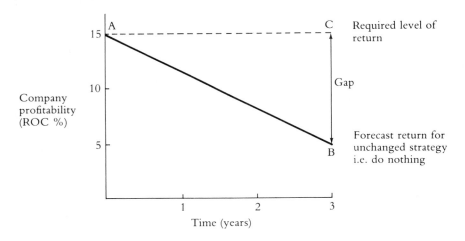

The company is currently operating at 15% return on capital and wishes to maintain that level. Increased competition, escalating labor costs and deteriorating machinery underlie the forecast of declining profitability unless current strategies are revised. BC represents the gap likely to exist in the 3 years time between required performance and actual performance. This gap needs to be "filled" by new strategies.

forecasting process, gap analysis can be difficult and time consuming. In addition, it is usually necessary to apply important measures other than profitability. Some of these may be easily quantifiable, such as productivity or volume of sales, while others may be more subjective, such as levels of quality or service.

Gap analysis is also used extensively in public sector planning, although in a somewhat different way. Here the strategic problem is often whether the future demands on a government service are likely to change to such an extent that the current resource provision will prove wholly inadequate. This is particularly important when considering the statutory obligations of many government services, such as hospitals, education, or social services. Demographic information is often of central importance in attempting to assess the likely gaps in provision as can be seen from Illustration 8.1.

8.2.2 SCORING METHODS

Scoring methods are a systematic way of analyzing *specific* options for their suitability or fit with the picture gained from the strategic analysis.

1. *Ranking* is the simplest type of scoring method where each option is assessed against a number of key factors the strategic analysis identified in the organization's environment, resources, and culture. Illustration 8.2 is an example of how such a ranking might be performed. One of the major benefits of ranking is that it helps the analyst to think

---

ILLUSTRATION 8.1   *Aging and Public Expenditure*

Gap analysis is very helpful in the development of public sector policies and spending plans.

One of the difficulties of public sector policy making is the long term nature of many commitments; often supported by mandatory legal obligations to provide particular services. For this reason it is essential to predict the likely level of demand for the various public services many years ahead in order to establish the strategic implications for policy making and budgeting. Planning is guided by an assessment of the gap which is likely to exist between current provision and expected future demands. These gaps vary by individual services and from one situation (e.g., country) to another.

One of the more important underlying trends which influences demand for public services is the age structure of a country's population. Analyses have predicted that by the year 2025 the ratio of government spending to Gross Domestic Product (GDP) will increase significantly in almost every advanced industrial country. This is attributed to the fact that people are living longer and producing fewer children, and the resultant growing cost of medical care and pensions is outstripping any possible decline in education costs.

Also, the pool of productive workers available to support the growing ranks of retired and elderly people will shrink, significantly raising the tax burden necessary to support social programs.

Comparisons between different countries are quite startling in terms of the gap which needs to be bridged. For example, in Canada, social spending is likely to fall as a percentage of GDP until 2010 and then show a modest rise. In the United Kingdom, a slow but steady rise is expected, accelerating beyond 2010 (post-war "bulge" retirements). By 2025, the impact of demographic change on the Japanese economy is likely to be the most extreme. This reflects the lateness and rapidity with which Japan began the demographic transition to a lower fertility rate and a higher life expectancy. Social spending is predicted to increase some 80% (as a percentage of GDP) by 2025.

The policy implications for bridging these gaps are significant. For example, decisions must be made about the possible need to contain the real increase in per capita benefits; limiting the growth in medical costs; the possibility of higher tax rates; and the desirability of raising savings and investment rates.

This policy debate at the national level clearly has to be paralleled at the local/regional level — where the picture is further complicated by population movements and major differences from average, country-wide statistics. Equally, the planning taking place in individual service departments will be strongly influenced by this changing population structure and by policy priorities.

Source: "Aging and Social Expenditure in the Major Industrial Countries 1980–2025," I.M.F. Occasional Paper No. 47, 1986.

through mismatches between a company's present position and the implications of the various strategic options. This is a useful preliminary step before a more detailed consideration. For example, one mismatch might be the lack of adequate production facilities to meet the output implied by a strategy. This would identify the need to assess the feasibility of a capital investment program to bridge this gap using some of the techniques discussed below. More sophisticated approaches to ranking[2] assign weightings to each factor in recognition that some will be of more importance in that evaluation than others. The method can also be combined with sensitivity analysis (see below) to test the likely impact on the company if the assumptions about each factor should change.

2. Chapter 4 discussed how the analysis of organizational resources in relation to the concept of the value chain could yield a picture of the organization's *distinctive competence* and identify those value activities crucial to particular strategies. Such an analysis, if extended into the future, provides a means of scoring a strategy in resource terms as shown in Table 8.1. This is often referred to as *resource deployment analysis*.[3]

The resource requirements of alternative future strategies should be laid out indicating the key for each strategy. For example, an extension of the home market would be critically dependent on marketing and distribution expertise together with the availability of cash to fund increased stocks. The resource analysis of the company should then be matched with the resource requirements of possible strategic options. In the example, it is clear that the company's resources are specifically geared towards the current product/market strategy and may represent a constraint to any change.

There is a danger that resource deployment analysis will simply result in organizations choosing strategies which most closely fit the configuration of their present

---

ILLUSTRATION 8.2   *Ranking options — an example, Chevron Foods Ltd.*

Chevron Foods began trading in 1976 and grew rapidly in its first two years of operation to an annual turnover of about $0.5m by 1978. This small private company imported orange juice under license from Florida and distributed the frozen juice to hotels in the UK together with a dispensing system which was installed and serviced free of charge. The key to the company's successful growth lay in this system which allowed hotels to serve high quality juice, at the right temperature, very quickly and efficiently during periods of high demand (breakfast). The company's sales had been largely confined to the larger hotels in the London area (with the exception of national chains which required a national service). The distribution of juice and installation/servicing of dispensers were subcontracted to independent operations.

In 1978, the company needed to decide to which of the many development alternatives they should give more detailed consideration, and a preliminary ranking of alternatives against a number of strategic factors was made (shown in the table).

Options	Desire for small company	Need to control quality of service	Dependency on supplier - license - credit	Threat of competition	Need for "big" outlets (To "pay" for cost of installation)	Need for high margins	Ranking
1. "Do Nothing" (i.e., current strategy)	↙	↙	Supplier wants growth(X)	X	↙	↙	C
2. Seek new suppliers	↙	↙	X	X	X	?	C
3. More customers of same type (in London)	X	↙	↙	Already large market share(X)	Best outlet already serviced(X)	↙	A
4. Expand nationally (in hotels)	X	Could lose control(X)	↙	↙	↙	↙	A
5. Expand product range (e.g., other juices)	↙	X	↙	X	X	↙	B
6. Seek new outlets (restaurants)	X	X	↙	May spread effort too widely(?)	Few large enough(X)	↙	A
7. Seek new outlets (hospitals)	X	X	↙	X	↙	X	B
8. Diversify (frozen foods)	?	X	X	X	X	?	B
9. Take over distribution and/or servicing	X	↙	?	X	X	?	C

↙ = Favorable influence   X = Unfavorable influence   ? = Uncertain or irrelevant
A = Appear most suitable   B = Moderately suitable   C = Appear least suitable

The ranking process is used to group the various options into three categories (A, B, C) in relation to their suitability. It should be noted that each strategic factor may not carry the same weight or importance: the need for growth to counter competition was in fact of overriding importance, so options 4 and 6 were identified as most suitable despite their lack of fit with other factors.

Source: "Chevron Foods Ltd.," Case Study by G. Johnson (1980). Available from the Case Study Clearing House of Great Britain, Cranfield.

Table 8.1 *Resource deployment analysis.*

(a)	(b)	Resource implications (c)					
Key resource areas	Present company situation	Strategy A (extend product range)		Strategy B (extend home market)		Strategy C (sell overseas)	
Financial							
Available cash	2	3	(1)	4	(2)	4	(2)
High inventories	3	2	(1)	4	(1)	4	(1)
Physical							
Modern machines	5	5	(0)	3	(2)	3	(2)
Distribution network	0	1	(1)	5	(5)	5	(5)
Human							
Skilled engineers	5	5	(0)	1	(4)	2	(3)
Marketing expertise	0	2	(2)	5	(5)	5	(5)
Other							
Reputation for quality	5	5	(0)	5	(0)	5	(0)
Overseas contacts	0	0	(0)	0	(0)	4	(4)
Degree of mismatch			(5)		(19)		(22)

(a) This would be produced from a strengths and weakness analysis (see Section 4.5 of Chapter 4).
(b) From previous resource analysis 0 = major weakness, 5 = major strength.
(c) 0 = unimportant, 5 = critical to success of strategy.

resources. It should be remembered that the real benefit of such an analysis should be the identification of those necessary changes in resources inferred by any strategy. This relates to resource planning which needs to take place during strategy implementation and will be discussed in Chapter 9. For example, in Table 8.1 both strategies B and C will require quite significant changes in resources.

3. In Chapters 4 and 6 it was stressed that if an organization's competitive position is to be sustained it will normally require a consistent theme — a generic strategy — to be supported by the resource base of the organization (its value chain). In particular, the *linkages* between value activities within the value chain and with the value chains of suppliers, channels, and customers are normally an important source of competitive advantage. Therefore, in screening specific strategies, it is useful to assess how far any new strategy would add strength to the linkages already in existence, or develop needs linkages competitors cannot match.

8.2.3 Decision Trees

Although decision trees[4] have been widely used in operational decision making, their use in strategy formulation has not, in general, received a great deal of attention. A typical strategic decision tree is illustrated in Figure 8.2. The alternatives listed at the end-point of the tree are actually discrete development opportunities as explained in Chapter 6 (Figure 6.1). However, the difference lies in how these options are screened for evaluation. Whereas previous methods have assumed that all options have equal merit (in the first instance), the decision tree approach ranks options by the process of progressively eliminating others. This elimination process is achieved by identifying a few key elements or criteria future developments are intended to incorporate, such as growth, investment, and diversification. For example, in Figure 8.2, the choice of growth as an important aspect of future strategies would automatically rank options 1 to 4 more highly than options 5 to 8. At the second step, the need for low investment strategies would rank 3 and 4 above options 1 and 2 and so on. Decision trees combine the identification of options with a simultaneous ranking of those options.

Perhaps the greatest limitation of decision tree analysis is that the choice at each branch on the tree can tend to be somewhat simplistic. For example, answering yes or no to diversification does not allow for the wide variety of alternatives which might exist

Figure 8.2   *A simplified strategic decision tree for a confectionary manufacturer.*

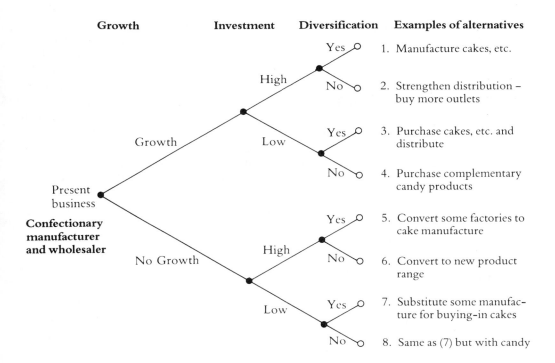

between these two extremes (see Chapter 6). Nevertheless, a decision tree can often provide a useful framework for beginning an evaluation.

Although the discussion of the decision tree has been confined to its use as a screening technique, readers should note that decision trees can also be used to evaluate specific aspects of strategic decisions. Historically, most emphasis has been placed on the assessment of the pay-off or profitability of alternative strategic decisions, such as investment programs or major R&D exercises. Such an analysis usually relies on forecasts of the profitability of various outcomes, or performance levels to be achieved. For example, probabilities must be assigned to the successful launch of a new product, the degree of market share gained, or the level of sales. It is not intended to discuss this particular use of decision trees here but readers should remember that the use of any evaluation technique at a strategic level is always limited by the difficulties of forecasting the factors used in the analysis. This can sometimes be forgotten when using neat techniques like decision trees.

8.2.4 SCENARIOS

A third approach to screening is that of scenario planning[5] which attempts to match specific options with a range of possible future situations (or scenarios). In other words, screening is used to categorize strategies as well as to eliminate some which do not fit any scenario. It is a particularly valuable approach where the future is very uncertain and the organization needs to be ready to respond to a range of different eventualities. The approach is essentially qualitative and is used as a means of addressing some of the less well structured or uncertain aspects of evaluation. It is often used to forecast the likely impact of possible environmental changes. Although scenarios are usually qualitative they are, nonetheless, detailed. They should identify key elements which could influence company performance such as competitive, economic, technical, social, or political forces. The type of scenario used will differ depending on the level within an organization. For example, in a multinational petroleum company such as Shell, the highest levels of management would be most interested in "global scenarios" — worldwide developments — while the focus would be narrower for specialized divisions, functions, or business sectors. Some aspects of global scenarios may, nonetheless, be relevant to more localized decision making — for example, developments in the Middle East will inevitably influence the local energy situation.

Scenarios are essentially a qualitative forecast of events but (unlike traditional forecasting) are based on the belief that the future is very difficult to measure and control.

The critical issue in scenario planning is that the organization should be clear on how it would respond to each scenario. This is usually formalized in terms of a set of *contingency plans* to meet the various scenarios. In other words, different strategic options would be implemented in each scenario. Equally important is the organization's ability to monitor the onset of a particular scenario in time to implement appropriate strategies. Illustration 8.3 provides some examples of scenarios.

ILLUSTRATION 8.3   *Examples of Scenario Building*

By taking a conceptual or qualitative approach to planning, management can vary its decision making according to a series of possible future outcomes or situations. Two examples are provided: the first is an example of "global" scenario building and the second details scenario building particular to one firm.

The Ten Americas Scenarios
The following is a very short summary of the ten scenarios to the year 2000 developed for the U.S. Environmental Protection Agency. These ten scenarios were developed to help the Agency plan for the kinds of varied national environments it might be faced with in the future.

"Hitting the Jackpot": Everything will be fine — abundant energy, widespread prosperity, highly responsible business leadership, and any environmental problem solved.

"Not-So Great Expectations": There will be a decline in energy supply, worsening climate, and food shortages along with a major depression, but social and economic institutions will survive.

"Apocalyptic Transformation": American society will be near collapse with an "energy bust" and a markedly deteriorating climate but people with adopt frugal values to survive.

"Journey to Transcendence": The standard of living will drop as inflation occurs and unemployment increases. Americans will adopt more frugal values and learn to live within the new limits.

"The Center Holds": The established order of big business, big agriculture, and big government is able to retain control despite energy shortages, bad climate, an eroding standard of living, and increasing political terrorism.

"The Boom Years": A recession will occur because of energy problems, but will be followed by better times as the climate improves and new energy sources are developed.

"The Industrial Renaissance": A recession and energy shortages curb economic growth, but new energy sources restore a slow, purposeful growth that is non-wasteful and non-polluting.

"The Dark at the Top of the Stairs": The world experiences continuing bad climate and recession leading to a withering of the Western industrial states with a grudging acceptance of a starkly frugal life-style.

"Mature Calm": After a period of frugal living, the energy problem begins to solve itself and the climate improves leading to an increase in the standard of living.

"Toward the Jeffersonian Ideal": There is a realization among Americans that they will have to temper the urge to be affluent with the realities of limited resources, and a national policy of zero energy growth will be accepted.

General Motors' Scenario-Strategy Matrix
The scenario-strategy matrix below is the outcome of a scenario building process at General Motors. Two scenarios were developed: one optimistic or the "best case," and the other pessimistic or the "worst case." The basic strategy options for the company were identified as: business as usual (no changes); reorganize the present business (regroup, transfer people, relocate or close plants, and so on); increase the level of vertical or horizontal integration; decrease the level of integration; or diversify into new businesses.

Scenario-Strategy Matrix

	Business as usual	Reorganize	More integration	Less integration	Diversify
Optimistic scenario	+ +	+	+ +	−	+
Pessimistic scenario	− −	+	−	+	+ +
Strategy	Business as usual	Reorganize	More integration	Less integration	Diversify

The outcomes of the various strategies were assessed for each scenario with plus or minus symbols (+ + being the best and − − the worst). In this example, the most advantageous strategies are to reorganize and to diversify because these will be the most successful under both the optimistic and pessimistic scenarios.

Source: "Alternative Futures for Environmental Policy Planning: 1975–2000," Washington: Environmental Protection Agency, 1975, (Doc. No. EPA540/9–75–027); Paul Dickson, *The Future File: A Guide for People with one Foot in the 21st Century*, (New York: Rawson Associates, 1977); M. E. Naylor, "Planning for Uncertainty-The Scenario-Strategy Matrix," in K.J. Albert, ed., *The Strategic Management Handbook*, (New York: McGraw-Hill, 1985), Chapter 22.

8.3 ANALYZING RETURN

An assessment of the *returns* likely to accrue from specific options is a key measure of the *acceptability* of options. However, there are different ways returns can be reviewed which require different approaches to the analysis of return. This section looks at two different assessments:

1. *Profitability* analyses which are important where financial return is of central importance — the situation which prevails in most commercial organizations.

2. *Cost/benefit* analyses where the returns are often less tangible, as occurs in many government or non-profit organizations where strategies are more likely to be justified in terms of improving provision rather than financial return.

8.3.1 PROFITABILITY ANALYSES

Profitability is a most important measure of financial acceptability.[6] For profitability measures to be useful they must relate back to a sensible basis for comparison. In strategic

Figure 8.3   *Some useful measures of profitability for strategic evaluation.*

a) Return on capital employment

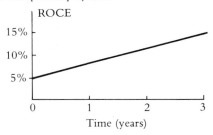

b) Payback period

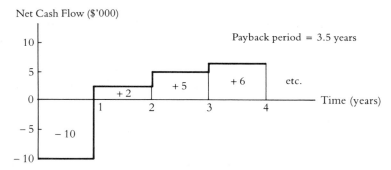

c) Discounted cash flow (DCF)

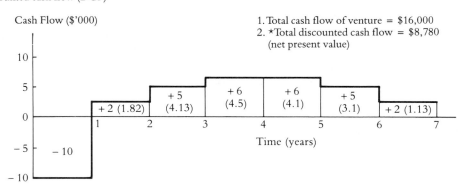

*Using a discounting rate of 10%
Figures in brackets are discounted by 10% annually

evaluation, the most useful measures are those which relate anticipated earnings to the amount of capital needed to generate those earnings.

A useful evaluative measure is the anticipated *return on capital employed* "x" years after a new strategy is implemented (e.g., the new strategy will result in a return on capital of 20% by 1992) — see Figure 8.3 a). Care must be taken to establish whether this measure is to be applied to the whole company or simply to the extra profit related to the extra capital required for a particular strategy. The former is more relevant to a company undergoing slow strategic changes while the latter would normally be applied to large investment programs.

When new strategies involve significant sums of capital investment then there are better measures of the relationship between capital expenditure and earnings. One such measure is that of *payback* which assesses the period of time required to pay back the invested capital.

In Figure 8.3 (b), the payback period can be most easily established by estimating the *net cash flow* of the project or strategy in each of the periods ahead. A typical investment would follow the pattern in the figure. The payback period is calculated by finding the time at which the cumulative net cash flow becomes zero — in the example, about three and a half years. The judgment is then whether or not this is regarded as an adequate outcome and if the company is prepared to wait that long for a return. This will clearly vary from one industry to another. In capital intensive industries, major investments normally have to be justified over a minimum of five years. In contrast, in fast moving consumer goods and services, payback is usually required more quickly. Major government ventures, such as bridge building, may well be assessed on a payback period of up to sixty years.

Discounted Cash Flow (DCF) analysis is perhaps the most widely used investment appraisal technique and is essentially an extension of the payback period type of analysis. Once the net cash flows have been assessed for each of the preceding years (see Figure 8.3 c)), they are discounted progressively to reflect the fact that funds generated early are of more real value than those in later periods (years). In the example, the discounting rate is 10% which reflects the value placed on money tied up in the venture. So, the projected net cash-flow of $2,000 in year 2 is discounted to $1,820 and so on. The Net Present Value (NPV) of the venture is then calculated by adding all of these discounted annual cash flows over the anticipated life of the project. DCF analysis is particularly useful for comparing the financial merits of two or more strategies which have very different patterns of expenditure and return. Most computer spreadsheet packages have an NPV function available for DCF calculations. Readers are referred to the references for a fuller discussion of these financial analysis techniques.

8.3.2 Cost/Benefit Analysis

In many situations, the analysis of profit is too narrow an interpretation of return, particularly where *intangible benefits* are an important consideration. This is very often the case in public sector projects, for example, when a site for an airport or a power station must be selected.

Cost/benefit analysis[7] attempts to put a money value on all the costs and benefits of a strategic option — including intangibles. Although this monetary representation of intangible costs and benefits can prove difficult in some cases this is not always true. Figure 8.4 is an example of the expected costs and benefits of a particular strategy and the basis for quantifying the intangibles. It can be seen that the basis of quantification needs to be justified carefully and is likely to be subject to disagreement from different interested parties. For example, the value put on the loss of an amenity (the public park) could be argued to be far greater than the proposed assessment if the general character of the city center is "spoiled" by replacing the park with a parking garage.

One of the greatest difficulties of cost/benefit analysis is deciding on the boundaries of the analysis. For example, in Figure 8.4 the increased attraction of shoppers to the city center will undoubtedly result in a diversion of spending from neighboring areas rather than an overall increase.

Despite the very real difficulties with cost/benefit analysis, it is a valuable approach when its limitations are understood. Its major benefit is in forcing people to be explicit about the variety of factors which should influence strategic choice. So, even if people disagree about the value assigned to particular costs or benefits, at least they are able to argue their case on common ground and decision makers are able to compare the merits of the various arguments. A detailed cost benefit analysis would proceed to assign weightings to the various items in Figure 8.4 in order to reflect their relative importance to the decision at hand.

Figure 8.4   *Cost benefit analysis – an example.*

A city council was considering whether to construct a new parking garage on the site of a city park.
The main costs and benefits were identified as:

Costs	**Bases of quantification**
1. Acquiring site	Already owned, market value known
2. Construction costs	Tenders obtained
3. Loss of amenity (park)	Known usage of park & notional entry charge (if privately owned)
4. Increased total transport costs	Differential between public and private (car) travel
Benefits	
1. Revenue	Demand & price forecasts
2. Reduced congestion in streets	Incremental increase in consumer spending due to easier access

8.4 ANALYZING RISK

The likely return from a particular strategy is an important measure of the acceptability of that strategy. However, there is another measure of acceptability against which strategic options might need to be assessed. This is the *risk* the organization faces in pursuing that strategy. This section outlines how this risk can be assessed as part of an evaluation of specific options.

8.4.1 FINANCIAL RATIO PROJECTIONS

One of the simplest analyses is the projection of certain key financial ratios[8] which give a broad measure of the risk the organization would be taking by pursuing various strategies. At the broadest level, an assessment of how the capital structure of the company would change by pursuing different options is a good general measure of risk. So, for example, options which would require the extension of long term loans will increase the leveraging of the company and increase its financial risk. The collapse of Dome Petroleum in the mid-1980s was a reminder of the dangers of funding capital investment extensively through long term loans (in the case of Dome, to the tune of $6.3 billion), particularly if market demand does not develop as forecast and interest rates rise. The level of financial risk created by funding a proposed strategy using long term loans can be tested by examining the likelihood of the company reaching the break-even point (see below), and the consequences of falling short of that volume of business while interest on loans continues to be paid. In this respect there is a clear link between the assessment of risk and the feasibility of alternative strategies.

It should not be assumed that these analyses of financial risk are entirely a matter for the private sector. New York City went through an extremely difficult period in the 1970s as it struggled to cope with a financial structure which was a legacy of the 1950s and 1960s.

At a more detailed level, consideration of the likely impact of an organization's *liquidity* is important while assessing options. For example, a small retailer eager to grow quickly may be tempted to fund required store renovation costs by delaying payments to suppliers and increasing bank overdraft. This reduced liquidity increases the financial risk of the business. The extent to which this increased risk threatens survival depends on the likelihood of either creditors or the bank demanding payment from the company.

8.4.2 SENSITIVITY ANALYSIS

Sensitivity analysis[9] is a useful technique for incorporating the assessment of risk during strategic evaluation. Its use has grown with the availability of computer spreadsheet packages ideally suited to this type of analysis.

The principles behind this approach are very straightforward. The technique allows each of the important assumptions underlying a particular option to be questioned and changed. In particular, it seeks to test how sensitive the predicted performance or out-

ILLUSTRATION 8.4   *Sensitivity Analysis*

Sensitivity analysis is a useful technique for assessing the extent to which the success of a company's preferred strategy is dependent on the key assumptions which underlie that strategy.

In 1987, the Dunsmore Chemical Company was a single product company trading in a mature and relatively stable market. It intended to use this established situation as a cash cow to generate funds for a new venture with a related product. Estimates had shown that the company would need to generate some $4m cash (at 1987 values) between 1988 and 1993 for this new venture to be possible.

Although the expected performance of the company was for a cash flow of $9.5m over that period, (the *base case*), management was concerned to assess the likely impact of three key factors:

a)   **Sensitivity of cash flow to changes in real production costs**

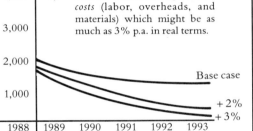

a)   Possible increases in *production costs* (labor, overheads, and materials) which might be as much as 3% p.a. in real terms.

b)   **Sensitivity of cash flow to changes in plant utilization**

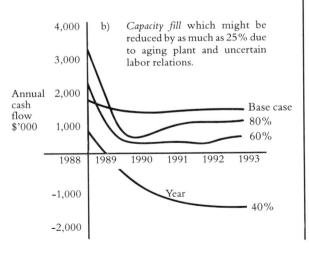

b)   *Capacity fill* which might be reduced by as much as 25% due to aging plant and uncertain labor relations.

c)   Sensitivity of cash flow
     to changes in real price

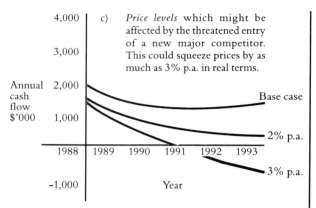

c)   *Price levels* which might be affected by the threatened entry of a new major competitor. This could squeeze prices by as much as 3% p.a. in real terms.

It was decided to use sensitivity analysis to assess the possible impact of each of these factors on the company's ability to generate $4m. The results are shown in the graphs.

From this analysis, management concluded that its target of $4m would be achieved with *capacity utilization* as low as 60% which was certainly going to be achieved. Increased production costs of 3% p.a. would still allow the company to achieve the $4m target over the period. In contrast, *price squeezes* of the order of 3% p.a. would result in a shortfall of $2m.

Management concluded from this analysis that the key factor which should affect their thinking on this matter was the likely impact of new competition and the extent to which they could protect price levels if such competition emerged. Therefore, an aggressive marketing strategy was developed to deter potential entrants.

Source: The Dunsmore example is by G. Johnson and K. Scholes and has been adapted for the North American edition. The calculations for the sensitivity test utilize computer programs employed in the Doman Case Study by P.H. Jones (Sheffield City Polytechnic).

come (e.g., profit) is to each of these assumptions. So, for example, the key assumption underlying a strategy might be that market demand will grow by 5% per annum, that the company will stay strike-free, or that certain expensive machines will operate at 90% loading. Sensitivity analysis asks what would be the effect on performance (in this case, profitability) if, for example, market demand grew at only 1% or as much as 10%. Would either of these extremes alter the decision to pursue that particular strategy? A similar process is repeated for the other key assumptions. This process helps management develop a clearer picture of the risks involved in making certain strategic decisions and the degree of confidence it might have in a given decision. Illustration 8.4 shows how sensitivity analysis can be used in strategic evaluation.

8.4.3 DECISION MATRICES[10]

There are many circumstances where specific aspects of strategic choice can be reduced to simple choices between a number of clearly defined courses of action. This is often the case when choosing between different development methods for a particular strategy. For example, an organization which has decided to expand its operations by developing a new geographical market may be faced with three different methods of achieving this: by building new premises; by buying and converting existing premises; or by leasing a purpose-built building. (See Figure 8.5) There is some uncertainty about the likely level of demand in the new market particularly in relation to obtaining one major contract. If the contract is won, demand is likely to be 20,000 units p.a., otherwise a demand of 10,000 units p.a. is anticipated.

Having analyzed the costs of these various options, the likely impact on unit production costs in each case is estimated, as shown in Figure 8.5 a). In deciding which option to choose, it is necessary (before any detailed analysis) to be clear about which type of *decision rule* would be used to weigh these options against each other. For example, in Figure 8.5, there are four different rules which could be applied:

1. The *optimistic* decision rule would choose the best of the best outcomes for each option. In this case, the best outcomes (i.e., lowest cost) for each option are $35, $33 and $40 respectively, so purchase and refit is chosen as the best of these three outcomes, since at $33 it represents the lowest possible cost situation.

2. The *pessimistic* decision rule would take the entirely opposite view. In this case, the best of the worst outcomes for each option is chosen. In the example, the worst outcomes for each option are $58, $56, and $50 respectively — hence the option of leasing would be chosen on this basis, since if demand proved to be only 10,000 units this option would have the lowest cost.

3. The *regret* decision rule would favor options which minimize the lost opportunity which might occur by choosing a particular option. So, in the example, if "purchase and refit" was pursued and sales turned out to be only 10,000 units then the wrong decision would have been made since leasing would have produced a lower cost. The regret with this choice would be $6 per unit (i.e., $56–$50). Similarly, if leasing had been chosen and sales turned out to be 20,000, the regret would be $7 per unit since option 2 would have been a cheaper alternative by that amount (i.e., $40–$33). Fig. 8.5 b) shows the regret table for each combination of option/outcome. The regret rule would give preference to "purchase and refit" since this minimizes the possible lost opportunity or regret.

4. The *expected value* rule introduces an important new dimension — namely, the *probability* that each outcome (demand) would occur. This can then be used to weight the outcomes for each option and, then, to compare the options on this basis. Fig. 8.5 c) shows how this process would be undertaken in a case where it was felt that the higher demand of 20,000 was only 30% certain. It can be seen that in these circumstances the leasing option would be preferred, since it has the lowest weighted average cost.

Figure 8.5   *Decision matrices: an example.*

a) Unit cost table for the options

Annual sales volume (units)

Option	10,000	20,000
1. Build new premises	$58	$35
2. Purchase and refit	$56	$33
3. Lease	$50	$40

b) Regret table for the options

Annual sales volume (units)

Option	10,000	20,000	Maximum regret
1. Build new premises	$8	$2	$8
2. Purchase and refit	$6	$0	$6
3. Lease	$0	$7	$7

c) Unit costs weighted by the probability of each outcome

Annual sales volume (units)

Option	10,000 (probability = 0.7)	20,000 (probability = 0.3)	Weighted average cost
1. Build new premises	$58 x 0.7	$35 x 0.3	$51.10
2. Purchase and refit	$56 x 0.7	$33 x 0.3	$49.10
3. Lease	$50 x 0.7	$40 x 0.3	$47.00

Although decision matrices are helpful in analyzing some aspects of strategic choice (as in the example), they clearly need to be tempered by other considerations not directly included in this simplified analysis. In the example, it may be that one reason for leasing the available premises is to deny a major competitor the opportunity of setting up quickly in that location.

8.4.4 SIMULATION MODELING

In the 1960s, there was great enthusiasm for the possibilities global strategic models[11] could bring to policy evaluation. Models of this kind attempt to measure and predict all the complex relationships which shape a company's future. For example, a model would include all the relevant environmental factors and the way they affect company performance, together with internal factors such as cost structure, deployment of assets, and so on. In other words, strategic models attempt to encompass all the factors considered by the separate analyses discussed in this chapter in one quantitative simulation model of the company and its environment. It should be no surprise that such global models have been virtually impossible to build. Nevertheless, the principle of *simulation modeling* is a useful one in strategic evaluation for those aspects which lend themselves to this quantitative view.

Financial models are often used to assess strategic options. *Risk analysis*[12] is a technique which seeks to assess the overall degree of uncertainty in a particular option by (mathematically) combining the uncertainties in each of the elements of the option. So for example, the likelihood of a particular profit projection is governed by the uncertainties surrounding costs, prices, and volume forecasts. Although risk analysis is theoretically much neater than sensitivity analysis (see above), it is less widely used. The main reason for this is that sensitivity analysis often more clearly depicts the strategic importance of this assessment of uncertainty. In other words, it is a better technique for communicating the key messages to decision makers.

One of the limitations on the use of strategic modeling is the need for large amounts of high quality data concerning the relationships between environmental factors and company performance. In this respect, the recent work of the Strategic Planning Institute (SPI) using the Profit Impact of Market Strategy (PIMS) data base[13] has been interesting (see Chapter 7). Research at SPI has tried to build a number of quantitative causal models (multiple regression) which explain how companies' performances have been influenced by up to two dozen different factors.

8.4.5 HEURISTIC MODELS

Many of the techniques applied to management decision making attempt to find the best or optimum solution to a problem or situation. In strategic evaluation, this is invariably very difficult due to the complexities of the situation and the high levels of uncertainty involved. It has also been acknowledged (in Section 8.2) that many strategic decisions are concerned with finding a satisfactory option rather than the "best" option.

Heuristic models[14] are a means of identifying satisfactory "solutions" in a systematic way. Perhaps the simplest forms of heuristic models are the "rules of thumb" managers use continuously in their day-to-day decision making and which are a central part of management intuition and judgment. Some examples might be:

"Always run the plant at 90% capacity fill."

"Have five times the number of sales leads as the order book."

"One doctor can cope with a 2,500 patient practice."

"Reorder when stock gets down to 200 units."

"If you get the right merchandise you can sell it off fish barrels."

Readers should note the strong link to discussion elsewhere in the book (particularly Chapter 2) concerning the importance of the "recipe" in guiding the actions of managers and also the dangers of sticking blindly to the historical recipe.

Where the situation is more complex — when many options are available to an organization and there are many different requirements to be fulfilled — a more detailed approach will be needed. This requires that all decision criteria be listed (e.g., "a satisfactory option must provide 5% p.a. revenue growth, labor productivity gains of 2% p.a., and must avoid closures in low income areas" and so on.) The various options are *searched* until one is found which satisfies all the criteria. This is not necessarily the best option. Indeed, the search can be continued to provide a short list of options which fit the criteria and in that sense could be used for screening. With the advent of cheap and powerful computers, heuristic modeling is becoming useful as an evaluation technique since the search process can be undertaken quickly even when many criteria need to be met and several hundred options exist.

8.4.6 STAKEHOLDER REACTIONS

There is some danger that the assessment of risk will be regarded as a totally dispassionate, objective analysis. In practice, the assessment of the *political risk* inherent in various strategies can be an important deciding factor between those strategies. For example, a strategy of market development might require the cutting out of middlemen (such as wholesalers), hence running the risk of a backlash which could jeopardize the success of the strategy.

A new strategy might require a substantial issue of new shares which might be unacceptable to certain powerful groups of shareholders since it would dilute their voting power. Plans to merge with other companies or to trade with new countries might be unacceptable to unions, government, or other customers. Clearly, in the government sector an understanding of these softer measures of risk is invariably important during strategic evaluation. It would be unwise to proceed with options likely to be permanently undermined by the political activity of either consumers or other organized groups. The key judgment is how long-lived these reactions are likely to be.

Often the most important issue is the likely reaction of competitors to particular strategic changes. Therefore, *game theory*[15] should, in principle, have some use as an evaluation technique. However, the difficulties of coping with the complexity of the strategic situation have limited the use of game theory to largely qualitative applications. Perhaps the biggest difficulty with using game theory lies in the assumption that the strategic competitive behavior of companies can be predicted by using simple rules. Readers should refer to the references for a fuller discussion of this technique.

8.5 ANALYZING FEASIBILITY

The previous two sections have largely been concerned with the acceptability of strategic options. This section looks at ways of assessing the feasibility of options although it should be remembered that many approaches actually combine a parallel assessment of both of these criteria.

8.5.1 FUNDS FLOW ANALYSIS

The assessment of financial feasibility would normally be an important part of any strategic evaluation. A simple and valuable piece of analysis is a *funds flow forecast*,[16] which seeks to identify the funds required for any strategy and the likely sources of those funds. For example, in Figure 8.6 the evaluation of a proposed strategy (*X*) would proceed by the following steps:

1. An assessment of the capital investment needed (e.g., new buildings, machines, or vehicles) — $13.25m.

2. A forecast of the cumulative profits earned over the period 1988–1990. "Funds from operations" of $15m are calculated from an estimate of future profits plus the adding back of any non-fund items such as depreciation, and represent the real flow of funds into the company forecast for that period.

3. An estimate of the necessary increases in *working capital* required by the strategy can be made by the separate consideration of each element of working capital (stock increases, increased creditors, etc.) or by using a simple *pro rata* adjustment related to the forecast level of increase in sales revenue. For example, if the present revenue of $30m requires a working capital level of $10m then a forecast increase in sales revenue to $31.65m would account for the anticipated increase in working capital of $0.55m. This type of *pro rata* adjustment would only be valid when looking at future strategies which are similar in nature to the present company activities.

4. *Tax* liability and expected *dividend* payments can be estimated (in relation to the anticipated profitability). In this case, $1.2m and $0.5m respectively.

5. The calculation so far leaves a shortfall in funds of $0.5m. The forecast is then finalized by looking at alternative ways of funding the shortfall and this is where the critical

Figure 8.6   *A funds flow forecast for strategy X (1988–1990), $'000.*

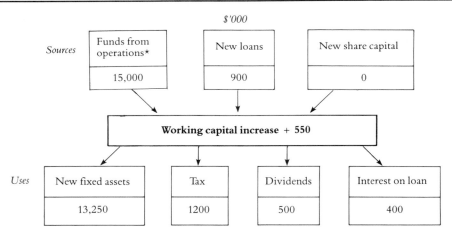

*Funds from operations = Profits corrected for non-fund items such as depreciation.

appraisal of financial feasibility occurs. In the example shown, this shortfall is to be funded by an additional short term loan of $0.9m (which in its turn will incur interest payments of $0.4m over the three year period assuming simple interest at 14.8% p.a.).

It should be remembered that funds flow analysis is a forecasting technique and is subject to the difficulties and errors of any method of forecasting. Such an analysis should quickly highlight whether or not the proposed strategy is likely to be feasible in financial terms and could normally be programmed onto a microcomputer should the model be repeatedly required during evaluation.

8.5.2 BREAK-EVEN ANALYSIS

Break-even analysis[17] is a simple, and widely used, linear programming technique helpful for exploring some key aspects of feasibility. In particular, it is often used to assess the feasibility of meeting targets of return (e.g., profit) and, in this way, it combines a parallel assessment of acceptability. As mentioned previously, this kind of analysis also provides an assessment of the risk in various strategies particularly where different options have markedly different cost structures.

Illustration 8.5 is an example of how break-even analysis can be used to investigate such issues as:

- The likelihood of achieving the levels of market penetration required for viability (in the static market situation).
- Whether competitors would allow profitable entry.
- Whether cost and quality assumptions are, in fact, achievable.
- Whether funding would be available to provide the required capacity and skilled labor to operate the plant.

ILLUSTRATION 8.5   *Using Break-even Analysis to Examine Strategic Options*

A manufacturing company was considering the launch of a new consumer durable product into a market where most products were sold to wholesalers who supplied the retail trade. The total market was worth about $4.4m (at manufacturer's prices) — about 630,000 units. The market leader had about 30% market share in a competitive market where retailers were increasing their buying power. The company wished to evaluate the relative merits of a high price/high quality product sold to wholesalers (Strategy A) or an "own brand" product sold directly to retailers (Strategy B). The table below summarizes the market and cost structure for the market leader and these two alternative strategies. The important conclusion is that the company would require about 22% and 13% market share respectively for Strategies A and B to break even.

Market and cost structure	Market leader	Strategy A	Strategy B
Price to retailer	$10	$12	$8
Margin to wholesaler	30%	30%	–
Wholesaler buys at	$7	$8.40	–
Variable costs/unit:			
raw material	$2.50	$2.90	$2.50
marketing/selling	0.50	0.60	0.20
distribution	0.20	0.20	0.20
others	0.30	0.30	0.20
total	3.50	4.00	3.10
contribution/unit	3.50	4.40	4.90
Fixed cost	500,000	600,000	400,000
break-even point (units)	$\frac{500,000}{3.50}$	$\frac{600,000}{4.40}$	$\frac{400,000}{4.90}$
	= 142,857	= 136,363	= 81,633
Market size	630,000	630,000	630,000
Break-even point (market share)	**22.6%**	**21.6%**	**13%**
Actual share	30%	0	0

8.5.3 OTHER ASSESSMENTS OF FEASIBILITY

It should be clear from the break-even analysis example that the assessment of feasibility is largely concerned with resource availability and assessment of capability against particular strategy options. This issue of resource planning is the subject of the next chapter. From this review of assessments of feasibility, it should be appreciated that it is difficult to divide discussion of strategic choice from that of strategic implementation.

Assessing feasibility is an important part of evaluation which, by necessity, requires a detailed consideration of the resource implications of implementation including the planning of *when* resources will be needed.

In the previous chapter, it was also argued that a key determinant in choosing strategies should be their "cultural fit" with the organization. This will be of central concern in a discussion of the implementation of strategies within the realities of an organization's structures, people, and systems (Chapters 10 and 11). So, in the same way as with resource planning, these factors are important considerations when choosing strategies as well as when attempting to make chosen strategies work in practice.

8.6 SELECTION OF STRATEGIES

The discussions in Chapters 7 and 8 have been concerned with how evaluation of strategic options can be undertaken both in terms of the general suitability of particular types of strategy and also the merits of specific strategic options. However, it is important for readers to recognize that these evaluations do not, by themselves determine which strategies should be *selected* for implementation. Readers are reminded of the discussions in Chapter 2 about the *process* of strategy development. There are three common ways strategies are selected.

8.6.1 SELECTION AGAINST OBJECTIVES

This is a common view[18] of how a rational choice of future strategies should occur, although it is normally impracticable to proceed entirely in this way. This method of selection uses the organization's objectives, quantified where possible, as direct yardsticks by which options are assessed. Evaluation methods are therefore central to the decision-making process and are expected to provide quantified answers regarding the relative merits of various options and to indicate the right course of action. In practice, however, even where this rational selection process occurs, it is very often the case that objectives need to be adjusted as the evaluation proceeds and become what is often called "post-rationalized." The objectives, therefore, fit the strategy and vice versa. In general, it is not a bad discipline to assess the extent to which strategic options might fit the preconceived objectives of the organization, provided it is recognized that this will give just *one* view of which strategies should be selected.

8.6.2   REFERRAL TO A HIGHER AUTHORITY

A common method of selecting future strategies in many organizations is by referring the matter to a higher authority as mentioned in Chapter 2. Those managers responsible for evaluation may not have the authority to give the go-ahead to the "solution." Equally, those senior managers who must decide on strategy may not have participated in the evaluation of options. This is a very important observation which should have a strong influence on how the results of evaluation are conveyed to senior management. In particular, it is very unlikely that senior managers will have the time or inclination to unravel all the detailed ramifications of an evaluation. They are more concerned with basing their judgment of the situation on the available facts and also with seeing how different strategies will fit the overall mission of the company. Thus, the evaluation process is best seen as a means of raising the level of debate which occurs among senior managers when they are judging the selection of strategy.

In large diversified organizations, (including government departments), there will be different types of evaluation occurring at the center than in the divisions, subsidiary companies, or (in government) the various service departments. The board of a conglomerate, for example, might look at their businesses using product portfolio analysis and buy or sell them to keep the portfolio properly balanced, without any detailed understanding of how each business operates. At the same time, the management of the parts of the business will be evaluating alternative strategies to convince their corporate masters that they should be given more resources to try out some new ideas.

8.6.3   OUTSIDE AGENCIES

Sometimes within organizations there are disagreements on strategy between parties who have similar power within the company. These may occur between management and unions, or between two different managers. In these circumstances, it is not unusual for an outside agency, such as a consultant, to evaluate the situation for the company. Very often this process of evaluation is described as an objective, rational process by virtue of the consultant's detachment from the situation. In practice, of course, all good consultants are aware of the political reasons for their involvement. To a large extent their role is one of arbitrator and their evaluation must reflect these circumstances. In multinational ventures, particularly where government is involved, it is very likely that consultants will be employed to assess the merits of the various strategies or at least to act in an advisory role to the decision makers.

8.7 SUMMARY

Strategic evaluation has often been presented as an exact science — a way of deciding what organizations should do. In fact, the analytical methods discussed in Chapters 7 and 8 are only useful as *sources of information* to makers of strategic decisions. It has been seen that the contribution various techniques make to improving the quality of strategic decision making will differ quite considerably. Some methods of analysis are valuable because they are eye-openers — they help managers see the logic or rationale behind strategies rather than assessing those strategies in detail. Other methods are more detailed and are useful ways of understanding how suitable, acceptable, or feasible a specific strategy might be.

However, even the most thorough strategic evaluation cannot possibly anticipate all the detailed problems and pitfalls which might be encountered in the implementation of a strategic change. So it is necessary to recognize that strategic decisions will be refined or even reversed as part their implementation. Implementation is discussed in the final part of this book.

References

1. J. Argenti, *Practical Corporate Planning* (London: George Allen & Unwin (Publishers) Ltd., 1980), describes an approach to corporate planning which is essentially focused around the idea of gap analysis.

2. A discussion of the "opportunity analysis matrix" can be found in F.F. Neubauer and N.B. Solomon, "A Managerial Approach to Environmental Assessment," *Long Range Planning*, Vol. 10, April 1977, pp. 13–20, and G. Johnson, "The Strategic Workshop," *Management Today*, October 1980, pp. 51–64. This extension of the technique is called "strategy mapping" by G. Johnson.

3. C. Hofer and D. Schendel, *Strategy Formulation: Analytical Concepts*, (St. Paul, Minn.: West Publishing Co., 1978), pp. 36–9 discuss the resource deployment matrix as a method of historical resource analysis. We have extended this idea into an assessment of the future (i.e., evaluation).

4. Decision trees are discussed in many books on management science and operational research. For example: P.G. Moore and H. Thomas, *The Anatomy of Decisions*, (Harmondsworth: Penguin Books Limited, 1976), Chapters 4 and 6; R.D. Harris and M.J. Maggard, *Computer Models in Operations Management*, 2nd edn., (New York: Harper & Row Ltd., 1977). Exercise 4 (p. 55) describes a computer package called *Decide* which uses a decision tree.

5. The following references provide useful discussions of scenarios: P.W. Beck, "Corporate Planning for an Uncertain Future," *Long Range Planning*, Vol. 15. No.4., Aug. 1982, pp. 12–21; J.H. Grant and W.R. King, "Strategy Formulation: Analytical and Normative Models," *Strategic Management*, edited by D.E. Schendel and C.W. Hofer, (Boston: Little Brown and Co., 1979), pp. 111–12; G. Steiner, *Strategic Planning*, (New York: Free Press: 1979), p. 235.

6. Most textbooks on financial management will include sections relating to the techniques discussed in the text. We would recommend J.M. Samuels and F.M. Wilkes, *Management of Company Finance*, 3rd edn. (London: Thomas Nelson and Sons Ltd., 1980), pp. 172, 217 and 218.

7. (a) A. Rowe, R. Mason, K. Dickel, *Strategic Management and Business Policy: A Methodological Approach*, 2nd edn., (Reading, MA: Addison Wesley, 1985), Chapter 9.
   (b) Cost benefit analysis is also included as a computer model in A. Rowe *et al.*, *Computer Models for Strategic Management*, (Reading, MA: Addison Wesley, 1987).
   (c) E.J. Mirsham, *Cost-Benefit Analysis*, 3rd ed., (George Allen & Unwin (Publishers) Ltd., 1982).

8. See for example Chapters 10 & 12 in Samuels and Wilkes, *Management of Company Finance*,

reference 6. Rowe *et al.*, *Computer Models for Strategic Management*, (reference 7b) has some useful computer routines for ratio analysis.

9. B. Taylor and J.R. Sparkes, *Corporate Strategy and Planning*, (London: Heinemann Educational Books International Limited, 1977), pp. 48–52 discuss the use of sensitivity and risk analysis as do Samuels and Wilkes, *Management of Company Finance*, p. 233, (reference 6), as methods of incorporating uncertainty into strategic evaluation. Computer spreadsheet packages are ideally suited for simple sensitivity analysis.

10. S. Cooke and N. Slack, *Making Management Decisions*, (Englewood Cliffs, N.J.: Prentice-Hall Inc., 1984), Chapter 7.

11. The use of corporate simulation models is discussed by J.H. Grant and W.R. King, "Strategy Formulation: Analytical and Normative Model," p. 109, (reference 5). For computer based strategic models see Rowe *et al.*, *Computer Models for Strategic Management*, (reference 7b).

12. A long-standing article on risk analysis is D.B. Hertz, "Risk Analysis in Capital Investment," *Harvard Business Review*, January-February 1964, pp. 95–106.

13. For details of the PIMS studies see Chapter 7.

14. See S. Cooke and N. Slack, *Making Management Decisions* (reference 10), and Rowe *et al.*, *Computer Models for Strategic Management*, (reference 7b).

15. The application of game theory is discussed in a number of texts. For example: J.H. Grant and W.R. King, p. 113, (reference 5); P. Kotler, p. 622, (reference 12); M.E. Porter, *Competitive Strategy* (New York: Free Press, 1980), pp. 88–107.

16. Most books on financial management will include a section on funds flow analysis. For example see J.M. Samuels and F.M. Wilkes, pp. 280–83, (reference 6). Also, Rowe *et al.*, (reference 7b) for a computer model.

17. Break-even analysis is discussed in J. Sizer, *An Insight into Management Accounting*, 2nd edn. (London: Pitman Publishing Limited, 1979).

18. For example: J. Argenti, *Practical Corporate Planning*, (reference 1), and D. Hussey, *Corporate Planning: Theory and Practice*, 2nd edition, (Oxford: Pergamon Press Limited, 1982).

Recommended Key Readings

An extensive discussion of approaches to strategic evaluation is C.W. Hofer and D. Schendel. *Strategy Formulation: Analytical Concepts*. St. Paul, Minn: West Publishing Co., 1978, also S. Tilles, "How to Evaluate Corporate Strategy." *Harvard Business Review*, Jul/Aug. 1963, pp. 175–85, is still worth referring to.

Readers should be familiar with the financial evaluation techniques discussed in the chapter. If they are not they should read relevant chapters in a financial management text. For example: J.M. Samuels and F.M. Wilkes. *Management of Company Finance*, 3rd edition. Thomas Nelson and Sons Ltd., 1980, or L.J. Gitman. *Principles of Managerial Finance*. New York: Harper & Row Ltd., 1976.

S. Cooke and N. Slack. *Making Management Decisions*. Englewood Cliffs, N.J.: Prentice-Hall Inc., 1984, is a comprehensive text on decision-making techniques.

A. Rowe *et al. Computer Models for Strategic Management*. Reading, MA: Addison-Wesley, 1987, provides some useful computer routines.

Part IV

Part IV
STRATEGY IMPLEMENTATION

Strategic analysis and choice are of little value to an organization unless the proposals are capable of being implemented. Strategic change does not take place simply because it is considered to be desirable; it takes place if it can be made to work. This part of the book deals with the vital problems of implementing strategy and with the planning of that implementation. Chapter 1 made it clear that one of the major characteristics of strategic decisions is that they are likely to give rise to important changes in the resources of an organization. Chapter 4 explained that such resources do not simply mean physical materials, plant, and finances but also include the people in the organization and the systems used to manage those people. So, when thinking about how strategic change affects the resources of an organization, it is necessary to think about all these sorts of resources.

- Chapter 9 is concerned with the planning of how resources will have to be reallocated given strategic change. This is discussed at two levels: at the corporate level where the problem is the allocation of resources between different parts of the organization as a whole (eg., between different businesses in a conglomerate); and at the operating (or business) unit level where the problem is the provision and allocation of resources between departments, functions, or projects, such as the phasing in of production, the addition or deletion of new products, the raising of finance, or the retraining of part of the work force. Strategic changes usually involve and affect many resource areas: they may be implemented on a day-to-day basis through the operating functions of the organization, but they need to be thought through as a whole to see if they form a coherent package. In Chapter 9, the approach is not to regard the implementation of strategy through resource management as a matter of functional planning but to look at the overall strategic planning of resources.

- A major resource of any organization is the people who work for it. How people are to be managed is obviously important: it is also clear that changes in strategy are likely to give rise to the need to reorganize how they are managed. The last two chapters of the book examine this problem. Chapter 10 concentrates on how people are to be organized in terms of who will be responsible for what: it is therefore concerned with structural questions — what shape should the organization take and at what level should different sorts of decision be made? The chapter also considers the conditions under which certain organizational forms might be more or less appropriate.

- Chapter 11 examines more specifically how strategic change might be managed through the people and systems of the organization. Here the problems and mechanisms of change are considered in terms of systems of control and regulation available to management; and also in terms of cultural and political systems.

Throughout Part IV of the book, it is important to remember the distinction between the planning of implementation and the carrying out of the tasks of implementation. The three chapters in Part IV move progressively from planning to the harsher and often problematic realities of implementation.

Chapter 9
PLANNING AND ALLOCATING RESOURCES

9.1 INTRODUCTION

The successful implementation of strategic change will invariably require some degree of change in the organization's resource profile. The careful planning of these resource changes is therefore extremely important. The discussions in Chapter 4 (resource analysis) highlighted the fact that the specific resource issues to be considered differ with the level in the organization at which the analysis is focused. This is equally true when detailed resource planning needs to be undertaken.

Resource planning usually entails two levels of consideration. First, the broader issues of how resources should be allocated between the various functions, departments, divisions, or separate businesses must be addressed. This analysis should be aided by an analysis of the balance of an organization's resources as referred to in Chapters 4 and 7. Second, a more detailed analysis of how resources should be deployed within any one part of the organization to best achieve the strategies must be done. This kind of analysis is concerned with the operational aspects of resource planning and is supported by a detailed assessment of strategic capability as discussed in Chapter 4 — in particular the value chain analysis. This chapter concludes with some practical advice on how organizations might develop resource allocation plans in a systematic way.

It is also important to emphasize again that when thinking through how a strategy will be put into effect, detailed attention must be given to the feasibility of its implementation. In this way, the planning of resource allocation is part of the evaluation of strategy. There is no sense in proceeding with the implementation of a strategy if, in planning how it should be done, it becomes clear it is unrealistic. Indeed, given the often generalized nature of strategic decision making as it occurs in reality, it may be that really detailed consideration of a strategic course of action does not actually take place until the planning of implementation begins. Managers should then realize that they are not simply planning how something is to be done but also whether or not it is possible or sensible to do it.

9.2 RESOURCE PLANNING AT THE CORPORATE LEVEL

At the corporate level in an organization, resource planning is mainly concerned with the allocation of resources between the various parts of the organization whether these are the business functions (marketing, finance, production), operating divisions, or geographical areas (e.g. in a multinational). Clearly, in large organizations this could consist of several layers or stages of resource allocation. This section looks at how these broader issues of allocation might be tackled in order to support the implementation of strategies. Figure 9.1 illustrates some commonly occurring approaches. It can be seen that the two most important factors in determining the general approach to allocation are:

1. The *degree of change* required in the resource base if strategic change is to be achieved successfully. This could be the extent to which the aggregate level of resources might need to change (e.g. growth or decline) or where significant shifts are required between resource areas within a largely unchanged overall resource.

2. The extent of *central direction* of the allocation process. Whether detailed allocations are dictated from the corporate level or are in response to the detailed plans and aspirations of the various units of the organization.

To illustrate these general approaches to resource allocation, the following three situations will be discussed:

1. Few changes in overall resources or in the deployment of resources.

2. Growth in the overall resource base.

3. Decline in the overall resource base or significant re-allocations within a static resource base.

In each case, the contrasting approaches of centralized or decentralized "control" of resource planning will be considered.

Figure 9.1 *Resource allocation at the corporate level.*

Extent of central direction	Degree of change: Low	Degree of change: High
High	"Formula"	Imposed priorities
Medium	Constrained bargaining	Constrained bidding
Low	Free bargaining	Open competition

9.2.1 FEW RESOURCE CHANGES

If the aggregate resources of an organization and the ways in which they are deployed are unlikely to change significantly with new strategies, then resource allocation tends to proceed along largely historical lines. In some circumstances, this could mean allocating resources by an agreed "formula." For example, an advertising budget might be 5% of sales, or revenue might be allocated on a per capita basis according to customers served. Often there is some room for bargaining around this historical position — for example, by redefining the formula or the way in which resources are measured (when resource sharing or central overhead charges are involved). Zero-based budgeting[1] (discussed later in the chapter) could be a means of building some fluidity into the resource planning process and avoiding some of the worst aspects of "formula" allocations which can be a particular problem where historically based formula allocations reflect the relative political strength of different groups[2] rather than their resource "needs."

9.2.2 ALLOCATIONS DURING GROWTH

During growth, resources can often be re-allocated in relative terms without any particular area of the organization suffering a reduction in resources — simply by directing new resources selectively across the organization. Some organizations will establish these priority areas centrally and impose the resource allocations from the center. At the opposite extreme, some companies adopt an openly competitive attitude towards the various parts of the business. Quite often the center of the organization operates as an "investment bank"[3] from which divisions or functions must bid for resources in an openly competitive way. This mechanism is quite common where new investment funds are being allocated. Clearly, the criteria for judging bids must relate to the chosen strategies of the organization and the resource profile needed to underpin them. Perhaps it is not surprising that most organizations during growth would tend to follow a middle path between these two approaches. This would be described as *constrained bidding*, where the various parts of the organization are able to bid for additional resources but within defined constraints. One of the political skills needed for managers within the units of a company is an understanding of the extent to which these constraints can be challenged and adjusted, as seen in Illustration 9.1.

9.2.3 ALLOCATING RESOURCES IN STATIC OR DECLINING SITUATIONS

The example of the computer company (Illustration 9.1) shows some of the resource allocation problems in an organization experiencing major growth. Many of the same issues apply in static or declining situations but there are important differences. In particular, resource re-allocation will require some areas to reduce in absolute terms to maintain other areas and/or to support new developments. There are differing approaches to these (often difficult) re-allocation problems. In some organizations, re-allocation is simply

---

ILLUSTRATION 9.1   *American Computer (UK)*

An American computer manufacturer operating worldwide through a range of sub-sidiaries developed a particular approach to resource allocation during rapid growth.

During the 1980s the American Computer company was committed to following the "natural" growth in the market (as high as 50% p.a. in the early part of the decade) in order to maintain its worldwide market position. This required very substantial efforts in terms of hardware development (particularly personal computers) and the redirection of the business from an old style hardware manufacturer to a service oriented business. Not surprisingly the company experienced considerable difficulty in following such a rapidly changing business situation and had some difficult resource planning decisions to make at the corporate level. Specifically, the following allocation issues had to be resolved:

- It was soon clear that a "fair-shares for all" policy between subsidiaries would be impractical and undesirable. The company followed a policy of internal competition for investment resources largely based on the previous year's performance against target. But this policy was only pursued within limits. So, for example, the most successful subsidiaries were only permitted to increase their resource base (particularly people) up to an agreed target "head-count." What happened in practice was that the more successful subsidiaries would always achieve sales beyond their target (based on head-count) and use this as a source of pressure to lift their head-count target in the next round of allocations.

- Difficult decisions had to be made at the parent company on how much resource to "cream-off" for new product development which was done centrally. Clearly, in such a fast moving market R&D could not be neglected, but the constant pressure from subsidiaries for more operational resources to support current activities made these investment decisions quite difficult.

- At the area level (e.g., Europe) there was rivalry between the various subsidiaries to be "top-dog" in their area. Although this was an understandable result of the internal competition for new resources, there was also recognition among the more astute managers that some time in the future operations within the area could well be rationalized (as had already occurred in mature multinational industries such as the automobile industry). A strong position in relation to other subsidiaries was needed once that time arrived.

- At the subsidiary level, there were different problems of allocation. During the middle part of the decade one of the major issues was the need to build up strength in the supporting functions such as software support, marketing, and technical support, from a situation where sales had been the one dominant function. Indeed, it required some considerable skill to ensure that these functions received more than their proportional share of new resources in recognition of their weaker starting point.

There was also a major shift in selling effort away from the traditional mainframe and minicomputers towards personal computers and this required the use of independent sales outlets rather than direct selling. This meant the diversion of some of the sales budget to establish a new selling arm to deal with these intermediaries.

imposed centrally as with some plant closures. In other circumstances, the re-allocation may be achieved in an openly competitive way, for example, a freeze may be imposed on all resource replacement by units, particularly employees who may not be automatically replaced as they leave. Vacancies are made subject to open competition and go to those units with the most pressing case. The most common situation lies between those two approaches, in other words constrained bidding for resources. In this case the competition is for resources which may be diverted from other areas. This competition is often made possible by earmarking a proportion of the total organizational resources for re-allocation to new ventures.

Many companies and government organizations experienced the difficulties of re-allocating resources during the 1980s.[4] Some of the ways re-allocation was achieved illustrate this situation:

- Often reductions were achieved by amalgamating related areas or activities. Although resulting resource savings were often explained by "cutting out overlap" or "economies of scale," usually neither of these were as important as the new opportunities which arose to prioritize within the new unit instead of the more difficult task of favoring one unit against another. For example, within a hospital two related specialisms may be merged under the same consultant.

- Paradoxically, another common solution was through the creation of new units outside the normal structure. This is particularly appropriate where the unit clearly supports the defined strategy. The unit was resourced by the marginal paring back of all other areas (hence maintaining "equality of treatment"). Once established, the new unit (if successful) was often the subject of some considerable rivalry and competition from the more established units. This rivalry and competition for resources occurs even though the more established units originally had devoted a portion of their scarce resources to help the unit develop. This competitive process often determined in which area of activity the new unit was assimilated into the mainstream. By this obtuse process, resource re-allocation occurred — often to a substantial degree.

- Of course there were some circumstances where resource allocation was achieved by a more overt and less subtle process — by simply closing down one part of the organization — and this has occurred in the automobile, steel, and mining industries.

9.2.4 RESOURCE SHARING/OVERLAP

One of the particularly difficult aspects of resource allocation at the corporate level is how much overlap, sharing, or duplication of resources should occur between the various parts of the organization. This problem arises in many different ways, such as how various services (e.g., secretarial) should be shared between departments and even grander issues such as whether two divisions should share their production capacity or have a common sales force. Issues of this type are very closely tied to the structure and systems of the organization and will be discussed in the next chapters.

9.3 RESOURCE PLANNING AT THE OPERATIONAL LEVEL

In the discussion of resource analysis (Chapter 4), the idea of the value chain was introduced as a means of analyzing the variety of ways an organization's capabilities relate to the strategies being pursued. It was emphasized that an organization needs to understand which particular value activities most contribute to the success of the organization's strategies — for example, through cost advantage or differentiation from competitors (or in the public services through cost efficiency or quality of service).

Clearly, during the implementation of new strategies, these same issues are of central importance in the resource planning which needs to occur:

- Resource planning must address resource requirements throughout the value chain, including linkages between resources and with the value chains of suppliers, channels, or customers.

- The planning must establish which value activities are of greatest importance to successful implementation of the selected strategies and ensure that these are given special care and attention.

In order to ensure that these issues are given proper attention in resource planning at the operational level, it is useful to ask a few questions of central importance to resource planning (see Figure 9.2). These questions will now be given some brief discussion before consideration is given to how they will be applied to the various activities of an organization's value chain.

9.3.1 CENTRAL QUESTIONS IN RESOURCE PLANNING

Resource Identification

The most basic requirement is the precise identification of the resources needed to carry out the strategy. Effective planning of resources depends on how clear the planner is about resource requirements. The danger is that resource requirements will be overlooked or that the assumption will be made that the resource needs of the past will cope with the

Figure 9.2   *Central questions in operational resource planning.*

---

1. Exactly what resources will a strategy require for
   its implementation?
   (Resource identification)

2. To what extent do these required resources build
   on or are a change from existing resources?
   (Fit with existing resources)

3. Can the required resources be integrated with
   each other?
   (Fit between required resources)

---

strategies of the future. The powerful influence of a recipe[5] on the views and practices of managers has already been pointed out: it is likely that both at an individual level and at a corporate or even industry level, managers manage very much on the basis of past experience. There is the danger that new strategies will be considered in the context of old expectations or existing bases of operating rather than in terms of what is required in the future. Illustration 9.2 shows how one company, Black & Decker, experienced declining sales and had to carefully focus its resources in a turnaround strategy.

In general, value chain analysis should help establish the value activities of crucial importance for maintaining the organization's competitive position. These are the areas where particular care and attention need to be paid to resource planning.

Fit with Existing Resources

Assuming the resources required to implement the desired strategy are identified, then it is possible to move to the next stage, which begins to clarify just how problematic implementation is likely to be. Strategic change may well entail important changes of resources. Since major resource changes will inevitably raise problems both of operational logistics and probably of conflict within an organization, it is important to be clear on the extent to which existing resources can cope, will need to be changed or added to, or perhaps will need to be replaced altogether. The likelihood is that some will be adequate and some will become redundant.

Chapter 4 emphasized that the strategic capability of an organization is not only determined by the intrinsic strength of its resources but also by the way the resources are deployed and controlled. These same considerations are extremely important when assessing the fit of new resources with old. For example, a company may choose to manufacture and market a new product range through a new division, or even a new company, to avoid problems of conflict with existing operations. So, the planning of resources also leads into structural considerations and issues of managing change which will be discussed more fully in the next two chapters. An assessment of this fit with existing

---

ILLUSTRATION 9.2 *Black & Decker's Refocusing of Resources*

After a period of decline, Black & Decker Corp. was forced to reassess its resources and utilize them to implement a turnaround strategy.

Black & Decker (B&D) Corp., a manufacturer of power tools, started experiencing serious problems in about 1981. Earnings dropped as the company faced strong Japanese competition and failed to market its products effectively. The strong US dollar made it more difficult to maintain foreign markets.

A new management team took over and introduced many cost-saving measures including the closure of several plants. In 1984, the company had acquired General Electric's small home appliance division and faced the additional challenge of making the acquisition profitable.

B&D identified three resource areas critical for returning the company to profitability: research and development, operations management, and marketing. Research and development was a key function as new, or redesigned, products had to be found and introduced. Development here resulted in about 12 new products being introduced a year.

At the same time, the company's manufacturing operations had to be completely reorganized. For example, too many motor sizes had been introduced because decentralized product decisions had been made at plants around the world. The resulting number of product variations was reduced when plants were organized around motor sizes, thus streamlining operations. Through this and other measures, capacity utilization was substantially increased to 75%.

Another resource area to receive attention was marketing, an area that had become weak. New power tool products were successfully launched, but the real challenge was to establish Black & Decker as a brand name in the kitchen. The company started transferring products from the General Electric brand name to its own, one product line at a time. The brand transfer was backed by advertising and appears to have been successful in establishing B&D as a brand name in small appliances.

Source: "How Black & Decker Got Back in the Black," *Business Week*, July 13, 1987, pp. 86 and 90.

---

resources establishes the extent to which implementation is likely to require major changes within the organization or is achievable by an adjustment of the current resource base. It also leads to a consideration of the current resources the organization possesses. New strategies may require a reconfiguration of the value chain and previously perceived strengths of the organization may not really be strengths at all.

Figure 9.3   *Some implications for resource integration in a product launch.*

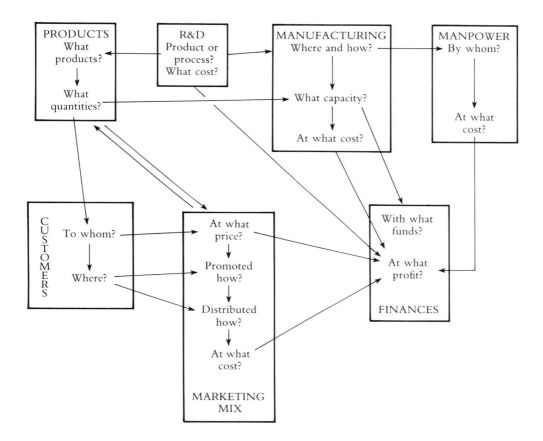

Fit Between Required Resources

One of the critical ingredients of successful strategies is the way in which the linkages between the important value activities and with the value chains of suppliers, channels, or customers are planned in order to give the organization a genuinely distinctive capability. For example, Benetton, ACA JOE, and Banana Republic have been successful in the 1980s through a strategy of product/market differentiation sustained by careful resource planning through the value chain. The procurement of merchandise, hiring of store staff, and store design and layout have been just as important as the product range, pricing, and promotion strategies. The fit between these various resources was critical to their success. Figure 9.3 shows some of the ways resource interaction occurs in a new product launch.

The remainder of the discussion in this section will be devoted to the resource planning which might be needed in each of the primary activities of an organization's value chain as new strategies are implemented. Within each activity three key issues will be considered: 1. overall requirements; 2. fit with existing resources; and 3. fit between resources. The implications of strategic change are summarized in Table 9.1

9.3.2 INBOUND LOGISTICS

The planning of resources is not confined to the internal resources of the organization. In many cases the distinctive strength of a company may arise from the skilful planning of the resource inputs to the organization and the linkages which exist with the value chains of suppliers.[6] Some important questions might be:

1. *What sources of supply* are available for new or changed products? Where are the locations of such suppliers and what sort of suppliers are they? Are the sources able to provide regular and reliable delivery?

2. *To what extent should there be a spread of supply?* There may be advantages in establishing a long term relationship with a limited number of suppliers, such as high levels of service and continuity of supply. This has to be set against the possibility that the organization may become so linked to one supplier that new ideas from other suppliers will be overlooked or more competitive prices ignored.

3. *Cost of supplies* is likely to be a major problem for new product initiatives. In early stages of growth the sales volume may be too low to achieve benefits of low costs through bulk buying. How are costs to be reduced?

4. *What are the financial requirements of the proposed strategy* in terms of current and capital expenditure? To examine this sensibly may require an exercise in both cash and capital budgeting (discussed later in the chapter) since the timing of financial support is of key importance. The identification of these requirements leads to considerations of the way in which such financing is to be obtained.

5. *What sources of product and process technology changes[7]* will be used? Will technological developments be in-house or through technology transfer? Will the company own exclusive rights to the technology (e.g., patents or license agreements)?

6. *What should be the R&D focus?* Should the firm concentrate on product development or process development and at what time should the emphasis switch? Product development will be of crucial importance during the development stage of a product life cycle, and process development and cost production will be as maturity approaches. But when should a company switch its R&D focus from one to the other? Too early and there is a risk that a competitor may develop significant product advantages; too late and the company runs the risk of an uncompetitive cost position.

7. *Is the R&D capability compatible* with the other operational areas of the organization? Is R&D effort being put behind a project that can be marketed, financed, and produced effectively, for example?

Table 9.1 *Some resource implications of strategic change.*

Resource planning issue	The value chain				
	Inbound logistics	*Operations*	*Outbound logistics*	*Marketing and sales*	*Services*
Overall resource requirement	Sources of supply Cost of supply Capital required Source of technology	Production capacity Location of plants Staffing levels/ skills	Transport Inventory Channels	Marketing mix (product, price, place, promotion) Subsidies	Product information Technical back-up Customer returns Maintenance Ancillary products
Fit with existing resources	Suitability of supplies Technology transfer Financial structure Working capital	Convert or new build Replace plant Training Staff reductions/ recruitment	Type of transport Choice of operators Storage and handling Ordering systems	In-house skills Outlets Agents Franchisees Role of sales force Merchandising	In-house provisions Service agents
Fit between resources	Make or buy Inventory policy	Make or buy Plant flexibility Staffing/downsizing Team development	Inventory Lead times Transport costs	Compatibility of costs and price production volumes	Cost of services

8. *Is there sufficient support from other areas* of the operation? One of the major reasons for the failure of R&D activity is the lack of resources due to current business pressures or problems of short term profitability.

9. *To what extent are existing suppliers suitable?* The decision to change a supplier is important: for example, a new model of a product may call for a component which could be made more cheaply by a different supplier; but a company may still be very reliant on their existing supplier for other components or for spares for existing models and, therefore, would wish to retain their goodwill.

10. The *make or buy* issue is important. To what extent is it advantageous to own sources of supply as distinct from buying them elsewhere? (Refer to Illustration 7.1.) This closely relates to the issue of vertical integration, and its advantages and disadvantages have already been covered in Chapter 6.

11. *To what extent is the image or reputation of a supplier* important to other aspects of the business? A new product could benefit (or suffer) considerably in the market if customers know of the use of a component manufactured by a particularly well known supplier.

12. *Is the project to be financed over time from internal[8] resources?* There are indications that management prefers this to be the case, if possible, and particularly in small firms. If this is impossible or not seen as sensible, then where are funds to be obtained? There may be a need for further equity capital, for example. Is this to be raised through a new share issue or by raising further equity from existing shareholders through a rights issue? Alternatively or in addition, *loan capital* may be more attractive. If so, from where is this to be obtained and on what basis? To what extent might third parties be willing to partly finance the venture?

13. *How is an increase in working capital* to be financed? There are two likely sources: tightening up the operation to provide increased profit margins through increased productivity, decreased wastage rates, or credit control, for example; or negotiating an increase in overdraft facility with the bank.

14. An examination of *sourcing of funds* may give rise to a need for change in the financial structure of the organization. When the company's profits are growing, a high level of debt may be advantageous since it increases earnings per share and retained earnings; but when profits are declining, high debt worsens the situation, both for earnings per share and retained earnings. Since the ability of a firm to generate funds for growth is likely to depend largely on the confidence of shareholders and the funds available for reinvestment from retained earnings, decisions on *levels of debt* become critically important.

15. A company which decides to raise capital by issuing *new shares* may also have problems: there may be further dilution of control, particularly for a private company, or the share price may be such that it would be more sensible to achieve an increase in that price before an issue of shares; there may even be fears that a failure to sell the shares might affect confidence in the company.

16.   In terms of both fixed and current assets, what policies will guide the *asset management* of the company? For example, what levels of cash are to be held? If the levels are too high then questions will be asked both by shareholders and potential buyers about why the company is not using or distributing the cash.

17.   Another important aspect of the management of assets is the *deployment of funds* within the enterprise. If funds are to be allocated to one division for a product development strategy, are there other divisions for which funds are not to be made available or curtailed?

9.3.3 OPERATIONS[9]

There are many questions to be addressed in planning the resources within the organization's operations.

1.   *What level of production capacity* is desirable? At least three levels can be considered. "Demand matching" entails attempting to match levels of demand with levels of production and is therefore likely to involve high costs through short production runs. "Operation smoothing" involves producing to average demand, building up stocks in low demand periods and drawing these off in high demand periods. "Subcontracting" entails producing at a minimum level and buying-in the remainder.

2.   *Where should plant be located?* Influences on this might include the proximity of markets, the cost of transport and access to supplies, the cost, availability and skills of labor, or the extent to which there are government incentives to move to an area. Economies of scale may also be an important consideration. For example, a choice between a large, single site with the benefit of economies of scale or several smaller sites nearer to local markets or raw materials might need to be made.

3.   *What should be the timing of investment in plant?* While demand may rise smoothly, costs of investment do not. These costs rise in a stepwise fashion resulting in periods of costly excess capacity, therefore, the timing of investment becomes important. Choices of timing are problematic: whether to be first with new plant and run the risk that later competitors will invest in improved plant; or to invest above levels of demand and accept overcapacity as the price of moving down the experience curve faster; or to introduce new plant later and run the risk of higher unit cost because of uncompetitive plant or inability to meet demand.

4.   *What skills are required*[10] to implement a course of action? These skills may be at a managerial or operative level. For example, a decision to move to a capital intensive, automated plant will necessitate acquiring quite different skills than a labor intensive plant.

5.   Associated with this may be the actual *size of the staff requirement* of the organization. In the case of a switch to automated plant, for example, the total number of staff may be reduced but the number required in specific skills may be increased.

6.   The *identification of training needs* is important. Which individuals need what sort of experience to develop general management and operating abilities?

7. In terms of changes in employment levels, how are numbers to be increased or reduced? In the case of reductions, will this be through *natural wastage, redundancy or redeployment*? Will needed skills be provided from within the organization or by recruitment?

8. What will be the *financial implications* of an extensive redundancy program? In the short term, redundancy payments can reach such high levels that they may mean the difference between relatively healthy overall profits and a loss.

9. Increasing emphasis is being placed on *team development* for managers and staff capable of working together productively. Has sufficient consideration been given to the teams of managers or staff needed to implement strategic change?

10. Given a change in production process, *is it more sensible to convert existing plant or to build new plant*? There may be arguments in favor of each. Conversion may be less costly in terms of capital investment but may mean that the downtime of plant during conversion is high. New plant may be more expensive to build but provide more efficient production on completion.

11. *Should the company make or buy the products*? If it makes or if it buys, to what extent should it do so? The issue is whether or not a company is well advised to tie up its funds in manufacturing when it could be investing in something else — more extensive marketing operations, for example.

12. *Is the production resource flexible enough*? As companies follow paths of increasing replacement of capital equipment for labor, there is the danger that expensive plant will need to be utilized to the full; if this plant is not flexible enough to handle different product ranges or variants then the only way full utilization can be achieved is by seeking extra volume of sales, usually at low margins, resulting in lower profits.

9.3.4 OUTBOUND LOGISTICS

For many organizations, success or failure can hinge on the way in which the shipments of goods to customers or outlets are handled. This may be a substantial element of cost for some companies and/or provide an important means of differentiating an organization from its competitors (e.g., through speed of delivery). In service organizations, many of the elements are equally important — particularly order processing systems. Some key areas are:

1. The *transport and inventory requirements* need careful assessment — particularly issues of centralization or geographical dispersal. Centralization may be cheaper but reduce the speed of delivery to customers.

2. The *type of transport* is also a crucial decision — especially for international operators. Other important decisions concern the choice of specific operators and whether they have experience in handling the types of product concerned (e.g., frozen or delicate goods).

3. The *ordering systems* may be important. In government services the equivalent would be the extent to which the organization's systems encourage or discourage use of the

service, for example, in a library. This is a major strategic problem in many government services.

4.   *Storage and handling facilities* may also be of central importance with particular types of products. For example, toxic substances and fresh foodstuffs.

5.   The choice of *distribution channels* will determine the speed and quality of delivery.

9.3.5   MARKETING AND SALES[11]

Issues concerning the market are of major importance in strategy formulation in both private and public organizations. Many of these broader issues concerning the choice of markets, the competitive position, and strategy have been discussed in previous chapters. However, ultimately the success of the product/market strategy is dependent on detailed and astute planning of the organization's marketing activities. Illustration 9.3 describes how some companies are altering their marketing resource planning to reflect a different approach to market segmentation. In government services these issues are equally relevant — although the term "marketing" tends not to be used — the need to plan services around the genuine needs of users is of great strategic importance.

Some of the questions which need to be addressed related to marketing are:

1.   *Product planning*: What range of products/services will be offered, on what quality levels, and to whom?

2.   *Pricing*: What price levels are appropriate to balance the financial needs of the organization and the attractiveness to potential consumers? Will customer *subsidies* be appropriate and available?

3.   Will *agents or franchises* be used?

4.   *Selling and promotion*: What will be the role of the sales force? Will merchandising activities be crucial? Will joint promotional activities (e.g., with outlets) be appropriate?

5.   *Choice of collaborators:* Even where the general marketing strategy looks fine, the specific choices of individual outlets, franchises etc., is a major influence on performance. Will the chosen individuals/companies enhance your performance/competitive advantage? Will they prove an important link in the value chain?

6.   Can the marketing requirements be met in terms of levels of *production*, at the *required quality and cost*, so as to market the product successfully and make it sufficiently profitable to be financially acceptable?

9.3.6   SERVICES

Many organizations neglect the services they provide in support of their products and in doing so weaken the overall value of their products in the eyes of potential consumers. Important areas are often:

1.   Good quality *information* about products/services.

2.   *Technical back-up.*

ILLUSTRATION 9.3   *Resource Planning — Marketing*

A new approach to marketing, segmenting the market by regions based upon ethnic, suburban, yuppie, or elderly characteristics, may lead to a new way of selling consumer products, and has many implications for how marketing resources are allocated.

Consumer product companies such as Campbell Soup, H.J. Heinz, General Foods, and ConAgra are experimenting with regionalizing their marketing efforts. Consumer products have been mass-produced to standardized specifications across the country. Companies are now realizing that a uniform, national market no longer exists. Market segments exist for working women, minorities, single parents, and older citizens, and different marketing approaches are required. Also, persons living in different geographical regions have different preferences. Instead of one set of products and a promotional plan for all consumers, products, promotion and sales efforts are being tailored to fit different markets or regions.

This new approach has several implications for how marketing resources are allocated in a company such as Campbell Soup. These implications include:

- Marketing will be decentralized to regions, 22 in Campbell Soup's case. Each region will have a sales and marketing staff to develop marketing strategies and media buying for the region. Less marketing will be directed from head office.

- There will be less national advertising and more local targeting. Instead of using national television, more advertising will be done in newspapers and on local radio. Promotion expenditures will be targeted through the use of coupons, sales promotions, and cooperative programs with retailers.

- Campbell Soup was traditionally a strong production oriented company and marketing was neglected. As sales of soup are growing slowly, new products are necessary to maintain growth. For the most part, these new products will be developed, marketed, and advertised at the local level. This results in a more decentralized organization with decisions being made on a divisional or business unit level where responsibility for profits and losses will also rest.

- Traditionally, mass marketing, that is, nationwide advertising, created a consumer pull of products through the system. Recently, with more sophisticated data collection with computers and automated checkouts, retailers have gained power over manufacturers. As retailers know exactly what brand items are selling, they can refuse to carry brands. Manufacturers are hoping to counter this trend with regional marketing efforts supported by new market research technologies able to provide consumer and consumption data.

This new approach is not without its problems. It might drive up manufacturing and marketing costs by reducing economies of scale. The decentralization of decision making will require substantially more coordinative and control mechanisms to insure that corporate objectives are being achieved.

Campbell Soup has also changed its approach towards its Canadian subsidiary. The Canadian operation is now much more independent of the parent company, and is allowed to develop and market products on its own. The subsidiary has been very successful and profitable, and Campbell Soup is considering similar decentralization in other foreign operations.

Source: Tony Thompson, "New Campbell Turns on the Heat," *The Financial Times of Canada*, March 16, 1987, pp. 1 and 24; "Marketing's New Look: Campbell Leads a Revolution in the Way Consumer Products are Sold," *Business Week*, January 26, 1987, pp. 64–9.

3.   Good systems for *handling customer returns*.

4.   A well-organized *maintenance network* (e.g., for consumer durables).

5.   Availability of *ancilliary products* (e.g., computer or video software) can be crucial, as shown in Illustration 9.4.

There is a feeling in many organizations that these items simply add cost (which they do) without recognition that they also add significant value to the product. As such they are likely to be important activities within the value chain.

9.3.7 KEY RESOURCES IN IMPLEMENTING GENERIC STRATEGIES

A useful way of bringing this section together is to return to the concept of generic strategies. Differentiation and cost leadership are basic strategic choices facing an organization: whether or not either can be put into practice will depend on the extent to which the organization has, or can configure, the set of resources and skills required for the generic strategy it chooses to follow.

A cost leadership strategy will require an emphasis on cost efficient plant and processes, with an ability to renew investment to maintain advantage in these areas. It is also likely that particular attention will be paid to achieving simplicity of operating processes and low cost distribution systems. An organization following a diversification strategy, on the other hand, is likely to require different sorts of skills and resources. In particular, there will be a need for strengths in marketing, research, and creativity with an emphasis on product development and engineering and strong links with the value systems throughout its distribution channel.

One of the problems organizations face is coping with the realities of resource requirements of this sort. In particular, problems can occur for diverse organizations seeking to pursue different generic strategies or focus strategies for different products. This requires specific configurations of resources for specific markets or market segments, and is likely to be difficult to implement for an organization with plant, labor and management held in common across products and services.

ILLUSTRATION 9.4 *Philips and the Compact Disc*

In assessing the ability of a company to pursue a new strategy, care needs to be taken not to overlook critically important resources outside the direct control of the company.

Although it was widely acknowledged that the Philips video cassette system (Video 2000) was technically superior to the Japanese VHS system, the product failed to make much impact on the market in the early 1980s. Indeed, it represented the most conspicuous product failure of the company for some years. The product failed partly because it was beaten to the market and partly because of the erroneous judgment that users would have little interest in renting commercially produced videos (mainly movies). They had, therefore, launched the hardware with no "software" back-up. After four expensive years they were forced to bring out their own VHS machine, using Japanese technology.

This experience was very influential in shaping the company's parallel efforts in the audio market, particularly in relation to compact disc machines. The technical know-how of Philips was "offered" to the Japanese electronics giants and Sony took the bait. The two companies agreed to develop the compact disc to a common standard. Ultimately the whole industry fell into line with that standard.

This experience illustrates the importance of two key resources partially outside the company's control. First, the ability to impose an industry technical standard/system and second, the availability of related products (in this case suitable "software" i.e., movies on video).

Source: *Management Today*, January 1986.

9.4 PREPARING RESOURCE PLANS

So far this chapter has dealt with some of the underlying principles behind the planning of resources at both a corporate and operational level and has discussed some of the detailed resource issues to be resolved during implementation. This final section is concerned with the *process* of resource planning and considers some ways resource plans can be prepared.

9.4.1 PRIORITIES AND KEY TASKS

It should be clear from the previous sections that organizations need to be clear about their priorities and the key tasks they should undertake to ensure successful implementation of new strategies. This kind of knowledge also provides the basis for the management and control of new strategies (which will be discussed in the next two chapters). Key tasks and priorities are different from each other. Key tasks are those tasks on which the strategic change is fundamentally dependent for its success. These may be the creation of new value activities, or the development of new linkages within the value chain or with the value chains of suppliers, channels, or customers.

Priorities, on the other hand, have more to do with timing: they are the actions which must be tackled to get the project underway. The design and commissioning of plant or ensuring that financial resources are available might be priorities in this sense. The identification of priorities and key tasks also provides a basis for the allocation of responsibilities. Who is to be responsible for each of the key areas? Where key areas interlink, who is responsible for coordination? It is also worthwhile to be explicit about what is *not* so important. What are the things which should or can be left until later or, more likely, which of the different priorities being advocated are to be followed up and which are not?

9.4.2 The Plan of Action

A plan is made up of responses to the series of questions raised so far in this chapter. It sets out which resources need to be obtained and which disposed of. A plan may well be in the form of a budget, but it might also be usefully expressed as a sequence of actions or a timetable. For example, an organization introducing a new product line would need a plan of action to coordinate the various aspects of its resource planning. For example, on-the-job production line retraining cannot begin until a production facility exists; until the company has examined in detail the timing of development, installation, commissioning, and completion of plant, it is not possible to examine fully the flow of funds required to finance the venture; until the company knows at what rate production is to be geared, it cannot take a sensible view of the extent of the product launch; that in turn means that the company will not have a clear idea of expected revenue flow, so again it cannot think sensibly about the requirement for funds.

The circularity of the problem is quite usual in developing a plan of action and raises the question of where to start — with a market forecast, an available level of funds, a production level constraint, or what? The answer is that it may not matter too much where the starting point is since the plan will have to be reworked and readjusted several times. A useful guideline is to enter the problem through what appears to be the major change area. So, an organization planning new strategies of growth may well start with an assessment of market opportunity. Someone starting a new business may well begin with a realistic assessment of how much capital they might have available. Many government services have been compelled to replan their resources to achieve particular levels of cost savings.

A plan of action should also provide the basis for understanding the impact of changes on the sequencing of activities. What would be the effect of a delay in one part of the program on the rest of the program? Are some areas of activity less sensitive to delays or change than others? It might be found that delays in the installation of plant do not have major impacts on the retraining program or even on the recruitment and activity of the marketing team, since both are fairly flexible. However, such a delay may have very serious marketing consequences if it means that the launch is delayed giving the competition time to react. The plan of action will also provide a means of monitoring and controlling the development of the project. It helps identify points in the program when certain key stages should be completed, for example.

9.4.3 THE RECOGNITION AND TESTING OF KEY ASSUMPTIONS

All plans are based on assumptions. They may be assumptions about resource availability, or the capacity of the organization to adapt existing resources or to coordinate the resource requirements of a new strategy. Assumptions may also have to do with the environment: that a market will grow, that funds can be raised or that suppliers will deliver on time. The questions raised so far in this chapter help identify the main assumptions on which a plan is based and these assumptions should be made explicit as part of the planning process.

The danger is that when a plan is drawn up, the assumptions built into it will take on the appearance of fact and become unquestioned. This is dangerous because the vulnerable areas of the plan are then disguised and the reasons for shortfalls or failures may not be recognized. If assumptions are made explicit, the plan can be used as a model to help both in the evaluation of strategy and also in the investigation of alternative means of implementation of strategy. Different assumptions about market conditions, price acceptability, competitive action, cost levels, and so on, can be tested to see how vulnerable plans of action are to different assumptions. So, too, can different assumptions about timing be tested: what effect would delays in a construction program have on capital requirements, for example? A common way of carrying out this sort of sensitivity analysis is to build "best," "worst," and "most likely" assumptions into budgets, models or a break-even analysis to see what the implications are. The best view would be a budget based on a relatively optimistic set of assumptions, the worst on a pessimistic set, and the most likely on what might be, for example, a consensus view of most reasonable assumptions. The resulting plans can be examined to see the implications of the differing assumptions.

9.4.4 FINANCIAL PLANNING AND BUDGETING[12]

Financial planning is concerned with translating the resource implications of decisions or possible decisions into financial statements of one sort or another. This is most commonly done through the various forms of budgets that managers use. Budgets have many uses and perform different roles in organizations. The concern here is with budgets as plans and models. Illustration 9.5 describes a company that places emphasis on financial budgets and controls.

A budget may take the form of a consolidated statement of the resource position required to achieve a set of objectives or put a strategy into effect. To generate such a statement it is necessary to identify and think through the required resource position of the organization. A budget expresses these in a monthly or yearly form, perhaps divided by departments in the organization. As such, it represents a plan of action for an organiza-

---

ILLUSTRATION 9.5   *Resource Planning — Financial*

Some corporations are known for their focus on resources in particular areas. American Home Products Corp. has a reputation for its strong financial cost controls.

American Home Products is a successful manufacturer and marketer of drug and household products and regularly records a return on equity of more than 30%. Some of its commonly known products are Chef Boyardee, Easy-Off oven cleaner, Dristan, and Woolite.

The company is know for its shrewd and strict financial planning and stringent cost control. Examples of this emphasis on financial matters include: the reviewing of expense reports by senior managers; the expectation of a one and a half year payback for new products instead of competitors' expected three or more years; and the lower allocation of funds to R&D expenditure (5% of sales versus other firms' 10% and more). The attitude is to save money everywhere, and critics suggest that this is hampering new product development.

It should not be concluded that American Home products neglects other function areas. For example, it is known for its marketing and promotional skills, but, the company makes sure that it gets its money's worth out of advertising agencies and media expenditures!

American Home follows what a recent *Harvard Business Review* article (referenced below) referred to as a "financial control" style of managing strategy in multi-business firms. The influence exerted by top or corporate management over the business units, or product divisions, focuses on short term budgetary control. The authors of the article claim that this style of managing strategy motivates managers to improve financial performance immediately, shakes managers loose from ineffective strategies, and is effective at developing managers. A shortcoming of the style is a tendency to ignore strategies and investments with long lead times and paybacks. The authors conclude that this style is appropriate for some firms in some situations, as might be the case for American Home Products.

Source: "Too Much Penny-Pinching at American Home?," *Business Week*, December 22, 1986, pp. 64–5; Michael Goold and Andrew Campbell, "Many Best Ways to Make Strategy," *Harvard Business Review*, November – December, 1987, pp. 70–6.

---

tion stated in resource terms. The process of budgeting also involves the thinking through of the resource implications of action and so has a useful role to play in forecasting the impact of decisions on the resources of an organization or part of an organization. For example, the planned launch of a new product might mean increased demands on the R&D department. That department would then undertake a budgeting exercise to forecast the resource implications for itself and may, as a result, come up with requests for additional resources.

Whether at an organizational or departmental level, a budget is in effect a model of required resources. A model can be examined, tested, and adjusted to see the implications of changes in assumptions about the future or changes in the progress that might be achieved in a project. Can the resources needed be sensibly coordinated or are there incompatibilities? Especially useful is the facility to examine the implications of changes in expected performance, or failure to meet required target deadlines and thus identify key tasks and priorities within the plan. This can be easily achieved if the budget is set up on a computer spreadsheet package.

There are different sorts of budgets.[13] It is always risky to say exactly which sorts of budget are most needed for resource planning, but the following might typically be used:

1. *Capital budgeting* is concerned with generating a statement of the fund flows related to a particular project or decision. A company may decide to invest in new plant or acquire a new business. A capital budgeting exercise might well seek to determine: (a) what the outflow and inflow of funds associated with that project will be; (b) what the implications of different means of financing the project would be (for example, how an acquisition financed by increased loan capital would differ from one financed by increased equity capital); or (c) some assessment of how worthwhile the project is through some measure of return of investment (discussed in Chapter 8).

2. *Revenue budgets* show the expected outcome of decisions in terms of changes in inventories, cash, debtors, and creditors. Underlying such an exercise would be decisions on expenditure and the management of working capital: it might be that the exercise would examine different policies on cash, inventory or creditor management.

3. *Departmental budgets* may be important if strategic changes are likely to affect parts of the business differently. As mentioned earlier, a decision to adopt a more aggressive product development program might well mean a much larger allocation of resources to departments, such as R&D, and a cutback in others.

4. *Consolidated budgets* and projected profit and loss accounts may well be useful in projecting, perhaps over a period of years, implications of decisions on an organization's overall performance. For example, a new venture might reduce a company's overall profits for many years before its benefits at an organizational level become apparent. This may, in turn, highlight as a key task the need to convince shareholders of the wisdom of the venture and the need for patience.

One of the very real difficulties experienced in budgeting is the extent to which the process actually helps the re-allocation of resources to fit future strategies. This is because the budgeting process is usually tied into the power structure in the organization as mentioned in Chapter 5. The types of re-allocation which may be necessary at both the corporate and operational level may well prove extremely difficult due to historical vested interests. This has been shown to be particularly problematic in government organizations where spending is justified against "need" rather than income and often subject to approval through a democratic, political process. The outcome is often the strong remaining strong even where there is agreement to a changing strategy.

To address these budgeting difficulties, some organizations have attempted to adopt a *zero-based budgeting*[14] approach where the historical size of the various budgets is given no weight in establishing the future deployment of resources (see Illustration 9.6). On the whole, this process has been unsuccessful unless tempered with some short term pragmatism. The most effective use of zero-based budgeting usually provides a "safeguard" whereby any individual budget will not vary by more than an agreed percentage from the previous year (this is the "constrained bidding" or "constrained bargaining" referred to in Figure 9.1). There are often good practical reasons for this. For example, the redeployment of resources from one area to another may be achievable, and even universally supported, if the pace of change does not lead to an unmanageable period of transition. In government, it is quite common to signal a commitment to redeploying resources (particularly people) by "red-circling" individuals within the organization. That individual is not redeployed but once he or she leaves, the post is automatically redeployed. The critical issue is whether or not future strategies can wait for redeployment to occur.

9.4.5 NETWORK ANALYSIS[15]

Network analysis, also known as critical path analysis, was developed for the purposes of military planning during the Second World War and has been adapted for management use since. It is a technique for planning projects by breaking them down into their component activities and showing these activities and their interrelationships in the form of a network. By considering the times and resources required to complete each of the activities, it is possible to locate the critical path of activities which determines the minimum time for the project. The network can also be used for scheduling materials and other resources and for examining the impact of changes in one subarea of the project on others. The technique is particularly relevant to projects with a reasonably definite start and finish.

This kind of analysis has been used very effectively in new product or service launches, construction of plant, acquisitions and mergers, relocation and R&D projects; the sort of activities relevant to strategy implementation. Figure 9.4 is an outline network analysis diagram for the launch of a new car. In fact, the analysis would probably be a great deal more detailed, but this example shows how this sort of analysis can help in resource planning.

- Network analysis demands the breakdown of the program of implementation into its constituent parts, by resource area.

- It helps identify priorities because it identifies activities on which others depend. For example, the network identifies that pilot building cannot take place before the development of tooling. Since the runout of the old model is not scheduled to start before the pilot-build, and may well need to be fitted into the selling and promotional calendar, network analysis places an emphasis on the priority of tooling which might not have been obvious at the outset.

ILLUSTRATION 9.6   *Zero-base Budgeting (ZBB)*

Zero-base budgeting (ZBB) arose in the private sector and the greatest potential for its use appears to be in government organizations. However, the difficulty with the ZBB approach is to apply it correctly.

Zero-base budgeting is an approach that requires managers to propose and justify their departmental budgets from scratch. The existence of a budgeted amount last year is not an acceptable argument for its retention in the next budgeting period. All requested funds must be justified in relation to their cost-benefit to the organization. Alternatives less expensive than current activities are sought, and managers can propose increases in departmental activities if these can be justified. Each activity level above the minimum increment covered by the budget is ranked by priority. The outcome of this process is referred to as a "decision package."

The budgeting approach is started at the lowest cost center in an organization and then proceeds up through each level. The total of the accepted decision packages becomes the organization's budget.

The approach originated in the private sector and was used by such companies as Texas Instruments Inc., Playboy Enterprises Inc., Ford Motor Co., and Bank of Montreal. In the 1970s, it became popular in governments and President Carter introduced it in the US federal government in 1977.

The advantage of the approach is that it is a bottom up technique which allows employees to participate in the budgeting process. Some organizations have had difficulty encouraging employee cooperation, and the process has been bogged down in excessive paperwork in some others. However, most organizations claim some benefit from the process.

A study by Stephen L. Gould *et al.* reported in *Canadian Public Administration* (Vol. 22, No. 2, 1979, p. 251–60) evaluated the introduction of ZBB in four departments of the Canadian federal government. The authors found that a positive consequence of the process was the participation of managers. They doubted that more and better information to support budgets was generated and it was not possible to conclude that different or better decisions were made.

However, the authors point out that the benefits of ZBB are long term with the first year or two of the approach not being a true indication of its value. They also indicate that the approach may be of greater value in some departments and programs than in others. It was concluded that forward planning was needed in the implementation of ZBB and that top management must give complete support.

Like the implementation of most management techniques, the approach and its the benefits should not be oversold or treated as a fad. The success of ZBB or other techniques is determined by the appropriateness of the implementation process. New techniques such as ZBB are useful to organizations and can contribute to an organization's success, but unfortunately they frequently suffer from misapplication.

- A network represents a plan of action. It enables the analyst to examine the implications of changes in the plan or deviations from the plan. The analyst can ask questions and follow through the implications for the whole program of development if tooling, engineering design, or the pilot-build program take a longer, or shorter, time than expected. So, a network is of particular value in thinking through the timing implications of a plan.

The network itself may be drawn up at several levels. The sort of network shown in Figure 9.4 may be fine as a generalization of a plan of action: however, there would need to be much more detailed planning at a departmental level, for example. There might be subnetworks for marketing and production or, indeed, a much more detailed overall network.

A common alternative or addition to a network is some form of departmental or project plan which details activities within the network, sets target dates for completion, and allocates clear responsibilities for completion of specific tasks.

There are a number of developments of network analysis methods which readers may find of interest. "Program evaluation review technique" (PERT) allows uncertainty about the times of each activity in the network to be taken into account. For example, in Figure 9.4 steps 4 to 6 would be so dependent on the outcome of the market research that, in reality, it may be difficult to make a precise estimate of the time needed for these activities. PERT would be a useful refinement in such circumstances.

Network analysis can be very valuable in establishing the sequence in which tasks need to be planned. A good network should also assist in drawing up a time schedule (i.e., the precise time when each task should start and finish). However, there are other techniques which can also be helpful in scheduling tasks, such as Gantt charts or route planning. The operations management literature is very helpful in this area of resource planning and should be consulted by readers who have a particular interest.

One specific approach to task scheduling which has received considerable attention and has proved to be of strategic importance to many manufacturing companies is "just-in-time."[16] Just-in-time is a simple philosophy according to which every stage in the manufacturing operation from receipt of materials to assembly and dispatch occurs precisely when it is needed — not before and never later. In effect, split-second timing is applied throughout the process, allowing a factory to work at the desired level of production with no idle inventory. An exceptional level of control is needed to ensure that there are no reject parts to be replaced, no shortages and, equally important, no surpluses. This technique has revolutionized the way in which some companies plan the acquisition of resources with the resultant reduction in costs and, at least in the short run, the potential of gaining competitive advantage on that basis.

9.5 SUMMARY

By looking at the resource planning process, this chapter has started to provide material for thinking through how strategies can be put into effect.

It has been seen that resource planning needs to occur at two general levels within

Figure 9.4 *A network analysis for the launch of a new car.*

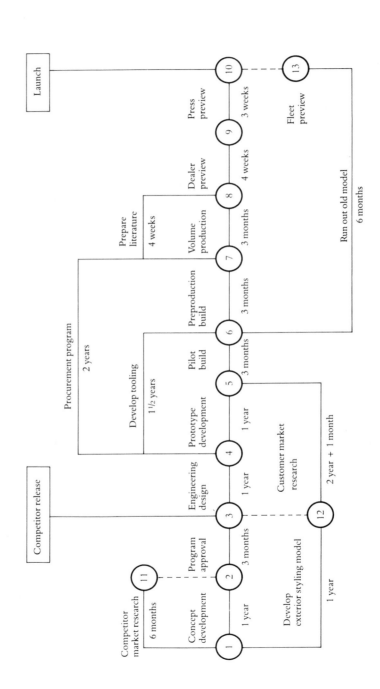

most organizations. First, there are the broad issues of resource allocation between different divisions, service departments, functions, or businesses within an organization. This has been referred to as resource planning at the *corporate level* where the focus is one of deciding how resources should be allocated in order to provide an appropriate balance to pursue the organization's overall strategies. A variety of methods is used to allocate resources at this level depending on the degree of change envisaged in the resource base and the extent to which priorities will be dictated centrally.

Second, the success of a strategy is dependent on a detailed consideration of the resources required at the *operational level*. The organization's value chain is a useful framework for identifying the resource requirements of any strategy.

While the people of an organization are a critical resource in determining the success or failure of strategic change, their influence on strategic implementation is more pervasive than that. Successful implementation also depends on the organization, motivation and control of people. The next two chapters look at these very important aspects of implementation.

References

1. A useful article on zero-based budgeting is D. Wise, "How to Make Bigness Better," *Management Today*, July 1986, pp. 72-75.

2. J. Pfeffer, *Power in Organizations*, (London: Pitman Publishing Limited, 1981), pp. 101-6, outlines the important links between resource allocation processes of power.

3. For example, T. Peters and R. Waterman, *In Search of Excellence*, (New York: Harper and Row Ltd., 1982), explain how an investment bank was operated in 3M's company.

4. P. Dainty, "How to Manage Retreat," *Management Today*, November 1985, pp.100-9.

5. The notion of the recipe as proposed by J-C. Spender, "Strategy Making in Business," (a doctoral thesis, University of Manchester), has to do with the "received wisdom" in an industry and is expressed in terms of how an organization should be operated. In this sense, the recipe is likely to encapsulate views about which resource requirements are particularly important. Also see P.H. Grinyer and J-C. Spender, "Recipes, Crises, and Adaptation in Mature Businesses," *International Studies of Management and Organization*, Vol. IX, No. 3, 1979, p.113.

6. Supplies strategy, important though it is, is not extensively discussed in the literature. However, there is some useful discussion of the area in a chapter by D.F. Cooper called "Corporate Planning and Purchasing Strategy" in D.H. Farmer and B. Taylor, eds., *Corporate Planning and Procurement*, (London: Heinemann Educational Books International Ltd., 1975). D.H. Farmer also discusses supplies strategy in *Insights in Procurement and Materials Management* published by the Institute of Purchasing and Supply.

7. R.E. Burridge, *Product Innovation and Development*, (London: Business Books, 1977) widely covers this field. Readers may also refer to G. Randall, "Managing New Products," *BIM Management Survey Report*, No. 47, 1980, which is a survey of activity and problems in the area, as is W.P. Sommers, "Improving Corporate Performance Through Better Management of Innovation," *Outlook*, Fall/Winter, 1981.

8. A sound general discussion of financial strategy and planning can be found in Chapter 5 of John Sizer, *An Insight into Management Accounting*, 2nd ed., (London: Pitman Publishing Limited, 1979). More detailed discussion of financial management as it relates to financial strategy is to be found in books on managerial finance: for example, J.F. Weston and E.F. Brigham, *Managerial Finance* (Chicago: The Dryden Press, 1978) or L.J. Gitman, *Principles of Managerial Finance* (New York: Harper and Row, 1976).

9. Many of the resource planning issues relating to operations are discussed in R. Wild, *Production and Operations Management: Principles and Techniques*, 3rd Edition, (New York: Holt, Rinehart and Winston, 1984), and T. Hill, *Production/Operations Management*, (Englewood Cliffs, N.J.: Prentice-Hall Inc., 1983).

10. G. McBeath, *Organization and Manpower Planning*, 2nd Edition, (London: Business Books, 1969) is still one of the most thorough treatments of manpower planning in relation to strategic change.

11. The discussion of marketing strategy in P. Kotler, *Marketing Management*, 4th Edition, (Englewood Cliffs, N.J.: Prentice-Hall Inc., 1980) is useful at this level.

12. As a general introduction to budgets and budgetary control, see John Sizer, *An Insight into Management Accounting*, 2nd Edition, (London: Pitman Publishing Limited, 1979).

13. Readers who are not familiar with these techniques should read any good book on management finance. For example, see L.J. Gitman, *Principles of Managerial Finance* (New York: Harper and Row, 1976) or J.M. Samuels and F.M. Wilkes, *Management of Company Finance* (London: Thomas Nelson and Sons Ltd., 1980).

14. See reference 2.

15. Network analysis is explained in almost any text on management science or operations management. So, for example, readers could refer to R. Wild's explanation in Chapter 13 of *Production and Operations Management*, (New York: Holt, Rinehart & Winston, 1979), or K. Howard in *Quantitative Analyses for Planning Decisions* (London: McDonald and Evans, 1975), or P.G. Moore, *Basic Operational Research*, 2nd Ed., (London: Pitman Publishing Limited, 1976), Chapter 2.

16. Just-in-time is explained in T. Hill, *Manufacturing Strategy*, Open University, 1985.

Recommended Key Readings

Chapters 11, 12 and 13 of G.A. Steiner. *Strategic Planning*. New York: Free Press/Collier Macmillan, 1979 provides a useful guide to the translation of strategic plans into functional and operational management, as does R. G. Murdick, R. H. Eckhouse, R. C. Moor and T.W. Zimmerer. *Business Policy: A Framework for Analysis*. Columbus, Ohio: Grid Publishers Inc., 1976.

As a guide to the sort of financial planning necessary: L.J. Gitman. *Principles of Managerial Finance*. New York: Harper and Row, 1976, or J.M. Samuels and F.M. Wilkes. *Management of Company Finance.* London: Thomas Nelson and Sons Ltd., 1980.

For an explanation of the techniques of network planning: R. Wild. *Production and Operations Management,* 3rd Edn. New York: Holt, Rinehart & Winston, 1984.

Chapter 10
ORGANIZATION STRUCTURE

10.1 INTRODUCTION

One of the most important resources of an organization is its people; therefore, how they are organized is crucial to the effectiveness of strategy. The last chapter dealt with how resourcing aspects of implementation might be planned. The next two chapters are primarily concerned with how strategy implementation is effected through the people in the organization.

Traditional views about regulation through an organization can be traced back to early 20th century management "scientists" and beyond.[1] Typically, such views hold that: (1) There is an optimum number of subordinates an executive can control and this dictates what the span of control should be in an organization. For instance, it is sometimes argued than no manager should have more than about six direct subordinates. (2) Everyone should have one boss only, with clear lines of reporting; so the flow of instructions and reporting goes up and down the organization. (3) There should be a clear delineation of who is responsible for what; jobs should be compartmentalized, usually functionally, so that individuals and groups can develop high degrees of specialist skills. (4) There should be clear rules and procedures to govern people's behavior in the organization.

These views are commensurate with a view of strategy making that is essentially top down, strategy is formed at the top and the rest of the organization is seen as a means of implementation; organization design becomes a means of top down control. Such principles of control are known as bureaucratic or mechanistic.[2] As was seen in Chapter 2, however, the idea that strategy is formulated in a top down way is questionable, and the extension of this, that mechanistic structures are necessarily appropriate, is therefore also questionable.

This chapter and Chapter 11 consider organizational design and control in the context of the strategic management of organizations. It is accepted that there is a need for the regulation of the implementation of strategy: but this needs to take into account many influences. For example, what are the sort of problems the organization faces in constructing strategy? Is it in a highly complex or changing environment or a fairly stable environment? How diverse is the organization; for example, are the needs of a multinational company different from a small local firm? To what extent is the organization reliant on simple or complex technologies? How answerable are the top executives to external influences, for example, is the organization a public body, perhaps answerable to a government minister; is it a privately owned firm; or perhaps a charity or a cooperative? All these different influences must have a bearing on the way the organization needs to be designed. It is not possible to have a simple set of rules to prescribe organizational structures and systems.[3] This chapter will examine the structure of organizations in two ways. First, it reviews the basic structural forms which exist. Second, the chapter considers what is likely to influence the sort of structure appropriate to an organization.

10.2   STRUCTURAL TYPES

Managers asked to describe their organizations usually respond by drawing an organization chart, in an attempt to map out its structure. These sorts of structures are like skeletons: they define general shape and facilitate or constrain certain sorts of activity; but they are incomplete in themselves without the sort of "flesh" dealt with later in this chapter and the next. It is also worth noting that the categories used here, although common, are not always employed. For example, in some texts a separate category for "holding company,"[4] or "conglomerate," is sometimes omitted. Other writers[5] split the general category of "multidivisional" into subcategories. However, what follows does provide a basic description of structural types.

10.2.1   THE SIMPLE STRUCTURE

A simple structure could really be thought of as no formal structure at all. It is the type of organization common in many very small businesses. There is likely to be an owner who undertakes most of the responsibilities of management, perhaps with a partner or an assistant. However, there is little division of management responsibility and probably little clear definition of who is responsible for what if there is more than one person involved. The operation is then run by the personal control and contact of an individual.

The main problem here is that the organization can only operate effectively up to a certain size of operation, beyond which it becomes too cumbersome for one person to control. What this size is will depend on the nature of the business: an insurance broker may personally handle a large number of customers, while a similarly sized business (in terms of volume) manufacturing and selling goods, may be much more diverse in its operations and therefore more difficult to control personally.

10.2.2   THE FUNCTIONAL STRUCTURE

A functional structure is based on the primary tasks which have to be carried out, such as production, finance and accounting, marketing and personnel. Figure 10.1 represents a typical organization chart for such a business. This structure is typically found in smaller companies or those with narrow, rather than diverse, product ranges. However, within a multidivisional structure, the divisions themselves are likely to be split up into functional management areas.

The functional structure has some advantages.[6] If the operation is not too large, the chief executive can keep directly in touch with the operations and this is likely to reduce problems of management control because the natural flow of information is vertical and lines of communication are short. There are also likely to be specialists in senior and middle management positions which, it is argued, improves the quality of the management of the functions. In functional structures, job roles are likely to be clearly understood and easy to define because they are based on the tasks the organization has to carry out.

There are some disadvantages too, particularly as organizations become larger or more diverse in their interests. Senior managers may become overconcerned and overburdened with routine matters, neglecting the strategic concerns facing the organization. If the organization's interests have become diversified then the functional structure may not cope easily with the different competitive environments in which it is operating. Suppose, for example, that a one-product company operating in one market develops a new product for a different market. Not only are the managers faced with understanding the demands of different markets, they may also have to cope internally with different technologies of production for the new products. A result may be that such organizations fail to adapt to changing competitive situations. It may be difficult for the organization to deal with these differences by continuing to manage on a functional, task-based structure since the environment and technology are no longer of the same kind. A further problem can arise when cooperation between functions is required, such as the planning of new products, which may need the coordination of marketing, production, and the finance and accountancy functions. If this has to be done by referring problems continually up vertical lines of authority for decisions, then cooperation may become a difficulty. Advantages and disadvantages of functional structures are summarized in Figure 10.1.

10.2.3   THE MULTIDIVISIONAL STRUCTURE

The main characteristic of a multidivisional structure is that it is subdivided into units responsible for defined market, service, or product areas of the enterprise. These divisions may be formed on the basis of products, as for example in Figure 10.2, there are, however, other bases for divisionalization such as geographical areas, or the processes of the enterprise. For example, a vertically integrated company might have manufacturing, wholesaling, and retail divisions. Illustration 10.1 shows how General Electric has within it

Figure 10.1   *A basic functional structure.*

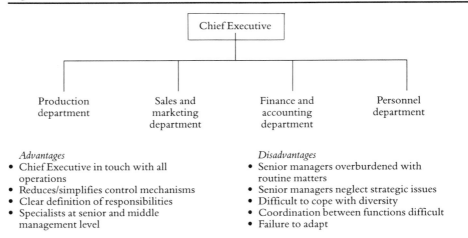

Advantages	Disadvantages
• Chief Executive in touch with all operations	• Senior managers overburdened with routine matters
• Reduces/simplifies control mechanisms	• Senior managers neglect strategic issues
• Clear definition of responsibilities	• Difficult to cope with diversity
• Specialists at senior and middle management level	• Coordination between functions difficult
	• Failure to adapt

different bases of divisionalization; some are product/market based, others are based on functions such as marketing and production; others are geographic and customer related.

The most popular structure now adopted in industrial companies is the multidivisional structure. In 1960, just one third of major manufacturing companies had a divisional structure. By the end of that decade over two thirds had such a structure. This dramatic change coincided with a major program of diversification by these firms, many of which were involved in extensive acquisition programs at that time. Divisionalization has then been a response to the need to manage diversity.[7]

This structural form has come about as an attempt to overcome the sorts of problems functional structures have in such circumstances. The main advantage of the multidivisional structure is that each division is able to concentrate on the problems and opportunities of its particular business environment. The product markets in which a multidivisional company operates are often so different that it may be impractical to bring the tasks together in a single body. It makes more sense to split up the company according to the different product markets or operations and then ensure that the needs of each division are met by tailoring the operations within the division to the particular business needs. The result can be quite a complex organization; for example a company may decide that it needs a number of levels of divisions in order to break up business activities sensibly. Figure 10.3 shows this. The company might be broken into a first level of divisions based on broad markets. Within each of these first level divisions, the businesses may again be split up, and in turn, these business units might be divided further. At some level in the organization, a division will then be split into functionally based departments dealing with the specialist tasks of that business.

Figure 10.2   *A multidivisional structure.*

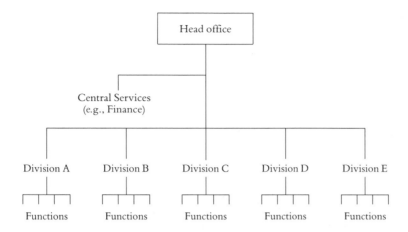

Advantages	Disadvantages
• Concentration on business area (e.g., product market)	• Confusion over locus of responsibility (centralization/decentralization confusion)
• Facilitates measurement of unit performance	• Conflict between divisions
• Ease of addition and divestment of units	• Basis of intertrading
• Facilitates senior management's attention to strategy	• Costly
• Encourages general management development	• Divisions grow too large

This raises another problem. Which functions are to be included at what level of divisionalization; and which functions are properly placed within the corporate head office rather than within any one of the divisions? For example, in Figure 10.3, where should a function such as financial planning be placed? Presumably, financial planning is required both at a corporate level and at some level within an operating business, but should this be at level one, two, or three? Similarly, at which level should personnel policy be decided or bargaining take place? Where should technology development best occur, or property decisions be made? There is no best way to place such functions in an organization. It is a matter of deciding on the most sensible design for the organization in structural terms and also at what level decisions need to be made.

Certain advantages arise from divisional structures. For example, because each division addresses itself to one business area it is possible to measure the performance of that division as a business unit. It becomes clear if a division is performing up to expectations

---

> **ILLUSTRATION 10.1**   *Divisionalization Within a Corporation: Examples at General Electric Co.*

Different organizations use different types of divisionalization. In addition, there is no reason why an organization cannot use several different types of divisionalization at different levels and parts of the organization.

General Electric (GE) Co., with sales of over $35 billion, is one of the largest industrial companies in the United States. Operating around the world, GE manufactures and markets a great variety of goods and services including: light bulbs, plastics, consumer electronics, home appliances, jet engines, power turbines, and railroad locomotives. It has made many acquisitions, for example, in the 1986 it acquired 80% of investment banker Kidder, Peabody & Co. for $600 million, and purchased RCA Corp. for $6.5 billion.

It is not possible to reproduce GE's complete organization chart on one or two pages. However, different parts of it are reproduced here to illustrate the variety of divisionalization approaches used by the company. These diagrams may not be completely up-to-date since GE is still undergoing reorganizations and restructuring (including the sale of some holdings).

Below are two primary divisions of the company, and it should be noted that the basis for divisionalization is by type of customer: consumer or industrial. Further, the breakdown under this initial division is for the most part by product, except for the Major Appliance Business Group which is organized by function, that is, marketing and production.

Figure 1

Consumer Products Sector	Industrial Systems Sector

Lighting Business Group
  Lamp Components and Technical Products
    Division
  Lamp Products Division
  Lighting Systems Products Division
Major Appliance Business Group
  Major Appliance Production Division
  Major Appliance Technology Division
  Major Appliance Marketing, Sales and
    Service Operations
  Major Appliance Marketing Division
  Major Appliance Sales and Service Division
Consumer Eletronics Business Operations
Mobile Communications Business Division

Industrial Electronics Business Group
  Factory Automation Products Division
Motor Business Group
  Motor Marketing Division
Construction Equipment Business Operations
  Construction Equipment Sales Division
Transportation Systems Business Operations
  Transportation Products Division
  Transportation Marketing Division
Semiconductor Business Division
General Electric Supply Company Business
  Division

GE's International Sector, shown below, is divided on the basis of geography such as Canada, Mexico, Brazil, and so on. In turn, operations in various countries are organized on the basis of product, function, and customer.

Figure 2

International Sector

International Trading Operations-GETC	General Electric do Brasil S.A.
Europe and Africa Operations	General Electric de Mexico, S.A. de C.V.
Middle East/Africa Business Development	Asia Pacific Division
Division	Canadian General Electric Company Limited
Andean Countries Business Division	

The figure below shows a corporate department, finance, which is organized by function, in this case, functions within finance such as accounting, auditing, and management.

Figure 3

Corporate Finance Staff

Corporate Accounting Operation	Corporate Financial Management
Corporate Treasury Operation	Corporate Investor Communications
Corporate Audit Staff	

or below par. So the company as a whole is able to measure more easily its performance in diverse areas of activity. Moreover, because these activities are set up as separate operating units, they are the easier to divest if necessary; a common phenomenon as North American corporations restructure themselves especially after a series of acquisitions. Divisionalization also facilitates the passing of profit and general management responsibility down the line. This can have two benefits: first it means that senior management in the parent company is more able to concentrate on strategic matters, and second it helps to develop general management ability at a lower level.

There are, however, disadvantages and difficulties with the multidivisional structure. One is the issue of devolution of responsibility. To what extent should responsibility be passed to the divisions? It may be accepted by all, for example, that operating responsibility to meet profit objectives or deadlines for new product launches should be devolved. But who decides on strategic objectives? Who decides if new product development should take place at all and in what areas? Who decides on levels of expenditure or borrowing? What about the responsibility for acquisition programs? If immediate action is required to counter a major competitive attack and that action could mean short or even long term reversals, at what level is the decision to be made? So, a problem divisionalized organizations face is defining the extent and nature of decentralization. This subject is returned to in Section 10.3.

Another problem is conflict between the divisions for the resources of the parent organization. On what basis should financial resources be allocated? How will the management of one division react if, despite meeting their budgets, some other division, deemed to have greater growth prospects, is favored more? Even further problems occur if there is intertrading between the divisions; how should transfer prices be fixed and what should the trading relationship be? The same sorts of problems occur if the divisions, based on different product markets, use common plant. Who controls it, who has first call on it, on what basis are the costs of raw material allocated? So, problems of operation and control are often far from straightforward in a multidivisional firm. These issues of control will be dealt with more fully in Chapter 11.

Another disadvantage often cited is that divisional structures are costly because they replicate management functions in each division and, with the addition of a central head office staff, this leads to high overheads. This argument is only valid if the cost of the overhead is greater than the cost of inefficiency which could result from an inappropriate structure: it is a matter of management judgment. Inefficiency may also arise because the divisions themselves become too big and cumbersome and "suffer from all the problems of oversized functional structures."[8] Figure 10.2 summarizes the advantages and disadvantages of multidivisional structure.

There has been some research work done on the financial performance of different structural forms.[9] This appears to show that, in general, multidivisional structures outperform other structural types. However, this does require some important qualifications. Divisionalized firms perform better than functional firms on measures of growth than they do on measures of rate of return; the gap between measures of return on investment and equity is marginal when compared to measures of growth in earnings and sales. But since divisionalization tends to occur when firms expand and diversify, it might be expected that firms with divisional structures should show higher growth figures. It appears that

Figure 10.3   *Levels of divisions.*

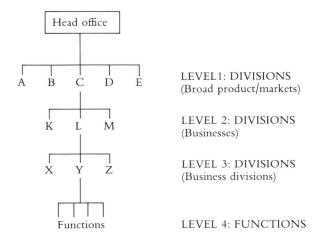

firms content to manage through a functional structure perform virtually as well on measures of return as those which opt for divisionalization. Indeed, it has been argued that companies emphasizing high growth best achieve this by divisionalization and fairly informal management styles, while those emphasizing profit performance may well be advised to look for a more functional structure with specialist senior managers and more formal management styles."[10]

10.2.4 THE "CONGLOMERATE" STRUCTURE

In its most extreme form, a conglomerate is really an investment company. It may simply consist of shareholdings in a variety of individual, unconnected, business operations over which it exercises little or no control. However, the term is also applied to an enterprise which, itself, operates a portfolio of virtually autonomous business units. Although part of a parent company, these business units operate independently and probably retain their original company names. The role the parent company takes may be limited to decisions about the buying and selling of such companies with very little involvement in their strategy. Many conglomerates have been formed in the past 25 years and Illustration 10.2 describes one of these.

An example of a conglomerate structure is given as Figure 10.4 The business interests of the parent company are likely to be varied, some of them may be wholly owned and some not, and there may be many business units within the group. To a large extent, the business units retain their own identity and perhaps their own individual structures. Central corporate staff and services may well be very limited. The essential differentiating feature for a conglomerate is, then, the extent of the autonomy of the business units particularly in relation to strategic decisions.

The advantages a conglomerate can offer are based on the idea that the constituent businesses will operate to their best potential if left alone. It has been argued that as business environments become more turbulent, and greater decentralization of strategic decision making is required, conglomerate structures facilitate decision making to a greater extent than formal divisionalization. However, Channon's study[11] of the UK service industry sector in the 1970s found that on all measures of performance the conglomerate structure performed worse in this sector than other structures: this led him to argue that there was a need for more central direction and control than conglomerates could exercise. The two views are, of course, not incompatible. It could be argued that the business environment is now a great deal more turbulent than it was in the 1960s and 1970s and that companies, particularly when they are faced with complex businesses to operate and such turbulent environments, cannot effectively exercise tight central control. This issue will be returned to shortly in a discussion of the advantages and disadvantages of decentralization.

There are other organizational advantages and disadvantages of conglomerate structures. For example, they do not have to carry the burden of a high central overhead since the head office staff of the parent is likely to be small. However, there are benefits for the

> **ILLUSTRATION 10.2**   *An Example of a Conglomerate*
>
> The bringing together of dozens of unrelated businesses under one umbrella organization, a conglomerate, has been common during the past 25 years. However, the composition of a conglomerate is constantly changing as acquisitions, divestments, and consolidations are made.
>
> Some of the well known conglomerates in the United States are ITT, Gulf + Western, Beatrice, Exxon, R.J. Reynolds, and Textron. This illustration looks at one of the largest and best known, ITT Corp. This highly diversified conglomerate has sales of about $18 billion and was created during the 1960s and 1970s by Harold S. Geneen. Among the businesses ITT was involved in were: semiconductors, financial services (Hartford Insurance), hotels (Sheraton), defense and space electronics, industrial technology (automotive parts), telecommunications (switching gear and long distance services), information services, fluid technology, and forest products.
>
> Conglomerates put together by assembling a group of mostly unrelated businesses can be easily disassembled also. For the past few years, ITT has been involved in divesting itself of under-performers, reshuffling assets, and overhauling some components. About 100 businesses have been sold in whole or part during the past eight years. These include: Canadian forest operations, an oil and gas company, Continental Baking, and C & C Cola. Many other parts of the organization are rumored to be for sale and these include parts of the natural resources and information services divisions.
>
> An example of the reshuffling occurring is the joint venture ITT entered into with Compagnie Général d'Electricité (CGE) of France. ITT's new telephone switching gear and other telecommunications operations were transferred, giving ITT a 37% interest in the new company called Alcatel.
>
> Many divisions, including hotels and industrial technology, are being overhauled. In 1980, sales were about $20 billion and employees numbered 348,000: in 1987 sales were about $2 billion less and employees numbered 123,000.
>
> ITT's advertisements have focused on the restructuring and the implications it has for the company. In an advertisement entitled "What is IT? IT is ITT" the company made the following statements:
>
> > ITT is a 17.4 billion dollar corporation that knows exactly where it is going.
> >
> > But it wasn't always this way.
> >
> > A few years ago, we were suffering from a kind of corporate split personality.
> >
> > There were businesses we could grow that were clearly "Us." And others that just as clearly weren't.
> >
> > We parted company with many, but held on to those product and service businesses which offered the chance for industry leadership.
> >
> > Then we rolled up our sleeves and went to work to help those businesses grow and prosper.

The advertisement claims that IT (ITT) is: one of the world's foremost producers of automotive equipment, one of the largest luxury hotel chains in the world, a leader in defense technology, an insurance company with assets of $19 billion, one of the fastest growing financial service companies in America, and a partner in the largest telecommunications manufacturing company in the world. The advertisement also outlines how the performance of its various operations has improved, and states that "we've only just begun."

Conglomerates go through stages of growth and contraction like most organizations. In ITT's case, the company grew rapidly in the 1960s and 1970s, appears to be retrenching and consolidating in the 1980s, and might well begin an expansion period in the 1990s.

Source: "Behind the ITT Deal: Will Araskog's Radical Surgery Work?," *Business Week*, July 14, 1986, pp. 62–4; "How Cleaning House May Help ITT Clean Up," *Business Week*, March 23, 1987, pp. 64, 68 and 72.

business units in a group, such as the offsetting of profits against others' losses, cheaper financing for investment from the parent company and, arguably, in bad times, the protection of the group. The conglomerate itself may also claim benefits such as the spreading of risk across many business ventures and the ease of divestment of individual companies. On the other hand, the businesses may run the risk of being sold off to make room for businesses which can perform better. There simply may not be the skills at the center to provide help since the aim is to keep the center as slim as possible. Perhaps the greatest weakness of this structure is, however, the possible lack of internal strategic cohesion and duplication of effort between business units. It is one thing to say that

Figure 10.4 *A conglomerate structure.*

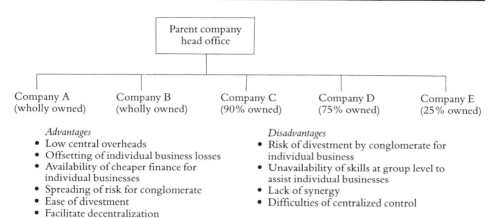

Advantages
- Low central overheads
- Offsetting of individual business losses
- Availability of cheaper finance for individual businesses
- Spreading of risk for conglomerate
- Ease of divestment
- Facilitate decentralization

Disadvantages
- Risk of divestment by conglomerate for individual business
- Unavailability of skills at group level to assist individual businesses
- Lack of synergy
- Difficulties of centralized control

business units operate better if they are given the profit responsibility to do so on their own: but in a large, perhaps multinational, operation there may be considerable pay-offs from having some sort of overall "logic" to the activities — some sort of horizontal integration[12] in the group. It may also be that the different parts of the corporation are difficult to control at times when the center would wish for such control. These advantages and disadvantages are summarized in Figure 10.4.

10.2.5 THE MATRIX STRUCTURE

A matrix structure is a combination of structures. It usually takes the form of product and geographical divisions or functional and divisional structures operating in tandem. Figure 10.5 is an example of a matrix structure and Illustration 10.3 describes how such a structure operates in one organization.

Matrix structures most often come about because an organization is involved in two distinct types of operation, both of which require substantial amounts of management emphasis making "pure" divisional structures inappropriate. For example, suppose a company increasingly extends its operations on a multinational scale and develops new product interests. It may regard geographically defined divisions as the operating units for the purposes of local marketing, and product divisions as responsible for the central worldwide coordination of product development, manufacturing, and distribution to the geographical divisions. Or, a group with a number of product divisions may argue that there is no benefit (and perhaps disadvantages) in having all functions in all divisions. It may make sense to have centrally organized selling (with a company-wide sales force) and manufacturing operations (particularly if different divisions are common manufacturing plants), with product development and marketing planning lodged in product divisions.

It is not necessarily the case that a matrix structure as such will result if there are two distinct types of operation in multinational firms. There are other ways of dealing with this situation which are discussed in Subsection 10.2.6. Also, matrix structures do not only arise in large, highly complex organizations, they are sometimes used in quite small, apparently straightforward organizations which have distinct types of operation or interest in them. For example, matrix structures exist in university departments and schools: one arm of the matrix might be responsible for academic, subject-based work and the other for administration and programming.

The benefits claimed for matrix structures[13] are several. It is argued that quality of decision making is improved in situations where there is a risk of one vital interest of the enterprise (e.g., the interests of a geographical area) dominating consideration of a problem at the expense of other vital interests (e.g., worldwide coordination of manufacturing). Formal bureaucracy is replaced by direct contact between individuals; the structure encourages informal exchanges of views across responsibilities. Linked with this, the matrix structure is supposed to increase managerial motivation, because of its participative nature, and managerial development because of the extent to which all levels of management become involved in activities.

ILLUSTRATION 10.3 *An Example of Matrix Structure*

In order to coordinate the implementation of plans, Delta Hotels Ltd. used a matrix structure but found there were problems.

Delta Hotels, an operator of hotels across Canada, attempted to design an organization structure which would allow it to adapt to new circumstances in the environment and to seek greater productivity and flexibility in its operations. Delta used a matrix structure to bring together employees from different departments to solve problems and develop projects.

The matrix structure functioned at all levels in the organization. The top level was comprised of the vice presidents of finance, human resources, marketing, and operations. At the next layer, four regional directors who reported to the Vice President Operations were involved. Finally, there was a layer at the hotel level made up of the general manager, chief accountant, sales manager, food and beverage manager, and head of housekeeping. The usual direct lines of authority still existed, but there was increased consultation and communication across operations as employees also reported to project coordinators at various times. Delta found that the matrix structure made top management and all employees more sensitive to the overall impact on hotel operations of plans or projects which had to be implemented.

The matrix structure was not used without some difficulty. Implementation required a change in behavior and the attitudes of managers and subordinates. Cooperation is required between the department heads and project coordinators, and sometimes the structure leads to a conflict someone at the top of the organization must resolve. It is estimated that between three and five years are needed to properly implement a matrix structure and that there is a possibility of some confusion, with decision making taking longer. Top management support for the matrix structure is critical, otherwise it would most likely not succeed.

However, Delta and companies which use the matrix structure, feel that the advantages outweigh the drawbacks. Users are convinced that the increased communication within the organization leads to better decision making and an overall more productive organization.

Source: James Walker, "Speeding the Decision Process: Matrix Management Eases the Flow of Communication," *Financial Times of Canada*, January 23, 1983, pp. 4 and 22.

However, many of these claims may not be borne out in reality. Matrix structures appear to have some very real problems associated with them. Peters and Waterman say their "favorite candidate for the wrong kind of complex response . . . is the matrix organization structure."[14] The problems are several. There is a high risk of a "dilution of priorities." That is, the risk is that the message to those in the organization is that everything matters equally and deserves equal deabte. The end result can be a sort of decision making paralysis. The time taken for decisions to be made may be much longer than in more "conventional" structures simply because the structure is designed to encourage debate between potentially competing interest groups. While joint responsibility may be conceptually laudable and it may appear to be clear in theory who is responsible for what, problems can arise. What happens, for example, in a multinational operation when the division responsible for Africa wants to reformulate a product and the central functions of manufacturing and worldwide marketing coordination insist on product uniformity? Who is actually responsible for marketing? This raises another problem. Exactly where does profit responsibility lie? The African division could argue that it cannot be held profit accountable if it does not control its own products. On the other hand, the central functions are not profit accountable because they are not responsible for selling and distribution. In fact, organizations with matrix structures may have to cope with a good deal of conflict because of the lack of clarity of role definition and responsibility. In such circumstances, a key issue in the effective working of matrix structures is the need for one arm of the matrix to be acknowledged as leading in order to minimize the risk of paralysis through bureaucratic procedures or sheer confusion. A summary of advantages and disadvantages is given in Figure 10.5 which also shows two matrix structures.

10.2.6 Intermediate Structures and Structural Variations

There exists a whole range of "shades of grey" between types of structures. Differences may arise for a number of reasons. It may be that there are problems of change from one sort of structure to another: for example, a wholesale move from a functional structure to a divisional structure may be difficult and very disruptive; some form of intermediate structure may make sense which might eventually evolve into a divisional structure. A company faced with this problem might find that problems arise with a functional structure as new products/markets compete for resources. Initially, these conflicts might be resolved by pushing the decision upwards until a sufficiently senior executive makes the decision. When too many conflicts need to be resolved in this way, new rules, guidelines, and procedures may be developed to advise people on how resources are to be shared between products. The next step may be to formalize these procedures in the planning process by, for example, allocating a budget to the new product/markets.

Until this stage, the problem has been dealt with by manipulating methods of control and operation rather than by structural changes. As the new products/markets become more important and create competition for resources, it may be necessary to create interdepartmental liaison roles. For example, marketing priorities may not be clear within the production function, so a committee may be set up with representatives from both departments or a temporary task force set up to advise on priorities. The next stage may be to create either permanent teams of coordinators or special coordinating jobs (the product manager is a good example). The last step which may prove necessary to maintain the functional structure is the creation of a department with the sole function of

Figure 10.5   *Two examples of matrix structures*

a) A multinational matrix structure.

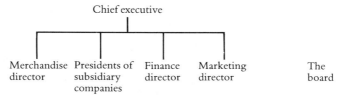

Chief executive

| Merchandise director | Presidents of subsidiary companies | Finance director | Marketing director | The board |

Subsidiary companies

| | Europe | South America | Far East |
Product divisions

Product group A

Product group B   The operations

Product group C

b) A matrix structure in a business school

Dean

Department leadership

| | Marketing | Finance | Accounting | etc. |
Student groups

Assistant Dean Undergraduates

Assistant Dean Graduates (MBA)

Assistant Dean Continuing Studies

Advantages
- Quality of decision making where interests conflict
- Direct contact replaces bureaucracy
- Increases managerial motivation
- Development of managers through increased involvement in decisions

Disadvantages
- Length of time to make decisions
- Unclear job and task responsibilities
- Unclear cost and profit responsibilities
- High degrees of conflict
- Dilution of priorities
- "Creeping bureaucracy"

coordination, a centralized planning department, for example. Ultimately, as the diversity increases, the organization may be forced to divisionalize since the costs of maintaining the functional structure will be unacceptably high or the administrative difficulties might become too great.

There are also some common intermediate structural answers to such problems. For some companies it might be more appropriate to describe their structure as "functional with subsidiaries."[15] Their main business, which employs by far the majority of employees, could be a straightforward functional structure; the more peripheral business interests could be the divisions. The converse of this is the company which is divisionalized except for certain key functions which remain at the center and have responsibilities across all the divisions. Channon[16] calls this a "critical function" structure and found it quite common in insurance companies where investment departments often remain a central function. In many divisionalized retail operations, too, there are central functions responsible for cross-divisional property dealings and, increasingly, for control of information systems.

Another intermediate structure often arises when there are development activities outside the responsibility of any one function or division, say a major capital project or new product development. Here it might make sense to set up a temporary full-time project team drawn from different functions or divisions. Peters and Waterman suggest that so-called "excellent" companies, characterized by their ability to continually change to meet the needs of the changing environment, are also characterized by the extensive use of such project teams and task forces.[17] They maintain a basic form of organization which is simple, lean, and easy to understand; they may change the precise configuration fairly regularly but its basic form remains the same. However, around that form, in order to respond to the different challenges they face, and to innovate and experiment, they set up *ad hoc* teams for short or long periods of time. In 3M, project teams with quite small numbers grow up around new ideas regularly; some die out fairly quickly, but it is quite possible that others will develop, together with their project, into new business ventures or even separate divisions.

Henry Mintzberg suggests that there is a new form of structure developing in those companies facing really complex and dynamic environments, especially where those companies are young, highly technical in their business base, and with many highly specialist roles for managers and staff to perform. This is the "adhocracy."[18] These are organizations with very little formal structure at all. They are groupings of specialists who work together through a process of mutual adjustment and professional understanding and training. There will be very few bureaucratic procedures — few job descriptions, or hierarchies, for example. It may be that the outside observer will have difficulty in seeing who is responsible for what, or indeed who is superior to whom. Such organizations do, of course, depend on high degrees of mutual respect and tolerance if they are to survive efficiently.

Another way of coping with the need for organizational change without fundamentally affecting what already exists, is to "externalize" the change by moving the responsibility for it outside the enterprise. There are many examples of this. In the past few years, governments have increasingly attempted to "privatize" some operations they previously performed themselves, for example, refuse collection, cleaning services, and the management of hospitals. Franchising is another means of structuring externally. Here the functions of marketing services, some elements of finance and accounting and perhaps manufacturing, are retained within the franchise operation while the local selling and cash collection may be dealt with by franchisees.

The disaggregation of organizations may, however, go much further than this. Some corporations, faced with the high cost of production in western economies are developing into "vertical disaggregated" companies or "dynamic networks." These companies essentially rely on other companies for manufacturing and many other business functions. Illustration 10.4 gives an example. The argument runs that, as western industrial society becomes more oriented towards high technology production and service industries, the production of commodity goods can be more cheaply done elsewhere. Such companies therefore seek to take advantage of low cost foreign labor and foreign technology by

---

ILLUSTRATION 10.4   *Disaggregation and Galoob Toys Inc.*

Could disaggregated structures become more popular as costs of production and management rise in Western economies?

Business Week reported on the organization structure adopted by Galoob Toys; a type of structure which, until the 1980s, was most uncommon but which has shown signs of becoming less so.

Lewis Galoob Toys Inc. is obviously a successful company. It sold $58 million worth of its sword-wielding Golden Girls "action figures" and other trendy toys last year — ten times the 1981 total. Its stock, issued in 1984 at 10, has soared as high as 15 and now sells for 13 1/2. Yet by traditional standards of structure, strategy, and management practice, Galoob is hardly a company at all. . . .

A mere 115 employees run the entire operation. Independent inventors and entertainment companies dream up most of Galoob's products, while outside specialists do most of the design and engineering. Galoob farms out manufacturing and packaging to a dozen or so contractors in Hong Kong, and they, in turn, pass on the most labor-intensive work to factories in China. When the toys land in the US, they're distributed by commissioned manufacturers' representatives. Galoob doesn't even collect its accounts. It sells its receivables to Commercial Credit Corp., a factoring company that also sets Galoob's credit policy. In short, says Executive Vice President Robert Galoob, "our business is one of relationships." Galoob and his brother, David, the company's president, spend their time making all the pieces of the toy company fit together, with their phones, facsimile machines, and telexes working overtime.

Source: "And Now, the Post Industrial Corporation," *Business Week*, March 3, 1986, pp. 64–71.

reducing their reliance on their own fixed capital, and looking for markets they can develop by buying-in products or services. In effect, parts of the value chain are externalized and the organization structure takes the form of a tight, small, central headquarters around which functions of the enterprise operate and are controlled. It may be that virtually all these functions are performed by other companies. There may be overseas suppliers, and home based distributors or marketing agencies, together with external accountancy services, designers, and so on.

There are advantages and disadvantages in such an arrangement. Such companies may be more agile and fast moving in exploiting markets. They certainly need less capital to do so and are likely to carry lower overheads; and with the flexibility to source from anywhere, their product costs are also likely to be low. On the other hand, the extent to which they can exercise control over production must be reduced, they are vulnerable to suppliers entering their own markets, are entirely reliant on the continuity of supply from companies outside their control, and they do, of course, demand a totally different sort of management skills to run the operation. It may be that such organizations can only operate on relatively small scales unless the type of business permits the breaking up and contracting out of services: for example, companies within the publishing industry are moving rapidly towards disaggregated operations in editing, production, and distribution. If such structures are to develop, it also probably means that businesses will have to be broken down into small operating units to avoid extremely unwieldy networks of operations.

10.2.7 STRUCTURAL TYPES IN MULTINATIONAL COMPANIES[19]

The growth in size and importance of multinational businesses warrants some special mention of the structural implications for such organizations. Since multinational activity usually involves some form of divisionalization, the discussion will also usefully point out that any one divisional type may have several variations. The most basic form of structure for a multinational is the retention of the home structure and the management of whatever overseas subsidiaries exist through direct contact between the manager of the subsidiary and the chief executive or some other manager in the parent company. In effect, there are no changes to the overall structure. This is most common in single-product companies or where the overseas interests are relatively minor, so it cannot be described as typical.

One of the most common forms of multinational structure is the *international division*. Here, the home-based structure may be retained at first — whether functional or divisional — but with the overseas interests managed through a special international division. In turn, it is possible that within an overall international division there will be other geographic divisions each reporting to a home-based head office. The international subsidiaries may draw in the products of the home company or, if large enough, may manufacture for themselves.

Such structures tend to work best where there is a wide geographical spread but quite closely related products. They tend to emphasize local responsibility rather than central control and so may be particularly useful where local knowledge or close relationships with national governments are important. The logical extension of this structure is that geographically based divisions or companies evolve which are part of a multinational whole, but operate essentially independently by country. In these companies virtually all the management functions are nationally based. In such circumstances, the control of the parent company is likely to be dependent on some form of planning and reporting system and perhaps the ultimate veto over national strategies; but the extent of control is likely to be low. However, there is one simple mechanism of control: since the national businesses are, for operational purposes, not dependent on the parent company, they can be disposed of relatively easily.

There has been a move away from the international divisional structure to what has become known as a *global product* or integrated structure.[20] Here the multinational is split into product divisions which are then managed on an international basis. The logic of such an approach is that it should promote cost efficiency (particularly of production) on an international basis and provide enhanced transfer of resources (particularly technology) between geographical regions. There is also a tendency for companies to move to global structures as foreign product diversity increases and as foreign sales, as a percentage of total company sales, increase.[21] There should also be better strategic planning on an international basis through the centralized product focus. In these organizations, control over manufacturing, for example, may well be coordinated internationally. The network of plants, each one in a separate country, may be making parts for cars which are assembled in yet another country: this manufacturing network may be supported by an international research and development network. Clearly, in such circumstances, the key requirement is planning mechanisms to coordinate the various operations, and it is in integrated organizations that planning and control systems are likely to be most sophisticated. Such structures may be beneficial where there is a diversity of products, a reliance on high technology, and a relatively low need to distinguish between different geographical areas.

However, research has shown that these benefits do not always occur.[22] Although cost efficiency is improved it does not appear that technology transfer is enhanced: technology transfer seems to be better achieved through geographic divisions than in a global product structure. Also, while the structure is well suited to promoting defensive or consolidation strategies, it does not seem to meet the expected benefits of heightened strategic planning and is not suited to the promotion of aggressive or expansion strategies. These difficulties may be accounted for in part by the almost inevitable separation of senior management of the global division from local problems; they are mainly concerned with central coordination and this reduces the sensitivity to local needs, particularly in terms of marketing needs and competitive activity. The tendency to move to global product structures is probably associated with attempts to rationalize the increasing diversity and problems of control within international divisional structures. Such rationalization has often taken place through some sort of portfolio planning which has tended to emphasize concentration on a more limited product range.

Matrix structures are also common in multinational organizations. Most typically, the matrix is based on head office responsibility for product and manufacturing planning and geographical divisions responsible for local administration, including selling and distribution. The argument for a matrix structure is that a multinational is just not suited to a hierarchical structure; decisions are better made through a "contractual" arrangement between central coordinators and local management. It certainly appears that the structure is better at promoting technology transfer, for example, but this has to be set against the costs of coordination and conflict discussed in 10.2.5 above. Matrix structures can provide greater flexibility in terms of geographical responsiveness in the global product structure while coping with a greater diversity of products and providing closer corporate control than geographic structures can. It also appears that matrix structures are better at promoting technology transfer. However, the problems of matrix structures previously discussed also hold for multinationals and in at least one major electrical company, decision making became so cumbersome in the late 1970s that managers openly campaigned for a shift to an alternative structure.

Doz[23] has argued that a multifocal strategy is evolving in some organizations in which there is no predetermined decision to follow a geographical route or a global product route. Rather, the extent to which the firm is integrated and controlled will depend on local market circumstances, as will the necessity to switch priorities and emphasis from one area of the world to another. In such circumstances, it is not possible to predetermine a structure which can exist over time and be relevant to operations in all parts of the world.

Table 10.1 *Advantages and disadvantages of different multinational business structures.*

	Geographic divisions	Global product divisions	Matrix
Diversity of products	L	H	H
High technology	L	H	H
Close corporate control	L	H	H
Close government relations	H	L	M
Resource allocation: priorities			
Product	L	H	M
Geographic	H	L	M
Functional	L	M	H
Relation cost	L	M	H

Key: H = high, M = medium, L = low

Source: Adapted from: J. Hutchinson "Evolving Organizational Firms," *Columbia Journal of World Business*, Vol. XL, 1976, p. 51.

There is likely, rather, to evolve the sort of adhocracy previously described in which there is a strong reliance on informal communication between top management on a global basis. Such top managers cannot expect to control the whole enterprise by formal systems, but rather, depend on establishing control mechanisms to access and analyze key data, establish clear overarching strategies which can be pursued by carefully selected management, and must be prepared to resolve conflicts of interests where they arise.

Davison and Haspeslagh's[24] research on 180 US-based companies in 1980 showed that the most common structure (in 32% of the companies) was the global product structure followed by the international divisional structure. This differs from the findings of Stopford and Wells[25] in the late 1960s when 52% of the multinationals they researched had international divisions and 18.5% had global product structures.

Table 10.1 summarizes some of the advantages and disadvantages of geographic global product, and matrix structures for multinational businesses.

10.3 CENTRALIZATION AND DECENTRALIZATION

When planning the implementation of strategy in organizational terms, structure is important because it creates what has previously been described as "the skeleton" to facilitate — and sometimes limit — the activities which need to occur. However, it is not enough to design an organization in terms of the "bones" of a structure. One divisional structure may be much the same as another in name and the sort of organization chart used to describe it: but that does not in itself help with some other vital aspects of organizational design. Another aspect to consider is what sort of decisions should be made at each level in the organization, and how this affects the ability to implement (and decide) strategy. This concerns issues of centralization and decentralization.

Decentralization means the extent to which power of decision making is devolved in an organization. This raises the question: "power over what?" Does this mean power to make decisions on operational issues — the scheduling of production or the hiring of executives, for example — or the power to make decisions about the strategic direction of the firm, i.e., to diversify or consolidate. Decentralization may mean either, which is one of the reasons there has been confusion over the use of the term: managers and consultants have too often assumed that decentralization of strategic and operational decisions necessarily go hand in hand, when they need not. For example, there is considerable decentralization of operational decisions in a company such as Unilever. A product marketing group in one of Unilever's subsidiaries would make decisions about substantial amounts of advertising expenditure and the scheduling of production in large manufacturing plants. But these decisions would be made within the context of a strategic framework for the subsidiary approved by Unilever itself. It would be highly unlikely, for example, that Walls Meat or Lever Brothers could make a decision to move outside their existing product market scope without the approval and active involvement of Unilever, which might well decide that such a new venture would be better lodged in some other subsidiary. On the other hand, it is quite possible that a business unit within another conglomerate might make decisions about such a move much more independently and even have the facility to raise funds to do it from outside the parent group. In the case of the Unilever, subsidiary *operational decentralization* is high and *strategic decentralization* more restricted: in the conglomerate case both operating and strategic decentralization are high. This distinction is important because there are indications that performance characteristics of firms may be influenced by the nature of decentralization.

It is argued that decentralization allows and encourages rapid managerial response to local or product specific problems. For example, if sales or profits drop in a particular market it is not necessary to refer the matter along hierarchical chains of decision making; a decision can be made by the manager responsible for that market. However, the speed of response may well depend on how well defined the responsibilities for strategic and operational decisions are at different levels of management. For example, if the decision has to do with a local distribution problem, then the local manager will probably have the authority to deal with it. But suppose the problem has important strategic implications: perhaps a product requires major redesign and its reformulation requires major funding; local management may not have the authority for this and the decision may have to be referred to more senior levels in head office. Unless the company is clear about what sort of decision making is to be decentralized and what is to remain centralized, delays and ineffectual decisions may result. In some organizations, inefficiencies may arise precisely because of the failure to decentralize operational decisions: for example, criticism of the services provided by governments often stems from the centralized nature of decision making which often results from the pressures of public accountability through statutory bodies or administrative channels.

Perhaps the most powerful reason for strategic decentralization is that it is necessary and beneficial when the complexity faced at the top of the organization is too great to be handled by senior management alone. Take the extreme example of a multinational operation with interests as diverse, dynamic, and complex as microelectronics, oil exploration, and communications technology. It is not conceivable that all strategic decisions could be made at the most senior level. Such decisions would certainly be decentralized to strategic business units such as divisions. Illustration 10.5 traces the decentralization process in one organization.

There are, of course, arguments for centralization. Coordination of activities may be facilitated by centralization. Senior management knows what is going on in all parts of the organization if decision making is routed through them. The need for complex control systems is reduced. Centralization of major strategic decisions could be important because it is only at the most senior level that an overall perspective of strategic implications can be appreciated and decisions about the overall aims and core strategies of the *whole* organization and funds allocation between competing claims can be made . Another argument for centralization is that it provides for speedier decision making. It is apparently the opposite claim to the first argument in favour of decentralization. Yet this may not be such a contradiction if the distinction between strategic and operational decentralization is

Figure 10.6 *Some benefits and difficulties of centralization and decentralization.*

	Benefits	Difficulties/problems
Centralization	• Ability to achieve and control consistent strategy • Coordination of activities • Simpler control systems • Allocation of resources facilitated • Speedier strategic decision making	• Failure to achieve response to local conditions • Difficulties in developing general management capabilities • Cumbersome and costly central overheads
Decentralization	**Operational** • Rapid response to specific or local problems • Improved motivation/ commitment **Strategic** • When environmental or decision making complexity too great to be dealt with at apex of the organization	• Definition of split of operational and strategic responsibilities • Failure to devolve *power* of decision making, resulting in: • Lengthy referral processes and delayed decisions • Frustrated management • Complicated control procedures

remembered. Decentralization speeds strategic management only if there is effective devolution of power to take strategic decisions and these do not need to be referred up and down management hierarchies for agreement. However, this may not occur for many reasons. For example, effective strategic decentralization would involve the authority to allocate funds to major projects: yet the sums of money required for major projects may be in excess of those under control of the business unit concerned. In such an event, the request for funds has to go to the parent group where it will be competing with other business units. Here, the responsibility for making strategic proposals has been devolved, and the authority to make the decisions has been centralized. The danger is that the process of proposal, discussion, and agreement or rejection will be institutionalized into a lengthy formal process which slows down strategic responses.

Figure 10.6 summarizes some of the benefits and difficulties (and problems) of centralized and decentralized organizational structures. Peters and Waterman have argued that a characteristic of the best performing organizations is that they are simultaneously able to retain control while maximizing the degree of flexibility, innovation, and contribution from lower levels. These organizations have "simultaneous loose-tight properties" of structure and control.[26] How this is done is not strictly a matter of structure but rather a matter of management style and corporate culture and is discussed in the next chapter.

The issue of decentralization is an important one, not least because the extent of decentralization seems to affect company performance according to the overall aims and strategy of those companies. Horovitz and Thietart[27] found that companies which successfully achieved high growth tended to be more decentralized than those emphasizing profits; however, they also found that high performing companies, whether on measures of growth or profits, tended to retain fairly high degrees of central control on matters of general strategic direction of the company.

There is no absolute "right" or "wrong" about the extent of decentralization. What matters is not so much whether an organization is centralized or decentralized, but the extent to which the design of the organization is internally consistent.[28] John Child has shown how, within the aircraft industry, companies operating in the same environment had varying levels of performance which could be explained in terms of how compatible the various aspects of their organizational structure were. Of the four airlines he discusses, two performed better than the others and were competitors. However, their structures were quite different. One was divisionalized, relatively decentralized (at least for operational decisions), and formalized in terms of its control and planning, which was on a long time horizon basis. The other successful airline was not divisionalized, operated on much shorter time horizons, and remained centralized with top managers meeting regularly to make the major decisions speedily. The point is that both organizations, though structured differently, operated an internally consistent structure enabling them to effectively handle the environment they faced. The poorer performing airlines, on the other hand, had inconsistent structures. For example, though nominally decentralized, they severely restricted authority for decision making, failed to monitor the project performance of divisions and had cumbersome decision making procedures. They were unable to respond as effectively to their trading environment.

It should be clear by now that there is an important distinction between decentralization and divisionalization yet the two terms are often used synonomously by both managers and management writers. The distinction is made clear by the Unilever example. Unilever is a divisionalized operation; certainly it has decentralized operating decisions but it has retained a large amount of central control over strategic decisions. Compare this to an advanced electronics company, for example, which could well be small and perhaps functionally organized yet where considerable strategic power may be decentralized to specialists. While divisionalization may make decentralization easier, the two do not necessarily go hand in hand.

10.4   INFLUENCES ON ORGANIZATIONAL DESIGN[29]

Why are organizations designed the way they are? Why are some organizations likely to have functional structures and others divisional structures? Why are some centralized and

---

ILLUSTRATION 10.5   *Decentralization at Great-West*

Many companies with international operations have decentralized for a variety of reasons. This has happened in the North American life and health insurance industry and an example is provided by Great-West Life Assurance Company.

Great-West Life Assurance Company is a large Canadian insurance company head-quartered in Winnipeg, Manitoba, that has been operating in the United States since 1906. Until the 1970s, there was little distinction made between the Canadian and American operations. However, environmental circumstances changed and forced the company to pay more attention to the American business as a separate operation. The main differences in the markets were the result of differing approaches to taxation, social security programs, and employee benefit plans.

Figure 1 shows Great-West in the early 1970s with an essentially functionally organized structure. However, even in this structure, the marketing function for the US portion of the business was performed by a separate section in Winnipeg. In 1973, this section was moved to the headquarters of the American operation in Denver. All other functional areas dealt will all products whether they were sold in the US or Canada. In reality, the company did not recognize the US market as a separate business.

Figure 1

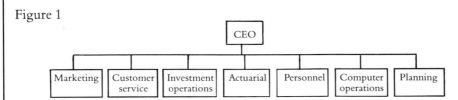

In 1976, the marketing function was formally split into US and Canada as shown in Figure 2. Other functions, including activities relating to individual versus group operations, remained centralized at the Winnipeg headquarters. The Marketing USA Divison was still located in Winnipeg.

Figure 2

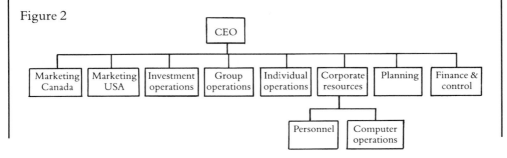

Figure 3 shows a further decentralization of operations. USA and Canada Marketing Divisions were established and made responsible for group and individual operations within each country. The USA Division was transferred to Denver between 1980 and 1982. Other functions, mainly staff or support activities, remained in Winnipeg. Corporate Resources and Investment have not been decentralized as the company either considers it inappropriate to do so given the nature of their business, or has not determined the best way to decentralize the activity.

Figure 3

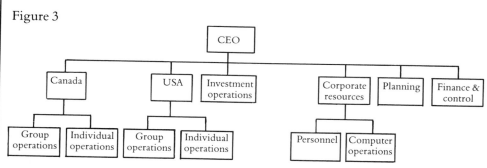

Great-West believes that the decentralization allowed for a transfer of authority to operating managers, increasing performance. Also, the decentralization sensitized the company to the nature of US business and the need to establish a separate image for Great-West in that market.

Source: Kevin Kavanagh, "Decentralization in the Life Insurance Industry — Great-West's Experience," *Business Quarterly*, Summer 1987, p. 102–5.

others decentralized? What influences other aspects of organizational decision? This part of the chapter summarizes some of the influences on organizational design and refers readers to further work in the area. Figure 10.7 provides a summary of the discussion.

In considering organization design, it is not enough to think about structural forms (functional, divisional, matrix) alone. It has already been seen that the extent of centralization and decentralization is important. Similarly, the management style of the organization is important; this will be discussed further in Chapter 11 (Section 11.3.4), but suffice it to say here that the extent to which the organization is bureaucratic (or mechanistic) or more informal (or organic), is an important aspect of organizational design.[30] So too is the extent to which parts of the organization are specialized in their tasks and roles. Lawrence and Lorsch[31] referred to this as "differentiation" within organizations and also pointed out that mechanisms of integration, necessary to coordinate specialist activities, are likely to be an important aspect of organization design. In considering influences on the design of organizations, it is important to consider more than purely structural forms.

Figure 10.7   *Influences on organizational design.*

		Structural form							Style	
		Functional	Divisional	Matrix	Centralized	Decentralized	Specialization/differentiation	Integration	Mechanistic	Organic
Strategies	Cost leadership						★		★	
	Differentiation					★		★		★
	Limited product/markets	★			★					
	Market development	★						★		
	Vertical integration						★	★		
	Diversification		★			★	★	★		
Technology	Separate technical processes			★						
	Integrated technical processes	★								
	Mass production				★				★	
	Non-standardized production					★				★
	Complex technology				?	?	★	★		★
	Level of innovation						★	★		★
Type of organization	Size of organization		★			★	★	★		
	External accountability				★			★	★	
	"Defenders"	★			★		★		★	
	"Prospectors"			★		★		★		★
Environment	Simple/stable				★					
	Dynamic				?	?		★		★
	Complex			★		★	★		?	?
	Competitive				?	?		★		
	Hostile				★					
	Multinational			★		★				

★ Likely effect of influence
? Likely to raise as key issue

10.4.1 THE INFLUENCE OF STRATEGY

Chandler[32] showed that a change in strategy is likely to result in structural changes, though the actual processes of change may well be problematic. A change in strategy is likely to give rise to administrative problems because the existing organizational structure is not adapted to cope with the new strategy. There may be resistance to change which gives rise to the sort of intermediate structures discussed earlier in the chapter. Nonetheless, different strategic developments generally tend to give rise to different forms of organization.

Chandler found in his historical studies that firms with limited product markets and fairly simple operations tended to adopt functional structures and be fairly centralized. The early development of such businesses tended to be through market development which allowed for the retention of functional structures but increased the need for integration through centralized control systems. He found that, typically, the next step in strategic development was vertical integration and this gave rise to the need for increasing specialization to deal with the balancing of flow of goods between different operations in the organization. This need in turn gave rise to specialist service functions in the center. Further strategic development tended to take place through product diversification and this tended to give rise to division structures and lead towards more decentralized structures and greater needs for specialization and integration of operations.

The extent to which diversity of operations leads to decentralization is not a phenomenon limited only to commercial operations. There have been signs in the public sector of the breaking up of centralized control into more autonomous units where speed of response and coping with diversity is important. In Canada, the federal government is decentralizing out of Ottawa some of its programs designed to stimulate regional economic activity to the areas of the country where they are supposed to provide assistance.

Different generic strategies will also require different forms of organizational design. The organization following a cost leadership strategy will need to find means of ensuring a cost efficient operation with an emphasis on cost control; whereas the organization following a differentiation strategy will need higher degrees of creativity and, probably, a rapid response to problems and opportunities. The likelihood is that the cost of leadership will require a more mechanistic system of control with clear job responsibilities, frequent and detailed reports on organizational efficiency and cost, and a clear delineation of responsibility for budgets and expenditure. The structure for an organization following a differentiation strategy, on the other hand, might need to be more organic in nature, with looser controls, a greater encouragement of informality and creativity within a more decentralized structure, but with a good deal of coordination between its various functions. The emphasis is likely to be more on groups of managers relating to problems and opportunities rather than on individual managers or departments being concerned with specific job functions.

It should be clear from this that those organizations which seek to follow focus strategies, in which they aim to achieve both cost leadership and differentiation for a particular market segment, are likely to find some conflicts in terms of organizational design, as will the organization which seeks to follow differentiation and cost leadership strategies for different parts of its business or product range.

10.4.2 THE INFLUENCE OF PRODUCTION PROCESS AND TECHNOLOGY

There are different ways product and technology influence structure. When products are manufactured by a sequence of separate, technical processes, companies may choose to forgo the possible economies of continuous production and create separate divisions to deal with each process of manufacture as a means of developing the highest quality of product. Conversely, where there is a highly integrated process, divisionalization is more difficult simply because the process is difficult to subdivide. Similarly, assembly and component manufacture, which are quite different in nature, allow components to be manufactured in separate divisions or to be subcontracted to other companies, as in the automobile industry. (Refer to Illustration 7.1.)

In terms of decentralization, there is much evidence to show that production process influences the ways decisions are made and the levels at which they are made. As long ago as 1965, Woodward's[33] research showed that there are links between types of production process and the nature of management. Mass production systems require the standardization of process and result in greater direction and control by senior managers: in short, there is a tendency towards centralization. Firms with less standardized manufacturing processes are more likely to have more decentralized and informal decision making processes. However, Woodward's findings have subsequently come under a good deal of critical scrutiny. In particular, it has been argued that the claim that standardized production systems result in formalized and centralized control is really only true within the production side of the company: other departments and the company as a whole may not be organized in the same way.

The last decade has seen an accelerating complexity in the technology used in organizations. The implications for structures are considerable. It would apear that the more sophisticated and complex the technology of an organization is, the more elaborate the structure becomes for a number of reasons. First, it is likely that a good deal of responsibility and power will devolve to those specialists concerned with the technology itself. This means that the need for liaisons between such specialists and the operating core of the business increases giving rise to an increase in integrating and coordinating mechanisms such as committees, joint working groups, project teams, and so on.

More sophisticated technology can give rise to increases in centralization or decentralization. For example, the advent of more sophisticated information technology may mean that it is possible for the center of the organization to cope with far more complex problems than hitherto; in retailing, the ability to record sales by electronic scanning in the store has provided retailers with greatly enhanced knowledge of rates of sales and inventories by product. This has facilitated much tighter central decision making on planning and store layout. Rapid transfer of information and computerized systems of control also allow companies like Galoob (see Illustration 10.4) to contract out services yet retain central control over operations. On the other hand, the same technology might also allow decentralization of support systems in organizations. For example, the functioning of the neighborhood offices mentioned above depends on local officers being able to communicate up-to-date information rapidly to central departments to provide a basis for localized decision making.

Finally, the extent to which the organization is required to be innovative in its approach to development of new services or products is likely to affect the extent to which experts have to be drawn from different disciplines, perhaps for short periods of time. Here we have a requirement for more organic approaches to organization and, in the extreme, a pull towards adhocracies.

10.4.3   THE INFLUENCE OF ORGANIZATIONAL TYPE

Other influences on organizational design stem from the size, accountability, and culture of organizations. It is inconceivable that all aspects of a large and diverse corporation could be organized except by splitting the tasks of management. The larger the corporation, therefore, the more there is the likelihood of divisionalization, a need for specialization and differentiation,[34] and in turn a need for increased coordination (or integration). The large corporation is also likely to move towards some form of decentralization although other circumstances which will be mentioned below may counter this tendency.

The nature of the accountability of an organization will also affect its organizational design. This is well illustrated by nationalized industries and in government bodies. Where government involvement is high, public accountability becomes an important influence; this is likely to give rise to a centralized structure of decision making where both power and accountability are in the hands of an easily identifiable team or individual at the center. Higher levels of decentralization would disperse authority more widely and make public accountability more difficult — or at least more difficult to demonstrate to the public. However, the price often paid for this ease of public accountability has been an inability to respond quickly to market and other environmental changes and has also often resulted in unwieldy systems of bureaucratic information and control in order to maintain this centralized structure.

In commercial enterprises where there is pronounced dependency on some external body such as a parent company or a powerful shareholder group, the same sort of result occurs.[35] There is a tendency towards centralization of decision making and, because external standards of performance are imposed, a tendency towards a more mechanistic style of management. Owner control may also be an important influence on structure. For example, many owner-controlled companies retain a high degree of centralization even when they grow quite large as the influence of the owner-manager continues.

The importance of an organization's culture has already been discussed in Chapters 2 and 5 and reference has been made to the "cultural web." Organizational structures over time come to reflect and support the organizational recipes which persist and the power structures associated with them. This is well illustrated by the work of Miles and Snow.[36]

The *defender* organization tends to specialize rather than diversify in terms of strategy. Structurally it is likely to be functional, permitting an emphasis on specialization at most managerial levels and emphasizing efficiency. The functional structure is likely to be mechanistic in management style with an emphasis on keeping costs down by minimizing cross-functional or cross-task training. Moreover, there will be a high degree of influence on decisions from the functions concerned with the maintenance of efficiency, such as finance and production.

The *prospector*, on the other hand, seeks actively for new opportunities so as to be first in the market. Here there is likely to be much less emphasis on control and efficiency and more on innovation. Strategically, there will be a greater diversity of interests and the pursuit of more, perhaps with teams to develop opportunities, and there may well be a tendency to decentralize and minimize top down control. The style of management will be organic, encouraging flair and risk taking, and there may be complex systems of coordination with, for example, specialist coordinating roles. Influence and power are likely to be lodged primarily in development areas of the business, such as marketing and R&D.

10.4.4 THE INFLUENCE OF ENVIRONMENTAL FORCES

The idea, introduced in Chapter 3, that environmental complexity and dynamism affect organization design will now be discussed. (Readers need to remember that by "dynamic" is meant the amount of change going on in the environment; and that "complexity" has to do with the amount of information an organization needs to deal with, or the range of inputs it is necessary to absorb, in decision making.) The main point is that dynamic or complex environments increase uncertainty in decision making. An organization can be thought of as a means of facilitating the processing of information or inputs for decision making purposes, so the form the organization takes is important as a means of handling uncertainty. Mintzberg[37] argues that the form of organizations is likely to differ in important respects according to different environmental conditions — differences summarized in Figure 10.8.

In an essentially simple environment, organizations gear themselves to operational efficiency. Not faced with high degrees of change, they can standardize their ways of operating, for example, in production terms and in their modes of management. Management styles tend to be mechanistic[38] or bureaucratic and management is fairly centralized. Mintzberg calls this type of organization "centralized bureaucratic." This type is exemplified by some mass production companies or raw material producers which, historically at least, faced fairly simple, stable environments. The danger, of course, for such organizations is that their environments cease to be benign and place them under threats they find difficult to handle.

Increasing complexity is handled by devolving decision responsibility to specialists. This means that organizations in complex environments tend to be more decentralized at least for operational purposes. Hospitals and universities are good examples of those which traditionally have been in fairly stable or predictable environments, but of a complex nature. They are "decentralized bureaucratic" organizations. The ongoing operational tasks — the operations management of a hospital, for example — are done in a standard way, often with a highly bureaucratic management style. The complexity of some of the aspects of patient care are then devolved to the specialist skills of the physicians, surgeons, psychiatrists, and so on.

Figure 10.8   *Environmental influence on organizational structure.*

	Stable	Dynamic
Complex	Decentralized bureaucratic (e.g., hospitals)	Decentralized organic (e.g., advanced electronics)
Simple	Centralized bureaucratic (e.g., mass production)	Centralized organic (e.g., retailing) or Decentralized bureaucratic

Source: Adapted from H. Mintzberg, *The Structuring of Organizations: A Synthesis of the Research,* Englewood Cliffs, N.J.: Prentice-Hall Inc., 1979 p.268. Reprinted by permission of the publisher.

In dynamic conditions, the need is to increase the sensitivity of managers to what is going on around them, helping them to identify change and respond to it. It is unlikely that bureaucratic styles of management will encourage such behavior so, as the environment becomes more dynamic, a more organic style is likely.[39] This is not to say that such organizations necessarily devolve authority for major decisions to lower management. In a simple but dynamic environment it may make sense to retain fairly centralized strategic decision making as a means of ensuring speed of decisions on important matters, while removing bureaucratic procedures, lengthy referral processes, extensive departmentalization, and layers of management. Mintzberg calls this type of organization "centralized organic." However, this may not be the only response to dynamic conditions. In situations of high levels of competition — which require rapid response and change — it has been noted[40] that organizations may decentralize decision making but ensure that overall control at a strategic level is monitored and planned through systematic, more formal, systems.

In such competitive environments, a key organizational issue is likely to be centralization versus decentralization. The answer is likely to depend on the circumstances of competition and the size of the organization. It would be difficult to centralize all strategic decisions in a conglomerate with a very wide diversity of business interests; here there needs to be some degree of decentralization, presumably at least to the business unit level.

The structure will also be dependent on the nature and degree of the competition and the sort of decisions which need to be made: for example, the greater the degree of competitive hostility, the more the organization will centralize, and also flatten the levels in the organization to speed up the response to competitive pressures. Indeed, it has been suggested that in extremely hostile circumstances organizations are likely, if only temporarily, to revert to "simple structures, becoming dependent for strategic discussions on a dominant leader."[41] On the other hand, if a necessary response to competitive pressures is the continual innovation of change — perhaps in the fashion industry, or the recording industry — then it is more likely that a much more organic system of management with a good deal of decentralization will be necessary.

What, happens then, when the environment is both complex and dynamic? These are the conditions in which Mitzberg suggests "decentralized organic" organizations may be found. Some of the firms operating at the frontiers of scientific development are in these conditions. Their environment is changing so fast that they need the speed and flexibility organic styles of management provide; and the level of complexity is such that they must devolve responsibility and authority to specialists. It is here the real decentralization of authority — operational and often strategic — to units within the organization takes place. These units may be divisions or they may be specialist departments, but they must respond to the change occurring so quickly around them.

10.5 COPING WITH THE PROBLEM OF ORGANIZATIONAL DESIGN

Choice of organizational design may not be all straightforward. There can often be conflicting influences on structure so, as with strategic choice, there are likely to be several possible structural designs and many influences on which of them is to be adopted. A common problem of the 1970s and 1980s has been the conflict between the influences of an increasingly turbulent environment and traditional technology. There are companies in which mass production core technologies had a major influence on the structure and nature of the organization. Such a company would very likely be fairly centralized and bureaucratic in its mode of operation. However, faced with a dynamic environment, the company may well have attempted to diversify away from its core technology. This strategic decision might argue for divisionalization and increased decentralization at least of operational decision making, while the nature of the environment and the need for innovation might demand more organic styles of management. Yet, the business may still be highly dependent on the traditional core technology and managers may be unwilling to decentralize authority. In such circumstances, the structural choice is not straightforward; there are different influences pulling in different directions. Illustration 10.6 shows how one organization has chosen to structure itself in a competitive industry with rapidly changing technology.

Given conflicting influences on organizational design, how is it sensible to set about dealing with the problem? There is no formula for doing this, no "right answer." It is again a question of analysis and in the end, judgment. However, it might be useful to ask these questions:

- What are the influences inside and outside the organization which affect how it should be structured? The influences discussed in this chapter should provide a basis for this.

- From these, which are the critical influences (that is, those which will either affect performance more than the others or those which simply override all others)? Readers

---

ILLUSTRATION 10.6   *Operating Structure at Magna*

Magna International Inc., a supplier of components to the North American auto-making industry, has implemented a growth strategy with an unusual structure.

Magna is a very successful producer of automobile components with plants in Canada and the US. It has a reputation for producing high quality products at low costs. In 1986, it had sales of over $1 billion.

There are three levels of responsibility at Magna: the operating unit, group management, and executive management. Each operating unit employs about 100 people and operates small, semi-autonomous plants with a General Manager and an Assistant General Manager who have authority and responsibility for the operation of their unit. The advantages of these small units are that they can provide flexibility by reacting quickly to market demands and the small number of employees enables management to maintain an uncluttered line of communication to employees. If a unit becomes larger than 100, a new unit is formed.

The operating units are grouped under a group management team with a Group Vice President responsible for all areas of activity in this group. The groups are: Magna Manufacturing (stamped, formed, and welded metal products); Maple (accessory drive sytem); Creative Mechanical Technologies (various mechanical assemblies); Decorative Products (trim components and plastic exterior components); and MACI (electromechanical devices, electronic components, and instrument clusters). Each group is supported by marketing, financial, and human resources personnel and oversees its own research and technology development. When a group gets to be about 20 operating units, or factories, a new group is formed. Most groups are publicly traded and are partly owned by employees.

The Executive Management level is a small policy and management resource group divorced from day to day operations and responsible for strategic management and the coordination and monitoring of the firm's fundamental business principles.

Source: Magna International Inc., *Annual Report*, 1985.

might consider from the example above, that the critical influence on the mass producer has become the dynamic nature of the environment; if the company does not cope with this, then its performance will continue to deteriorate.

- Given the identification of these critical influences, it may be that some clear structural implications emerge, or it could be that there are options. If there are options, then it is sensible to consider the advantages and disadvantages of each in the context of the strategy the organization wishes to follow.

- The final point is too often overlooked. No matter how elegant a structure is, the most important point is that it has to be workable. How will the structure be put into effect? If divisionalization of a conglomerate is recommended then exactly what is going to happen to the chairmen of the many virtually autonomous businesses which are to be rationalized into a few divisions? Who is to report to whom in this new organization? Where will decisions of what sort be made? If substantial decentralization is to take place in the divisions, will more senior management accept it and will more junior management be able to handle it? Part of the evaluation of structural alternatives, just as for strategic alternatives, is to consider feasibility.

10.6 SUMMARY

This chapter has concentrated on structural implications of organizational design. It has been argued that strategic implementation is effected through the people in the organization, and of key importance is the way in which those people are organized. To help readers understand how this might be accomplished, the chapter has reviewed the various forms of structures in common use, together with their advantages and disadvantages. It then examined the sorts of influences within the organization and from outside which may affect structure. The chapter concluded by discussing how consideration of the most appropriate structure might take place.

However, this chapter has only touched on a second, equally vital aspect of organization: how the people within the structure are to be managed. This issue is considered in the next chapter.

References

1. Some of the early writings on organization are brought together in a volume of readings edited by Derek Pugh, *Organization Theory*, (Harmondsworth: Penguin Books Limited, 1984). They include papers by Fayol and Taylor, the proponents of "scientific management."

2. There is further discussion of the definitions of different management styles, including mechanistic and organic styles, in Chapter 11. However, the terms originate from the work of T. Burns and G.M. Stalker, *The Management of Innovation*, (London: Tavistock Publications, 1968).

3. Perhaps the most extensive study of how different organizational structures are adapted to different strategic and environmental influences was carried out in the series of studies known

as the Aston Studies, which promoted the idea of a contingency theory of organization. There are a number of papers written on this particularly towards the end of the 1960s, for example, see D.S. Pugh, D.J. Hickson, C.R. Hinings, and C. Turner, "The Context of Organization Structures," *Administrative Science Quarterly*, Vol. 14, No. 1, 1969, pp. 91–114.

4. For example, R. Rumelt does not include the category "holding company" in his book on American industry strategy, *Structure and Economic Performance* (Cambridge, Mass: Harvard University Press, 1974).

5. P. Grinyer and J-C. Spender, *Turnaround — Managerial Recipes for Strategic Success*, (London: Associated Business Press, 1978), use subcategories of the term "multidivisional" which they describe as "diversified majors and passive or acquisitive conglomerates." These are terms we return to later in the chapter to differentiate between the nature of different multidivisional organizations. Also, see P.H. Grinyer and J-C. Spender, "Recipes, Crises and Adaptation in Mature Businesses," *International Studies of Management and Organization*, Vol. IX, No.3, 1979, p. 113.

6. A good summary of the advantages and disadvantages of different structures is given in an article by M. Davis, "Current Experiments in Management Structure," *Reviewing the Management Structure* (London: British Institute of Management, 1972). Readers may also care to refer to the discussion of the problems of functional structures in T. Peters and R. Waterman, *In Search of Excellence* (New York: Harper and Row, Ltd. 1982), and by Henry Mintzberg, *The Structuring of Organizations* (Englewood Cliffs, N.J.: Prentice-Hall, Inc., 1979).

7. The view of divisionalization as a response to increasing diversity was put forward by A.D. Chandler, Jr., *Strategy and Structure*, (Cambridge, Mass.: Harvard University Press, 1962). It is supported by other writers, for example, Derek Channon, *The Strategy and Structure of British Enterprise*, (New York: Macmillan, 1973).

8. This quotation is taken from page 314 of T. Peters and R. Waterman, *In Search of Excellence* (see reference 6).

9. The books which most thoroughly examine the relationship between basic organizational structures and performance are based on data of the 1960s and 1970s. See R. Rumelt, *Strategy, Structure and Economic Performance*, (Cambridge, Mass: Harvard University Press, 1974); and Derek Channon, *The Service Industries Strategy, Structure and Financial Performance*, (New York: Macmillan, 1978).

10. See J.H. Horovitz and R.A. Thietart's research summarized in "Strategy, Management Design and Firm Performance," *Strategic Management Journal*, Vol 3, No. 1, 1982, pp. 67–76, and J. Child, "Managerial and Organizational Factors Associated with Company Performance: Part II: A Contingency Analysis," *Journal of Management Studies*, Vol. 12, No. 1, 1975, pp. 12–27.

11. See reference 9.

12. The benefits of horizontal integration are discussed by Michael Porter in *Competitive Advantage*, (New York: Free Press/Collier Macmillan, 1985).

13. The benefits and problems of matrix structures are discussed more fully by K. Knight in "Matrix Organization: A Review," *Journal of Management Studies*, Vol. 13, No. 2, 1976, pp. 111–30.

14. This quotation is taken from page 306 of T. Peters and R. Waterman, *In Search of Excellence* (see reference 6).

15. "Functional with subsidiaries" is a term used by R. Rumelt, reference 4.

16. D.F. Channon uses the description "critical function" structure in his study of structure and performance in the UK service industry: see reference 9.

17. T. Peters and R. Waterman have found the extensive use of project teams and task forces in the excellent companies they reported on (see reference 6).

18. For a discussion of "adhocracy" see Henry Mintzberg, *The Structuring of Organizations*, (Englewood Cliffs, N.J.: Prentice-Hall Inc. 1979).

19. For a more extensive treatment of the structure of multinational companies see: M.Z. Brooke and H.L. Remmers, *The Strategy of Multinational Enterprise* (London: Pitman Publishing Limited, 1978. (Ch. 2) and Y. Doz, *Strategic Management in Multinational Companies* (Oxford: Pergamon Press Limited, 1986).

20. "Integrated Structures" is a term used by Y. Doz (see reference 19).

21. J.M. Stopford and L.T. Wells, *Managing the Multinational Enterprise*, (New York: Basic Books, 1972) found this tendency. However, it should be noted that their findings are based on 1968 data.

22. These findings are from research published by W.H. Davidson and P.C. Haspeslagh, "Shaping a Global Product Organization," *Harvard Business Review*, July-Aug., 1982, pp. 125–321.

23. See reference 19.

24. See reference 22.

25. See reference 21.

26. "Loose-tight" is an expression used by T. Peters and R. Waterman (see reference 6) and explored in more detail in Section 11.6 of Chapter 11 of this book.

27. See reference 10.

28. Both P.N. Khandwalla, "Viable and Effective Organizational Design of Firms," *Academy of Management Journal*, September 1973, pp. 481–95, and J. Child, *Organization: A Guide to Problems and Practice*, (New York: Harper and Row Ltd., 1977) have found this relationship between the consistency of an organization's structure and its performance.

29. Overall, the most thorough treatment of influences on organizational design is the volume by Henry Mintzberg (see reference 19) which is also summarized in *Structure in Fives: Designing Effective Organizations* by the same author (Englewood Cliffs, N.J.: Prentice-Hall, Inc. 1983).

30. See reference 2.

31. See P. Lawrence and J. Lorsch, *Organization and Environment* (Homewood, Illinois: Richard D. Irwin Inc., 1969).

32. A. Chandler's work, *Strategy and Structure*, (Cambridge, Mass.: Harvard University Press, 1962) began a whole series of investigations into the relationship between strategy and structure. It is a fine study of the historical development of American industry but, in drawing conclusions about organizations in the 1980s it should be remembered that the period being studied was the 1940s and 1950s, a time when the influences on business were somewhat different from the 1980s.

33. See J. Woodward, *Industrial Organization: Theory and Practice* (Cambridge: Oxford University Press, 1965).

34. A major study highlighting this is that of P. Lawrence and J. Lorsch, (see reference 31). Similar findings are, however, reported by D. Pugh *et al.* as a result of their research program which has become known as the Aston Studies (see for example, "Dimensions of Organization Structure," *Administrative Science Quarterly*, Vol. 13, No. 1, June 1968, pp. 65–105); and P.N. Khandwalla discusses relationships of size and structural characteristics in *The Design of Organizations* (New York: Harcourt Brace, 1977).

35. This has been found to be the case in several studies: Henry Mintzberg, *The Structuring of Organizations*, (Englewood Cliffs, N.J.: Prentice-Hall Inc., 1979), pp. 288–91; D. Pugh *et al.*, "The Context of Organisation Structures," *Administrative Science Quarterly*, 1969, pp. 91–114, and B.C. Beimann, "On the Dimensions of Bureaucratic Structure: An Empirical Reappraisal," *Administrative Science Quarterly*, 1973, pp. 462–76.

36. The work and findings of R.E. Miles and C.C. Snow, *Organizational Strategy, Structure and Process*, (New York: McGraw-Hill, 1978), have been discussed earlier in Chapters 2 and 5 and readers should refer to this discussion for a more detailed explanation of their organizational types.

37. See reference 18.

38. Mechanistic management is a term used by T. Burns and G.M. Stalker (see reference 2) to describe a management system which is fairly regulated and prescribed. Managers are likely to have clearly defined job roles with specified reporting relationships and a clear idea about who makes decisions about what sorts of things.

39. Again it is T. Burns and G.M. Stalker (see reference 2) who use this term. Organic styles of management are much less formal with less clearly defined job roles, responsibilities, and reporting relationships. There may, then, be a good deal more conflict and apparent confusion, but the likelihood is that managers will more likely be aware of and sensitive to changes outside their immediate day-to-day jobs.

40. This association between high levels of competition and decentralization combined with formalization is supported empirically by studies by C. Perrow, "The Bureaucratic Paradox: the Efficient Organization Centralizes in Order to Decentralize," *Organizational Dynamics*, Spring 1977, pp. 2–14.

41. This point is made by H. Mintzberg and Waters, "The Mind of the Strategist(s)," S. Srivasta, ed., *The Executive Mind*, (San Francisco: Jossey-Bass Publishers, Inc., 1983).

Recommended Key Readings

A clear exposition of the different basic organizational structures together with a summary of a good deal of research on structure is in J.R. Galbraith and D.A. Nathanson. *Strategy Implementation: The Role of Structure and Process*. St. Paul Minn.: West Publishing Co., 1978.

A good summary of the influences on organizational design is to be found in Henry Mintzberg. *Structure in Fives: Designing Effective Organizations*. London: Prentice-Hall International, 1983.

Two articles giving other perspectives on structure are:

Ian C. MacMillan and Patricia E. Jones. "Designing Organizations to Compete." *Journal of Business Strategy*, Vol. 4, No. 4, p. 11–20.

Danny Miller. "Strategy Making and Structure: Analysis and Implications for Performance." *Academy of Management Journal*, Vol. 30, No. 1, p. 7–32.

For a useful insight into the organizational workings of multinationals see Yves Doz. *Strategic Management in Multinational Companies.* Oxford: Pergamon Press Limited, 1986.

Chapter 11
PEOPLE AND SYSTEMS

11.1 INTRODUCTION

Implementation of strategic change requires the identification of the key tasks needed to effect that change as discussed in Chapter 9, and a proper consideration of the organizational structure and design to facilitate those changes, as discussed in Chapter 10. However, the success with which the key tasks are actually performed, and strategic change occurs, depends on the way people within and around an organization are managed and controlled. The ways different systems of control in the organization may be employed to implement strategy are the subject of this chapter.

Strategic changes can take place over long periods of time and give rise to considerable differences in the way an organization operates. As a result, the process of implementing strategic change generates a great deal of uncertainty within the organization which, in turn, triggers off political and social activity as groups and individuals try to cope with the consequences of change. Mumford and Pettigrew[1] have shown how this uncertainty "cascades" down through the organization triggering off more uncertainty as a consequence. This process is demonstrated in Illustration 11.1. Faced with such uncertainty, groups and individuals in the organization tend to seek to reduce that uncertainty and; as was seen in Chapter 2, they are likely to do this by relying more on the sorts of organizational systems, routines, and rituals with which they are familiar. Managing strategic change is, therefore, problematic.

Broadly speaking, there are two ways this problem of achieving change can be coped with. The first has to do with the employment of systems of control and regulation to ensure that the tasks of implementation are clear, that their execution is monitored, that individuals and groups have the capabilities to implement change, and that they are rewarded for so doing. Secondly, interaction between groups and individuals is also important on a social basis. It is therefore important for those trying to implement change to understand and work within the social, political and cultural systems (discussed in

Chapter 2 and 5) which regulate organizational behavior, and can give rise to the resistance to strategy change, but which can also be employed to help achieve successful strategic change.

Figure 11.1 is a framework demonstrating how the implementation of strategic plans might be undertaken through different systems existing in organizations. It will be used as the structure for this chapter and is now briefly reviewed. The framework suggests that the implementation of strategic change can be considered under four broad headings (although as will be explained later in the chapter, these should certainly not be conceived of as being entirely distinct from each other).

Strategic change requires that the sorts of key tasks identified through the planning processes discussed in Chapter 9 are implemented. It is therefore important that mechanisms exist to ensure that people in the organization follow the plans and procedures necessary. This chapter deals with how this might be achieved under the same four headings used in Figure 11.1

1. *Control and Information Systems*. Control and monitoring systems, usually quantitative in nature, can be employed to provide information to establish whether or not a course of action is being followed or desired results achieved.

2. *Regulatory Systems*. There are procedures which can be followed to regulate or guide behavior: these could include training to ensure people have the capabilities to implement strategy; systems of incentives and rewards to encourage compliance with required change; the changing of organizational routines and work systems to modify established ways of operating; the management style of the organization; and as already discussed in Chapter 10, the changing of organizational structure.

These are ways in which managers seek to ensure that the plans necessary for the implementation of strategic change are complied with. Such action does not, however, necessarily mean that groups or individuals in the organization will accept the need for change or feel happy about it: in other words, such action might achieve compliance without identification or internalization of the need for change.[2]

3. *Culture Change*. The successful management of strategic change is most likely to be achieved if the sort of uncertainty and resistance discussed at the beginning of the chapter can be avoided or overcome. Desirably, this requires that the need for change be accepted by those involved in making it work; that they identify with the change or really believe it necessary. This is likely to mean that the existing recipe has to be changed and its constraining cultural influences minimized.

The problem is, then, one of culture change. This will be discussed in this chapter in terms of means of achieving *recipe change*, by which is meant that people in the organization actually change the ways in which they perceive their organizational world. Some of the mechanisms relevant to this process are discussed in this chapter including means of "unfreezing" the status quo, challenging recipes, and changing power structures. *Symbolic action* as an influence on culture change will also be considered.

4. *Political Systems and Strategic Change*. It is also recognized that all this activity goes

---

ILLUSTRATION 11.1   *Cascade of Uncertainty*

The rapid development of microcomputer technology during the late 1970s caused a considerable amount of political activity at one university.

For many years, the provision of computer facilities had been an important strategic issue for universities due to their high cost and their importance to teaching and research. Up until the late 1970s, a mainframe computer provided the only source of computing. However, by 1978, microcomputers had reached a level of development where senior management in one university had to consider whether they should begin to make use of this new technology. Being a recent innovation, most of the microcomputers did not have a proven track record, leaving senior management uncertain as to whether they needed microcomputers at all and if they did need them, which system would be most appropriate.

At departmental level there was uncertainty about the outcome of senior management's deliberations, triggering off political activity among groups. The computer services department, which operated the university's mainframe computer, pressed for its upgrading, realizing that the widespread introduction of microcomputers would erode their power. Their main weapon was their expertise, and as senior management was lacking in this area, the computer services department was able to get representatives onto the committee advising on computer provision. The other tack of their argument was that there would be government funding for the upgrading of the mainframe computer resulting in an improved facility with no direct cost to the university.

The other groups involved in the political activity were the user departments. They faced the uncertainty brought about by the seemingly impregnable position held by the computer services department and the fear that the decision to upgrade the mainframe would be pushed through quickly. The user departments (who preferred microcomputers) attempted to delay the decision to allow departmental members to improve their knowledge of computer systems and so enable them to challenge the computer services' arguments. They also tried to discredit the quality of service provided by the mainframe computer, suggesting that departmental microcomputers would provide the type of service the users required. The various user departments also formed alliances in order to create a more powerful lobbying force within the university's formal decison-making structure.

The user departments' response, (the pursuit of greater computing knowledge and a justification for departmentally-based microcomputers) in its turn led to uncertainty for the individual members of the departments who responded in differing ways. Those who were familiar with computers realized the opportunity to enhance their own position within the department, while others, who were previously uninterested in the role of computers in teaching, saw the need to gain such knowledge quickly. The course leaders encouraged the use of microcomputers as a means of enhancing the image of their particular course. However, a minority responded by suggesting that microcomputers were a "passing fad," and sought to emphasize the traditional role of the teacher.

The response of senior managment to this political activity was to permit the purchase of a limited number of microcomputers, partly as a result of the users' arguments, but also because not buying them may have jeopardized the university's claim for a large sum of money from the government to upgrade the mainframe computer. To some extent this could be regarded as a "side-payment" to allow the main decision to proceed.

on in a political context. Therefore, how strategic change might be managed through political systems is also discussed at the end of the chapter. Here the concern is with the way in which individuals and groups, in their interaction, can achieve conditions to exercise the power to implement strategic change.

Finally, the chapter concludes with a discussion of how all these systems — the more formal control systems, the regulatory systems, the cultural and political systems — might combine in so-called "excellent" organizations to provide a system of relatively continual change and avoid the dangers of strategic drift noted in Chapter 2.

Figure 11.1 *Strategy implementation: the influence of organizational systems.*

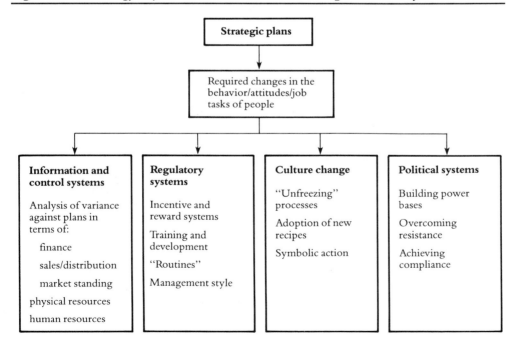

11.2 CONTROL AND INFORMATION SYSTEMS[3]

The successful implementation of strategic change may involve steering the organization into areas where there is little previous experience. Even strategies of consolidation, which were discussed in Chapters 6 and 7, may require modified production systems, changed incentive schemes, or relocation of salespeople. When the organization becomes involved in the real problems of implementing strategic change, managers need some means of identifying how implementation is proceeding and the extent of variance from the plan.

Figure 11.2 sets out some of the bases of analysis for providing data for control and strategy implementation. Essentially, these build on many of the sorts of analyses discussed previously in the book. For example:

- Different means of financial analysis (similar to those shown in Chapter 4) can be used to measure the extent of variance from financial plans.

- Market analysis may well take a form similar to that outlined in Chapter 3 in trying to establish the extent to which strategic plans are achieving improved competitive standing, for example, by monitoring the changes in demand in the market and changes in market share achieved.

- Sales and distribution analysis can monitor the extent to which sales budgets or planned distribution levels are being achieved.

- Physical resource analysis concerns itself with the plant and materials of the organization and, again, may take form in some of the measures discussed in Chapter 4.

- Human resource analysis examines the productivity and stability of the work force and the capabilities of those concerned with the implementation of strategy to put it into effect.

Many of the bases of control outlined here are therefore also bases of strategic analysis. As was pointed out in Chapter 1, the control and information systems used as means of implementing strategy are also means of analyzing strategic performance. This serves as another reminder that the process of strategic management is continual and cannot be thought of simply as a step-by-step process.

Certainly, organizations without some such systems of monitoring the implementation of strategy will find major difficulties in achieving change. However, the introduction of such measurements is not in itself sufficient to ensure successful implementation of strategy. Rather, it is important to consider carefully how such information and control systems should be designed to aid the implementation of strategy and help ensure useful feedback for further analytical and planning purposes. The following guidelines, also summarized in Figure 11.3, are designed to identify some of the key issues in achieving this.

1. *Distinguish between various levels of control.* Anthony[4] has suggested that control

needs to take place at three levels he calls the strategic, management, and operational levels. Implementation of new strategies requires control at all these levels, each of which will have a quite different purpose and require different information. For example, a venture into new overseas markets would require controlling at the strategic level through an overall budget, at the management level by monitoring expenditures and motivating employees, and also at the operational level by ensuring that routine tasks are properly performed. If strategy implementation is to be successful the control systems need to take these different levels into account. Operational control will normally require more detailed information and should be dealt with by line managers. In contrast, strategic control may consist of a few global measures monitored by senior management.

Figure 11.2 *Some analyses for controlling strategy implementation.*

Type of analysis	Used to control
1. *Financial analysis*	
Ratio analysis	Elements of profitability
Variance analysis	Cost or revenue
Cash budgeting	Cash flow
Capital budgeting	Investment
2. *Market analysis*	
Demand analysis	Competitive standing
Market share analysis	
3. *Sales and distribution analysis*	
Sales budgets	Sales effectiveness and efficiency
Distribution analysis	Distribution effectiveness
4. *Physical resource analysis*	
Capacity fill	Plant utilization
Yield	Materials utilization
Product inspection	Quality
5. *Human resource analysis*	
Work measurement	Productivity
Output measurement	
Labor turnover	Work force stability
Needs assessment	Skills capability

Figure 11.3   *Guidelines for the effective control of strategy*

1. Distinguish levels of control.
   (e.g., strategic control/management control/operational control)

2. Identify responsibility centers.
   > revenue centers
   > cost centers
   > profit centers
   > investment centers

3. Identify key factors and collect relevant information to control them.

4. Allow diversity of control.
   (e.g., avoid the temptation to have universal standards such as sales volume)

5. Use a sensible time period.
   (e.g., where investment is involved use a realistic measure of payback period)

6. Avoid misleading measurement.
   (e.g., the use of surrogate measures can be misleading)

7. Avoid purely "negative" monitoring.
   (e.g., only identifying performance below plan)

2.   *Create responsibility centers.* The complexity of strategic change usually requires the subdivision of control within a company. These smaller units can be regarded as responsibility centers.[5] They are identifiable parts of the whole organization and are responsible for a certain aspect of the business; their performance is measured and controlled accordingly. There are a number of bases on which this responsibility can be apportioned as shown in Table 11.1. The limited devolution of responsibility represented by revenue or cost centers has the advantage that senior management is more able to control the political activity between groups; but the disadvantage that the degree of motivation the control system provides to individuals or groups may be quite limited. In contrast, the creation of profit or investment centers may provide motivation to perform but create political tensions within the company which may be difficult to control.

3.   *Select key factors and collect relevant information.* It is crucial to identify those aspects critically important to the success or failure of the strategy. These should have been identified during resource planning (Chapter 9). It is then necessary to ensure that information *relevant to those key factors* is made available and known to be the most significant measure of performance. There are often cases where companies recognize the need to be selective but either do not identify or fail to monitor performance in those areas. For example, an organization may become obsessed with a single measure of performance,

Table 11.1 *Different types of responsibility center.*

Type	Examples	Control exerted over	Typical controls
1. Revenue center	Sales department	Income	Sales targets
2. Cost center a) Standard cost centers b) Discretionary expense centers	Production dept. (manufacturing) R & D Administrative dept.	Cost of labor, materials, services, etc. Total expenditure	Detailed budgeting Standard product costing Budget
3. Profit centers	Internal services (e.g., design) Product or market division Subsidiary company	Profit	P & L accounts
4. Investment centers	Subsidiary company	Return on capital	Complete financial accounts

such as volume of output or sales, without assessing how this fits the overall objectives of the company. This can be a severe constraint when new strategies are introduced which do not neatly fit this yardstick. A company wishing to introduce a low volume, high profit product into its traditional range of high volume, low profit lines would have great difficulty if they continued to measure the performance of the sales staff entirely by volume.

4. *Allow diversity in control.* The previous example also illustrates the danger of assuming that all an organization's activities can be controlled by a single, all-embracing system. Not only is this not achievable in practice, but is not desirable when attempting to control strategic implementation. The fact that strategic decisions are long term and made in conditions of uncertainty is in itself sufficient reason for requiring the more liberal application of control.

The continued evolution of new strategies requires this diversity of control. The most obvious example is the lack of profitability of new products during their early days. Chapter 7 explained the importance of a balanced portfolio of products or activities. The profitability of cash cows and stars would not be expected to be the same since the strategic purpose of those two groups of products is different. Their contribution to the company may have to be measured and controlled differently.

5. *Avoid misleading measurements.* Control relies heavily on measurement, but many aspects of strategy are difficult to measure quantitatively. This can lead to situations where the pressure to produce quantitative measures distorts the process of control and, in some cases, leads to poor performance. The police force has a problem in this respect as the assessment of how well law and order is being maintained is very difficult. In the absence of any precise measures, there is a tendency to develop surrogate measures, ie. those

---

ILLUSTRATION 11.2   *Control Systems in Two Integrated Multinational Corporations*

Systems of control and information play important roles in achieving integration worldwide at IBM and between the various subsidiaries of Ford Europe.

IBM

One way the management at the center of IBM can evaluate progress and determine priorities for its subsidiaries is through its planning and accounting processes. Planning at IBM is a two way process. Corporate headquarters may set targets and plans for local subsidiaries: however, local subsidiaries can also put forward their plans to the center and, if not approved, can appeal to the Corporate Managing Committee, comprised of the top three IBM executives. For each subsidiary, plans include financial and operating statements on strategy which are used consistently throughout the group to measure performance of subsidiaries. Thirteen different elements of performance are monitored against plan by corporate staff; and volume and staffing measures are reviewed regularly by a Corporate Managing Committee. Corporate staff also report to this committee about any substantial deviations on any of the other measures. Since high and low parameters for performance are set within the budget, any deviations by subsidiaries outside these are also subject to more detailed studies by staff functions. The same measures in the plan are also likely to be used for any bases of incentive policy for managers of subsidiaries.

Ford of Europe

In the 1960s, Ford of Europe operated in a far less integrated way than it does in the 1980s. Sales subsidiaries, for example, bought cars from national manufacturing companies at "export prices" set by the manufacturing companies. Since the center measured the performance of subsidiaries in terms of net profit, these subsidiaries were primarily concerned with maximizing their performance with the risk that they might not be benefiting the corporation as a whole; for example, they might promote products on which they made the greatest margins and cause an imbalance of production throughout Europe. A different means of accounting was introduced in an attempt to integrate and track profitability on a European-wide basis. This allowed for the identification of the contribution made by sales of specific models by country, thus providing information to managers of subsidiaries about the extent to which they were contributing to the performance of Ford of Europe as a whole, and the means of measuring the contribution of sales subsidiaries themselves. A Ford manager explained it as follows:

> Our accounting system now allocates a share of the corporate (Ford of Europe) operating profits to the various national subsidiaries. This is accompanied by an annual business plan for each company. Before this accounting allocation system

was implemented the managing directors of the sales companies had no idea of the overall profitability of what they were doing. Now the impact of their actions on corporate profits can be measured and they are evaluated on what they generate for the corporation as a whole. This plays an important role in shifting the focus of our sales companies from that of internal agents to that of real businesses, run by general managers, and playing their part in the whole corporation.

Source: Y. Doz, *Strategic Management in Multinational Companies*, (Oxford: Pergamon Press Limited, 1986).

things which are measurable. In the case of the police, surrogate measures might be the number of arrests, convictions, or proportion of cases solved. A police force which had extremely good relations with its local community might score badly by these measures.

6. *Beware of "negative" monitoring.* There is the danger that the systems will concern themselves with purely negative monitoring of performance [6] (for example, only with highlighting variances which are below plan). The result can be that departments and individuals become overconcerned with minimizing the risk of such negative variances. This can lead to a situation where risks are avoided or attempts are made to transfer the blame for poor performance onto other departments or individuals. It is important that monitoring systems be present to ensure that everyone knows how performance against plan is being achieved and to highlight excellent performance as well as negative performance. One of the implications here is that the agreement of objectives against which performance is to be measured usually benefits from participation in setting those objectives rather than them being prescribed by top management alone. In this way it is more likely that the objectives will be "owned" by those responsible for achieving them and, in turn, that they will regard them as useful measures against which to monitor their own performance, rather than as the heavy hand of top management.

Systems of control are particularly important in complex organizations to ensure that the various parts of such organizations are integrated sufficiently to implement corporate strategy. Illustration 11.2 shows how the implementation of integrated multinational strategies at IBM and Ford Europe depends heavily on such systems.

11.3 REGULATORY SYSTEMS

Information is not the only basis of control open to organizations. There exist other means by which a change in the behavior of those who must implement strategy might be attempted. These vary from fairly formalized organizational systems — such as training and reward systems or changes in work practices — to the management style adopted in the organization. These will be discussed in this part of the chapter.

11.3.1 REWARD SYSTEMS

Reward systems[7] are an important means of achieving compliance with planned strategic change. They can be monetary reward systems such as graded pay schemes, bonuses, profit sharing schemes, and productivity schemes and also nonmonetary reward systems, such as promotions and increased status. It is also important to remember that reward systems have both positive and negative impacts. The failure to achieve rewards, or the withdrawal of rewards, may be perceived as "punishment." In addition, the nature of the rewards needs to be carefully considered in terms of the objectives to be achieved; for example, if long term growth of profits is the aim then rewards based on short term achievement of sales targets are not likely to be helpful. This section considers how reward systems might affect the behavior of people and therefore be important in the management of strategic change. It does this by considering some of the key issues likely to arise in implementing strategic plans and how reward systems might relate to these issues. Since the particular issues likely to be important will vary by context, the reader should bear in mind that there is no one correct way of designing reward systems; the "package" of rewards needs to be designed for the circumstances faced by the organization, and the groups and individuals within it.

1. *Short versus long run perspectives.* As has already been indicated, the nature of rewards needs to vary according to the time horizons of the plans to be implemented. In general, the shorter the time horizons, the more important it is that any incentives, such as bonuses, should be based on clear quantitative measures of performance relating to the short term. On the other hand, the longer the time horizons, the more likely it is that more qualitative measures may be appropriate for basing incentives, unless quantitive measures can be made relevant to long term performance; for example, some companies have recently begun to give bonuses or share options based on the rise in real earnings per share over a number of years. A common problem is that organizations expect managers to devote effort and attention to long term problems when rewards are mainly tailored to short term performance. It is unrealistic to suppose that managers will jeopardize the achievement of short run goals in the long term interest of the organization, particularly when their renumeration is based on the attainment of such term goals. However, there is a trend to pay a higher portion of compensation based on performance, including performance in the longer term. To do this, it is necessary to provide the right rewards to managers for meeting strategic performance objectives. For example, bonuses as rewards tend to reinforce short term, yearly performance while stock options to be exercised in the future focus on the longer term.[8]

2. *Risk aversion and risk taking.* Slater[9] suggests that an organization wishing to encourage greater risk taking among its managers is likely to find that more qualitative measures of performance on which to base bonus awards or share options will be beneficial. Quantitative measures of performance may result in minimizing behavior to avoid failure rather than risk taking behavior to achieve results even greater than expectation. However, it is equally important that executives expected to take risks be provided with both salaries and incentives commensurate with the business and personal risks likely to be involved.

3.   *Profits versus volume/size.* Researchers have observed that organizations under managerial control (as opposed to those with marked shareholder influence) tend to follow strategies of growth and the achievement of size sometimes at the expense of profit performance.[10] There is also evidence that chief executives in managerially controlled organizations tend to be remunerated on the basis of size and scale of operations, whereas those in organizations with dominant shareholder influences are more likely to be rewarded in terms of profit performance.[11] Those concerned with designing reward systems should bear in mind that there may exist expectations about the bases of reward systems rooted in the ownership and control structures of the firm; those in managerially dominated firms may expect to be rewarded in terms of scale of operations, whereas those in which shareholders play a more dominant part may expect to be rewarded in terms of profit performance. For the change agent, perhaps trying to move the organization towards a greater profit focus in a managerially dominated firm, the implication is that the package of rewards designed to achieve such ends will have to be especially sharply focused towards the achievement of profit objectives.

4.   *Rewards for individuals.* An important issue is to consider how reward systems can or should reflect individuals' *capabilities*, direction and degree of *effort*, and *job satisfaction*. The Human Relations Movement of the 1930s[12] saw job performance as primarily related to job satisfaction. Others[13] have seen rewards and payment as a major stimulus to effort and emphasis has been placed on payment by results (e.g., piece work, sales commissions, etc.). In other organizations, rewards tend to reflect capability, for example, where skilled workers are paid more than unskilled workers. It is important to bear in mind that reward systems geared to only one aspect, such as effort, can have a negative effect on people's performance in other ways. For example, the satisfaction and compliance of a departmental manager may be undermined by a productivity scheme (effort related reward system) which results in his operatives earning higher wages than he does. Table 11.2 illustrates the range of reward systems commonly available and the aspects each reward system is designed to deal with. For example, graded pay systems are designed to reward capabilities, even to the extent, in some organizations, of giving increments of pay to those who

Table 11.2   *Types of reward systems.*

Type of reward	*Factor being rewarded or stimulated*		
	Capability	*Effort*	*Satisfaction*
Monetary	Graded job/pay system Bonuses (e.g., for qualifications)	Piecework Productivity schemes Profit sharing	Differentials important
Nonmonetary	Promotion (dependent on qualifications)	Promotion Dismissal	Promotion More autonomy Bigger budget Status symbols (car, office, carpet, etc.)

possess certain qualifications irrespective of job performance. In contrast, nonmonetary rewards such as cars or size and location of offices, are often a method of improving job satisfaction.

Illustration 11.3 describes how one organization changed the way it rewarded employees, in this case how compensation was paid.

5.   *Individual or group rewards.* Rewarding individuals for effort and performance can prove difficult unless the organizational structure and the systems of control allow an individual's performance to be isolated from the efforts of others. From a strategic point of view, therefore, it may be an important consideration as to whether reward systems should

---

ILLUSTRATION 11.3   *The Reward System at A&P*

Sometimes employees will go to extraordinary lengths to help insure the survival of the company for which they work. An example is provided by A&P.

A&P supermarkets in the United States were in serious difficulty and thousands of stores had been closed between 1974 and 1982. In 1982, A&P and the United Food and Commerical Workers (UFCW) entered into an experimental arrangement at 60 stores in Philadelphia which had been closed. Employees accepted a 25% cut in wages in exchange for a promise that if employees kept labor costs at 10% of sales, they would receive a cash bonus equal to 1% of the store's sales (0.5% at eleven percent or 1.5% at 9.5%)

Performance improved markedly. Management attributes about 80% of the increase in operating profits in 1984 to the plan, which has spread to 281 stores. Management wants to extend the plan to 850 A&P stores. Employees are also happy with the plan. Their earnings are now comparable to others in the industry. Their productivity has increased and they are more enthusiastic about their work. They are making suggestions on how to improve productivity and increase sales.

Unions do not usually support profit sharing of any form as it places part of an individual's earnings at risk. However, when closure is the alternative, such plans are considered more seriously. Others in the industry feel that the 1% bonus is high given that profit margins are not much higher. Since the plan has been so successful for A&P, other firms in the industry are taking another look.

Environmental factors have had major impact on the supermarket industry. Competition has increased and the format of food retailing has changed. The events at A&P illustrate how environmental trends impact on strategy and how a reward system is important to strategy implementation.

Source: "How A&P Fattens Profits by Sharing Them," *Business Week*, December 22, 1986; Bill Saporito, "Just How Good Is the Great A&P?," *Fortune*, March 16, 1987, pp. 92–3.

Table 11.3   *Managerial rewards — individual and group incentives.*

Aspects to be considered	Schemes based on individual performance	Schemes based on group performance
Managerial contribution to company performance	(a) Appropriate where individual's contribution is relatively independent	(a) Appropriate where individuals' contributions are relatively interdependent
	(b) Appropriate where performance standards are relatively variable (i.e., some managers at much higher standard than others	(b) Appropriate where performance standards are relatively uniform
Type of behavior	Encourages entrepreneurial, self-reliant, or creative types of behavior	Encourages greater cooperation, coordination, and team management
Flexibility of scheme	Scheme can be negotiated individually; or can be uniform	Scheme can be negotiated individually, but is more likely to be standard or uniform
Administration	Administrative requirements relatively great	Administrative requirements relatively slight
Discrimination	Relatively easy to achieve high discrimination between different levels of performance	Discrimination can be achieved between different groups or teams, but not so easily between individuals

Source: Angela M. Bowey, ed., *Handbook of Salary and Wage Systems*, 2nd. edn., Aldershot: Gower Publishing Company Limited, 1982, p. 254.

seek to influence the behavior of individuals or groups. A manufacturer of quality silver-plated tea sets,[14] attempting to move from a craft based operation to a light engineering operation, found problems as a result of its payment schemes. The existing piece rate scheme had been effective when the craftsmen had control of the whole process and took personal pride in product quality: but when it was applied to the new production process, quality dropped significantly. The company found it necessary to phase out piecework payment and move to a factory bonus scheme rewarding consistent quality of output for the factory as a whole.

Organizations choosing to introduce incentive schemes for managers face similar problems in deciding whether the scheme should be based on the performance of each individual manager or on the management team as a whole.[15] Table 11.3 summarizes the pros and cons of each system. This list is useful in choosing reward systems since it helps in matching the conditions described in the table with the type of strategic change being undertaken. For example, individual incentive schemes are clearly more appropriate for strategies which are independent of other company activities and where performance can

Table 11.4   *A weighted-factor approach used to reward achievement of strategic goals.*

SBU* Category	Factor	Weight
High growth	Return on assets	10%
	Cash flow	0%
	Strategic funds programs	45%
	Market share increase	45%
		100%
Medium growth	Return on assets	25%
	Cash flow	25%
	Strategic funds programs	25%
	Market share increase	25%
		100%
Low growth	Return on assets	50%
	Cash flow	50%
	Strategic funds programs	0%
	Market share increase	0%
		100%

*SBU = Strategic business unit

Source: P.J. Stonich, "Implementing Strategy," Cambridge, Mass.: Ballinger Publishing Company, 1982, p. 136.

be easily measured. In contrast, a group incentive would be better where a high level of overlap exists between activities, or where many (perhaps specialist) managers are involved, or where performance is difficult to assign to individuals.

6. *Business unit versus corporate perspective.* Care has to be taken to balance corporate interest against business unit interests. For example, a distributor of cars moved to a geographically based divisionalized structure and at the same time introduced divisional profit targets upon which bonus schemes were based. Prior to these changes, garages in different parts of the country had accommodated each others needs, informally, by transferring cars at short notice to meet customer requirements. After the changes, such transfers became much less common as managers were wary of releasing cars and therefore possibly missing sales.

The greater the independence of the units from the center or from each other, the more it is likely that unit based reward systems will be sensible. Similarly, the more removed the individual manager or group within the unit is from influencing corporate performance, the more sensible it is to have unit based reward systems. However, real problems occur in the case of divisional or unit based general managers and directors. Such managers typically have dual influences; both on their unit performance and on contributions to corporate well being. Considerable care has to be given to a sensible balance of rewards which are likely to focus attention on the areas of greatest concern or

Figure 11.4   *Reward systems and strategic change: a checklist.*

1. Which aspects of the strategy will rewards be most concerned with? e.g.
   • Profits or volume
   • Risk or stability
   • Short versus long time horizons
   • Quality
2. Should reward systems focus on groups or individuals?
3. Should reward systems focus on the business unit or the corporation?
4. Should the systems reward effort or capability?
5. Should rewards be mainly monetary, promotion or status?
6. What sanctions and punishments, if any, are needed?
7. Is there a sensible balance between types of reward systems to achieve strategic objectives?
8. Are political consequences of reward systems likely to help or hinder strategic change?

priority and minimize the risk of negative influence either at unit level or at corporate level.

These are some of the key issues to be considered in designing reward systems. It is increasingly being realized that there is no one best way to design such systems to achieve strategic change. More organizations are moving towards a mixed basis for remuneration, depending on the strategic requirements of the organization. Table 11.4 gives an example of such an approach, showing how different performance measures might vary according to growth objectives for different business units within a corporation. The measures of performance are all the same but the weight given to the mix of remuneration depends on the strategic circumstances of the organization. Illustration 11.3 also shows how the system of remuneration was altered to fit the company's need to implement a turnabout strategy.

In summary, the design of reward systems is a key element in creating a climate for strategic change. The need is to decide what the most important issues are for the reward system to deal with. Figure 11.4 is a checklist of some of these issues and summarizes the discussion above.

11.3.2 Training and Development

One of the most difficult aspects of implementing strategic change is ensuring that the employees are able to undertake the key tasks the change requires. During strategic change, the nature of people's jobs might alter, with the result that their *capability* in their new role or their *identification* with the required changes may be in question. Either of these problems will reduce the possibilities of successful implementation of strategy. Illustration 11.4 describes how one organization uses in-house "colleges" in implementing strategic change.

Strategic change in organizations is likely to require that individuals cope with a good deal more uncertainty and ambiguity[16] than when they are faced with operational change only. A new work practice may raise problems enough in trying to get people familiar with new techniques, and it can raise problems of resistance to change because people do not identify with such change. Strategic change, however, is the more difficult because the emphasis is more likely to be on getting people to accept new ways of thinking about their roles — for example, new attitudes to customer service, or a greater level of risk taking. These are not matters which can be dealt with by providing people with information or skills training alone. Rather, they need individuals to adopt both new operational skills and to cope with and help resolve situations of uncertainty. As explained in Chapter 2, the extent to which new ways of doing things will be accepted may be particularly small in organizations where there is a long established recipe and cultural web: while programs of training and development can help manage such change, they probably also need to be considered together with the means of culture change discussed later in the chapter.

A precursor to the design of training and development programs is a reassessment of the roles and responsibilities of people within the organization. A proper understanding of people's ability to operate in different ways is essential to implement change. This underlines the need for an analysis of an organization's human resources, as discussed in Chapter 4. Approaches to training and development[17] will then vary according to the extent of changes and the capabilities of individuals and groups identified in the assessment. Figure 11.5[18] not only provides a checklist of training aims and methods, but also suggests that the greater the degree of strategic change, the more likely it is that suitable methods of training and development will be needed to provide bases for understanding and internalizing change and experiencing the results of change. Such aims are unlikely to be achieved through programmed learning techniques, but are more likely to be achieved through group discussion work and, particularly, on the job, practical and project based experience related to the changes. Some corporations wisely regard such development, not merely as a matter of training, but as a matter of career planning; they ensure that managers gain a breadth of experience needed at higher levels for managing change during their careers by undertaking jobs and experiencing situations in different parts of the corporation. Certainly in Japanese companies, the development of such a breadth of experience is seen as essential to the development of management.[19]

11.3.3 ORGANIZATIONAL ROUTINES

There is another major influence which will regulate behavior within an organization. Nelson and Winter refer to "routines" as "a general term for all regular and predictable behavioral patterns of firms . . . from well specified technical routines for producing things, through procedures for hiring and firing, ordering new inventory, or stepping up production of items in high demand, to policies regarding investment, R&D or advertising, and business strategies about product diversification and overseas investment.[20] In many

---

ILLUSTRATION 11.4   *Corporate Colleges*

There are several approaches to training and developing employees. Some organizations even operate their own "colleges" where they train and educate employees in classroom settings.

McDonald's is famous for its "Hamburger U." where it trains franchisees and supervisory management in all aspects of fast food restaurant operation. In its advertisements, Tilden Car Rentals (National Car Rental in the US and Europcar in Europe) claims that its employees spend up to 200 hours in classroom sessions, on home study, and at refresher courses. One of the most intensive and systematic corporate colleges is operated by General Electric (GE) Co.

GE operates Crotonville Management Development Institute at Ossing, NY. The purpose of the in-house college is to develop managers, to help assimilate diverse operations, and to spread the company's vision or philosophy. The college teaches accounting, finance, and marketing, but also conducts sessions on problem solving. The college is attempting to mold a common GE culture, and courses include sessions on GE's objectives and philosophy.

The 2,500 college graduates GE hires each year are required to attend a two and a half day session. Managers at upper levels in the company attend month long programs. The college has its own staff but also relies on GE executives and visiting professors as instructors. Even Chairman John F. Welch Jr. instructs in some courses on his vision of the company.

Critics of such in-house colleges argue that there is a danger that the curriculum is too insular and inward focused. GE counters that its college fosters commitment to corporate objectives and helps reinforce a corporate culture.

Source: Janet Guyon, "Culture Class: GE's Management School Aims to Foster Unified Corporate Goals," *The Wall Street Journal*, August 10, 1987, p. 25; "GE's Training Camp: An 'Outward bound' for Managers," *Business Week*, December 14, 1987, p. 98.

---

respects, these routines are the institutionalized "ways we do things around here" which tend to persist over time and guide how people do their jobs. It may, of course, be that an organization which becomes particularly good at carrying out its operations in particular ways achieves real competitive advantage in so doing and therefore searches for strategies which best utilize such advantages[21] — though here there is a need to be aware of the chances of strategic drift discussed in Chapter 2.

Certainly the power of such routines is clear enough when they need to be changed in order to accommodate some new strategy. As one manager explained about the implications of a strategic change in his organization: "it's like turning an oil tanker; you may

Figure 11.5 *Methods of training and development for managing strategic change.*

	Information Transfer	Cybernetic	Cognitive	Experiential	Social influence
Examples of methods of development	Lectures Programmed learning	Simulations Business games	Case studies Discussions Reflection	Action learning Job rotation Project assignments	Rituals of induction and change
Aims of methods	Providing information	Providing feedback on abilities/skill application	Providing basis for knowing/ internalizing issues/change	Providing basis for experiencing needs/results of change	Reinforcing and affirming need for change socially

The chart above the table shows an S-curve rising from OPERATIONAL to STRATEGIC Change (vertical axis), across the columns Information Transfer, Cybernetic, Cognitive, Experiential, Social influence.

know that you want to go somewhere else but the systems keep grinding on and you can't turn the ship." The result is that attempts to change strategy may fail because implementation must be accommodated within existing routines. The logic of the strategy may be to change the routines but these are in fact what define the organizational work patterns for perhaps thousands of individuals. Managers often make the mistake of assuming that because they have specified a strategy requiring operational changes in work practices, and have even identified to more junior management what such changes are, the changes will necessarily take place. They may well find that reasons such changes should be delayed or cannot occur have to do with the persistent influence of long standing routines. Just as it was argued earlier with regard to control systems, there is a need to identify the priority areas for changes in such routines. It is then important that senior management, responsible for the strategic changes, take personal responsibility for ensuring such changes in routines occur. A few examples make the point:

- Buyers in a major retailer had always "bought long" to obtain the greatest discounts: a new president wanted a more responsive fashion oriented operation and insisted on cutting buying lead times by half.

- The new chief executive of an engineering firm, appointed to turn the business around, found an unacceptably high level of inventory, particularly in small items. These were kept in "bins" in the stockroom. He ordered that the bins be replaced with smaller ones and the size of the stockroom be reduced.

- The new personnel director of a firm trying to diversify away from its traditional base in heavy chemicals noticed that recruitment practices were biased towards recruiting chemical engineers. He reduced the space available in application forms to do with past career and qualifications and requested that applicants write about possible future company strategy. He also changed the journals in which advertisements were placed and involved more outsiders in the interviewing procedures.

11.3.4 MANAGEMENT STYLE

The management style of an organization is, in the end, an expression of the nature and characteristics of the managers, those they manage, the tasks in the organization, and the organizational culture.[22] These aspects have been discussed elsewhere in the book (particularly in Chapters 2 and 5). Management style, however, also has to do with how the different systems of control and regulation are put into effect and this is likely to differ between organizations. Chapter 10 began by explaining that, traditionally, organizations were conceived of as machines with clear structures and mechanisms for working. This has become known as a bureaucratic or mechanistic approach to organization.[23] It is not, however, the only way organizations may work. It may well make sense for organizations to be less mechanistic, or "more organic," in some circumstances than in others. Figure 11.6 contrasts mechanistic and organic systems of organization. Organic systems assume that the ability and efficiency with which individuals work together is not so much reliant on formal standardization of work patterns or job descriptions, so much as on the commitment of the individuals to organization wide concerns and the organization's ethos. The result is a more fluid system of management in which it may be more difficult to determine exactly who reports to whom or precisely what job is done by any one individual. Such systems are characterized by their informality and their loose rather than tight definition of work practices.

Again, just as there is no right or wrong about levels of centralization in organizations, there is no absolute right or wrong as to whether an organization should sensibly be organic or mechanistic, or something in between. The point is, in different circumstances different systems of organization are more, or less, sensible and this was made clear in discussing different influences on organizational structure in Chapter 10. For example, for the organization facing very stable environmental conditions and with established work practices, it may make sense to exercise control through mechanistic systems. This would, however, be inappropriate for an organization in a rapidly changing environment where more organic systems of management control would be more appropriate.

The impact of a CEO's management style on an organization is described in Illustration 11.5.

ILLUSTRATION 11.5   *Andy Grove's Management Style*

Sometimes, "how things are done" in a company is influenced to a substantial degree by one individual. An example of such a situation is provided by Andy Grove, CEO of Intel Corp.

Intel Corp is a very large manufacturer of microprocessors and semiconductors. The company's CEO is the author of two books on management, *High-Output Management* and *One-on-One With Andy Grove*. His theory of management is based on the assumption that a manager's job should be controlled with the same precision as a factory. In other words, Grove advocates very tight controls over managers.

Grove is known as a very "hands on" manager who has had a high involvement in operations. He is a person who pays attention to detail. This has resulted in a tightly centralized management structure at Intel, and many independently minded managers have left. The culture at Intel reflects Grove's beliefs, for example, employees work in cubicles with his own being only slightly larger, employees are encouraged to speak out, and there is a procedure for every contingency.

As Intel is growing, the question is whether or not such close control is still possible. But, decentralization is not easy to implement as managers are not used to operating on their own and Grove may find it difficult not to get involved. Grove is attempting to decentralize responsibility and to loosen his grip on operations. Examples of such attempts to decentralize include: delegating budgeting to operating managers, a plan to divide manufacturing operations along product lines, and a reorganization of the company's sales force.

Whether or not Grove's style will enable these changes to be implemented is not known. But, "how things are done" at Intel reflect the wishes of one man.

Source: "Can Andy Grove Practice What He Preaches?," *Business Week*, March 16, 1987, pp 68–9.

11.4   ACHIEVING CULTURE CHANGE

Managing strategic change is, in the end, about achieving a change in the culture of the organization;[24] that is, a change in the recipe and the aspects of the cultural web which preserve and reinforce that recipe. It is unrealistic to suppose that strategic change can be implemented if the current beliefs, assumptions, and ways of doing things remain the same. This section examines some of the processes important in recipe change: and goes on to discuss why changes in the symbols of organizational life can be important.

Recipe change essentially has to do with cognitive change; that is, changing the way in which members of the organization make sense of their organizational world and its

Figure 11.6 *Characteristics of mechanistic and organic systems in organizations.*

Mechanistic	**Organic**
1. Specialized differentiation and definition of tasks in the organization.	1. Contributive nature of special knowledge to the total concerns of the organization.
2. Hierarchical supervision and reconciliation of problems.	2. Redefinition of tasks and responsibilities through interaction with others.
3. Precise definition of job responsibilities, methods, rights, and obligations.	3. Commitment to the organization beyond any technical/precise definition: such commitment more valued than loyalty.
4. (Perceived) location of superior knowledge at the top of the hierarchy.	4. Network structure of control, authority, and communication.
5. Vertical interaction of individuals between subordinate and superior.	5. Omniscience not imputed to senior executives; knowledge located anywhere in the organization and this location may become center of authority for given issue.
6. Insistence on loyalty to organization and obedience to superiors.	6. Lateral rather than vertical direction of communication.
7. More prestige attached to job (and locale) than to more general knowledge, experience, and skills.	7. Communication consists of information and advice rather than instruction and decisions.

environment. Broadly, two stages can be discerned in the process of cognitive change. The first is the process of "unfreezing" or breaking down the beliefs and assumptions which currently exist. Second is the process of reformulation, that is the assertion and adoption of new sets of beliefs;[25] in effect, the acceptance of a new recipe. This is discussed below and summarized in Figure 11.7.

11.4.1 THE UNFREEZING PROCESS

Unfreezing the existing recipe might be achieved in a number of ways.

1. As was seen in Chapter 2, there is likely to be the need for some form of organizational *trigger* to signal the need for change. Typically, this is a downturn in performance or market share, or perhaps a threatened takeover. Such triggers may, or course, be deliberately manipulated by management on occasion to create a climate in which change may occur more readily.

2. *Challenge and exposure* of the current recipe is likely to be required. The mechanisms by which such challenge may occur can be varied. It may be as formalized as a deliberate planning procedure, or as informal as management meetings which begin to question ways of operating. It may also be that such challenge takes on a more symbolic dimension:

Figure 11.7   *Achieving culture change.*

Recipe change through

- **Unfreezing processes:**

    The need for a *trigger*
    Challenging/exposing the recipe
    Reconfiguring *power structures*
    Involving *outsiders*

- **Adopting a new recipe**

    Showing through *deeds*
    Enhancing or diminishing *status*
    Participation and *partial implementation*

- **Symbolic activity**

for example, Schein[26] tells of a new chief executive who, on taking over his job in a transport company, ordered that the signs on all the vehicles be removed and the vehicles painted plain white. Despite initial objections, the new chief executive insisted and when managers then asked how they should repaint the vehicles, his answer was to ask them to make proposals. In effect, he was asking them to rethink what the business was about without the preconceptions rooted in its history.

3.   It is likely that there will be a need for the reconfiguration of *power structures* in the organization. This may well go hand in hand with the legitimizing of dissent from those in the organization who are questioning the existing ways of operating. In order to effect this reconfiguration of power it is likely that the momentum for change will need *powerful advocacy* within the organization, typically from the chief executive, a powerful member of the board, or an influential outsider. It is not unusual, in such circumstances, to find that a new chief executive is appointed to take on the role of change agent.[27]

4.   Major change is often accompanied by the intervention of an *outsider*, maybe in the form of a new chief executive, senior executive, or perhaps a consultant. An outsider is not defined here as someone necessarily physically from outside the company, though this is quite likely to be the case, but rather as someone with little or no commitment to the existing recipe[28] who can therefore more easily perceive its limitations. Moreover, the role of the outsider may be very specific in terms of reformulating the strategy itself. It is not suggested that outsiders necessarily "invent" totally new solutions, rather that they may import or borrow from their previous experience, relevant new approaches. In effect, that outsider brings to bear his or her past experience but applies that experience to new situations.[29]

11.4.2   THE ADOPTION OF A NEW RECIPE

A new view of the organizational strategy, perhaps brought by an outsider, is in itself no guarantee that members of that organization will accept such views and beliefs and change their ways of perceiving the organization. Nor does unfreezing the current recipe mean that new beliefs and approaches will be accepted. Indeed, the unfreezing and reformulation process may be seen by management as destructive because it takes apart that which already exists.[30] At such times, the organization is likely to go through a period of turbulence during which there is a risk that it could revert back to old ways of operating. There need to be means, therefore, by which new ideas gain the confidence of management and other stakeholders. There are a number of ways in which this may occur:

1.   There is evidence to suggest that the most powerful mechanism for the adoption of new strategy is *showing through deeds*[31] the effectiveness of new strategies. Concrete performance improvement or real, visible signs of change are much more powerful than analytical arguments about the need for change.

2.   The acceptance of new strategies is likely to be linked to the extent to which such change enhances or diminishes *status*. For example, it is quite common for a new chief executive, when taking over, to remove all or part of the old board of directors. Not only may this have the effect of removing resistance to change and signifying the intent of change, but it also may mean that more junior managers are provided with opportunities for advancement, and this will increase the likelihood of their accepting change.

3.   Acceptance of such change may also be assisted by managers' *participation* in discussions about the change and its *partial implementation*, perhaps in some test market activity or in the formulation and implementation of trials to examine the feasibility of new strategies. This is one reason why the use of project teams and task forces which come together to introduce new strategies may be a useful means of implementing strategic change.[32]

4.   Finally, *symbolic activity* may play an important role in achieving acceptance of recipe change. For example, organizational and personnel changes which symbolize the irreversibility of change may be very powerful: the example given above of the replacement of a board by a new chief executive is a common signalling of such permanence of change. However, there are other ways in which symbolic activity can be a powerful means of achieving and cementing culture change, and these now will be discussed.

11.4.3 Symbolic Action and Strategic Change[33]

Four years before *In Search of Excellence* was published, Tom Peters argued that managers needed to understand better that "the mundane tools that involve the creation and manipulation of symbols over time have impact to the extent that they reshape beliefs and expectations."[34] The point is that managers need to understand that for change to be meaningful for individuals in the organization, that meaning must be apparent in their day-to-day experience in the organization: and the day-to-day "reality" of organizations is represented by the many mundane aspects of organizational life which come to take on symbolic significance. These include the sorts of stories people tell, the rituals that take place, the status symbols, such as cars or sizes of offices, and the type of language used. They also include the very systems discussed elsewhere in this chapter and the last; the sorts of reward, information, and control systems people become accustomed to; the "ways of doing things around here" that have been termed organizational routines; and the organizational structures which indicate reporting relationships and often status. In addition, the budgeting and planning systems discussed in Chapter 9 come to take on symbolic significance insofar as they come to represent to individuals the reality of day-to-day organizational life. As previously explained, these cultural devices preserve and legitimize the recipe: they are part of the cultural web which represents the reality of the organization to its members. Changing them, or employing them to signify or emphasize change, can be a very powerful mechanism for change. For example:

1. *Organizational rituals* are important means of regulating behavior within organizations and also, potentially, for changing behavior and challenging and changing recipes. Trice and Beyer[35] argue that there exist six different types of rites (or rituals) organizations typically employ to cement or change existing modes of behavior and organizational assumptions: these are shown in Table 11.5 the last column of which has been added to give some examples of how such rituals are used for the purposes of promoting or consolidating recipe and culture change.

2. Formal *control mechanisms* may also take on symbolic significance and be important for promoting change; a computerized inventory control system which may have the apparent aim of minimizing inventory, may also be used in a retailing operation to challenge managers' assumptions about what can and cannot sell in a store. Rates of depreciation, apparently an accountancy measure, also encapsulate whole sets of assumptions about degrees and rates of change, so changing them may challenge expectations of change. Targets set for managers may demand that they think outside their current horizons and invent new ways of approaching old problems.

3. Organizational *stories (or myths)* can also be an important vehicle for stimulating change, because they communicate in ways readily understood the "vision of the organization's mission or role."[36] The importance of quality at Mars is enshrined in the story of Forrest Mars throwing Mars bars at his managers on finding just one miswrapped in a store.[37] One company faced with significant resistance to change found acceptance accelerated rapidly when word spread that one of the long serving senior executives had "been converted" to the new approaches being introduced. In another, stories about the "irreverent" behavior of a new chief executive towards a long established family-

Table 11.5   *Types of rites (rituals) and their roles in culture change.*

Types of rites	Social consequence	Role in promoting and consolidating culture change	Examples
Rites of passage	Facilitate transition of people into social roles and statuses new for them.	Consolidate ways people carry out social roles.	Induction of new recruits.

Types of rites	Social consequence	Role in promoting and consolidating culture change	Examples
Rites of degradation	Dissolve social identities and their attendant power.	Provide public acknowledgment that problems exist. Defend group boundaries by redefining who belongs and who does not. Reaffirm social importance and value of role involved.	Firing and replacing top executives.
Rites of enhancement	Enhance social identities and their attendant power.	Spread good news about the organization. Provide public recognition of individuals for their accomplishments and motivate others to similar efforts. Emphasize social value of performance of social roles.	Award ceremonies at company conferences.
Rites of renewal	Refurbish social structures and improve the ways they function.	Reassure members that something is being done about problems. Focus attention on some problems and away from others. Legitimate systems of power and authority.	Problem-centered/ project task forces. Appointment of consultants on specified projects.
Rites of integration	Encourage and revive shared feelings that bind people together and keep them committed to a social system.	Permit venting of emotion and temporary loosening of various norms. Reassert and reaffirm, by contrast, moral rightness of usual norms.	Office Christmas parties.
Rites of conflict reduction	Reduce conflict and aggression.	Reestablish equilibrium in disturbed social relations. Compartmentalize conflict and its disruptive effects.	Internal appeal systems. Union–management committees.

Source: adapted from H.M. Trice and J.M. Beyer, "Using Six Organizational Rites to Change Culture," in R.H. Kilman *et al.*, (eds), *Gaining Control of the Corporate Culture*, San Francisco: Jossey-Bass, Publishers, Inc., 1985, pp. 374–5.

dominated board, spread through the company before he had made any formalized changes.

4. More generalized *symbols of change* can also be important. Declining performance required Tandem Computers CEO Jimmy Treybig to give up his laid-back managerial style symbolized by Friday afternoon "beer blasts," lack of an organization chart, and informal communications. Now, committees exist which meet on a regular basis, cost controls have been implemented that include the automatic turning off of lights, and more formal communication methods are used, such as electronic mail. These actions symbolized change at Tandem.

In a university business school, a new director, instead of merely trying to explain the need for a greater orientation towards research for the staff, moved his study and computer terminal to a position adjacent to the lobby: there he was visible to the staff as they entered each morning, doing his own research. Symbols of change might include relocation of offices, changes in furnishings and decor, changes in logo or house style, changes in the clothes people wear, and so on.

5. The sorts of *structural changes* discussed in Chapter 10 are also of symbolic significance. The replacement of a board of directors, the amalgamation of divisions or the splitting of a division into smaller parts, and the change from functional to divisional structure are not merely structural changes; they also signify changes in the expectations of those making such changes.

Illustration 11.6 outlines how one organization is attempting to achieve cultural change.

11.5 MANAGING STRATEGIC CHANGE THROUGH POLITICAL SYSTEMS

One of the themes running through this book is that management should be seen not only as an analytical and planning activity, but as a political process. It is therefore important to consider how strategic change might be implemented from a political perspective. Managers need to realize that analysis and planning may themselves take on political dimensions. A new marketing director of one company commissioned market research on customer perceptions of service and found the results were highly critical. The director found that the presentation of the findings to the board gave rise, not to analytical debate, but to systematic "trashing" of the research report. As he later stated, he failed to realize that it was "not so much an analytical statement, as a statement of political threat."

11.5.1 POWER AND THE MANAGEMENT OF STRATEGIC CHANGE

Chapter 5 discussed the importance of understanding the political systems of an organization. Having established this understanding there is also a need to plan the implementa-

---

ILLUSTRATION 11.6   *Strategic Change at Bank of America*

When initiating strategic change in an organization, it is necessary to consider the implications for reward systems, management style, culture, and the political system, if the change is to be successful.

In 1982, Bank of America in California reassessed its status in the financial services market and shortly afterward assessed its culture. The findings were that the bank was in the aging phase of its cycle and that it lacked the vitality and aggressiveness with which it had conducted business in the past. The results of the cultural assessment were somewhat distressing. Employees seemed to have the following beliefs:

- They had become risk averse with short term perspectives and felt that the company did not value risk takers.

- They were "division" focused as each division operated as a profit center and was largely self-sufficient. This attitude made it difficult for customers to obtain service from across divisions.

- They were complacent, and reluctant to question plans, programs, strategies, and products.

- They felt that performance was not to be worried about especially since merit pay was usually across the board.

These findings presented a challenge as the company was also facing a changing environment necessitating strategic change. Deregulation of the financial services industry meant that new products and services would be offered by the competition, and customers would expect to receive more services from the bank. Shifting markets meant that many branches were no longer viable and would have to be closed. New products would have to be introduced and employees would have to be trained to provide them.

Top management recognized the need for a market driven strategy and the need to introduce strategic change from the top down in the organization. The change process was started by forming a team of top corporate executives and by developing a CEO change agenda. There was a need to develop a shared business vision as employees were committed to division activity and lacked an understanding of where the bank was going. In order to do this, it was necessary to determine what desired changes in behavior and values would be required from employees. Then the strategic change could be set in motion with the CEO providing leadership.

It was ascertained that attitudes would have to shift from products, service, and profitability by division to customer satisfaction, market share, growth, and total corporate performance. The power system of the organization would have to be reoriented to support the new attitudes or values, and it would be necessary to use high-impact systems and operating mechanisms to accomplish this reorientation.

The bank defined its vision and and determined that the following values would be important:

- Place the Customer First — to provide customer service which would lead to profits.
- Respect, Recognize, and Reward — to respect customers and employees, to recognize the needs of individuals, and to reward employees and shareholders.
- Make the Most of Technology — to use technology to improve customer service and to make employee's work easier.
- Share Our Strategy, Strengthen Our Team — to communicate bank strategy to employees to create a "team."

The strategic change had to be introduced carefully as it involved a substantial change in management style. Several initiatives were undertaken to build awareness and integrate the change throughout the business. One hundred executives were informed of the change plan and were provided with guides for communicating it to their subordinates. Aspects of the change were communicated through the bank's in-house newsletter, at managers' conferences, in management schools, and in employee training programs. All these approaches talked about the vision, the values necessary, and the strategies involved, and why the change was important. Symbols of change were also used to reinforce the change, for example, there was a CEO's pin for managers who performed at levels exemplifying the new values.

High-impact systems were also used to reinforce the change. Management development programs, performance evaluation, compensation schemes, staffing, and career progression all focused on the change and the values necessary. More training was done in-house so that bank values could be emphasized. Prior to 1982, bonuses had been paid regularly but now were paid only on the basis of performance evaluation, and more compensation was based on performance than had been previously. There was a continuing emphasis on "Performance Planning, Coaching, and Evaluation" sessions by all managers at all levels through such approaches as mutual goal setting, periodic meetings, and end-of-year assessments and appraisals.

Leadership practice inventories and other surveys attempted to measure the change. In 1987, it was felt that some progress was being made in changing employee and customer satisfaction. The shareholders' perspective was not as favorable because the financial performance of the Bank of America had suffered because of loan write-offs. However, management believed that the bank was better positioned to take advantage of the changing environment in the industry.

Source: Robert N. Beck, "Visions, Values, and Strategies: Changing Attitudes and Culture," *The Academy of Management Executive*, February 1987, pp. 33–41; James E. Olson and Thomas A. Cooper, "CEOs on Strategy: Two Companies, Two Strategies (ATT and Bank of America)," *Journal of Business Strategy*, Summer 1987, Vol. 8, No. 1, pp. 51–7.

tion of strategy within this political context. The approach developed here draws on the content of Chapter 5 and also some of what has been discussed in this chapter to provide a framework for considering such political activity: Table 11.6 summarizes some of the "power games" which occur in organizations.[38] These include the manipulation of *organizational resources*, the relationships between powerful groupings, or *elites*, activity with regard to *subsystems* in the organization, and *symbolic activity*. All of these may be used to a) build a power base, b) overcome resistance, and c) achieve compliance.

1.   The control and manipulation of organizational *resources* was shown in Chapter 5 to be a source of power. For example, acquiring additional resources or being identified with important resource areas of expertise, and the ability to withdraw or allocate resources, can be valuable in overcoming resistance or persuading others to accept change, and the careful use of information or news to counter that being used to justify opposition may be important.

2.   How existing powerful groupings (or *elites*) in the organization are handled is likely to be of crucial importance. Association with an existing elite, or support by that elite, can help build a power base. Similarly, association with a change agent who is respected or seen to be successful can help a manager overcome resistance to change. It has already been seen in this chapter that the breaking down, or indeed, dismantling of such elites is also a powerful means of overcoming resistance and signalling change.

3.   Similarly, how the *subsystems* of organizations are handled will be important. Building up alliances and a network of contacts and sympathizers, even though they may not be powerful themselves, may later be important in overcoming resistance from more powerful groups. Certainly the building of a team of individuals, perhaps within a manager's own department, strongly supportive of the activities and beliefs of that manager, will be helpful. The danger here is that existing elites may regard the building of a strong team around a manager as a threat to their own power which needs to be minimized. Resistance to change is unlikely to be overcome by attempting to convert the whole organization to an acceptance of change; it is, however, likely that there are parts of the organization more sympathetic to that change than others. It is these the change agent will work on to develop momentum. Moreover, if that group can visibly be rewarded for such enhanced momentum, this can speed the process of overcoming resistance. The danger, however, is that change will be seen as a short term hiccup; that strategic change will be temporary and the organization will slip back into former patterns of behavior.

The main vehicles for implementing change are therefore to do with communicating and consolidating its acceptance throughout the organization. While it is important that the most senior levels in the organization, and particularly the chief executive, are visibly seen to be associated with and committed to the change implemented, it is also vital that processes be underway to achieve compliance throughout the organization. The management of change throughout the subsystems of the organization could begin within the phase of overcoming resistance; for example, it may be that the change agent has set up

Table 11.6 *"Power games" in organizations.*

Activity areas	Mechanisms				Key problems
	Resources	Elites	Subsystems	Symbolic	
Building the power base	Control of resources Acquisition of/ identification with expertise Acquisition of additional resources	Sponsorship by an elite Association with an elite	Alliance building Team building	Building on legitimation	Time required for building Perceived duality of ideals Perceived as threat by existing elites
Overcoming resistance	Withdrawal of resources Use of "counter intelligence" information	Breakdown or division of elites Association with change agent Association with respected outsider	Foster momentum for change Sponsorship/ reward of change agents	Attack or remove legitimation Foster confusion, conflict and questioning	Striking from too low a power base Potentially destructive: need for rapid rebuilding
Achieve compliance	Giving resources	Removal of resistant elites Need for visible "change hero"	Partial implementation and participation Implantation of "disciples" Support for "young Turks"	Applause/ reward Reassurance Symbolic confirmation	Converting the body of the organization Slipping back

committees or projects with representatives throughout the organization testing out the feasibility of certain changes. In such circumstances, these individuals not only are likely to become identified with and party to the changes but also to be involved in the partial implementation of those changes: it may be that these individuals will go back into their functional operations as disciples of change. It is also possible that groupings of change agents will grow up within the organization itself; these "young Turks" might be given active and visible support from the top.

4.   Finally, as has been seen, the conscious employment of *symbolic mechanisms* of change is likely to be useful. From a political point of view this may take several forms. First, the manager needs to realize that these symbols act to preserve and reinforce the recipe: so, to build power, the manager may consciously seek to identify with such symbols — to work within the committee structures, become identified with existing organizational rituals or stories, and so on. Second and conversely, to break resistance to change, the removal of challenging or changing rituals and symbols may be a very powerful means of achieving the questioning of what is taken for granted. Third, symbolic activity can be used for consolidating change: by concentrating attention or "applause" and rewards on those who most accept change, its wider adoption is more likely; and there may be means of confirming through symbolic devices such as new structures, titles, and systems of control, that the change is to be regarded as important and not reversible.

11.5.2 Problems with Managing Political Systems

The management of change through political mechanisms, though likely to be necessary, is a difficult and potentially hazardous task. Table 11.6 summarizes some of the problems. The problem in building a power base is that the manager may have become so identified with existing power groupings that he or she either actually comes to accept their views or is perceived by others to have done so, thus losing support among potential supporters of change. Building a power base is a delicate path to tread.

In overcoming resistance, the major problem may simply be the lack of power to undertake such activity; attempting to overcome resistance from a lower power base is almost bound to be doomed to failure. There is also a second major danger: that in the breaking down of the status quo, the inevitably destructive process in the organization is so fundamental, and takes so long, that the organization cannot recover from it. If the process is to be gone through, then its replacement by some new configuration of beliefs and the implementation of new strategy is vital and needs to be speedy. And, as already identified, in implementing change the main problem is likely to be carrying the body of the organization with the change. It is one thing to change the commitment of a few senior executives at the top of an organization; it is quite another to convert the body of the organization to an acceptance of significant change. Individuals are quite likely to regard change as temporary: something they need to comply with only until the next one comes along.

11.6 ACHIEVING EXCELLENCE THROUGH PEOPLE AND SYSTEMS

It has been seen that, over time, organizations are likely to get out of line with the forces at work and requirements of their own environments: this is the phenomenon of strategic drift. Researchers who have examined so called "excellent" companies[39] argue that the reason for such excellence is that these organizations are able to avoid such drift; are better able to maintain an alignment with the requirements of their environment more or less continually. How is this possible?

Managers do not reinvent their organizational world every time they face a new situation. They have to employ some set of assumptions or guiding principles to make sense of that world — what is referred to in this book as a recipe. However, if the recipe is necessary for managers to operate effectively, it is also dangerous because it is likely to create the sort of drift the organization must avoid. There is, then, a need for the maintenance of a system of beliefs, but at the same time the ability to challenge and change that system of beliefs. "Excellent" organizations appear to have the ability to do this simultaneously; they are what Peters and Waterman call "simultaneous loose-tight" organizations.[40] How such companies manage through the organizational system can be used to draw together much of what has been covered in this chapter.

These organizations have a "clear culture." That is, members of the organization clearly identify with what that organization is about. However, within such an organization, there is also the facility to readily challenge assumptions and current ways of operating. Managers in those organizations seek to encapsulate core, underlying strategies into overarching goals and expectations to form a coherent philosophy for that organization; they have a clear mission which is owned throughout the organization. Further, it is likely to be reflected and sustained in the everyday language and working practices of the organization. The mission is not just a set of ideas, it permeates the organization. Peters and Waterman provide the example of Walt Disney Productions. Here the mission is one of providing happiness through entertainment and this is translated into a set of values and messages which are simple to understand, but also require total commitment and intense training to carry out. Customers are "guests" who form an audience; employees are "cast members" and the personnel department is "casting;" when the employees work with the public they are "on stage." The point is that the strategy is not shrouded in the obscure detail of objectives and plans. These may exist in the organization but their manifestation is in the everyday lives of those who work at Disney.

Such organizations are also likely to demonstrate other "loose-tight" properties. The mechanisms for analysis, planning, and systems of control in such organizations will be highly developed; there may be centralized decision making and control systems which allow very fast response to change; it is usual in such organizations to be able to get decisions made quickly from the top. However, in addition to this, there is likely to be the facility for the challenging of taken for granted assumptions. This may take many different forms; it may be achieved through the organic management systems which exist, giving rise to high degrees of informality between levels of management; it may be that the organization has a high level of internal competition and an expectation, built up over time, that managers will question and challenge each other; it is likely that in such organizations the onus will be on experimentation rather than just "doing your job." In such organizations, the emphasis will be on systems and structures which encourage the exchange and challenging of ideas across groups and between levels of management, and minimize the extent to which powerful groups can isolate themselves from others or force their views and ways of doing things on others.

These systems which lead to the ability to challenge and question are likely to be supported in a number of ways. There may be visible "change heroes" within the organization; role models with whom employees can identify a successful ability to maintain change. In some organizations this may very well be the chief executive, but not necessarily so. Structures are likely to be flat, with the minimum degree of enforced hierarchy and the ready ability to cut across functions and job roles. It is likely that, in addition to any formal structures, there will be task force or project groupings around particular issues.

Senior managers in such organizations are likely to adopt a "hands-on" approach to management. They may be strategists but they are also involved in the organization, continually prompting the sort of change and innovation that they expect to see coming up from below. They will also appreciate the importance of symbolic support of change. For example, the adoption of modes of behavior in line with such challenging and questioning, will be reinforced through visible reward; the rituals and stories evident in the organization will be about change rather than history; there will be an avoidance of an emphasis on formal systems to maintain the status quo; and, rather, an emphasis on such

Figure 11.8 *Managing change in "excellent" organizations.*

Clear mission/corporate values
- Owned throughout the organization
- Relevant to the market

"Loose-tight" systems
- Analysis/planning/control *but*
- Informality/organic management
- Internal competition
- Challenging/questioning approach
- Experimentation

Supported by
- Top management visibility
- "Change heroes"
- Absence of political elites
- Flat, integrative structures
- Task forces, project teams
- Symbolic communication

systems which underline the need for change or continual questioning. For example, reward systems, accountancy measures, inventory control systems, and so on, may actually be used to challenge current management thinking about what can be achieved and how. In these organizations, the aim is to overcome many of the problems of the formulation of strategy seen in Chapter 2. The aims are to speed up the triggering of the perceived need for change, the lag which can exist between individuals spotting the need for change, and their response in an organizational sense; and to ensure that the response to change is not so dictated by "managerial experience" that the maintenance of existing strategy becomes inevitable. Figure 11.8 summarizes some of the mechanisms by which this may be achieved.

11.7 SUMMARY

The implementation of strategy involves both the planning of resources and the management of the people in the organization. Chapter 9 dealt with the planning aspects of strategy implementation. Chapters 10 and 11 dealt with some of the ways people involved in implementing strategy might be managed through the structural and systems designs of organizations. This chapter, in particular, has "highlighted the need to consider how systems of control and regulation, and the cultural and political systems of organizations, are important for achieving strategic change. The chapter has also served to remind readers of the integrated nature of the strategic management problem: in considering how organizational systems might contribute to — or constrain — the implementation of strategy, and by putting into effect systems of control, managers are also involved in activities of resource analysis, the analysis of cultural and political systems, the examination of the feasibility of strategies, and the planning of strategy implementation.

References

1. E. Mumford and A. Pettigrew, *Implementing Strategic Decisions*, (London: Longman, 1975), is a report on the research into the introduction of large scale computer systems in four large organizations. The process of implementation was monitored over a period of two to five years.

2. For a fuller discussion of the notion of "compliance" see A. Etzioni, *A Comparative Analysis of Complex Organizations*, (New York: Free Press, 1961).

3. Useful references on control systems are R.N. Anthony and J. Dearden, *Management Control Systems; Text and Cases*, 3rd Edition, (Homewood, Illinois: Richard D. Irwin Inc., 1976), and the section on the Control Process in Chapter 7, L.G. Hrebiniak and W.F. Joyce, *Implementing Strategy*, (New York: Collier Macmillan, 1984).

4. See reference 3.

5. Responsibility centers are a useful means of dividing control systems. They have been discussed by many authors, for example: R.N. Anthony and J. Dearden, *Management Control*

Systems ; Text and Cases, (see reference 3) and R.F. Vancil, "What Kind of Management Control Do You Need?," *Harvard Business Review*, March/April 1973, pp. 75–86.

6. The dangers of negative monitoring are discussed by L.G. Hrebiniak and W.F. Joyce, (see reference 3), pp. 200–01.

7. A useful review of research on the relationship between rewards and strategy can be found in J.R. Galbraith and D.A. Nathanson, *Strategy Implementation: The Role of Structure and Process* (St. Paul, Minn.: West Publishing Co. 1978), pp 81–5.

8. See "Rewarding Executives for Taking the Long View," *Business Week*, April 2, 1984, pp. 99–100 and 108.

9. See M.S. Salter, "Tailor Incentive Compensation to Strategy," *Harvard Business Review*, March/April 1973.

10. A number of researchers have pointed out that managerially controlled firms tend to follow a growth and size objective in business organizations; for example see R. Marris and A. Wood, *The Corporate Economy* (New York: Macmillan, 1971); and W.S. Baumol, *Business Behavior Value and Growth* (New York: Harcourt, Brace and World Inc., 1967).

11. For discussion of the relationship between ownership and managerial compensation see L.R. Gomez-Mejia, H. Tosi and T. Hinkin, "Managerial Control, Performance and Executive Compensation," *Academy of Management Journal*, Volume 30, No. 1, March 1987, pp. 51–70.

12. F.J. Roethlisberger and W.J. Dickson, *Management and the Worker* (Chicester: John Wiley and Sons Ltd., 1964), is an interesting book written by two of the Hawthorn researchers of the 1930s. Pages 517–35 describe how cash incentives are not the prime motivation to perform well.

13. Payment by results is discussed in most texts on rewards, personnel management, and often operations management. A useful discussion can be found in G.H. Webb, "Payment by Results Systems," in A.M. Bowey, ed.,*Handbook of Salary and Wage Systems*, (Aldershot: Gower, 1975).

14. This example is taken from the case study on "Executive Holloware" by Kevan Scholes available from the Case Clearing House of Great Britain.

15. This issue of group versus individual rewards for managers is discussed by M. White, "Incentive Bonus Schemes for Managers," in A.M. Bowey, ed. *Handbook of Salary and Wage Systems*, (see reference 13).

16. J.R. Galbraith and D.A. Nathanson, *Strategy Implementation: The Role of Structure and Process*, (see reference 7, pp. 86–7) explain more fully a number of research findings in the link between "tolerance for ambiguity" and performance.

17. For a review of different methods of management development see A. Hcuzynski, *Encyclopedia of Management Development Methods*, (Aldershot: Gower, 1983).

18. Figure 11.5 is based loosely on a paper by J. Burgoyne and R. Stewart, "Implicit Learning Theories Determinants of the Effects of Management Development Programs," *Personnel Review*, Volume 6, No 2, 1977, pp. 5–14.

19. Chapter 2 of W. Ouchi, *Theory Z — How American Business can meet the Japanese Challenge*, (Reading, Mass.: Addison-Wesley Publishing Ltd., 1981), explains how such an attitude towards

the development of individuals contrasts with many American and UK companies where specialization is all-important. Ouchi cites this as an important reason for the success of Japanese companies.

20. See R.R. Nelson and S.G. Winter, *An Evolutionary Theory of Economic Change*, (Cambridge, Mass.: Harvard University Press, 1982), p. 14.

21. S.A. Lippman and R.P. Rumelt, "Uncertain Imitability; An Analysis of Inter-Firm Differences in Efficiency under Competition," *Bell Journal of Economics*, Volume 13, No. 2, 1982, pp. 418–38.

22. Charles Handy, *Understanding Organizations*, (Harmondsworth: Penguin Books Limited, 1976) is a useful reference for understanding components of management style more fully.

23. The terms "organic" and "mechanistic" systems of management were introduced by T. Burns and G.M. Stalker, *The Management of Innovation*, (London: Tavistock Publications, 1961).

24. Readers who would like to refresh their memory about the use of the term culture in this book should refer back to Chapter 2 (Section 2.4).

25. The idea of unfreezing and reformulation in achieving change is not new. Kurt Lewin, *Field Theory in Social Science*, (London: Tavistock Publications, 1952), and Edgar Schein, "Personal Change Through Interpersonal Relationships," in W.G. Bennis, D.E. Berlow, E.H. Schein and F.L. Steel, *Interpersonal Dynamics*, (Homewood, Illinois: Dorsey Press, 1973), pp. 237–67 developed the models of change processes on which this discussion is based.

26. This example is taken from Edgar Schein, *Organizational Culture and Leadership*, (San Francisco: Jossey-Bass Publishers, Inc., 1985). Chapter 12 includes a number of examples of culture change mechanisms.

27. The role of a new chief executive in promoting strategic change is noted by both P.H. Grinyer and J-C. Spender in "Recipes, Crises and Adaptation in Mature Businesses," *International Studies of Management and Organization*, 9, 1979, pp. 113–23, and also by Stuart Slatter, *Corporate Recovery*, (Harmondsworth: Penguin Books Limited, 1984).

28. Edgar Schein (reference 26) refers to members of the organization who are not wedded to the recipe as "hybrids."

29. The notion that the outsider, in effect, applies his old experience (or old recipe to the new situation) is proposed by Grinyer and Spender (reference 27) and supported by Gerry Johnson, *Strategic Change and the Management Process*, (Oxford: Basil Blackwell Publishers, 1987).

30. The term "destructive processes" is used by N.W. Biggart in describing the processes of change he observed in the US Post Office described in "Creative-Destructive Processes of Organizational Change: the Case of the Post Office," *Administrative Science Quarterly*, 24, 1977, pp. 410–26.

31. The importance of "showing through deeds" the effectiveness of change in order to consolidate that change is argued by V. Sathe, *Culture and Related Corporate Realities*, (Homewood, Illinois: Richard D. Irwin Inc. 1985).

32. The usefulness of project teams and task forces is particularly emphasized as a means of partial implementation by T. Peters and R. Waterman, *In Search of Excellence*, (New York: Harper and Row Ltd. 1982).

33. The importance of symbolic activity in managing change is referred to by a number of writers; for example, see N.W. Biggart (reference 30), D.M. Boje, D.B. Fedor and W.M. Rowland, "Myth Making: a Qualitative Step in OD Interventions," *Journal of Applied Behavioural Science*, 18(3), 1982, pp. 17-28 and Tom Peters, "Symbols, Patterns and Settings: an Optimistic Case for Getting Things Done," *Organizational Dynamics*, Autumn, 1978, pp. 3–22.

34. This is a quotation from page 11 of Tom Peter's paper (reference 33).

35. See H.M. Trice and J.M. Beyer, "Using Six Organizational Rites to Change Culture," in R.H. Kilman (ed.), *Gaining Control of the Corporate Culture*, (San Francisco: Jossey-Bass Publishers, Inc., pp. 374–5.

36. See A.L. Wilkins, "Organization Stories as Symbols Which Control the Organization," in L.R. Pondy, P.J. Frost, G. Morgan and T.C. Dandridge (eds), *Organizational Symbolism*, (Greenwich, Conn.: J.A.I. Press Inc., 1983).

37. This story is told by Tom Peters and N. Austin, *A Passion for Excellence*, (New York: Random House, 1985), pp. 278–81.

38. This discussion is based on observations of the role of political activities in organizations by, in particular, Henry Mintzberg, *Power in and Around Organizations*, (Englewood Cliffs, N.J.: Prentice-Hall, 1983), and Jeffrey Pfeffer, *Power in Organizations*, (London: Pitman Publishing 1981).

39. See T. Peters and R. Waterman, *In Search of Excellence*, R.M. Kanter, *The Change Masters*, (New York: Simon and Shuster, 1983), T. Peters and M. Austin, *A Passion for Excellence* and J.B. Quinn, *Strategies for Change*, (Homewood, Illinois: Richard D. Irwin Inc., 1980).

40. The term "loose-tight" is taken from T. Peters and R. Waterman, *In Search of Excellence*, p. 318.

Recommended Key Readings

The fullest discussion of control systems remains that in the writings of R.N. Anthony. Particularly, *Planning and Control Systems: A Framework for Analysis*. Harvard Graduate School of Business: 1965 and R.N. Anthony and J. Dearden. *Management Control Systems: Text and Cases*. Homewood, Illinois: Richard D. Irwin Inc. 1976.

Other perspectives on control and information systems are:

Peter Lorange and Declan Murphy. "Considerations in Implementing Strategic Control." *Journal of Business Strategy*, Vol. 4, No. 4, Spring 1984, pp. 27–35.

Georg Schreyogg and Horst Steinmann. "Strategic Control: A New Perspective." *Academy of Management Review*, Vol. 12, No. 1, 1987, pp. 91–103.

John M. Ward. "Integrating Information Systems into Business Strategies." *Long Range Planning*, Vol. 20, No. 3, 1987. pp. 19–29.

For further discussion of reward systems and their links with strategy see: J.R. Galbraith and R.K. Kazanjian. *Strategy Implementation: Structure, Systems and Process*. St. Paul, Minn: West Publishing Co., 1986.

M.S. Slater. "Tailor Incentive Compensation to Strategy." *Harvard Business Review*, Mar-Apr., 1973, pp. 94–102.

Paul J. Stonich. "Using Rewards In Implementing Strategy." *Strategic Management Journal*, Vol. 2, No. 4, 1984, 15–25.

For a discussion of the relationship between strategic management and leadership styles see:

L.J. Bourgeois, III, and David R. Brodwin. "Strategic Implementation: Five Approaches to an Elusive Phenomenon." *Strategic Management Journal*, Vol. 5, No. 3, 1984, pp. 241–64.

Milton Leontiades. "Choosing the Right Manager to Fit the Strategy." *Journal of Business Strategy*, Vol. 3, No. 2, 1982, pp. 58–69.

Paul C. Nutt. "Identifying and Appraising How Managers Install Strategy." *Strategic Management Journal*, Vol. 8, No. 1, 1987, pp. 1–14.

Andrew D. Szilagy, Jr., and David M. Schweger. "Matching Managers to Strategies: A Review and Suggested Framework." *Academy of Management Review*, Vol 9, No 4, 1984, pp. 626–37.

Bernard Taylor. "Strategic Planning — Which Style do you Need?" *Long Range Planning*, Vol. 17, No. 3, 1984, pp. 51–62.

The fullest account of training and development techniques is to be found in A. Hcuzynski. *"Encyclopedia of Management Development Methods."* Aldershot: Gower, 1983.

For illustrations and explanations of strategic change through cultural and political processes see:

Jay B. Barney. "Organizational Culture: Can It Be a Source of Sustained Competitive Advantage?" *Academy of Management Review*, Vol. 11, No 3, 1986, pp. 656–665.

Gerry Johnson. *Strategic Change and the Management Process*. Oxford: Basil Blackwell Publisher, 1987.

Ralph H. Kilmann, Mary J. Saxton, Roy Serpa and Associates. *Gaining Control of the Corporate Culture*. San Francisco: Jossey-Bass Publishers, Inc. 1985.

Jay W. Lorsch, "Managing Culture: The Invisible Barrier to Strategic Change. "*California Management Review*, Vol. XXVIII, No. 2, 1986, pp. 95–109.

Howard Schwartz and Stanley M. Davis. "Matching Corporate Culture and Business Strategy." *Organizational Dynamics*, Summer 1981, pp. 30–48.

For illustrations and explanations of strategic change through cultural and political processes see Gerry Johnson. *Strategic Change and the Management Process*. Oxford: Basil Blackwell Publisher., 1987.

There have been a number of books published on "excellence" in organizations. For example, T. Peters and R. Waterman. *In Search of Excellence*. New York: Harper and Row, 1982, T. Peters and N. Austin. *A Passion for Excellence*. New York: Random House, 1984, and M. Kanter. *The Change Masters*. New York: Simon and Schuster: 1983.

EPILOGUE

Of necessity, textbooks need to be structured and written in a way which allows the reader to systematically develop an understanding of the subject. However, there are dangers in this since the reader may gain an insight into the "building blocks" which make up the subject but fail to appreciate its "wholeness." This is a particular concern with the study of strategic management since the essence of the subject is that of "wholeness" rather than the intensive study of the parts.

The point was made at the beginning of the book that the adopted focuses of analysis, choice, and implementation may not take the form of a step-by-step process in practice. They are likely to be interrelated and, indeed, it is likely that the emphasis placed on each will differ according to the organization and its circumstances.

The simplest way to understand this is by looking at some of the examples discussed in various parts of the book. The purpose of doing so is to show that strategic management in all organizations is concerned with managing strategic change but that this process may be achieved in different ways.

- In a large conglomerate or divisionalized company, those employed at the center or head office may be primarily concerned with *analysis*, trying to understand the company's position, its balance of activities, and the opportunities which exist, perhaps through a corporate planning department. In contrast, managers in each division may spend most of their time on *resource planning* and implementing new strategies.

- In a multinational company, corporate management may be absorbed in aspects of *company structure*. For example, whether the company strategy will be more efficient if lines of responsibility are shifted from global product divisions to international divisions.

- In contrast, the owner of a small, fast growing company may be mainly worried about obtaining the *resources* to capitalize on the opportunities which have been opened up. At a later stage, as growth slows, the search for new *strategic options* may dominate strategic thinking in the company.

- Many industrial companies need to spend large sums of money on capital equipment and therefore, pay a great deal of attention to the *analysis* and *evaluation* of capital expenditure projects. Retailing companies, however, may have little money tied up in fixed assets (properties are, after all, saleable) and may develop new strategies by a series of small incremental steps where the company learns through *implementation* of ideas.

- In government organizations, there may be a special need to understand the *political environment* within which decisions are made and implemented.

- In Japan, the process of *strategic evaluation* is much more overtly political in the sense that acceptability of proposed changes tends to be tested out much more fully during evaluation than tends to be the case in Europe and North America.

ILLUSTRATION E.1   *Strategic Management at General Motors — Continued*

Roger Smith and other managers at General Motors Corp. (GM) appreciate the "wholeness" of strategic management. This illustration summarizes some of the dimensions of strategic management at GM and provides an example of now management is attempting to get strategic analysis, strategic choice, and strategy implementation to fit together as a comprehensive strategy.

About ten years ago, General Motors Corp. recognized the need and importance of a serious strategic management approach. By early 1988, it was clear that many initiatives had been taken in response to a dynamic marketplace. Roger Smith has been quoted as saying that GM is "running scared" due to all the challenges presented by the environment!
   Some examples of the strategic choices GM has made follow:

- Initiated a program to modernize assembly plants.
- Formulated plans to close 16 plants by 1990.
- Reassessed the degree of vertical integration, that is, the proportion of components made in-house.
- Introduced new models.
- Attempted to increase export sales made possible with the declining dollar.
- Initiated a cost reduction program.

These choices were reflected in strategy implementation and have involved initiatives such as:

- A restructuring of the organization resulting in fewer levels of management, reduction in management overhead, and the decentralization of decision making closer to the marketplace.
- A new attitude toward employee-management cooperation with promises of "secured employment levels," the establishment of joint labor-management committees at the plant level, and changes to the compensation and benefits package including profit sharing, merit pay, and pay based on performance.
- A program to get GM's vast array of office, engineering, and manufacturing computer systems to communicate with each other was started.
- Marketing approaches are being reassessed, including use of sales incentives, lower prices, and inclusion of extras as standard equipment.
- In early 1988, GM launched a major campaign to change its image from a problem plagued firm to one that was "moving ahead" and was "doing well." The campaign included network television interviews, a huge exhibit focusing on high-

technology at New York's Waldorf-Astoria Hotel, and an eight page advertising insert in major consumer publications. The campaign was an attempt to restore GM's credibility with stakeholders, customers, employees, suppliers, dealers, financial analysts, journalists, and shareholders.

The environment has forced strategic change throughout GM resulting in an attempted rejuvenation unprecedented for a corporation of this size. But, managers are faced with the challenge of keeping new car development, production modernization, marketing initiatives, and new approaches to employee relations all on track at the same time. Roger Smith believes that the worst is over and that most of the necessary strategic changes will be accomplished by 1990. Observers of GM can now see how strategic management is fitting together and you will be able to assess whether or not GM has been successful at its strategic management.

- Finally, General Motors was used as an example of strategic management in Chapter 1. Illustration E.1 outlines some aspects of how GM is attempting to manage strategic change.

In all the situations described above, the development of strategy will depend on the development of an understanding of the strategic position (strategic analysis), choosing between possible options (strategic choice), and planning and executing the strategy (strategy implementation). But where the process begins and what the focus of attention is, are likely to change over time, or depend on the position in the organization from which corporate strategy is viewed.

There is, of course, a danger associated with these differences in emphasis or focus. The danger is that an organization, or a manager, may come to see strategy in too limited a way, that some of the "building blocks" will be emphasized at the expense of the "wholeness" of the problem. A theme throughout this book has been that strategic decision making will depend on the interaction of many management issues and activities, but that above all, it is necessary for management to be sensitive to, and develop an understanding of, the overall nature of strategic problems. It is common for managers to fail to do this. They become so familiar with their own functions, or the particular way they have been used to approaching problems, that they find it difficult to conceive of wider issues. Communication on matters of strategic importance is often difficult between different levels of management or between different functions, for example. Managers cannot be expected to conceive of problems or opportunities in strategic terms unless they are familiar with concepts and practices of strategic management wider than their own particular experience. The view expressed in this book is that the sort of flexibility, sensitivity, and imagination required of managers today at all levels in an organization can be enhanced by their "exploring strategic management."

Index